Children's Literature Association Centennial Studies

1. *Beatrix Potter's* Peter Rabbit: *A Children's Classic at 100*, edited by Margaret Mackey. 2002.
2. *L. Frank Baum's* World of Oz: *A Classic Series at 100*, edited by Suzanne Rahn. 2003.
3. *E. Nesbit's Psammead Trilogy: A Children's Classic at 100*, edited by Raymond E. Jones. 2006.
4. *J. M. Barrie's* Peter Pan *In and Out of Time: A Children's Classic at 100*, edited by Donna R. White and C. Anita Tarr. 2006.

J. M. Barrie's *Peter Pan* In and Out of Time

A Children's Classic at 100

Edited by
Donna R. White
C. Anita Tarr

CHILDREN'S LITERATURE ASSOCIATION
CENTENNIAL STUDIES SERIES, NO. 4

THE SCARECROW PRESS, INC.
Lanham, Maryland • Toronto • Oxford
2006

SCARECROW PRESS, INC.

Published in the United States of America
by Scarecrow Press, Inc.
A wholly owned subsidiary of
The Rowman & Littlefield Publishing Group, Inc.
4501 Forbes Boulevard, Suite 200, Lanham, Maryland 20706
www.scarecrowpress.com

PO Box 317
Oxford
OX2 9RU, UK

British Library Cataloguing in Publication Information Available

Library of Congress Cataloging-in-Publication Data

J.M. Barrie's Peter Pan in and out of time : a children's classic at 100 / edited
by Donna R. White, C. Anita Tarr.
    p. cm. — (Children's Literature Association centennial studies ; no. 4)
Includes bibliographical references and index.
ISBN-13: 978-0-8108-5428-4 (alk. paper)
ISBN-10: 0-8108-5428-7 (alk. paper)
 1. Barrie, J. M. (James Matthew), 1860-1937. Peter Pan. 2. Barrie, J. M.
(James Matthew), 1860-1937.—Criticism and interpretation. 3. Children—
Books and reading—Great Britain—History—20th century. 4. Children's
stories, English—History and criticism. 5. Peter Pan (Fictitious character)
I. Title: Peter Pan in and out of time. II. White, Donna R., 1955– III. Tarr, C.
Anita, 1953– IV. Series.

PR4074.P33J53 2003
822'.912—dc22

                                                                    2005032787

⊚™ The paper used in this publication meets the minimum requirements of
American National Standard for Information Sciences—Permanence of Paper
for Printed Library Materials, ANSI/NISO Z39.48-1992.
Manufactured in the United States of America.

Contents

Introduction

Donna R. White and C. Anita Tarr

THE PARADOX OF *PETER PAN*

J. M. Barrie's literary reputation rests on one work: *Peter Pan*, the play, first performed in 1904 to wildly enthusiastic audiences and still performed successfully today. The character of Peter Pan, the boy who would not grow up, has become iconic in popular culture as well as in children's literature. Peter's story has survived charges of sentimentality to emerge periodically but predictably in every generation to renewed impact. We celebrate the centenary of *Peter Pan* with this book: a collection of essays devoted to *Peter Pan* as a work that brought together various strains of influences during Barrie's own time; a work that still confounds readers in its narrative complexity; and a work that, simply, refuses to die but keeps on ticking through our cultural changes to underlie our ideologies about children and the literature we provide for them. Peter Pan is immortal.

By the time Barrie wrote *Peter Pan* (and rewrote and rewrote it until the published iteration of 1928), he was already a highly successful novelist and playwright, as well known for his eccentricities as for his fanciful stage productions.[1] Alone of all of Barrie's literary works, *Peter Pan* remains vital today because it speaks nostalgically about our wishes to keep children young, while reminding us mercilessly about how cruel childhood can really be. Neverland is never innocent, nor is it heaven or hell, nor reward or punishment, but rather an imaginary place individual to each child, reeking with desires for safety and home as strong as those that lured each child away from home in the first place.[2] Neverland is never just one idea, just as Peter Pan is never just one boy or girl, but betwixt and between, and just as *Peter Pan* is not only a play for children but also one for adults, indulgently sentimental, joyful and tragic, about a dead boy who never dies.

Peter Pan is mired in the times of its creation, but it is also timeless. It is outside of time even as it follows us all with a ticking clock. Our deaths are simultaneously imminent and escapable. We cannot completely comprehend *Peter Pan,* but we always remember it. We are Peter Pan; we are Wendy. We are, hopefully, an open window to our imaginations.

PETER PAN AND THE PANTOMIME TRADITION

Anyone who has ever tried to write about Peter Pan has quickly discovered the protean nature of the subject. What are we to make of a boy who can fly without the benefit of wings—except when he forgets he knows *how* to fly? A boy with an extremely limited short-term memory and no long-term memory at all who nevertheless remembers running away from home when he was only one day old? A boy who successfully refuses to grow up but sometimes seems to be a baby, sometimes a pre-teen, and occasionally a god? When the dastardly Captain Hook asks the direct question, "Pan, who and what are thou?" Peter replies, "I'm youth, I'm joy . . . I'm a little bird that has broken out of the egg" (*Peter and Wendy* 188). As a definition, Peter's response leaves much to be desired. It sounds remarkably similar to playwright James Barrie's response when Nina Boucicault, the first actress to play Peter Pan, asked for some insight into her character. All Barrie would say was, "Peter is a bird . . . and he is one day old" (qtd. in Hanson 36).

The text is just as amorphous as its main character. Is it a novel or a play? If a novel, which one? As for the play, in *The Road to the Never Land*, R. D. S. Jack identifies more than twenty variants written by Barrie, who, incidentally, often claimed that he was *not* the author of *Peter Pan* and had no clear idea who was. There is no definitive text of *Peter Pan*, but there *is* a textual history. The first appearance in print of a character called Peter Pan occurred in 1902 in a novel Barrie wrote for adults, *The Little White Bird.* The book recounts the friendship between the narrator and a poor but well-born young couple and their son. Over the course of several chapters, the narrator tells the boy, David, a story about a one-week-old baby who flies out of his nursery to return to the island of the birds—a baby named Peter Pan. The author's whimsical notion is that all babies were once birds; that is why there are bars on nursery windows—to keep the babies from flying away if they forget they are no longer birds. In *The Little White Bird*, the infant Peter Pan has many adventures in Kensington Gardens, where he lives among the birds and the fairies, apparently forever.

Barrie himself claimed that an earlier work was really the basis for Peter Pan: a privately published photograph album with fictional commentary called *The Boy Castaways of Black Lake Island*, which Barrie had printed in 1901. Only two copies of this volume were printed, and one was immediately lost on a train. This album recounted the imaginary adventures of three young friends of Barrie: George, Jack, and Peter Llewelyn Davies. The boys acted out the adventures as Barrie directed them. Barrie portrayed Captain Swarthy, a villain similar to Captain Hook. Although some of the adventures in the album influenced the later play, the character Peter Pan does not make an appearance. *The Boy Castaways* is really what we might call an Ur-text, only tangentially related to the textual history of Peter Pan. However, the Llewelyn Davies boys were vitally involved in the *creation* of Peter Pan since the stories that appeared in *The Little White Bird* had originally been told to George and Jack, and the infant Peter Pan was at first their baby brother Peter.

In 1904, two years after *The Little White Bird*, the play entitled *Peter Pan* was first produced in London. But Barrie, a well-known playwright by then, was a hands-on writer, and the production the audience saw on opening night was considerably different from the handwritten manuscript conserved at the Lilly Library in Indiana. And the play seen by another audience four nights later contained two additional scenes. Barrie constantly rewrote the play during rehearsals and even during the run of the play that first year. Each year thereafter until his death in 1937, a new production was mounted every Christmas and Barrie tinkered with the text some more.

The next item in our textual history was published as a children's book, *Peter Pan in Kensington Gardens*, in 1906. This, however, consisted only of the Peter Pan chapters from *The Little White Bird*. The main attraction of the book was the addition of illustrations by the famous Arthur Rackham. A novelized version of the play appeared in 1911 with the title *Peter and Wendy*. It is considerably different from the play, although the structure of the adventures remains the same. Barrie elaborates on characterization, adds numerous scenes, and provides much authorial commentary. This is the book most people think of as *Peter Pan*. The title *Peter and Wendy* was changed to *Peter Pan and Wendy* in 1924 and later became simply *Peter Pan*, thus usurping the title of the play and causing great confusion for scholars and bibliographers.

Finally, in 1928, Barrie published the play itself—or at least, one version of it. This too was titled *Peter Pan*. The textual history makes it difficult to know what scholars are talking about when the subject is Peter Pan. The editors of this volume do not propose to make things any easier. We have another answer to Captain Hook's question, "Pan, who and what are thou?" We say *Peter Pan* is a pantomime. The *Peter Pan* we are referring to at this point is the play produced in 1904 and every year thereafter. However, we are not the first to call it a pantomime. Barrie himself said he was writing a pantomime. Contemporary audiences and theater critics knew it was a pantomime. As late as 1937, George Bernard Shaw referred to it as a pantomime (qtd. in Mander 44). More recent literary critics, however, particularly American ones, do not know this, and would not be much enlightened if they did, because they would not know what a pantomime is.

Pantomime is a peculiar British phenomenon, with the accent on peculiar. It is a form of popular entertainment produced at Christmas time, featuring stock characters, standard plots, and extravagant sets and stage effects. To quote from one history of pantomime,

> It takes its name from classical times and changes the meaning, its characters from Italian comedy and changes their names, its stories from continental fairy tales and mixes historical figures, then adds every conceivable trick and resource of the theatre, opera, ballet, music hall and musical comedy. It has moulded all these elements together over the past three hundred years into something which no-one but the English understand, or even want! (Mander 1)

By Barrie's time, pantomime had become a Christmas extravaganza for children, but it certainly did not start out that way. During the first decade of the eighteenth century, the traditional Italian *Commedia dell' Arte* characters were introduced to English audiences by acting troupes from France that performed in English theaters and at fairs. In 1716 an enterprising London theater manager, John Rich, who was also an actor and a gifted mime, started adding a silent pantomime based on the Italian characters to the end of an evening's double bill. On the English stage, the most popular of these characters became known as Harlequin and Columbine, the lovers; Pierrot, the clown; and Pantaloon, the old skinflint. Rich's pantomimes were so successful that other theaters began to copy him. Eventually a standard form developed for these entertainments. First there was an Opening, which told a familiar story or classical legend in verse and song—sometimes burlesquing the latest Italian opera playing at the Queen's Theatre in Haymarket but usually serious in tone. Then, by means of a magician or other benevolent agency that thwarted the powers of evil, the characters were transformed into Harlequin, Columbine, Pantaloon, Pierrot, and other Italian types, who went through a series of usually comic and acrobatic adventures mimed to music, known as a Harlequinade. The Harlequinade featured elaborate sets and costumes, and much stage machinery was employed to create impressive effects, such as characters flying or ascending into heaven (or, in one production, ascending into hell).

Audiences loved it. Alexander Pope was disgusted:

> See now what Dulness and her sons admire!
> See what the charms that smite the simple heart,
> Not touched by nature, and not reached by art.
> . . . .
> Behold a sable sorcerer rise,
> Swift to whose hand a winged volume flies;
> All sudden, gorgons hiss and dragons glare,
> And ten-horned fiends and giants rush to war,
> Hell rises, Heaven descends; and dance on earth,
> Gods, imps and monsters, music, rage, and mirth,
> A fire, a jig, a battle and a ball,
> Till one wide conflagration swallows all.
> Thence a new world, to Nature's laws unknown,
> Breaks out refulgent with a heaven its own;
> Another Cynthia her new journey runs,
> And other planets circle other suns.
> The forests dance, the rivers upward rise,
> Whales sport in woods, and dolphins in the skies;
> At last, to give the whole creation grace,
> Lo! one vast egg produces human race! (qtd. in Mander 8)

The public did not care about the opinions of the literary elite. They came to pantomimes in droves. In fact, pantomime's popularity brought in so much revenue for the London theaters that it was virtually underwriting the productions of more purely literary plays. As the form developed during the eighteenth century, the Harlequinade characters began to speak and sing. In the nineteenth century, pantomime became more closely associated with the Christmas season, and the plots were drawn from popular stories and fairy tales rather than from classical myth and legend. The shows became longer, stand-alone productions, and pantomime became more and more a family entertainment. Even the literary elite began to enjoy the shows. Charles Dickens was a fan; he even edited the memoirs of the great Grimaldi, the most famous of the pantomime clowns.

The Victorian Era was the heyday of pantomime. By the mid 1800s it had become a lavish children's entertainment produced only at Christmas. In the 1850s elements of burlesque theater were introduced into pantomime, adding popular songs and new stock characters like the comic Dame played by a man in drag. The special effects grew more and more elaborate, as did the casts, which needed lots of extras to portray fairy troupes or comic armies. Every theater in London as well as regional theaters throughout the country produced a pantomime for Christmas, and much of the rest of the year went into planning and preparing for these productions.

At the beginning of the twentieth century, when Barrie began to escort the Llewelyn Davies boys to annual Christmas pantomimes, "panto," as it is often called, was a long-standing English tradition. The Harlequinade itself had shrunk to a short final scene at the end of an extravagantly produced fairy tale or other popular story. Aladdin and Cinderella were favorite pantomime subjects, and so was Robinson Crusoe, although it was not a Crusoe Defoe would have recognized. Children sat entranced by amazing transformation scenes that created magical fairy lands using every imaginable trick of lighting and stagecraft.

In 1901 Barrie took his young friends to a new Christmas pantomime called *Bluebell in Fairy Land*, written by its male star, Seymour Hicks. Unlike most pantos, which remounted the same popular stories again and again, *Bluebell* boasted an original plot not based on any traditional fairy tale. Several biographers suggest that this may have given Barrie the idea of writing his own original pantomime, although they also mention a private pantomime called "The Greedy Dwarf," which Barrie wrote, produced, and performed in his home on January 7, 1901. In any case, Barrie cannot be credited with being the first writer to conceive of an original story for a pantomime. Nor could Hicks. In pantomime's then two-hundred-year history, original stories had been introduced now and again, after which they soon became "traditional" stories, as indeed *Peter Pan* was to become the "traditional" Christmas entertainment for English children for over a century.

In 1904, the original audience would have easily recognized *Peter Pan* as a pantomime. First of all, it was produced as one, scheduled for a short run during the Christmas season. The only unusual aspect of this panto, besides the original story, was the fact that it was written by a famous playwright of the legitimate stage. Despite (and maybe because of) its immense popularity, pantomime was still viewed as Pope had seen it: vulgar entertainment for the uneducated masses. Becoming a children's entertainment had actually improved pantomime's reputation among the intelligentsia. Even though children, like the masses, have not developed any discernment in theatrical matters, the late Victorians and the Edwardians had an idealized view of childhood and valued it highly. Most newspapers reviewed the pantomimes just as they would a new production of *Hamlet*, only with a difference in tone: arch or whimsical or patronizing. Nevertheless, one seldom found a well-known playwright contributing to the pantomime tradition. The mass appeal of pantomime is also why it has often been overlooked in literary history, just as early histories of children's literature ignored such widely popular forms as dime novels and penny dreadfuls and comic books. Most of the standard sources a Barrie scholar would consult never mention pantomimes.

Barrie's first audience also would have recognized and accepted numerous elements in *Peter Pan* as part of the pantomime. For example, the matter of casting provides important evidence. Peter Pan has almost always been played by a woman. This cross-gendered casting has puzzled some critics and Barrie biographers. They have come up with interesting and sometimes convoluted reasons to explain it. The favorite theory is that Barrie was working around a British law that made it illegal to have children under fourteen on stage after 9:00 at night. Casting a grown woman as Peter meant that the other children's roles could be scaled according to her height rather than a boy's, allowing older children to play younger parts (Birkin 105). Other scholars suggest that the part of Peter Pan was so demanding that a child could not have handled it. However, the most logical reason for the cross-gendered casting is that the male lead of a pantomime was always played by a woman. One of the burlesque elements introduced into pantomime in the 1850s was the practice of cross-gendered roles, usually for comic effect. Thus, Cinderella's ugly stepsisters were usually played by men, preferably big, hairy men. Similarly, the young male lead was a role called Principal Boy, always played by a woman. There was a Principal Girl too, also played by a woman. In *Peter Pan*, Wendy is the Principal Girl. There was never any question that Peter Pan would be played by an actress. All but one of the Lost Boys were also portrayed by women, as was one of Wendy's younger brothers. The other brother, John, and the sixth Lost Boy were tall young male actors, and their size in comparison to the others was used for comic effect.

Ever since John Rich first introduced pantomime to an English audience, the serious Opening had ended with a benevolent agent transforming the classical characters into the humorous stock characters of the Harlequinade. The actors thus performed double roles in every pantomime. By Barrie's day, the Opening had itself been transformed into a humorous fairy play and the Harlequinade had all but disappeared, but the tradition of double casting is reflected in the dual role of Mr. Darling/Captain Hook. This hybrid character is a kind of Pantaloon figure: the enraged father chasing the trickster Harlequin, who has eloped with daughter Columbine. Why does Hook hate Peter Pan and constantly seek to kill him? Because Peter is Harlequin, and Pantaloon always goes after Harlequin.

Peter is clearly a Harlequin figure. According to Peter Holland, the role of Principal Boy originated as Harlequin (198). Harlequin was the star of the Harlequinade; he was adept at disguise and mimicry and was a gifted acrobat, musician, and dancer. Mostly, though, he was an inveterate trickster and magician. Peter Pan's antics and actions retain much of Harlequin's personality. His self-identification as "a little bird that has broken out of the egg" may actually be a tribute to John Rich, the original English Harlequin, who always portrayed Harlequin hatching from an egg—a famous bit of stage business (Wilson 22).

In a similar fashion, Columbine became Principal Girl, or Wendy in *Peter Pan*. The focus of Harlequin's affections, Columbine willingly ran off with him (though usually not with two younger brothers in tow) and participated in his various tricks and transformations. The Principal Girl, states Holland, is "a fantasy of girlhood. . . . Pretty but not beautiful, wholesome and innocent, the Principal Girl is the fantasy of the girl-next-door. . . . The figure is de-eroticized: a focus not for sexual desire but for sentimentalized, non-sexual, romantic love" (199). In Wendy's case, of course, her Harlequin, Peter Pan, seeks maternal love rather than romantic love, but with that exception, Holland's description fits Wendy perfectly.

Another type of pantomime character used in *Peter Pan* was the animal character. Actors call such roles "skin parts." Wendy and her brothers have a large Newfoundland dog as their nursemaid. Nana, the dog, was usually played by a man, but never by an actual dog, although Barrie claims he allowed his pet Newfoundland to do a walk-on one night. In more minor roles, *Peter Pan* features several wolves and a very large crocodile. Individual actors were in the wolf costumes, but the crocodile had two actors—a front half and a back half. This was typical of traditional pantomimes, which often featured actors in animal costume. After all, most of the plots came from fairy tales. What would *Puss in Boots* be without Puss? Dick Whittington was also a favorite subject for pantomime, and his cat played an important part. *Mother Goose* always included a large goose, and *Robinson Crusoe* featured a dog. Animal characters were so popular that they were often introduced into stories that did not originally include animals, for example, a dog in *Aladdin*. Pantomimes were populated by comic cows, chickens, monkeys, storks, and other livestock.

The diminutive fairy Tinker Bell was also derived from the pantomime tradition. The Victorians had popularized fairylands in their pantomimes. *Bluebell in Fairy Land*, the panto some think inspired Barrie, had lots of fairies. The closing scene of *Peter Pan* also contained hundreds of fairies. Representing fairies by means of bells and stage lights was the normal practice, but seldom were they used as effectively as in the portrayal of Tinker Bell. Variations of the tinkling bell and the flickering light created the illusion of a real person with a complex personality. In this, as in many other ways, Barrie improved on usual pantomime practice.

Besides characters, much of the stage business in *Peter Pan* comes from the pantomime tradition. As Michael Booth explains in *Victorian Spectacular Theatre,*

> In a real sense melodrama and pantomime were creations of technology. The very existence of new materials, new stage machinery, and new methods of lighting impelled them into a dramatic structure which in part existed to display the ingenuity of machinist, gasman, head carpenter, costume designer, and stage manager. (64)

Pantomime was thus ostentatious, extravagant, and elaborate, and it provided a grand display of technical virtuosity. All of Barrie's biographers have commented on the difficulties of producing *Peter Pan* because of these very elements. They focus particularly on the problem of flying across the stage. Although Barrie is often credited with inventing stage flight for *Peter Pan*, characters had been flying on stage in pantomime since the early 1700s. Barrie improved on the practice by hiring a professional aerialist to invent a new kind of harness. To protect himself and the theater, he required his actors to take out insurance policies before they learned to use the harness.

Elaborate sets and stage effects such as those in *Peter Pan* were standard in pantomime. Towards the end of every panto there was a transformation scene that was expected to outdo all the previous sets and effects. A character would cross the stage and wave a magic wand, then cue the music and the curtain. When the curtain rose on the transformation scene, the audience should gasp in wonder and continue to do so as the transformation unfolded. Booth describes the process:

> The effects of a transformation, which might take twenty minutes to unfold, were dependent upon a combination of machinery, lighting, changing scenic pieces and gauzes, and the display of a large number of beautifully costumed women, some floating high above the stage. More than half the machinery for a transformation scene was worked from beneath the stage, and basically what happened was that a large platform suspended by ropes and counterweights rose through an opening in the stage created by removing that section of the stage floor during the preceding scene. On this platform were about twenty fairies, mermaids, waternymphs, angels, or the like. . . . While this was going on the lighting intensified, gauzes were raised, scenery changed, the orchestra played, other performers appeared on stage, and the transformation moved in a leisurely way toward a climax. (80)

In the orginial production of *Peter Pan*, the transformation scene began when the minor character Liza, a housemaid (who was also in Barrie's whimsy listed on the program as author of the play), walked across the stage with the magic wand, which in the stage directions was referred to as Harlequin's wand, and initiated the transformation. The curtain opened on a scene of Peter's little house in the treetops, where Wendy is saying good-bye after her annual visit to do his spring cleaning. She leaves, and dusk settles as Peter plays his pipes and thousands of fairy homes start to twinkle around him. Music, lights, and set combined to create stage magic. This one scene is proof enough that *Peter Pan* is a pantomime because its only reason for existence is the pantomime tradition. The scene contributes nothing to the story of Peter Pan; the previous scene in the children's nursery was the natural end of the play.

Song and dance were also required elements in pantomime. However, pantomimes were not musicals the way *My Fair Lady* or *Oklahoma* is a musical; in panto the songs did not help to develop character and plot or set the mood. Years later there would be a musical version of Peter Pan on Broadway, not to mention the Disney musical cartoon, but the first production used music in a different way. It was musical like a variety show. There were set pieces so that various actors and actresses could show off their singing and dancing talents. In the opening scene, Mrs. Darling sang an old lullaby to her children and Peter performed a shadow dance. Later the pirates sang pirate songs, the Indians performed a tribal dance, and one of the Lost Boys did a well-received pillow dance. The songs and dances often changed from one production of *Peter Pan* to the next, according to the talents of the cast. For example, the pillow dance was the specialty of American actress Pauline Chase. After she was promoted to the role of Peter in later productions, the Lost Boys no longer did a pillow dance. This kind of change is a common feature of pantomime, as are elaborately staged mock battles like those between the Lost Boys and the pirates and between the Indians and the pirates.

One of the most famous moments in *Peter Pan* occurs when Tinker Bell has drunk from a poisoned cup to save Peter's life. Peter turns to the audience to save Tinker Bell, asking them to clap if they believe in fairies. And, of course, the audience claps resoundingly and Tinker Bell revives. According to most of Barrie's biographers, this was seen as a bit of risky stage business. What if the audience did not clap? However, it was not as risky as some people think. Audience participation was a standard part of pantomime, rather like melodrama, in which the audience is expected to boo and hiss when the villain enters and cheer the hero. In pantomime, ritual dialogues developed between characters and audience, and shouting back at the actors at set times was part of the entertainment. Although *Peter Pan* does not offer that level of audience involvement, Barrie could count on the fact that the audience was trained to respond to an actor's appeal, so they were bound to clap to save Tinker Bell.

Other common features of pantomime included panoramic tableaux and formal processions. As the play has come down to us, *Peter Pan* no longer contains either of those elements, but the first production featured both. When Wendy persuaded the Lost Boys to return with her to England, there was a procession of beautiful mothers who came to claim their lost sons. In fact, there were far more mothers than there were Lost Boys to be claimed. And after Peter vanquished Captain

Hook, the curtain opened on a Napoleonic tableau—Peter as a victorious Napoleon on the ship, with the other characters posed appropriately around him wearing French officers' uniforms. The scene was presented without motion or dialogue.

The main feature of the early pantomime—the Harlequinade—had shrunk almost out of existence by Barrie's day, but it was still the final scene of many pantomimes. The original manuscript for *Peter Pan* ends with a Harlequinade set in Kensington Gardens. Captain Hook appears as a schoolmaster; there are six schoolgirls accompanied by a governess, a couple of Lost Boys, Peter, and Tinker Bell (called in the manuscript Tippytoe). In this scene Peter and the boys are transformed into clowns (as Pierrot became known), the schoolgirls into Columbines, and the governess into Harlequin (Jack, "The Manuscript" 105). By this point in panto's development, Clown had replaced Harlequin as the trickster, with Harlequin relegated to a dancing role; thus Barrie transforms Peter into a clown rather than a harlequin. The clowns vanquish the schoolmaster, who then is finished off by a crocodile. According to Denis Mackail, Barrie's first biographer, "a harlequin and columbine flitted across the stage in the first acted version—who take part in a kind of ballet with a corps of assistant-[school]masters" (352). This scene was dropped amost immediately, but it provides more evidence that Barrie was writing a pantomime. The governess was clearly meant to be a comic Dame and would have been played by a man in drag. The only sign of the Harlequinade that remained in the early productions of *Peter Pan* was the stage direction for the transformation scene, which specifically states that Liza carries a Harlequin wand. From its earliest days, pantomime included this object, often called Harlequin's bat and viewed as a phallic symbol. Harlequin used it as a magic wand to transform characters and scenery into new and unusual people and things. Liza and the Harlequin wand did not make it into any of the published texts of *Peter Pan*, so all traces of the Harlequinade have disappeared.

Peter Pan would not exist if not for the pantomime tradition. Pantomime was at the back of Barrie's mind even in *The Little White Bird*, which contains an episode featuring figures from a Harlequinade. From his first appearance in print, Peter was associated with panto, a term which might have been Barrie's inspiration for calling his most famous creation Peter "Pan." Even if pantomime remains a mere inkblot in the history of theater, it deserves to be remembered for this contribution to children's literature. Of course, it is also only one of many influences on a play that transcends any kind of literary dissection, as we hope this collection of essays will show.

PETER PAN'S REVERBERATIONS

Peter Pan seems to be the mightiest figure in children's literature, for most writers, especially fantasy writers, have to wrestle with his image at some point, either happily admitting the influence or so steeped in it that they do not even recognize it. He is a slippery sort, leaving his traces on our stories or his shadow to haunt us. He engages us in secret dialogue so that we continue the conversation that Barrie began, arguing the silliness of Neverland even as we manage to squeeze Peter into our literary dreams.

We grew up with Peter Pan in the 1950s and early '60s with two separate versions: Disney's animated film (1953) and the frequent showings on television of Mary Martin's flying acrobatics.[3] Of course, we all know how Disney appropriated the story and well-nigh galvanized it into a simple tale that belies both the complexity of Barrie's story and of growing up in general. Then there was mother-obsessed Steven Spielberg's *Hook* (1991), which drew on pop psychology's concept of the inner child as Robin Williams's Peter Banning, who has grown up to resemble the piratous Hook, realizes that he has to recover his lost childhood in order to become a better parent. Offering an early celebration of the one-hundredth anniversary of the play, P. J. Hogan's *Peter Pan* came out as a live-action film in 2003, one that makes clear the seductive relationship between Peter and almost every other major character as it attempts to give Wendy more agency; she is sexually frustrated, but then so are Tinker Bell and Tiger Lily and the mermaids (and probably even Hook). The most recent movie to tackle Peter Pan is *Finding Neverland* (2004). Unlike the earlier versions, which tried to repeat or revise the original play, *Finding Neverland* somewhat inaccurately examines the creation of Peter Pan, drawing a sentimental (albeit engaging) portrait of Barrie, Sylvia Llewelyn Davies, and her boys. Continuing the sexual overtones of 2003's *Peter Pan, Finding Neverland* attempts to retrieve Barrie's virility, suggesting a physical relationship with his wife Mary Ansell as well as posing star Johnny Depp as a cricket player, sitting on a bench with legs askew and looking as though his machismo is latent but not absent.[4] Although the film reenacts the first production of *Peter Pan* with the title character played by an actress, it is clear that Barrie's Peter Pan is male.

The centenary of *Peter Pan* reminds us how influential Barrie's story has been and continues to be; not just popular culture but also much of children's literature is informed (and misinformed) by Barrie's ideas. Some novels are strongly redolent of Barrie, as is Natalie Babbitt's *Tuck Everlasting* (1975). Here, Peter is embodied as Jesse Tuck, part of a family who once drank from a mysterious stream and have not grown older for decades; Jesse looks and acts 17 but is really 104. Wendy becomes Winnie, who is attracted to the winsome boy, especially when he gives her some of the magic water and tempts her to drink from it when she turns 17 so that they can wander around the world in never-ending youthful gaiety. The other members of the Tuck family are clearly miserable, wishing they were mortal; Angus Tuck explains to Winnie that they are excluded from the cycle of life and are unnatural. Readers are left guessing until the end of the novel as to whether or not Winnie drinks the water; a final scene set many years later shows the Tucks returning to Winnie's town and visiting her grave.

Even more than *Tuck Everlasting*, which tries to warn young readers of the inappropriateness and unnaturalness of everlasting life, Nancy Farmer's *The Ear, the Eye and the Arm* (1994) offers readers both characters and plot that parallel that of *Peter Pan*. Set in Zimbabwe in 2194, the story involves three children who are kidnapped but also includes several characters who cannot or will not grow up: Trashman, who is mentally challenged and has no short-term memory, and the Mellower, who is the children's irresponsible nanny/storyteller (who also is afraid of being thrown to the crocodiles). Clearly these characters, although quite likeable, are not to be admired. Tendai, the oldest child, wonders, "What would it be like to go outside the way everyone else did and fly—all alone, without bodyguards or the police or Father—to a magical place none of them had seen before?" (24). The places the children are taken to are far from magical. Even Resthaven, where time has essentially stopped in order that a select few people can maintain the tribal lifestyle of an earlier century, is dangerous because it is stagnant; and Tendai, while at first tempted to stay, eventually sees how it is suffocating him and his siblings. Throughout, Farmer tries to both borrow from and argue with Peter Pan's legacy, especially when the children's father, who had kept them isolated and inexperienced within their highly guarded enclave, says after they have been kidnapped, "Why, why didn't I let them grow up?" (51). *The Ear, the Eye and the Arm* is a warning to parents and children that staying child-like is just plain dangerous; survival requires that children be taught how to take care of themselves, to be wary rather than naïve, self-reliant rather than dependent.

More recently, Phyllis Shalant's *When Pirates Came to Brooklyn* (2002) tries to dramatize the enormous effect the several popular productions of *Peter Pan* had on children: in 1960, two lonely girls—one Christian, one Jewish—develop a friendship based on their re-enacting the adventures of Peter Pan.[5] They fight pirates and practice flying, while slowly helping their parents let go of their religious prejudices. The novel is realistic, but it contains one brief foray into fantasy: Lee actually does fly once to visit her friend, and there is a bit of evidence to show that the event was not a dream.

Dave Barry and Ridley Pearson's *Peter and the Starcatchers* (2004) is currently getting the most attention, perhaps because it is billed as a prequel to Barrie's story. *Starcatchers* attempts to explain Peter's ability to fly and the original identities of Hook, the pirates, the redskins, the mermaids, and the Lost Boys. The major female, Molly, has more in common with Avi's Charlotte Doyle than with Wendy, as the authors deliberately allow her to display as much or more derring do as Peter himself. *Peter and the Starcatchers* is admittedly an engaging adventure story, but any attempt to explain Peter Pan and Neverland—to logically figure out how Peter got there—seems somehow dull and unmagical, even though *Starcatchers* itself employs fantasy in the guise of alien fairy dust, which is what enables Peter to fly. This novel tries to take away the veil, to expose the falsity of the magician's trick, while replacing the veil with another, less fascinating one. *Starcatchers* is not complex enough or imaginative enough (or controversial enough) to have the continuing influence of Barrie's creation.

As much as these contemporary stories seem to want to revise the image of Peter Pan and impress upon child readers the necessity of growing up, they actually revise only Disney's popular image of Peter Pan, not the Peter Pan of Barrie's play and novel. As many readers come to realize, and as Barrie himself tells us, *Peter Pan* is a tragic tale. Even as children, we know it is not just that "[a]ll children, except one, grow up" (*Peter and Wendy* 1) but that all children, except one, *want* to grow up; and as adults we feel like the grown-up Wendy, "a grown woman smiling at it all, but they were wet smiles" (218), feeling his loneliness, his bravado, his loveless life. Peter Pan does not love us and does not remember us, and that is exactly why we love and remember him, because we know what he is missing.

THE ESSAYS

The fifteen essays in this collection offer a wide array of new readings of *Peter Pan*, interpretations that challenge our smug belief that we already know all there is to know about this story. The essays are highly provocative and enlightening and, though diverse, all connect with the theme of time—whether examining the contemporary influences on Barrie as he created *Peter Pan* (Part I: In His Own Time); the impact *Peter Pan* has had on children's literature and culture in the ensuing decades in the United States (Part II: In and Out of Time—*Peter Pan* in America); the problematic narrative and time structures of the play and novel (Part III: Timelessness and Timeliness of *Peter Pan*); and recent feminist approaches to the texts (Part IV: Women's Time). These essays document the continuing interest of *Peter Pan* not just to children but to children's literature criticism as it connects to cultural, psychoanalytical, feminist, historical, and linguistic theories.

Part I: In His Own Time. We begin our centenary celebration of *Peter Pan* with a lively essay by Karen Coats, who discusses the relationship between Hook and Peter in terms of child hatred in "Child-Hating: *Peter Pan* in the Context of Victorian Hatred." Drawing on James Kincaid's theories of pedophilia and Christopher Lane's theories of Victorian misanthropy, Coats argues that Hook represents our societal need to manage our general hatred of children. Coats's essay is followed by "The Time of His Life: Peter Pan and the Decadent Nineties," in which Paul Fox reads Barrie's story as a reflection of Walter Pater's aesthetics. Drawing parallels with both Pater and Oscar Wilde, Fox posits Peter Pan as a successful aesthete, living in the moment, continually recreating himself in order to defeat creative stagnation—that is, time. Our third contributor, Christine Roth, argues that *Peter Pan*, long considered the exemplar of the Cult of the Boy Child, is instead a carryover from the Victorian Cult of the Girl Child. Tracing the transformation of focus from boy as simultaneously mature and boyish, Roth's "Babes in Boy-Land: J. M. Barrie and the Edwardian Girl" shows how Barrie's female characters display alternating visions of the girl as innocent and worldly, daughter and mother, Wendy and Mrs. Darling. From the Cult of the Girl Child we move on to what might be called the Cult of the Pirate with Jill May's "James Barrie's Pirates: *Peter Pan*'s Place in Pirate History and Lore," which examines the influence of pirate lore—from operettas to childhood adventure stories to biographical accounts—on Barrie's creation of Captain Hook. The final essay in Part I is Kayla

McKinney Wiggins's "More Darkly down the Left Arm: The Duplicity of Fairyland in the Plays of J. M. Barrie." Wiggins tracks the emergence of fairy lore in three of Barrie's plays: *Peter Pan*, *Dear Brutus*, and *Mary Rose*. All three employ elements of British (and particularly Celtic) fairy stories, drawn from Barrie's Scottish childhood.

Part II: In and Out of Time—Peter Pan *in America*. In "Problematizing Piccaninnies, or How J. M. Barrie Uses Graphemes to Counter Racism in *Peter Pan*," Clay Kinchen Smith uses Derrida's concept of the grapheme to argue that Barrie is attempting to undermine racial stereotypes. Unfortunately, Barrie's political agenda has been overshadowed by the many revisions of his work, especially Disney's 1953 film, that reinscribe the racialist characterizations. Following Smith's contribution, Rosanna West Walker tackles Barrie's influence on Willa Cather in "The Birth of a Lost Boy: Traces of J. M. Barrie's *Peter Pan* in Willa Cather's *The Professor's House*." Walker offers a convincing argument that Cather was engaging with Barrie's myth, notably in her focus on the avoidance of maturity in the major male characters of her 1925 novel *The Professor's House*.

Part III: Timelessness and Timeliness of Peter Pan. Part III opens with Irene Hsiao's "The Pang of Stone Words," which examines the binary of print literacy and orality and how this opposition structures the characters in *Peter Pan*. Even though Peter Pan is illiterate and too forgetful to tell a story, while Hook is a noted raconteur, these two characters are remarkably alike. From print literacy we segue to computer literacy with Cathlena Martin and Laurie Taylor's "Playing in Neverland: *Peter Pan* Video Game Revisions." Martin and Taylor contend that because of its origin in oral storytelling and because of the modular structure of the story, *Peter Pan* is ideally suited to video game narratives and offers potential for opening up the story for more participation by female characters and female players. In "The Riddle of His Being: An Exploration of Peter Pan's Perpetually Altering State," Karen McGavock examines the fluidity of Barrie's story and main character. The gender uncertainty, the playful narrator, and Barrie's constant revisions of the story all display the same fear of fixity and stagnation. Similarly, in "Getting Peter's Goat: Hybridity, Androgyny, and Terror in *Peter Pan*," Carrie Wasinger writes that the indeterminacy of gender, though common to Victorian audiences, was both threatening to Victorian gender distinctions and progressive. Wasinger argues that *Peter Pan*'s unstable narration allows readers to better identify with Peter's gender uncertainty. A different kind of uncertainty—the anxiety of influence—concerns John

Pennington in "Peter Pan, Pullman, and Potter: Anxieties of Growing Up." This essay highlights Philip Pullman and J. K. Rowling, who both publicly claim they dislike *Peter Pan* and the concept of never growing up, but who are nevertheless indebted to Barrie. Both reject Barrie's emphasis on maintaining innocence and make the dark undertones, the tragedy, more overt, allowing their characters—pushing their characters—into emotional, social, and sexual maturity. The last essay in this section offers a provocative Lacanian reading of *Peter Pan*: David Rudd's "The Blot of Peter Pan." Drawing on Barrie's short story of the same name (1926), Rudd argues that Peter Pan acts as "the maternal phallus" in his pre-Symbolic state.

Part IV: Women's Time. Neverland is an unconscious creation of Mrs. Darling, says M. Joy Morse in "The Kiss: Female Sexuality and Power in J. M. Barrie's *Peter Pan*." Explaining first the historical context for the ambivalent position of wives and mothers in the late nineteenth century, Morse goes on to show how Mrs. Darling's ambivalence over her societal roles is reflected in her dream about Neverland. Like Morse, Emily Clark is interested in women's roles in Victorian England, but in "The Female Figure in J. M. Barrie's *Peter Pan*: The Small and the Mighty," she examines those roles against the backdrop of British colonialism. Focusing on the physical attributes and dialogue of Wendy, Tinker Bell, and Tiger Lily, Clark finds that all three characters overcome their liminality to some degree by appropriating agency for themselves.

Through these essays, our understanding of *Peter Pan* is broadened, our own boundaries of meaning stretched, and our fixed borders torn down. Truly, Barrie's creation is an evocative text, still flirting with readers to declare new meanings. It is nevertheless nice to know that *Peter Pan* will never be settled, but will always be controversial and always, we hope, read.

NOTES

1. When Barrie wrote the play *Peter Pan*, his name already adorned twenty published volumes (novels, collections of stories, nonfiction) and twelve London plays. Several of the books were best sellers, and one of the plays was *The Admirable Crichton*, the most popular and critically acclaimed of Barrie's plays for adult audiences.

2. Barrie's original name for his imaginary wonderland was The Never Never Never Land. He soon edited it to The Never Never Land, then to The Never Land, and finally to Neverland.

3. Mary Martin's debut as Peter Pan on Broadway, which coincided with the release of Disney's animated film (1953), was staged live on television in 1955 and again in 1956. In 1960, Martin's performance was videotaped and was shown several times through the 1970s.

4. In real life, Barrie was an avid cricket player. He was the captain of a private cricket team, the Allahakbarries, composed mostly of artists and authors and better known for socializing than for winning cricket games.

5. The characters discover a male cologne called, oddly, Pirate's Booty. Even more bizarre is a snack food by Robert's American Gourmet called Pirate's Booty that can be found now in grocery stores. The sexual meaning of the modern slang word "booty" seems to have escaped both children's authors and snack food manufacturers.

WORKS CITED

Babbitt, Natalie. *Tuck Everlasting.* 1975. New York: Farrar, Straus and Giroux, 1985.

Barrie, J. M. *The Boy Castaways of Black Lake Island.* N.p.: Privately printed, 1901.

———. *The Little White Bird, or Adventures in Kensington Gardens.* London: Hodder & Stoughton, 1902.

———. *Peter and Wendy.* 1911. New York: Scribner's, 1935.

———. *Peter Pan in Kensington Gardens.* London: Hodder & Stoughton, 1906.

———. *Peter Pan; or, The Boy Who Wouldn't Grow Up.* Duke of York's Theatre, London. 27 Dec. 1904.

———. *Peter Pan; or, The Boy Who Would Not Grow Up.* London: Hodder & Stoughton, 1928.

Barry, Dave, and Ridley Pearson. *Peter and the Starcatchers.* New York: Hyperion, 2004.

Birkin, Andrew. *J. M. Barrie & the Lost Boys: The Love Story that Gave Birth to Peter Pan.* New York: Clarkson N. Potter, 1979.

Booth, Michael R. *Victorian Spectacular Theatre 1850–1910.* Theatre Production Studies. Boston: Routledge & Kegan Paul, 1981.

Farmer, Nancy. *The Ear, the Eye and the Arm.* 1994. New York: Puffin, 1995.

Finding Neverland. Dir. Marc Forster. Perf. Johnny Depp, Kate Winslet, Dustin Hoffman. Miramax, 2004.

Hanson, Bruce K. *The Peter Pan Chronicles: The Nearly 100 Year History of "The Boy Who Wouldn't Grow Up."* New York: Birch Lane P, 1993.

Holland, Peter. "The Play of Eros: Paradoxes of Gender in English Pantomime." *New Theatre Quarterly* 13 (1997): 195–204.

Hook. Dir. Steven Spielberg. Perf. Robin Williams, Dustin Hoffman, Julia Roberts. Columbia/Tristar, 1991.

Jack, R. D. S. "The Manuscript of *Peter Pan.*" *Children's Literature* 18 (1990): 101–113.

————. *The Road to the Never Land: A Reassessment of J. M. Barrie's Dramatic Art.* Aberdeen, Scot.: Aberdeen UP, 1991.

Mackail, Denis. *Barrie: The Story of J. M. B.* New York: Charles Scribner's Sons, 1941.

Mander, Raymond, and Joe Mitchenson. *Pantomime: A Story in Pictures.* New York: Taplinger, 1973.

Peter Pan. Dir. Clyde Geronimi and Wilfred Jackson. Disney Studios, 1953.

Peter Pan. Dir. P. J. Hogan. Perf. Jason Isaacs and Jeremy Sumter. Universal Studios, 2003.

Peter Pan, the musical. Dir. Vincent J. Donehue. Adapted and choreographed by Jerome Robbins. Perf. Mary Martin, Cyril Richard, 1960.

Shalant, Phyllis. *When Pirates Came to Brooklyn.* New York: Dutton, 2002.

Wilson, A. E. *The Story of Pantomime.* 1949. Totowa, NJ: Rowman & Littlefield, 1974.

I

IN HIS OWN TIME

1

Child-Hating: *Peter Pan* in the Context of Victorian Hatred

Karen Coats

J. M. Barrie's *Peter Pan* is one of the most beloved and enduring works of children's literature of all time. Its wistful celebration of childhood freedoms and specifically boyish confidence induces in readers a nostalgia for something that probably never existed for most of us, but exerts a strong pull nonetheless. Indeed, the idea that there is a place outside of real-world constraints—where children have power and the pesky confines of things like gravity and calorie-counting don't matter in the slightest—animates our most compelling fantasies; the continental drift of our inner geographies always seems to tend toward the Neverlands of the Emerald City, the other side of the looking glass, Narnia, and Hogwarts, to name but a few choice destinations. In these fanciful locations, adult preoccupations are explicitly or implicitly called into question, and we emerge with a fuzzy memory of the sweetness of our sojourn there. This memory, however, is more or less faulty, insofar as it glosses over a certain dark side that persists in each of these fantasy worlds—a force that does not cherish our presence there and, indeed, threatens it. The fantasy spaces of childhood are not safe places; they are not places where children are universally loved and protected. Instead, they almost always include beings that hate both the state of childhood and children themselves.

Such is the case with Neverland, the home of Peter Pan. When Wendy and her brothers travel there, they realize very quickly that it is a treacherous place, a place where their lives are endangered on a regular basis and thrills are always linked to violence. This sort of excitement is exhilarating at first, but it induces a careless forgetfulness and irresponsibility to others that Wendy finds disturbing. Her sense of values, even her sense of humanity, is strongly linked to home and family, and if that means going home and accepting the responsibility of growing up, then so be it. It might even be said that, to some degree, Wendy's ambivalent relationship to childhood is both a necessary and desirable attitude to foster in children: as much as she may enjoy the relatively carefree state of childhood, she doesn't really regret its passing overmuch. This romantic celebration of childhood, limned by the inevitabilities of growing up, is standard fare in children's books. But there is a force at work in *Peter Pan* that goes beyond a tolerant regret over something we must always inevitably lose. In his authorial asides as well as in his plot structure, Barrie sets up a deliberately antagonistic relationship between childhood and adulthood, and in the characters of Peter Pan and Hook, he reveals the truly violent nature of that relationship and its groundedness in an irrational hatred. Barrie sets up a stark choice for both Wendy and the Lost Boys: to choose home, hearth, and a loving family means to reject the heartlessness of Peter Pan (which is how Barrie characterizes his essential childness) and to revoke citizenship in Neverland forever. Hence this beloved book that seemingly focuses on a love of all things childlike has at its core a hatred—a hatred that is often overlooked.

Interestingly enough, it is this undercurrent of hatred that places this "timeless" book squarely in the context of its time and place. Although we generally tend to think of Victorian and Edwardian society as models of decorum, civility, and philanthropy, we must attend to the currents of misanthropy, imperialism, and outright hatred of otherness that bubbled under the surface of these prim, elite folk. Such attention will force us to challenge the most prevalent ideology of turn-of-the-century child-adult relations, as articulated by James Kincaid, as well as to question anew why Barrie's work continues to resonate so much with us today.

In his smart though somewhat campy book, *Child-Loving: The Erotic Child and Victorian Culture*, Kincaid claims that since Victorian times, we have all become child-lovers on some level and, paradoxically, that we have created the figure of the monstrous pedophile in order to set up a distance between a proper fascination with children and that which would be considered improper. Kincaid says that, insofar as we construct the child as desirable, we need someone to desire him.

Desire, however, is a greedy thing with a tendency to stretch into all sorts of morbidity. Hence we are led to ask: what would happen if our desire for the child that we have constructed ran amok, got out of control? Enter the pedophile, who acts as a repository for all the possible ways that our own tame, respectable desire might reach its extremity. Indeed, Kincaid claims, in order to set limits on child-loving, culture needs the pedophile, who will violate those limits, activate our revulsion, and send us scurrying back to the right side of the imaginary line separating child and adult in terms of erotic desire. The pedophile thus occupies the position of the abject—that which haunts the borders of propriety and respectability, keeping those borders permanently brittle so that we must maintain our vigilance against it.

Despite my emphasis so far on child-hating, I don't wish to argue with Kincaid, who gets it right, I think, on this point. He has hit on the psychoanalytic truth of perversion: the pervert serves the cause of conservatism by acting out the unconscious fantasies of the mainstream, thus allowing those fantasies to remain unconscious and allowing culture to congratulate itself on its moral rectitude. This argument is advanced in psychoanalytic circles with regard to adult sexual, particularly homosexual, activity, but it is even more apt in our relations with children. According to Kincaid, we have evacuated the child of any particular sexual qualities in order to render her innocent and turn her into a screen for our own projections. Following this, he says, "*I* want to claim that the way in which we have constructed the child, the way in which it has been constructed historically, makes its desirability inevitable" (198). Here desirability is construed in its most ordinary garden variety, as something deliciously yummy, something worth having, worth preserving in its current form. Desire equals love—specifically, an idealized love of the pure object. We want to capture childhood like a dragonfly in amber so that we may look at it from a distance as a static, inviolate object. The pedophile wants to violate that space of childhood, but not out of aggression. According to Kincaid, rather, he wants to touch the child out of a desire to enter into its purity— pedophiles are sweeties, really, who undoubtedly have boundary issues, but are on the whole quite gentle and often, under Kincaid's rendering, could be viewed to represent our best selves rather than our worst. It is almost as if Kincaid feels responsible for those who fill the role of the pedophile; if we as a culture have created them and we use them to keep our own errant desires in line, then we need to exercise some measure of compassion for the monsters we have created.

Moreover, Kincaid maintains that the pedophile is a textual construct, which would make his or her crimes predicated neither on sex
nor on violence, but on textuality.[1] He uses real-life and textual examples of pedophilia interchangeably in his work, which is troubling, especially since the brutal truth of his thesis is that we are all pedophiles,
separate only from the perpetrators of actual criminal acts by a matter
of degree. This blurring of actual and textual subjectivities, however, is
quite common practice in post-Nietzschean discourse, though a similar
line of reasoning can be found in the Pauline letters of the New Testament. Nietzsche would suggest that the subject emerges in a discourse
of accountability; likewise, Paul indicates that we only have a sense of
ourselves as transgressors of a law because we have prior exposure to
the written law that puts us in that position. But whereas Paul holds us
accountable for that position, Kincaid is more ambiguous about where
responsibility lies. As Judith Butler puts it,

> [A] set of painful effects is taken up by a moral framework that seeks to
> isolate the "cause" of those effects in a singular and intentional agent, a
> moral framework that operates through a certain economy of paranoid
> fabrication and efficiency: *the question, then, of who is accountable for a
> given injury precedes and initiates the subject, and the subject itself is
> formed through being nominated to inhabit that grammatical and ju-
> ridical site.* (4–5)

In other words, in our textual constructions of the inevitably desirable
child, we have created an anxious space for the child-desirer to occupy; the notion of child-loving, and of the potentially injurious nature
of child-loving, must be in place before we have anyone to embody
those positions.

Kincaid, however, doesn't tell the whole story of our vexed notions
of the child and the relationships we build in light of them. In focusing
on the ways that we love and have loved children, for instance, he sup-
presses the ways we have hated them. Kincaid situates most of his arguments and evidences for child-loving in Victorian culture, even as he
effectively shows how little we actually know of that time and place.
Primarily, though, he is using Victorian culture as a lens through which
we may view our own cultural attitudes and practices. The point he
hammers home, and the most striking similarity between Victorian culture and ours, is the multivocality and variety of discourse on both
childhood and sexuality. Since his main thesis depends on linking the
discourses of childhood and sexuality, his readings of texts seek ways

in which they may be read alongside each other, to the exclusion of other possibilities.

Clearly, *Peter Pan* offers an amiable text through which one may link discourses of childhood and sexuality, and Kincaid does not disappoint. His reading of *Peter Pan* locates Peter as the inviolate signifier of desire for the viewer, a desire that is pedophilic in more than one sense. First, there is the nostalgia for an everlasting childhood—a love, then, for the child-like itself, as heartless, irresponsible, and carefree as it can be—but also, the more erotic fascination with the beautiful, "cocky," naked boy. The scene where Hook shimmies down Slightly's tree to find Peter, who has "[o]ne arm dropped over the edge of the bed, one leg . . . arched, and the unfinished part of his laugh . . . stranded on his mouth, which was open, showing the little pearls" (121), is deliberately provocative in its composition, according to Kincaid. But with this scene we reach a sort of limit to the thesis of child-loving. Had Hook been able to dislodge himself from Slightly's tree, Peter would surely have been violated, not in an act of eros, or love, but in an act of hatred, or violence: Hook surely would not have caressed the sleeping boy, but killed him.

I am, of course, not naively suggesting that the two actions are incompatible; indeed they are as often linked as not in the following way: to pursue either pedophilia or child-hating, we have to make the figure of the child into an object and enter into a relation of unequal power with regard to his or her subjectivity. That is, instead of engaging children at the level of subject to subject, we must enter into a relationship with them in terms of subject (us) and object (them). This requires a distancing, a sense of oneself as other than a child, that is, an adult. Presumably, many child readers, rather than view the children in the book as objects or others, will instead identify with them. These identifications will lead them to put the adult into the position of object, rather than a child, reversing the polarity of the relationship. Either way, we (whether child-subjects or adult-subjects) are no longer ethically bound to preserve the freedom of our objects and can thus manipulate them at will. Kincaid doesn't posit what goes on from the position of a child reading a child, but he figures that adult readers empty the child out, make him a cipher so that we can imagine him any way we need to. He follows this argument by describing two ways in which the child was given substance in Victorian culture—as what he calls "the gentle child" and "the naughty child." These two types of children play directly into pedophilic fantasies by performing their roles as

submissive, either to caresses or spankings. As such, they are in fact not
"other" at all, though we (and Kincaid) imagine them as such. Instead,
they are extensions of ourselves, necessary complements to our roles as
benevolent caretakers and wise teachers. We need them, in other
words, to complete our own roles. But Peter Pan, Kincaid admits, fits
neither profile. "Otherness cannot be made into a formula with these
characters [indicating both Peter and Alice, another child who does not
fit his formulas]," says Kincaid. However, he is wrong insofar as his first
two types—gentle and naughty—are not, as I have indicated, "other,"
though they are formulaic (276). I have argued elsewhere that Alice,
though I agree she is neither gentle nor naughty, is vexed as to her status as Other—she functions more as what Lacan calls an *objet petit a*, an
object with only a little otherness, understood as more of an extension
or completion of the self than a separate entity.[2] Peter Pan is different.

To suggest that something is empty, as Kincaid maintains of our construction of the child, is to imply that it might alternately be full. This is
the case with Peter Pan. It is not Peter Pan's emptiness or vacancy that
establishes our relationship to him, but his plenitude. But whereas Barrie insists that no woman can resist Peter, I know several adult women
readers who despise him and many other people of both genders who
are singularly unmoved by his story. His desirability, as it turns out, is
not inevitable. In fact, insofar as Peter seems to have no lack, he is a
difficult character to love. Wendy must convince herself that he is sin-
cere in wanting a mother, but that becomes a harder fantasy for her to
sustain as she comes to spend more time with him, and indeed Barrie
lets the reader know quite clearly that Peter is simply playing on
Wendy's desire to be his mother in order to keep her on as a chronicler
of his exploits. As a hero, he lacks only a bard to make him famous, but
his perpetually presentist way of being in the world makes this a luxury, not a necessity. Peter really doesn't have some disguised vulnerability that allows space for an other to penetrate and take up residence
in his heart. But since Kincaid and others have admirably articulated
the persistence of his power as a cultural icon (that is, the relationship
between Peter Pan and his audiences over time) and still others have
woven captivating tales of his relationship to his author, I'll do a rather
unfashionable thing here and stick with the relationships inside the
text. Of those, it is clear that the women and girls in the book (with the
exception of Nana) all adore Peter—Mrs. Darling, Wendy, Tinker Bell,
Tiger Lily, the mermaids, and even the Never Bird are all attracted to
Peter on some erotic level or another. They do not, however, all love

each other: Tinker Bell "hated [Wendy] with the fierce hatred of a very woman" (46), and the mermaids hate everyone except Peter. Mr. Darling and the pirates, on the other hand, don't seem to feel any compelling bent in Peter Pan's direction, though they are drawn into his games through circumstances beyond their control. Mr. Darling, however, is interesting in his own relationship to children. Repeatedly we find him hesitating over their desirability, figuring it in terms of cost-value ratios, and whether or not they admire him sufficiently. Obviously there is much irony here, but it points to an ambivalence that is amplified to hatred in Mr. Darling's Neverland counterpart, Captain Hook. Throughout the history of the play, in fact, a single actor has been dually cast as both Mr. Darling and Captain Hook, invoking nothing so much as a Jekyll/Hyde split in the character of Mr. Darling. Nana mistrusts the young scamp Peter Pan but desires only to keep her charges safe from his attraction, not feeling it herself. Finally, Hook may be said to be attracted to Peter, but it is the allure of an obsessive hatred, which we will need to locate with some specificity if we are to understand its position in a Victorian narrative.

What I am suggesting here, then, is that we need to unpack and perhaps deconstruct Kincaid's notion of the inevitability of the desirability of the child as such, which he claims is bequeathed to us from the Victorians. Moreover, I want to wrest *Peter Pan* from the traditional way of viewing the book and play as atemporal expressions of a timeless, indeed impossible, space of universal childhood. It can be argued that even Kincaid participates in this discourse to some extent by locating Peter outside of the two conventional Victorian portraits of the child that he identifies. However, I think there is much to be gained by reading *Peter Pan* as a text with primarily Victorian, though sometimes more Edwardian, concerns. As the two epistemes overlap, it is difficult and often unnecessary to disentangle their respective ideologies, especially in terms of an underlying hatred of the other that was subtended by an isolated nationalism and a class-based elitism, and was perhaps even more prevalent under the reign of Edward than during Victorian times. But we shall start, as Kincaid does, with the Victorians. Since hatred and antisocial, even murderous, impulses are so much a part of the relationships in this text, however, we shall depart from his preoccupations with children and sexuality, and focus on the tensions Victorians felt between the pull of community and the antisocial, misanthropic impulses and *schadenfreude* (that is, joy in the misfortunes of others) that infected their social life.

As Christopher Lane traces in his recent *Hatred and Civility: The Antisocial Life in Victorian England*, there is more evidence of hatred in Victorian literature than civility, more antipathy than sympathy. Lane points out that commentators of the period were holding forth regularly on nearly every conceivable type of hatred: "The Hatred of England," "The Hatred of Authority," "The Hatred of the Poor for the Rich," "Holy Hatred," "Racial Hatred" are but a few of the articles that ran in journals in the 1880s and 1890s (11). He offers compelling readings of the works of Edward Bulwer-Lytton, Charles Dickens, George Eliot, Charlotte Brontë, Robert Browning, and Joseph Conrad to show the varieties of contempt in which fictional characters held the masses. As Lord Goring says in Oscar Wilde's *An Ideal Husband*, "Other people are quite dreadful. The only possible society is oneself" (xvii). Lane uses this quote to note a shift in the understanding of misanthropy from the Romantics, who saw such a stance as a moral victory over corrupt society; for Victorians, the misanthrope was pathological and in need of a social cure. Reflecting this belief, the most common mode for representing Victorian hatred in fiction of the period was to have characters whose hatred was, in fact, punished and/or repressed in favor of a more sociable ethic. Hence, for instance, the "proud, niggardly, reserved, and suspicious" Bentley Drummle from *Great Expectations* (203) is killed during an act of his own viciousness, while the "silent and sullen and hang-dog" misanthrope, Sydney Carton, of *A Tale of Two Cities* is allowed the qualified redemption of self-sacrifice (169). But the authors Lane explores in detail, as well as Barrie himself, I think, offer hatred and antisocial behavior as a more complicated phenomenon with a less satisfying remedy.

For these authors, the problem of hatred emerges in the context of the transitional feelings that haunted Victorian society. As Walter E. Houghton notes in *The Victorian Frame of Mind, 1830–1870*, Victorians had a self-conscious experience of being in transition from old ways of thinking into modern ways. Houghton quotes John Stuart Mill as saying that "mankind have outgrown old institutions and old doctrines, and have not yet acquired new ones," indicating that the old institutions and doctrines are not those of the long eighteenth century, but of the Middle Ages (1). On social, political, religious, economic, intellectual, and domestic fronts, Victorians were having trouble accommodating the rise of a lifestyle founded on industrial, bourgeois capitalism. One of the prevailing feelings of the day was a profound nostalgia for a lost sense of security and community—one may have been on the wrong side of a feudal hierarchy, but at least one knew where one stood and what one could expect from life. However, when Victorians tried to engage with community, they met with competition and treachery as often or more often than they met with fellow feeling. Consider the fate, for instance, of Silas Marner, who was repeatedly beset by communal hatred and betrayal. Yet Victorians were repeatedly told by social commentators that community was what would save them. According to Lane, Victorians believed much more strongly than their predecessors that hatred had a social remedy, that companionship and warm domestic relations would provide the answer to their problems of isolation and nostalgic longing. He offers William Morris as a poignant example: Morris wrote that "fellowship is heaven, and lack of fellowship is hell," yet he also admitted that "[a]part from the desire to produce beautiful things, the leading passion of my life has been and is hatred of modern civilization" (qtd. in Lane xviii). Lane asserts that the tension between rancor and civility is systemic in Victorian culture "because it stems from impulses, emotions, and forms of rebellion that society can't integrate" (xlv). One of these emotions, demonstrated less often (perhaps because more likely to offend) but certainly highlighted in texts such as *Oliver Twist*, *The Water Babies*, and *Peter Pan*, is the hatred of children, as we shall see. Despite the prevalent and systemic nature of the hatred, however, the Victorians themselves tended to scapegoat the misanthrope as an aberrant, rather than necessary, condition of social life.

We can make a connection, then, between Kincaid's pedophiles (both textual and actual) and Lane's (textual) misanthropes: they are pathological limit cases, figures who voice an undercurrent made necessary by the particular forces of repression operative in their time. If, on the one hand, desire for a child must be curbed by the limits made plain by the pedophile who crosses them, then hatred, especially of the child, sets the limit in the opposite direction but with the same urgency in regard to cultural need. We mustn't hate children—how monstrous!—and hence we have figures like Hook and the exploitive bosses in Charles Kingsley's *The Water Babies* who do engage in the practice of hating children in order to manage readers' tendencies toward such hatred. Indeed, if Butler is correct in her assertion quoted earlier, textual figures such as these open up spaces for actual child-haters who will exploit and harm children without regard for any fragility that might render them worthy of protection. Victorian social activism on behalf of child laborers points to a manifest concern for the welfare of children, which in turn is subtended by a casual indifference to their fate, an idea that children, especially poor children, being as plentiful as rats, were more or less expendable. *Oliver Twist* and *The Water Babies* are exemplary here—the orphaned child on whom we are to take pity is surrounded by scoundrels and spoiled brats for whom such pity is less well-deserved. George Eliot's descriptions of the Victorian cult of babies, particularly in *Middlemarch*, are delivered with sardonic tones that barely conceal their ambivalence toward the creatures in question. Most telling, however, is the prevalence of tales of the dead or dying child. It is as if to maintain the illusion of a child's innocence and desirability, one must be unburdened by the more complicated presence of the child itself, who will never measure up to any ideal representation. Motives for reading such fare are assuredly complicated. On the one hand, such texts offer consolation to bereaved parents. On the other hand, to take pleasure in reading of the untimely and tragic death of anyone, let alone a child, can point to a tendency toward *schadenfreude*, or at least a bit of better-him-than-me, in one's personal taste. It does us well to remember that this is the context in which Mrs. Darling first heard of the legendary Peter Pan, who, she seems to remember, escorted dead children on their journeys so that they wouldn't be frightened. What a lovely and sentimental way of perceiving a character who, as it turns out, is not interested in guiding children gently on their way to a happier, safer existence, but in fact lures them from the safety and love of family to a much more dangerous place.

As Peter Pan tells it, "I ran away the day I was born. . . . It was because I heard father and mother talking about what I was to be when I became a man. . . . I don't want ever to be a man. . . . I want always to be a little boy and to have fun" (26). Peter is voicing a misanthropic sentiment here that is as profound as it gets; rather than participate in society under the terms of Victorian manhood, he opts out of life altogether. The question that immediately comes to mind for me is, what is so wrong with the image of manhood during this time period that Peter Pan simply cannot face it? Barrie offers us two portraits of men, one Victorian and seemingly more than sufficient to account for Peter's abhorrence for adult masculinity, and the other more properly Edwardian, with which Peter finds a strange affinity, as we shall see. Mr. Darling, the quintessential Victorian male, is presented as petty, miserly, and obsessive before the children leave for Neverland. He is overly concerned with what people think of him, and he frets continually about who is admiring him and who is not. After the children leave, he resolutely devolves; he makes a spectacle of his failure to keep his family from danger by going about in Nana's kennel, gaining fame and hence a bit of pleasure from his debasement. He is a failed patriarch, and as such shows us something of what Peter would have to lose (that is, quite literally, his "cockiness") were he to become a man under the specifically embattled conditions in which men, caught between the conservatism of Victorianism and the tenuous rebellions and fierce imperialism of the Edwardians, found themselves.

Eric Laurent historicizes the problem in psychoanalytic terms:

> The phallus that the father used to promise through his "My son, one day you will be a man" was all right for Kipling and the formation of the imperial man. But the modern subject is the subject of de-colonisation more than the subject of Empire, and we know that his status is that of refuse, that which falls as lost wrappings. In this sense we are all the abortions of a desire, of whatever remains of a desire that sustained us. In thus defining ourselves, we do so not on the basis of the signifier of that desire, which is the phallus, but of the refuse. (qtd. in Rodriguez 172)

In *Peter Pan*, Barrie introduces us to the transitional subject, the subject between Edwardianism and modernism. Peter aborts the desire of his parents, but the other Lost Boys are more literally Laurent's lost wrappings, having fallen out of their carriages and been lost while attended by careless nannies. One of the boys even takes the name Slightly from a label he found on his nightshirt; it was secondhand and marked "slightly soiled," so the boys figured that was his name. Peter's status as refuse is more on the order of a volitional *refusal* to achieve his parents' desires for him. Until or unless these boys are ready to take up their position with respect to the phallic signifier, to take their medicine like men or be revealed as "cowardy custards," they can only ever exist in a Neverland, which, paradoxically enough, is inhabited by the very figures of colonialist hate and fantasy: indigenous "redskins," murderous pirates, and equally treacherous mermaids. Barrie presents us with an apparent paradox of a colonialist impulse in a boy who refuses Kipling's manhood, but then he complicates it by introducing an important difference between the virtual interiority of Peter's island and the real worlds of colonial aggression. In Peter's world, a genuine reciprocity between the Lost Boys and the redskins is necessary to keep the games alive, so much so that Peter has been known to change sides if the battle appears too uneven. The goal is not to conquer but to keep

the play active and interesting. In fact, at one point Peter expresses regret that he has given the birds on Neverland "such strange names that
they are very wild and difficult of approach" (126), a gentle but telling
dig at the exoticizing and appropriating activity of the Victorian imperialist strain in scientific "discovery." Peter's refusal to be a man can't be
read wholly as a refusal to be an imperial man, but it does reflect the
signs of the growing resistance to the totalizing fantasy of the subject
of Empire.

In fact, though, Peter's decision to escape the inadequacies and
villainies of Victorian masculinity seems a heady victory until one
reads it in the eerie light of Matthew Arnold's "Lines Written in Kensington Gardens," the site where Peter ran away and lived until he
moved to Neverland:

> In the huge world, which roars hard by,
> Be others happy if they can!
> But in my helpless cradle I
> Was breathed on by the rural Pan . . .
>
> Calm soul of all things! make it mine
> To feel, amid the city's jar,
> That there abides a peace of thine,
> Man did not make, and cannot mar.
>
> The will to neither strive nor cry,
> The power to feel with others give!
> Calm, calm me more! Nor let me die
> Before I have begun to live. (qtd. in Houghton 81)

Arnold's desire to live in the peaceful bliss of harmonious fellow
feeling, a gift of "the rural Pan," is challenged and soundly parodied by
Barrie's rambunctious boy, who prefers to die rather than live in such
empathetic community. Like Arnold, Peter Pan is not content to join
the huge roaring world, or, as Morris called it, the "vapour-bath of hur-
ried and discontented humanity" (qtd. in Lane xviii), nor has he any desire for a contented life in a domestic circle within such a world, especially if it means that he has to think of other people. Surely, Peter
saves the lives of Wendy, John, and Michael, as well as Tink, Tiger Lily,
and the Lost Boys, on regular occasions. But as Barrie's narrator tells
us, "you felt it was his cleverness that interested him and not the saving of human life" (37). So far is he from the desire to possess "the
power to feel with others" that he is quite indifferent to the discomfort

of the others who cannot, with him, pretend that they are full from an imaginary meal, nor does he have any inkling as to what Tink or Wendy wants from him in terms of affection.

Peter's antisocial (and scandalously Victorian) impulses are so strong that, for him, "adventure" is the equivalent of murder, real or imagined, and remorse is impossible because he can't even hold his deeds in memory. The narrator's utterly casual tone in recounting this very inhuman attitude reinforces its antipathy: "He often went out alone, and when he came back you were never absolutely certain whether he had had an adventure or not. He might have forgotten it so completely that he said nothing about it; and then when you went out you found the body; and, on the other hand, he might say a great deal about it, and you could not find the body" (74). He even forgets that he saved his companions from his archenemy Hook, indicating that he cares as little for his friends as his enemies:

> "Don't you remember," she [Wendy] asked, amazed, "how you killed him and saved all our lives?"
> "I forget them after I kill them," he replied carelessly. (161)

On the one hand, the narrator would seem to chalk up this blithe forgetfulness and lack of shame to a feature of childhood generally. He repeatedly reminds us that children are "gay and innocent and heartless" (168), "rubbishy" (151), "wicked" (32) brutes possessed of an "awful craftiness" (31) who think of no one but themselves. But in a strangely uncomfortable moment, Mr. Darling also forgets his children, asking his wife from his kennel to close the nursery window as he feels a draught (152). As this would prevent his children from entering the nursery should they return, the casual disregard for that which should be most precious is not limited to children after all.

Peter's carelessness with regard to human life might make him seem oddly innocent if it stopped at a confusion between real and pretend murders or lives taken in combat, but it does not. When Peter is angry, we find him volitionally attempting mass murder: " . . . he breathed intentionally quick short breaths at a rate of about five to a second. He did this because there is a saying in Neverland that, every time you breathe, a grown-up dies; and Peter was killing them off vindictively as fast as possible" (107). In addition to caring nothing for other people, Peter Pan, as captain of the Lost Boys and chief inhabitant of Neverland, encourages as much mayhem as possible. He despises peace and "hates lethargy" such that his entire island comes to murderous life with his arrival (47). Things are fairly calm on Neverland without Peter: "The fairies take an hour longer in the morning, the beasts attend to their young, the redskins feed heavily for six days and nights, and when pirates and lost boys meet they merely bite their thumbs at each other" (47). Peter's arrival sets off a panic of aggressive activity, with each group chasing another in a circle, the beasts chasing the redskins, the redskins chasing the pirates, the pirates chasing the Lost Boys, "all want[ing] blood" (48). Hardly the Arnoldian vision of the calm a rural Pan bestows on his charges.

While Barrie's Peter Pan is thus a ruthless parody of both the rural god who shares his name and the sensibilities that Arnold so passionately expresses, the poem does offer us a glimpse into why Hook hates Peter so much—that is, he suggests in his second stanza the yearning that fired the Victorian imagination, inspiring both its nostalgic longings and its restless ambition. He wants a peace that passes understanding. In a society where social relations and intellectual frameworks are fraught with instability and doubt, it makes sense that people would want something that is changeless over time, which by necessity would be outside the realm of human manufacture and custom. Moreover, that "something" would have to answer to the malaise, ennui, and depression that Houghton argues characterized contemporary urban life (54–89). What Hook finds in Peter Pan is indeed something that he believes "[m]an did not make, and cannot mar," but it is not peace. Nor is it something that Hook necessarily desires, which skews Kincaid's reading of Hook's child-loving response to Peter. What Hook hates in Peter is, as I indicated above, his plenitude. In giving up his position in life as a potential man, Peter enters into the space containing that which "men did not make, and cannot mar"—not a peaceful place, necessarily, but a place of fullness, a place where one's own bliss has not been renounced, in Benthamite fashion, for the greater good.

In order to participate in social life, one must give up at least some of one's essential selfishness. Barrie is keenly aware of this, particularly when it comes to adults making some sort of room for children. He figures it variously—Mr. Darling comically calculating what it might cost per child per annum, figuring that if he gives up coffee at the office, and even the typically Victorian charity of giving a pound to the poor who show up at one's door, they might be able to keep all three of the children. Later, the Lost Boys and he both figure the accommodations they will have to make to fit in the house, including searching for an imaginary drawing room and settling on corners where they might lie doubled up if necessary. For Mrs. Darling, the sacrifice is less material. Barrie's narrator says slyly, "until Wendy came her mother was the chief one" (1), indicating that mothers, no matter how attractive, are usurped by their children. But he goes to great lengths to suggest that Mrs. Darling hasn't given up everything and that what she hasn't given up is related to Peter Pan. He draws attention to the enigma of her romantic mind as a set of tiny boxes and a kiss on the righthand corner of her mouth, saying that when Mr. Darling got her, "[h]e got all of her, except the innermost box and the kiss. He never knew about the box, and in time he gave up trying for the kiss" (2). That which "man cannot mar," indeed. Peter Pan, on the other hand, is "very like Mrs. Darling's kiss" (10), which he takes with him when he leaves the Lost Boys, who are to stay with the Darlings for good (161).

The conjoined figures of the kiss and Peter Pan hint at the profundity of the sacrifice one makes for the privilege of being among other people; what is gained and what is lost are not symmetrical, nor can one have both. As Peter looks in on the scene of the Darlings' reunion with their children, the narrator says, "He [Peter Pan] had ecstasies innumerable that other children can never know; but he was looking through the window at the one joy from which he must be for ever barred" (156). The figure of the box also returns later, when the narrator recounts that "Wendy was a married woman, and Peter was no more to her than a little dust in the box in which she had kept her toys" (162). Wendy has made a choice to renounce Peter, and that which he represents, in favor of marriage and family life, giving up many ecstasies for the arguably paler consolations of family life. Hence Barrie cleverly sets in opposition the social and antisocial drives that haunt Victorian culture: while the strong pull of misanthropic rejection may drive the more energetic, exciting parts of the narrative, Barrie leaves room for the sentimental dream of a peaceful, Victorian domestic life.

The reader is left to make his or her own choice as to which is better, but Peter Pan himself remains resolutely on the side of misanthropy, as does Hook. Peter is perfectly happy with the adventures that not caring for people affords him; he would suffer the love of a mother only if it came with no strings attached. Indeed, he repeatedly expresses his disdain for mothers, considering them "very overrated persons" (23). What he understands is what Wendy, in her acquiescence to the Victorian deification of domestic life, resolutely refuses to acknowledge, that "one can get on quite well without a mother, and that it is only mothers who think you can't" (107). Hook understands the matter a bit more complexly—he is profoundly dejected when he learns the boys have found a mother, because it signals to him that civilization and sociability might infect the island, that the pleasures of hating that he and Peter Pan enjoy might come to be repressed in favor of love and concern for others. Such a possibility shakes Hook to his core, threatening his very identity. Addressing his own ego, he says, poignantly, "'Don't desert me, bully'"(85), revealing that he defines himself by his ability to hate.[3]

He needn't have worried, however, as Peter is completely unwilling to give up the ecstasies that he has for the more tepid pleasures of home and hearth. He plays at them, certainly. When John and Michael first come to the island, Peter makes great sport of sitting around and doing nothing, which is what good little Victorian boys seemed to do all day. He, rather anxiously, plays at being their father, but he eventually despises that role as well. Indeed, in his antisociality, he finds more satisfaction in playing at being Hook, especially after Hook dies. Peter sequesters himself in Hook's cabin, dresses in his clothes, and crooks his finger like a hook, implying that he identifies with the man who has made a career out of hating him. What Peter has, what Hook despises in him, is an unself-conscious joy that exists in contrast with and won't be contained by Hook's beloved "good form." The enmity that Hook feels for Peter Pan is closely akin to the prevailing sentiments found throughout the poetry of Robert Browning—a sentiment that Lacan calls "life envy." Particularly in the poem "Cleon," Lane claims, Browning links such life envy to the schism between youth and adulthood, concluding that "life's inadequate to joy," that is, that we painfully perceive "the gap between absolute joy and [our] own paltry ability to feel it" (Lane 140). Though Lane does not cite Barrie, the affinities between Barrie's ideas and those of Browning are clear, the more we read one in tandem with the other. According to the work of both writers, we envy those who don't seem to experience this gap. Unlike ordinary jealousy, life envy, says Lacan, "is the jealousy born in a subject in his relation to an other, insofar as this other is held to enjoy a certain form of *jouissance* or superabundant vitality, that the subject perceives as something that he cannot apprehend by means of the most elementary of affective movements" (Lacan S VII 278).

I have argued elsewhere that Peter Pan represents as full a picture of the various kinds of *jouissance* that Lacan identifies as we could hope to find in literature.[4] Hook's major objection to Peter's way of being in the world appears to be located in what Lacan calls feminine *jouissance*—a *jouissance* that female subjects have but about which they know nothing, not because they are naïve or ignorant but because such *jouissance* is inimical to knowledge itself. Knowledge cuts the world up into manageable pieces of the known and the unknown and imposes value judgments and a locus of control based on methods of knowing, not unlike Mr. Darling's obsessive totting up of balance sheets or Hook's accounting of good and bad form. *Jouissance*, on the other hand, is the pleasure of plenitude, which could, in fact, be figured as the otherworldly peace, not made by men and hence not able to be marred by them, that Arnold is looking for. In Peter Pan's case, though, it is characterized more by his "superabundant vitality" (278). Peter Pan doesn't *have* joy, he *is* joy, and insofar as Captain Hook can't be him, he is reduced to a manic envy of the boy. The fact that the quality of *jouissance* probably doesn't even exist does nothing to mitigate its power to elicit jealousy and hatred in others who assume that it does and that they can't have it. Hook is identified as having a "touch of the feminine" (85), which allows him enough intuition to know about the existence of things like Mrs. Darling's innermost box, another figure of feminine *jouissance*, but not enough to give him access to it. Peter, on the other hand, doesn't know that a schism could even exist between absolute joy and his ability to experience it—for Pete's sake, the kid can fly! If Peter could be said to possess a kind of knowingness about his own connection to *jouissance*, it is a knowing how to enjoy, rather than a knowledge that such ability is always already lost to the subject who has ceded his will to the common run of humanity. Since Peter hasn't, he is, literally, full of himself, and that, more than anything, incites Hook's hatred.

Barrie's narrator offers us this:

> Peter was such a small boy that one tends to wonder at the man's hatred of him. True he had flung Hook's arm to the crocodile; but even this and the increased insecurity of life to which it led, owing to the crocodile's pertinacity, hardly account for a vindictiveness so relentless and malignant. The truth is that there was something about Peter which goaded the pirate captain to frenzy. It was not his courage, it was not his engaging appearance, it was not—. There is no beating about the bush, for we know quite well what it was, and have got to tell. It was Peter's cockiness.
>
> This had got on Hook's nerves; it made his iron claw twitch, and at night it disturbed him like an insect. While Peter lived, the tortured man felt that he was a lion in a cage into which a sparrow had come. (115–16)

Obviously, there is enough potentially erotic imagery (in Peter's symbolic castration of Hook contrasted to his own "cockiness") in this portrait to sustain Kincaid's eroticization of Hook's relationship to Peter. But the thing about life envy is that, as Lane points out, following Lacan, it requires no "primal basis in love" (150). Rather, its primal basis is a desire for death. Peter makes the vow "Hook or me this time" (Barrie 127), but that either him/or me has been motivating Hook the entire time. So long as Peter is alive, he taunts Hook with his ability to enjoy. As a pirate, Hook's modus operandi is theft—he can kidnap the boys, take their mother—but Peter's joy is something he simply cannot steal. Moreover, he irrationally believes that Peter's ability to feel such undiluted joy somehow interferes with his own contentment. So, insofar as he fails in being able either to access Peter Pan's *jouissance* or to eliminate it, he is undone. Finally, then, Hook's acceptance of his own death at Peter Pan's hand devolves into a pale *schadenfreude*, a desire to see Peter Pan compromise himself on Hook's terms by exercising bad form.

Good form has been Hook's compensation for the inability to experience the superabundant vitality that comes so easily to Peter Pan. That is, if Peter has forsaken society without ever knowing it, Hook still retains memories of a time when he lived in the company of respectable people. Thus good form forges a tenuous link for Hook to the society of men, a link he has all but severed in order to pursue the more salacious pleasures of his hatred for Peter Pan. Unlike *jouissance*, good form is a species of social behavior, whereas *jouissance* is emphatically not. Men make good form, and they can mar it. But the tragic part of this is that Peter cares not a wit for good or bad form since his lack of memory renders him immune from its effects. When Hook bites him, he chafes at the unfairness but soon forgets it. Barrie's narrator makes a point of insisting that, for most children, this encounter with the unfair, or with bad form, marks the beginning of something like knowledge in the child. As Barrie says, "No one gets over the first unfairness; no one except Peter. He often met it, but he always forgot it. I suppose that was the real difference between him and all the rest" (87–88). It doesn't faze Peter because his *jouissance* is unaffected by it; form and *jouissance* exist in entirely different economies. This, finally, explains why Hook hates Peter so much. Lacan, interpreting Freud's discussion of how and why children love their elders, says "he whom I presume to know, I love" (S XX 64). What irritates Hook so much is that Peter does not know anything about form, good or bad, which is part of the social substitution we make when we choose society over isolation, particularly in Victorian and even more so in Edwardian cultures, when form and appearance came to matter so much. Peter only knows how to exercise his joy. Tim Dean argues that when we take up a position as cultural subjects, we enter into a contract with society to contain our desire, to keep it within the limits of good form, as Kincaid similarly points out. Hence we may, like Hook, experience life envy with regard to those whose desires and joys go over the limit. Hook thus shows us the truth of Dean's compelling extrapolation of Lacan's thesis, "*he whom I suppose to know how to enjoy, I hate*" (127, italics in original). Such heightened agitation toward enjoyment would have been especially prevalent in Victorian culture as the Victorians struggled to create a civil society that squeezed out disruptive frivolity and antisocial impulses.

In highlighting Victorian preoccupations with society as the cure for misanthropy and hatred, Lane quotes Thomas Carlyle: "Society is the genial element wherein [man's] nature first lives and grows; the solitary man were but a small portion of himself and must continue for ever folded in, stunted, and only half alive" (qtd. in Lane xx). Both Hook and Peter demonstrate versions of the solitary man. Each shuns society, and each could therefore be said to be stunted and only half alive, but in different ways. Peter is emotionally stunted in terms of fellow feeling, and though he gives the impression of being deliriously alive, we mustn't forget that he is not—he is a child who has chosen not to live. Hook's life envy for Peter is thus revealed as an irrational hatred, since it has no basis in anything possible. Both are quite willing to accept death at the hands of the other, simply because they are not tethered to life by the bands of love for other people. Yet Barrie has portrayed their hatred in devilishly clever ways to create surprising affective states for the reader; we may find ourselves cheering the boy's hatred of the man even while we identify in some ways with the man's hatred of the boy. In either case, we find ourselves indulging in the pleasures of hating, and perhaps very like the Victorians, as glad of the existence of Neverlands as we are of our own protected hearths.

NOTES

1. Taken to its extreme, obviously, such dismissal of material responsibility in favor of analytical causality sets the stage for ethical misconduct, which is

unfortunately often the case in contemporary juridical proceedings. Causes become mitigating excuses for malignant behaviors; Kincaid's argument, whether it intends to or not, fosters a displacement of responsibility from individual criminals to systemic culpability.

2. See Coats, 77–88.

3. According to the OED, "bully" at this time was used both as a term of affectionate connection and also to indicate a violent ruffian.

4. See Coats 89–95.

WORKS CITED

Arnold, Matthew. "Lines Written in Kensington Gardens." *Empedocles on Etna, and Other Poems.* London: B. Fellowes, 1852.

Barrie, J. M. *Peter Pan.* 1911. New York: Bantam, 1985.

Butler, Judith. "Burning Acts: Injurious Speech." Unpublished manuscript, 1995.

Coats, Karen. *Looking Glasses and Neverlands: Lacan, Desire, and Subjectivity in Children's Literature.* Iowa City: U of Iowa P, 2004.

Dean, Tim. *Beyond Sexuality.* Chicago: U of Chicago P, 2000.

Dickens, Charles. *Great Expectations.* 1860–61. New York: Penguin, 1996.

———. *A Tale of Two Cities.* 1859. New York: Penguin, 1985.

Eliot, George. *Middlemarch.* 1871–72. New York: Penguin, 2003.

Houghton, Walter E. *The Victorian Frame of Mind, 1830–1870.* New Haven, CT: Yale UP, 1957.

Kincaid, James R. *Child-Loving: The Erotic Child and Victorian Culture.* New York: Routledge, 1992.

Kingsley, Charles. *The Water Babies.* 1863. New York: Puffin, 1995.

Lacan, Jacques. *The Seminar of Jacques Lacan Book VII: The Ethics of Psychoanalysis, 1959–60.* Ed. Jacques-Alain Miller. New York: Norton, 1992. (S VII)

———. *The Seminar of Jacques Lacan Book XX: Encore, 1972–73.* Trans. Bruce Fink. New York: Norton, 1998. (S XX)

Lane, Christopher. *Hatred and Civility: The Antisocial Life in Victorian England.* New York: Columbia University Press, 2004.

Rodriguez, Leonardo. *Psychoanalysis with Children: History, Theory and Practice.* London: Free Association Books, 1999.

2

The Time of His Life: Peter Pan and the Decadent Nineties

Paul Fox

> He will realize himself in many forms, and by a thousand different ways, and will ever be curious of new sensations and fresh points of view.
>
> —Oscar Wilde, "The Critic as Artist"

Time tick-tocks its way inexorably through J. M. Barrie's *Peter Pan* in the lumbering form of Hook's nemesis, the crocodile. The centrality of time and its relationship to play and a creative aesthetic situate the text very much as a product of the literary interests of its contemporary moment. Indeed, the moment itself, neglecting past and memory, future and all but immanent desire, is focused in the character of Peter and is the basis for the ludic creativity of life in Neverland (the name itself playing upon the possibility of a space existing outside time). Peter's willed capacity to "forget" enables the continuation of the ludic moment in perpetuity, to be created and recreated for its own sake, unburdened by memories of the past. Thus, the eponymous hero might be seen to be the personification of *art pour l'art*, the repeatedly reimagined present as an end in itself.

"Art for Art's own sake" was the rallying call for the aesthetes of late Victorianism in England, and the basis of their aesthetic program was a concern with, and attempted overcoming of, the atrophic power of time. I will argue that the aesthetic of Decadence, culminating in the

1890s (the name of the artistic movement itself underlining the delete-rious effects of time), consistently informs the themes of *Peter Pan* and the characterization of its hero. In examining the "Conclusion" of Wal-ter Pater's *Studies in the History of the Renaissance* and Oscar Wilde's *The Picture of Dorian Gray* as two of the informing texts of 1890's aes-theticism, I suggest that Barrie has produced a portrait of the *fin de siè-cle* artist/e, the creative role-player, the actor of his own drama who creates his moments as ends in themselves, simultaneously forgetting the past and creating anew each present moment. It is this conceit of the "moment" when time stands still, in which the artist sees himself and the world of his making as all that there is and has ever been, that allows a transcendence of the atrophy that linear time enforces. Yet change and the passing of time are employed as the means by which creative sterility is avoided, affording to the aesthete new momentary stages on which to re-play his or her world and identity. The aesthete lives *as if* each moment is an eternity unto itself, but rewrites anew every moment that time's passing allows to him or her. This "grammar of time" is the informing structure of the 1890's Decadent aesthetic.

Peter, like Oscar Wilde's Dorian Gray, never ages, and he employs artfulness as the vehicle of his self-perpetuating youth and identity. This disinclination to be affected by time is central to Barrie's (and Wilde's) aesthetic and is clear evidence for viewing *Peter Pan* as being strongly redolent of the British Decadent movement. Self-engendering, not once but recurrently, is the *modus vivendi* of those who live only in the play of the present. It is in this manner that *Peter Pan* portrays a successful revision of the failed aesthete portrayed in Wilde's novel *The Picture of Dorian Gray*, in which Dorian cannot forget his past and recurrently worries about his future. Peter's capacity to willfully disregard both past and future marks his signal success in creating a reality and an identity for himself that precludes the angst and obsessions of his Wildean coun-terpart. Dorian wishes to be his own and sole progenitor, but he cannot escape the fascination of viewing himself as reproduced by his portrait.

As to Peter's relationship to his past, it is notable that he becomes ex-tremely agitated when required to relate the "truth" of his family back-ground. For him his life began when he abandoned his parents, and he thereby entitles himself to create his own genealogy by eventually re-peating his choosing of a mother when it is time for a "spring cleaning," referring as much to the sweeping aside of his own past as to the mun-dane affairs of housekeeping in Neverland. The demise of Hook, caused by the pirate's inability to free himself from the societal strictures of the past and his constant desire for a Peter Pan-less future, is an example of the calamity awaiting those unable to live in and for the moment. The tick-tocking crocodile consumes the present when we will not fully live our own lives.

The centrality of time to the story of Peter Pan is apparent from the opening section of Barrie's 1911 novel *Peter and Wendy*, the prose version of the original play produced seven years earlier. Recounted to us is two-year-old Wendy's first appreciation of the fact that she is an individual subject who will age. Barrie writes the scene as the child's becoming self-aware, of comprehending the adult realities of life and time, and he specifically emphasizes "knowledge" as the basis of the traumatic change in the child's perceptions. Wendy plucks a flower in the garden, and runs to present it to her mother:

> I suppose she must have looked rather delightful, for Mrs Darling put her hand on her heart and cried, "Oh, why can't you remain like this for ever!" This was all that passed between them on the subject, but henceforth Wendy knew that she must grow up. You always know after you are two. Two is the beginning of the end. (69)[1]

This is a strikingly similar situation to Dorian Gray's loss of innocence when hearing the delightful aesthetic, the "New Hedonism," of Lord Henry Wotton. Mrs. Darling's cry echoes almost exactly Dorian's chagrined outburst to himself when he sees his magnificent portrait, only to realize that it will taunt him with his erstwhile beauty as he himself grows older. In the second chapter of Wilde's novel, Dorian and Lord Henry are in the garden of the artist Basil Hallward, Dorian enjoying the scent of the lilac bushes and finally plucking a bud. Lord Henry relates his theory of Youth, the moment which influences Dorian's future so fatefully:

> When your youth goes, your beauty will go with it, and then you will suddenly discover that there are no triumphs left for you. . . . Time is jealous of you, and wars against your lilies and roses. . . . Ah! realise your youth while you have it. . . . The moment I met you I saw that you were quite unconscious of what you really are, of what you might really be. There was so much in you that charmed me. (31)

Dorian, now conscious of this youthful charm, loses his innocent regard for himself and the world, and the lilac spray falls from his fingers to the ground.

Barrie appears to have rewritten Wilde's introduction of Dorian Gray in the opening presentation of his heroine Wendy. As in Lord Henry's eulogy upon Youth, Barrie presents to his readers a fall from innocence in a beautiful garden. He emphasizes the deleterious effects of time, indeed, the fall *into* time. We are shown the moment the sense of self is divided into two: a past, remembered self, never to return, and a new consciousness of the self as a "subject" aware of a future over which one is bereft of control. The echo of the "Ah!" of Lord Henry in the "Oh!" of Mrs. Darling and the plucking of a flower signaling the beginning of the end punctuate Wendy's introduction to her life in linear time.

The "escape" of Wendy into Neverland allows her the aesthetic ability to recreate her identity as the mother of the boys on the island. But she never fully forgets her past and, as such, is not fully included in the ludic creativity of the boys' games. The character of Wendy exists in a liminal position in the drama. She role-plays the mother of the Lost Boys at Peter's behest, remaining capable of comprehending Neverland in childish delight, yet knowing her delight is childish.

If Wendy has lost her innocent perception of a timeless world, she has not developed an adult view just yet. She can still partake of Neverland along with her younger brothers and her newly adopted ragamuffin brood. It is worth noting, however, that Wendy is described as spending the major portion of her time in the home underground, domestically harried (although thoroughly enjoying the role) with darning, washing, and cleaning. Her place in Neverland, as with her role as mother, is performed in liminal spaces, neither a full party to Peter's adventures nor disbarred from them as an "adult" nurturing a family.

But if the role is traditional, the family certainly is not. This is no picture of late-Victorian, nor of Edwardian, domestic bliss (neither is the family life of the Darlings in the adult world for that matter, happy though it might have originally been). And it cannot be overemphasized that Wendy is indulging in a performance and indulging Peter and his Lost Boys at the same time. Positioned in the time between childhood and adulthood, Wendy constructs an identity which is distinctly her own in a momentary act of aesthetic self-definition. It is only in this transition from childhood to adulthood, in the liminal space of Neverland, that Wendy can stage a reality which is both serious and farce in equal measure. If Peter can create his own origins, so too can Wendy create a character to act out an apparently traditional female role, but in *acting* the part she subverts it, constructing it as a performance-piece, a make-believe, dress-up.[2]

If Neverland itself is seen as a liminal space, it is also primarily presented as inflected in time. The grammar of time is the foundation of the novel, at one point Barrie as author inserting himself into the story, suggesting a possible alteration to the text, justifying his choice of language and explaining his employment of the pluperfect tense (112). In her analysis of time in children's literature, Maria Nikolajeva remarks upon the use of the narrative present throughout *Peter Pan*, stating that it acts as "a sure marker of iterative frequency, expresses the recurrent nature of the events; it has always been like this and will always be like this, before Wendy's visit and after" (91).[3] Whilst this recurrence is precisely that which the repeated aesthetic moment seeks to indulge, Nikolajeva portrays recurrence and difference as being mutually exclusive. In the aesthete's creation of each moment *as if* it were an eternity unto itself, Neverland displays a constant return of difference under the pretence of the unchanging eternal, that is, what will always be and has always been, as Nikolajeva suggests. Ann Yeoman in her study of *Peter Pan* writes "that imagination . . . must undergo constant renewal, otherwise it may become petrified and petrifying" (166). To exist solely in the moment in reality would be to suffer a creative death. The grammar of time is the present under the guise of constancy but open to the reinterpretative energies through which the past is renewed and to the creative will that welcomes the new. It is the creation of the moment as if each moment, as it comes, is all that there is, has always been, and will be. This is the Neverland of *Peter and Wendy*.

The name of Neverland, then, divulges to the reader the place's nonexistence in any traditional, linear conception of temporality. According to editor Peter Hollindale's note upon the name of the island, "Peter Pan's island was called the Never, Never, Never Land in the first draft of the play, the Never, Never Land in the play as performed, the Never Land in the play as published, and the Neverland in *Peter and Wendy*" (*Peter and Wendy* 232). The complexity of repetition, negatives multiplied, is a playful nod to the impossibility of locating Peter's home as real or unreal at any point in time. Is "Neverland" a placename or a statement that there cannot ever be such a place?

In her psychoanalytic analysis of closure in children's fantasy literature, Sarah Gilead says of *Peter Pan* that the "true paradox of the 'never' in Neverland is in its double meaning of stark denial—on the one hand, the refusal of the self to conceive of its own end and, on the other, the absolute reality of death" (286). I believe that the aesthetic that Peter embodies and lives out displays exactly this paradox: the need for

change, and thus endings, to enjoy difference and newness, but the desire for life exterior to the atrophy of time's passing.[4] It is in the aesthetically conceived moments of Neverland as eternities unto themselves that the dilemma is overcome. The two contraries are married
into the fabrication of an existence consistently acted out as an unchanging reality from moment to moment.

To fabricate a reality is to suspend traditional judgments of time and
space, to accept the pretence of a show being staged. If Wendy rehearses her role for the day when her act becomes a reality, Peter has
created a world, that of Neverland, within which to stage his dramatic
adventures. It is obvious in Barrie's descriptions of the island that the
entirety of its life thrills to the aesthetic will of Peter, who dominates
every scene in which he appears, not surprisingly, as he has created
every scene even down to the background stage-sets: for example,
when tracking Hook and the pirates toward the conclusion of the story,
Peter "regretted now that he had given the birds of the island such
strange names that they are very wild and difficult of approach"
(185–86). The position of Neverland is one of the contingent realities
of performance because to Peter "make-believe and true were exactly
the same thing" (128), and again, "[m]ake-believe was so real to him
that during a meal of it you could see him getting rounder" (135).

What makes this precarious ontology possible is Peter's voracious
appetite for the variety of stories and his capacity to forget. The smallest details, the nuance and color of every scene, are produced from Peter's extraordinary will for novelty. He can repeat performances for the
simple reason that once they have been acted, he no longer recalls
them. He can invent or re-invent new situations on a whim. Novelty is
the confluence of the aesthetic will and willed amnesia. Nikolajeva
sees this loss of memory in *Peter Pan* as "the worst curse of Neverland
. . . because . . . without memory, there is no real life" (93). Sarah Gilead
suggests a similar psychic tragedy when she writes that "Peter, forgetting the past, is entrapped in an eternal present . . ." (287). But this is
precisely why forgetting is the *sine qua non* of life in Neverland and
the basis of the aestheticism of the British Decadents. Real life is the linear flux of change and inconstancy. The creative life is willed illusion
and the justification of the real as being capable of being borne. It is
only because Peter on occasion is forced to recall his past (by Wendy
or in his dreams) that he has moments of suffering in the novel. When
one remembers nothing, everything is new. As such, forgetting is a lib-
erating essential to an aesthetic life—not its tragedy, but its justification.

If Barrie has shown the influence of the previous decade's aesthetic in his story, this will for experiencing novelty comes directly from the literary progenitor of those aesthetic Nineties, the writer who made Victorian prose purple and gave literature a Yellow hue, Walter Pater. It is difficult nowadays to appreciate just how much influence Pater cast over the literature and thought of the last twenty-five years of the nineteenth century and the early years of Modernism. *Studies in the History of the Renaissance*, first published in 1873, was the inspiration for a generation of new writers and artists, Wilde being only one of many. In *The Picture of Dorian Gray*, Lord Henry's "New Hedonism" is directly descended from Pater's aesthetic, albeit perverted from the course of its main argument, the encouragement to live fully, enacting experience for its own sake. In the famous "Conclusion" to the book, Pater used as his epigraph a quotation from the philosopher Heraclitus, which he translated as "all things give way: nothing remaineth" (174). This ontological vision of the world given in the "Conclusion" bears a remarkable similarity to that directed by Peter. Pater writes,

> To regard all things and principles of things as inconstant modes of fashion has more and more become the tendency of modern thought. . . . Fix upon . . . life . . . in one of its more exquisite intervals, the moment, for instance of delicious recoil from the flood of water in summer heat. (150)

The Darling children literally enjoy this "delicious recoil" in *Peter and Wendy*, lolling on the rock in the Lagoon during long summer days at play. Pater's passage as a whole concentrates life down to those particular moments which can be enjoyed in and of themselves and for their own sake. The moment is described as an "interval" in time or, more precisely, between times, when the flux of change becomes focused in the singular experience of the individual. Pater continues,

> What is the whole physical life in that moment but a combination of natural elements to which science gives names? But those elements . . . are present not in the body alone: we detect them in places most remote from it. Our physical life is a perpetual motion of them – . . . like the elements of which we are composed, the action of these forces extends beyond us: it rusts iron and ripens corn. . . . This at least of flame-like our life has, that it is but the concurrence, renewed from moment to moment, of forces parting sooner or later on their ways. (150)

Neverland can be viewed as an expression of Peter's own moments of concurrent renewal, extending beyond his own frame into the world at large. His whims are flighty, flickering, and variable like the "flame" of Pater's ontology.[5] And he concentrates life into the roles that he plays. His impressions are absolutely true to him from moment to moment; their expression creates a world within which he can *live*. Neverland is a Never Land because it does not exist in real time, the movement of flux, of change and aging, but is created outside this linearity in a concentration of moments and elements. Time is relative between the adult world and that of Neverland. Its passage in Peter's world is presented as a series of moments, lived as moments, to the extent that, barring Wendy, his troop has no conception of how long they have been there. The question concerns how we *live* time, whether as the adults and Hook do, dwelling upon (and in) the past and future (Hook's memories of schooldays, Mr. Darling's concern with finances), or as Peter does, glorying in the opportunities of each moment as it occurs and living that moment to the full with no concern about what has gone before or what might occur afterwards. Pater expresses such an individual perception, and it serves as the consummate description for the character of Peter Pan:

[An impression] is limited in time. . . . [A]ll that is actual in it being a single moment, gone while we try to apprehend it, of which it may ever be more truly said that it has ceased to be than that it is. To such a tremulous wisp constantly re-forming itself . . . what is real in our life fines itself down . . . that continual vanishing away, that strange, perpetual, weaving and unweaving of ourselves. (151–52)

Within such an ontology, the action of memory becomes a remembering, a re-presentation of the past in new guise and in new configurations, such as Peter and his Lost Boys playing the role of the pirates after the demise of Hook and his men. Memory becomes not a reconstitution of the past as it was but the re-membering of a past as a new and present moment, the basis of creative activity. As Yeoman puts it, "re-membering and re-collecting . . . restore life to lost possibilities" (66). Peter can make the pirate's role his own, and he swiftly forgets the name and person of his erstwhile nemesis, before forgetting that guise for another. Once more, the centrality of a willed forgetting can be seen not as a "curse" but as an aesthetic blessing (in disguise).

Barrie himself reflects this attitude in his constant textual revisionism. Hollindale writes,

[N]one of his play-texts is ever fixed and stable. In successive preliminary drafts, then during rehearsal, then in the light of initial production expe-

rience . . . even when a play is fully established in the repertoire, he is
ceaselessly modifying, experimenting, refining, improvising possible variations, or simply changing his mind. (*Peter and Wendy* ix–x)[6]

As each production becomes an end in itself, each new version of
the story becomes *the* version, until the next moment of presentation
comes along. The acting of the drama can thus be seen as a metaphor
for Peter's own aesthetic, one in which, in the midst of time's flux, en-
actments of one's own life are privileged as authentic from one production to the next.

One remarkable instance of Barrie's tinkering with the versions of
his story presented upon the stage is the unique incidence of what became "An Afterthought" in the published version of the drama, in
which Peter reappears in the adult world, meeting a grown-up Wendy
and her infant daughter, Jane (*Peter Pan* 155 63).[7] This scene was written into the 1911 novel *Peter and Wendy* but was acted out upon the
stage only once, on the last night of the 1908 season.[8] It seems to me
that this variant operates as a functioning non-ending, the proliferation
of the continual cycle of Peter's "mothers" through generations, the
perpetuation of removing moments from the context of the adult world
of linear time. Originally the play closed with Peter sitting piping to a
massed audience of birds and fairies. The single performance of the
1908 act, combined with its inclusion in the printed prose version of
the tale, remarks the expression of the moment as both unique and
perpetual: to view a Paterian contingency is to perceive it as a recon-
figured constant, rather akin to Peter's presumption that each new generation of Wendy's family is the same mother he has always had. In Pater's words, the moment must be "fixed upon" and in its acting out as
fixed, we may live (150). It is the reiteration of life in its variance, as being constituted from moment to moment as all that there is and has
been and will ever be. Identity is momentarily renewed, but for that
moment it is everything. Hence the Lost Boys' nervousness when acting out one of Peter's whimsical scenarios. It might change at any time,
but it must be, for that moment, their entire world.

Pater's infamous final thoughts in the "Conclusion" propose a means
to live:

How shall we pass most swiftly from point to point, and be present at the
focus where the greatest number of vital forces unite in their purest energy? To burn always with this hard, gem-like flame, to maintain this ecstasy, is success in life. . . . While all melts under our feet, we may well
catch at any exquisite passion. . . . Not to discriminate every moment

some passionate attitude . . . is, on this short day of frost and sun, to sleep before evening. (152)

The aesthetic that Pater has presented here is that which is embodied in Peter throughout the drama. On the Lagoon with Hook, Peter is "tingling with life," and when asked by the pirate who and what he is at their final confrontation, Peter replies, "I'm youth, I'm joy . . . I'm a little bird that has broken out of the egg" (*Peter and Wendy* 145, 203). The image of birth might stand for every moment that Peter lives, engendering himself repeatedly, and is the expression of life itself, full of the eagerness and delight that speaks to the "passionate attitude" for which Pater calls.

Peter's ultimate passion is for stories, and this is emblematic of his desire to create both himself and the world through his aesthetic will. It is the prime reason that he acquires a "mother" (beyond his desire for a new role to play), and it allows him the pretence of creating his own genealogy. Stories exist in the drama of life in Neverland as the expression of creative adventuring. The boys retell their own experiences on the island, often embellishing, always alive to the opportunity that to relate a story is to make its details so.[9]

The one Lost Boy who recalls something of the adult world is Slightly. It is not surprising then that his attempt to tell a story goes awry, Barrie writing of the effort that "the beginning was so fearfully dull that it appalled even himself, and he said gloomily: 'Yes, it is a dull beginning. I say, let us pretend it is the end'" (*Peter and Wendy* 163). In the adult world, the vitality of the moment simply does not impress itself upon individuals. It is interesting to note, however, that even Slightly, in an act of speech ("I say"), compresses the failed tale, calling for pretence, into a moment, with the simultaneity of the beginning finally being the end. Even he, with the least appreciation of the power of stories and the imagination required to create them anew for each hearing, knows that the momentary configuration of narrative expresses the truth of life. And this is where Pater's dramatic influence upon his times is evident: life is impression; things are true inasmuch as they are perceived by the individual. But, just as Peter Pan's character makes abundantly clear, Pater suggests that there is a hierarchy of abilities in life, that there are those who can compress experience into the passing moments and can simply be more often "present at the focus where the greatest number of vital forces unite in their purest energy" (152). This world of experience is not based on a tawdry aesthetic relativism, nor does Barrie present his Neverland as being formed from such. Some stories and their tellers are simply better than others.

Wendy is retrieved from the adult world to relate stories to Peter's clan. Mothers are said by Peter to be very capable in this role. But there is one story that Wendy insists upon telling that is much to Peter's distaste, and it is a displeasure based in a forced immersion in the flux of linear time. Indeed, this particular story seems to cause Peter pain, for he groans during its telling. Wendy presents to the Lost Boys the narration of her and her brothers' own journey to Neverland, with the addendum that they will one day return and grow up to be normal, social adults. In mimicry of the sentimental fiction of the day, Barrie writes,

> "See, dear brothers," says Wendy, pointing upwards, "there is the window still standing open. Ah, now we are rewarded for our sublime faith in a mother's love." So up they flew to their mummy and daddy; and pen cannot describe the happy scene, over which we draw a veil.
>
> That was the story, and they were as pleased with it as the fair narrator herself. Everything just as it should be, you see. (*Peter and Wendy* 166)

It is the picture of adult motherhood and of growing older, of becoming socialized, of everything *being* rather than becoming, that Peter feels gnawing at his heart. It is the beginning of the end for the children's adventure, for the conversation that ensues drives the Darlings to set out for home.

A primary example of the confusion that results whenever "adult" attitudes and standards intrude into the ludic world of Neverland is evident in Peter's disquiet when confronted by Wendy about their relationship. One can read Peter's rejection of Wendy's advances as based on his detestation of any static, essentialized role, such as that of "husband" or "father." His utter ignorance of stable, adult relationships is well chronicled throughout the text, with his three female admirers, Tinker Bell, Tiger Lily, and Wendy, all making attempts to bind him to themselves in greater affection than he knows how to return. But Peter also fears any attempt on his would-be consorts' parts to realize these new affections; Barrie makes this clear with a conversation between Peter and Wendy about their roles as pretend mother and father:

> "Dear Peter," she said, "with such a large family, of course, I have now passed my best, but you don't want to change me, do you?"

"No, Wendy."

Certainly he did not want a change, but he looked at her uncomfortably; blinking, you know, like one not sure whether he was awake or asleep.

"Peter, what is it?"

"I was just thinking," he said, a little scared. "It is only make-believe, isn't it, that I am their father?"

"Oh yes," Wendy said primly. (*Peter and Wendy* 161–62)

In Pater's terms, there is most certainly a combination of elements occurring here: the role-playing of Wendy; the "fatherhood" of Peter; the actuality of those roles creeping into the pretence; the affection Wendy feels for Peter; his discomfort in the possibility that the roles may become reified through this affection; her incipient awareness of the "proper" manner to be displayed discussing things sexual; the liminal position, between dream and the real, of life in Neverland; and, at base, the importance of change in the adventuring of the children. Barrie states that Peter does not want to change anything, but this, of course, refers to the role played by Wendy and the stories that she tells. It is clear that the relationship between Wendy and Peter can and does change in the story, Peter becoming "father" after the Indians begin naming him as such. To change Wendy would be to end the possibility for change, for she brings variety into the lives of the Lost Boys with her storytelling. But to ask the question pulls aside the stage curtain to reveal the players as only players. And this is what causes fear and confusion in Peter. He is forced to consider the pretence of their roles when confronted by the possibility that they may be actual and stable. It is similar to the situation at the start of the story when Peter is asked how old he is by Wendy and becomes discomfited: "I don't know," he replied uneasily, "but I am quite young" (*Peter and Wendy* 92).

The liminal position of the moment, between the actual and pure fancy, is developed by Barrie when he describes Peter's nightmares. He writes,

> Sometimes, though not often, he had dreams, and they were more painful than the dreams of the other boys. For hours he could not be separated from these dreams, though he wailed piteously in them. They had to do, I think, with the riddle of his existence. (81)

This existential "riddle" must refer to Peter's origins and, thus, his identity in the adult world of linear time. It is usually only in his dreams that

Peter is confronted with the actuality of the question of his historical selfhood. The suggestion of the irruption of the hyper-real (the adult world) in dreams perhaps derives from the burgeoning importance given to Freud's revolutionary work, *The Interpretation of Dreams* (1900), which had been published a few years before Barrie's drama. Nevertheless, it is certainly only in the creative moment when the vital energies of life are concentrated that Peter is comfortable. In the dreamscape, he is tortured with the real world of linear time, where his past is forced upon him and he is reminded that even he can grow, and has grown, older. No wonder then that Peter would prefer to avoid Wendy's questions, her story about the "real" world, and the temporal patterning he must avoid at all costs to preserve his Neverland.

This psychological wear upon Peter Pan is concretely reproduced in the dissolution of his band, for with the departure of the Darlings, the Lost Boys, invited to go along, snatch at the chance for a new experience. "That strange, perpetual, weaving and unweaving of ourselves" talked about by Pater (152) exists not only for Peter's lived experience but also for those around him. The band unravels in a moment, and Peter is left to re-generate a new life for himself with the fairies, the birds, and the occasional visit from a descendent of Wendy. In his version of time and change, Barrie narrates (as do his contemporaries Henri Bergson and Wilde) the playing out of theories of evolution and dissolution, progress and decay, which had been of seminal interest to the Victorian era.

At the time, perhaps the most shattering critique of *fin de siècle* aestheticism-cum-decadence was Max Nordau's vituperative *Degeneration*, translated into and published in English in 1895. The very name of Decadence, as referring to the artistic movement of the 1890s, suggests a cultural atrophy that was very much part of the narrative of contemporary social theories. Speaking about Nietzsche and his theory of time, one which mirrors Pater's theory closely, Nordau froths,

> Blow away the lather from these phrases. What do they really say? The fleeting instant of the present is the point of contact of the past and future. Can one call this self-evident thought a fact? (418)[10]

But that is precisely the point. It is not a "fact" but a creative expedient, contingent upon the moment and beyond a linear time that necessarily brings atrophy and dissolution to the self. It is only in living the moment that the self *can* be evidenced to the mind of these aesthetes.

It is a fabrication, a pretence, a beautiful lie. But it allows one to *live*. This was Pater's theory, as it was Wilde's, and it is also that of Peter Pan's lived experience. The aesthete was, simply put, the next stage in the evolution of man.

One of our first views of Neverland expresses this strange evolution working on the island. Peter's role in vitalizing the inhabitants is again emphasized:

> In his absence things are usually quiet on the island. . . . But with the coming of Peter, who hates lethargy, they are all under way again: if you put your ear to the ground now, you could hear the whole island seething with life. . . . [T]he lost boys were out looking for Peter, the pirates were out looking for the lost boys, the redskins were out looking for the pirates, and the beasts were out looking for the redskins. They were going round and round the island, but they did not meet because all were going at the same rate. . . . [W]hen they have passed, comes the last figure of all, a gigantic crocodile . . . but soon the boys appear again, for the procession must continue indefinitely until one of the parties stops or changes pace. Then quickly they will be on top of each other. (*Peter and Wendy* 112, 116)

With this cycle of life, from reptile (crawled from the swampy Lagoon), to the (described as such) primitive redskins, to the barely civilized and bloodthirsty pirates, to the Lost Boys, to Peter who is sought but not yet present, the evolutionary round is played out. Peter is the absent animator of life, the god-like father-figure whose return rekindles the energies of Neverland. Time, in the figure of the clock-swallowing crocodile, comes at both the end and the beginning of the cycle in the manner of Barrie's description. The circle is an unending round and comes into being only with the immanent authority of Peter's aesthetic will. A collapse by one of the parties will end the cycle, but that is possible only at an "indefinite" time. Peter brings the definition of moment to the island, and it is his dynamism that staves off the descent into chaos and confusion. Regression is thus stasis, breaking the rhythm of life (this is Dorian's criminal mistake, and also Hook's, obsessed by the forms of the past). Barrie artfully crafts glimpses of his aesthetic frame through the "evolving" procession of characters on the island: from animal to savage, from the barbaric to an incipient aestheticism in search of the creative spirit in love with life. Change animates, and under all lies the cycle, not the linearity, of time.

The cycle of time: the only manner in which the moment is repeated is in its difference.[11] In this sense, Peter is emblematic of the aesthetic moment: he is the unchanging lover of an ever-changing life. Every moment is both a repeated and a new beginning. Similarly, decadence can be read both as Nordau's dissolution of identity and values and, according to Pater's and Wilde's construal, as the necessary passing away of one moment to give birth to the next. Peter's love of novelty is not cultural regression but the aesthetic pinnacle of evolution. Forgetting one's past and creating one's own identity are the privilege of the thoroughly modern individual, living momentarily. A repeated return to beginnings is nothing to be feared; rather it is a necessity to be embraced. It affords the aesthete ever-proliferating opportunities for new experiences and new configurations of meaning.

This pattern of aesthetic existence is reflected in Barrie's singular narrative style. Once more, I would suggest that Barrie is indebted to his aesthetic forebears, Wilde and Pater. Wilde's use of language to effect a reversal of expectation plays with contemporary views of meaningful linear progress, and Pater's repeated grammatical deferrals require a constant reconstitution of meaning by the reader in his texts; both narrative methods are much in evidence in both the dramatic and prose texts of Peter's story.

Wilde's wit was infamous, and his *bons mots* were the talk of London in the years before his downfall.[12] The consummate use of language displayed in his life and art functions as a destabilizing influence on traditional Victorian values, reversing norms and expectations, reconstituting language as creative rather than as referential. As Ruth Robbins remarks,

> [L]anguage itself, the only medium in which truth might be told, distorts rather than mimetically represents the real. . . . [L]anguage is non-representative and intransitive. . . . [I]t does not necessarily refer to the world beyond itself, it does not make sense of the world, and nor does it make things happen in the world. (109–10)

The "real world" in both Wilde's and Barrie's art is problematic (and it is that world to which Robbins refers). Language for Wilde's aesthetes and for Barrie's Peter Pan is used whimsically to *create* worlds, meaningful only for the moment because in constant flight. Meaning alters with each new utterance as language re-construes existence. I have stated above that Peter and the Lost Boys apply language to life to bring things, as they are said, into being, not to describe or relate events as objective reality. There is no mimetic correspondence between the word and the world; in fact (or rather in fictions) words create the world.[13] And these momentary worlds express the true subversion of Neverland vis-à-vis the adult world of the Darlings with its traditional perspectives. They are the fabrication of contingent meaning, the "grammar of time" to which I referred earlier in the essay.

The reversal and repetition of construal in language make a non-sense of meaning progressing through a text to a given conclusion. Comprehension must be renegotiated after the fact. There *are* no conclusions, no ultimate meanings. As Pater suggests, dissolution and reconstitution are the conditions of existence, conditions which the aesthete embraces as an opportunity for experiencing life in all its variety. And in his own prose style, Pater reflects this view. In her *Language and Decadence in the Victorian* Fin de Siècle, Linda Dowling makes note of Pater's use of euphuism as a method of writing that reclaims archaism and simultaneously employs neologisms to express meaning (121–26). Reconstituting anew what has gone before whilst simultaneously creating the novel: this is the linguistic expression of the aesthetic described in the "Conclusion" to *Studies in the History of the Renaissance*. Dowling writes that Pater

> puts off the moment of cognitive closure, . . . And he does this not simply by writing long sentences, but by so structuring his sentences as to thwart—at times even to the point of disruption—our usual expectations of English syntax. Hence, for example, Pater's use of proleptic reference, his habit of introducing and then widely separating a pronoun from its referent. (130)

What Wilde does with language, Pater does with syntax. Meaning is deferred, anticipated, diverted from its traditional courses, the subject of a sentence appearing almost as having different identities grammatically, pronoun and referent being distanced through a sentence, thereby mirroring the reconstitution of the subject as the moments of apparent apprehension pass.

Barrie's grammar, as befits a book read by children, might not retain Pater's complex syntactic legerdemain, but in combining the influences of Wilde and Pater, Barrie also presents a narrative which defers meaning by reversing expectation. One of many examples is the famous conclusion to Barrie's *Peter and Wendy*, which states that Peter's abduction of "mothers" will continue indefinitely: "and thus it will go on, so long as children are gay and innocent and heartless" (226). The final word alters the meaning of the sentence as expected at that point, thus deferring comprehension to an end that reverberates back along the sentence and, indeed, through the text itself. The story must be reread and re-construed in light of its final word, and thus reversal of expectation and deferral of meaning reconstitute the conclusion as the point at which understanding must be once more negotiated and begun again. The repetition of stories among the children makes of their world an ongoing narrative, full of asides, alterations, hyperbolic restatements; the consequence of Barrie's "conclusion," if it can be deemed such, is to open out the narrative into futurity, suggesting the continuation of the drama with different actresses (and new roleplaying Lost Boys, perhaps) playing the same role. The predicate of the performer is deferred with no ultimate referent, for it is only in the role that identification is constituted. Similarly, the predicated role of mimetic language in Pater's texts is syntactically subjugated to the nonreferential cognate, reflecting back upon itself and meaningful only within its own momentarily recognized context.

The subjugation of meaning to contingency is reflected thematically in Barrie's text in the character of the redskins and the critique of the imperialist and essentializing view of race. The nomenclature employed by Barrie makes occasionally for uncomfortable reading to a modern audience and seems to place the text firmly in the tradition of colonial masculine romance, of the boys' own adventure stories made so popular in the late nineteenth century by writers such as H. Rider Haggard, Robert Louis Stevenson, and Rudyard Kipling. Peter adopts a swaggering *noblesse oblige* when the redskins call him "Great White Father."[14] For the first time in the novel, he seems to be a stereotype, a shallow caricature mouthing racial platitudes and incapable of making a role his own.

However, I believe Barrie subverts this essentialized justification of the empire of cultural superiority and the natural servitude of the "darker races" and accomplishes this, once more, through the emphasis upon roles being played. The Indians live in Barrie's text according to expectation, as clearly demonstrated in the narrative of their massacre by Hook and his pirates. But with this episode, Barrie writes a superbly subversive satire of accepted accounts of so-called brutal and crafty primitives and the white man attacked by treachery and in an uncivilized fashion:

> By all the unwritten laws of savage warfare it is always the redskin who attacks, and with the wiliness of his race he does it just before dawn, at

which time he knows the courage of the whites to be at its lowest ebb. The white men have in the meantime made a rude stockade . . . and . . . there they await the onslaught. (*Peter and Wendy* 173)

Hook, on the other hand, knowing these "unwritten laws," attacks the Indians first, well before dawn, and massacres them. In mocking the literary tendency to trot out repetitively standardized narratives of colonial derring-do, containing static characterizations of the participants, Barrie reverses his audience's expectations and has the Europeans sneak-attacking the "savages." Barbarism begins at home.

What then of Peter's stereotypical role as "Great White Father"? Imperialism's tendency toward an essentializing of the subject, a diminution of a people's varied identities to the lowest common denominator, operates both upon the self-proclaimed superior and upon the subjugated. To essentialize a subject is, of course, absolutely counter to the aesthete's tendency to recreate his or her sense of self from one moment to the next. Peter would seem to have been affected by the ideological baggage of the adult Victorian world of empire, but Barrie critiques the idea of essentialism as cultural damnation, no matter to whom it might be applied, and presents in its place an ethical aestheticism which is ennobling inasmuch as it proceeds upon an understanding of life in its variability.

This critique of essentialism is of utmost importance in Barrie's text, whether it is temporal, semantic, or ontological. Racial identity is as fluid as the passing moment, the reversals of linguistic meaning, or the sense of the aesthetic self. Peter Pan's role as "Great White Father" is just that, a role. He certainly does not feel it to be a natural one based upon a racial right. How could it be, when he alters his identity constantly throughout the story? It is not a part which he will play any longer than any of the others. At the battle of Slightly Gulch, when the redskins are still the boys' enemies, Peter switches sides in the middle of the battle by switching identities, deciding for that day to be a redskin (138). This mockingly aesthetic version of Kipling's "going native" fascinates the Indians, who agree to be Lost Boys for that day and proceed to battle again—hardly evidence of the essentializing tendency inherent to imperialism and counter to 1890's aestheticism.

Nevertheless, as mentioned earlier in the essay, there is a clear aesthetic hierarchy and evolution in the story. It is in their playing to the imperialist gallery's essentialist expectations that the redskins are massacred. They go to sleep expecting to fulfill their assigned roles at dawn, only to have Hook steal their own part, attacking them first. It is not so much the pirates themselves who are more aesthetically developed than the Indians, for just as the Lost Boys without Peter shamble through their everyday existence, without Hook, the pirates are simply another motley bunch of misfits on the island. But Hook is in many ways the most aesthetically intriguing character in Neverland, and with the massacre he displays the capacity to act out roles unwritten for him. It is impossible to define Peter's character because it is multiple; it is only in the manner of his becoming that he can be described from moment to moment in the narrative. Wendy is playing a role throughout the story, in a liminal position between the adult reality and the aesthetic fictions of the island. Her character is defined in relation to her positioning between these two worlds. But Hook is different.

I would suggest that Hook, as Wilde's Dorian, is an example of an unethical and failed aestheticism. He is certainly described as a Dandy:

> In dress he somewhat aped the attire associated with the name of Charles II, having heard it said in some earlier part of his career that he bore a strange resemblance to the ill-fated Stuarts; and in his mouth he had a holder of his own contrivance which enabled him to smoke two cigars at once. (*Peter and Wendy* 115)

A fop then, indulging in contrivances, even, we are told, particularly sensitive to shades and nuances, being frightened only by the sight of his own blood, "which was thick and of an unusual colour" (115). The one obsession (beyond the death of Peter) to which Hook is in thrall is that of the question of good and bad "form." His childhood days linger to haunt him with the idea of what is and is not acceptable in the realm of the Victorian public school: "Good form! However much he may have degenerated, he still knew that this is all that really matters" (188).[15] A degenerate, well-educated dandy, obsessed with "form": this is surely society's conception of the 1890's aesthete writ large. The literary style of the later Victorian period, much influenced by Pater, held form to be of the utmost import. In his essay "The Decay of Lying," Wilde wrote,

> Art takes Life as part of her rough material, recreates it, and refashions it in fresh forms, is absolutely indifferent to facts, invents, imagines, dreams, and keeps between herself and reality the impenetrable barrier of beautiful style, of decorative or ideal treatment. (1078)

Hook realizes that Peter lives good form naturally and unselfcon-
sciously, that in the boy's very lack of awareness as to his identity
through time, beyond each moment, resides the "pinnacle" of the pirate's own desires (*Peter and Wendy* 203). This is the basis of Hook's
detestation of Peter and his "cockiness," which is simply another manner of saying Peter's delight in his character as its novelty impresses itself upon him from moment to moment. Michael Egan makes a similar
point in his analysis of *Peter Pan* as Oedipal drama, when he says that
Peter is "Youth" and that "[t]hroughout the story Barrie has suggested
that what Hook finds most irritating in Peter is his boyishness, his
'cockiness'" (52). Peter does not age because he lives in the eternal moment. Hook is imprisoned by the past, by the linearity of time, thwarted
in his inability to slough tradition and the expectations as to the form
his life should take. His incapacity to live, as Peter does, solely in the
moment negates his aesthetic capacity and makes his life the true
tragedy of Barrie's story.

Bad form is bad art and an inadequate aesthetic. In Peter's ability to
raise creative aesthetics to a means of living, we have touched upon
the heart of what was often misconstrued by the critics of Wilde and
Pater: that their art was a highly evolved ethical system. If one lives, experiencing all that one can of what life has to offer, overturning the presumptions of traditional dogma and conventional moral stricture, then
the world becomes the theater of independent and creative acts. These
are not to be indulged in selfishly, for the question of selfhood is contingent upon the moment, and this realization is Hook's curtain-call.
Artful whim serves life, and in serving life, we can serve the world. As
Yeoman remarks upon play and fantasy (or the imagination), "They le-
gitimize our re-formation and re-creation of the world, allowing us to
re-member and so re-deem the scattered fragments of ordinary life"
(151). The aestheticized "higher ethics" of Peter Pan allows to all who
follow his form of creativity the opportunities he already enjoys. Difference, not conformity, becomes the standard of the aesthetic community, and it is appreciated in and for itself. This is what Pater and
Wilde, their contemporaries in the Aesthetic movement, and, I would
claim, Barrie and his Peter Pan, sought to deliver. This is their version
of the Beautiful, and it justifies the world.

Barrie's 1937 obituary in the *Times Literary Supplement* suggests that
the aesthetic of *Peter Pan* can indeed, and beneficially, effect a creativity in those who can enjoy the moments as they come:

If this be true, it means that Barrie had the power which is much greater than that of storytelling of compelling successive generations to invent his story afresh, to tell it to themselves and in their own terms—that is to say, he was able not merely to instruct and to entertain but to impregnate the collective mind of his audience. (qtd. in *Peter and Wendy* xxvi)

Echoes of Pater: this is the moment in which to begin.

NOTES

1. In this quotation, note both the psychological and general meaning in reading the term "subject." Much might also be made of Barrie's statement, "You always know after you are two." There are obvious parallels with Jacques Lacan's mirror stage for both Dorian and Wendy: Dorian's portrait is described in Wilde's story as "the most magical of mirrors. As it had revealed to him his own body, so it would reveal to him his own soul" (84).

2. It has been suggested that the name "Wendy" was invented by Barrie for his story. Whilst this would make Wendy a literal "new woman" with no referent behind her identity, the suggestion seems not to be accurate. See Adams.

3. Nikolajeva charts the progress from circular, mythic time in children's literature to the linear temporality of "traditional" adult narratives. However, I would suggest that the aesthetic of the 1890s and Barrie's *Peter Pan* marry these two views of time: because of the passing of linear time, the return of new moments, lived as eternal, is possible.

4. In psychoanalytic readings of *Peter Pan*, desire is seen as being founded in a "lack" or "need" and frames a conception of Neverland as a literary representation of the Freudian unconscious. For example, "Barrie unconsciously created a vast, symbolic metaphor . . . of the child's id" (Egan 37). My reading of desire is that it proceeds from an overabundance of life, not a "lack," and that the unconscious is present throughout the entirety of Barrie's novel, in both the adult world and that of Neverland. Peter's ego, his aesthetic individuality, informs the chaos that Neverland would be without him. He forgoes the strictures of societal standardization, the superego, as it is present in the adult world, where ego is crushed into authoritarian non-individuation. It is in the combination of the unconscious memory (the chaos that linear time brings) and the ego (self-produced, particularized moments) that the renewed present of Neverland can exist. My reading of *Peter Pan* as being representative of a late Victorian aesthetic is at odds with the psychoanalytic tendency to read Peter as "neurotic." I agree with Marie-Louise von Franz's analysis that Peter Pan lives a "provisional life" and one of "asocial individuation" (2), but I see this in an aesthetically positive rather than a psychically negative light.

5. Michael Egan is one of several psychoanalytic critics who has remarked upon the "sense of psychic fracture" that Peter displays (39). Rather than reading Peter's fragmentary identity as neurotic, I would suggest that this is symptomatic of the repetition of created, role-played identities that are willed by Peter in each and every aesthetic moment.

6. Hollindale also quotes Humphrey Carpenter's statement that Barrie had no recollection of having written the story of Peter (*Peter and Wendy* xxvi). This "forgetting" is, of course, perfectly commensurate with the aesthetic in Barrie's text.

7. For Hollindale's analysis, with other referred commentators, see *Peter Pan and Other Plays* vii.

8. For details of this unique performance, see Green 109–12.

9. The boys' use of hyperbole can be seen reflected in Barrie's own directions concerning the acting of his play. These directions indicate once more the links between Barrie and the aesthetic of the 1890s, that the importance of artifice and role-playing is privileged over the real: "No doubt there should be a certain exaggeration in acting, but just as much as there is in stage scenery, which is exaggerated, not to *be* real, but to *seem* real" (Green 105).

10. See Nietzsche 179. Nordau's statement refers to this passage, in which the gateway engraved "Moment" is happened upon by the eponymous hero. Nietzsche's text was published in 1884, the year before Pater's *Marius the Epicurean*, a story presenting the philosophy of *Studies in the History of the Renaissance* in novel form. I would suggest that the appearance of the two texts at virtually the same time is an example of precisely those confluences of dynamic forces that Pater suggests "make up" existence itself.

11. Here I read Nietzsche's idea of the Eternal Return as another version of Pater's aestheticism. The similarities are startling, excepting the fact that both philosophers predict such confluences, in this instance intellectual, in time.

12. Wilde was convicted in 1895 of gross indecency under Section 11 of the Criminal Amendment Act (1885) and given the maximum sentence of two years hard labor. At the time of his arrest, he was at the pinnacle of his success. With his conviction, his West End plays were taken off the stage and even association with Wilde could blight a career, such as that of Aubrey Beardsley, who was dismissed as art editor of *The Yellow Book*. The end of Decadence as an artistic movement in England is often dated to Wilde's imprisonment, although the aesthetic would obviously continue to influence artists beyond 1895.

13. As Wilde says in his essay "The Decay of Lying," "Life imitates Art far more than Art imitates Life" (1091). In this quotation, we see both the form and the contention of Wilde's reversals of expectation.

14. According to Green, "The Great White Father" was one of the earliest titles of *Peter Pan* (43).

15. Schools referred to as "public" in Britain are known as "private" elsewhere.

WORKS CITED

Adams, Cecil. "Was the name Wendy invented for the book "Peter Pan"? 17 Dec. 2002. *The Straight Dope*. Ed. Ed Zotti. 15 Jan. 2004 <http://www.straight dope.com/mailbag/mpeterpanwendy.html>.

Barrie, J. M. *Peter Pan and Wendy*. New York: Scribner's, 1911.

———. *Peter Pan in Kensington Gardens; Peter and Wendy*. Ed. Peter Hollindale. Oxford: Oxford UP, 1999.

———. *Peter Pan and Other Plays*. Ed. Peter Hollindale. Oxford: Oxford UP, 1995.

Dowling, Linda. *Language and Decadence in the Victorian* Fin de Siècle. Oxford: Princeton UP, 1989.

Egan, Michael. "The Neverland of Id: Barrie, *Peter Pan*, and Freud." *Children's Literature* 10 (1982): 37–55.

Gilead, Sarah. "Magic Abjured: Closure in Children's Fantasy Fiction." *PMLA* 106.2 (March 1991): 277–93.

Green, Roger Lancelyn. *Fifty Years of Peter Pan*. London: Peter Davies, 1954.

Nikolajeva, Maria. *From Mythic to Linear: Time in Children's Literature*. Lanham, MD: Scarecrow, 2000.

Nietzsche, Friedrich. *Thus Spoke Zarathustra*. Trans. R. J. Hollindale. London: Penguin, 1961.

Nordau, Max. *Degeneration*. 1895. Lincoln: Nebraska UP, 1993.

Pater, Walter. *Studies in the History of the Renaissance*. Oxford: Oxford UP, 1906.

Robbins, Ruth. *Pater to Forster, 1873–1924*. New York: Palgrave Macmillan, 2003.

Von Franz, Maria-Louise von. *Puer Aeternus*. 2nd ed. Santa Monica: Sigo P, 1981.

Wilde, Oscar. "The Decay of Lying." *Collin's Complete Works of Oscar Wilde*. Centenary ed. Glasgow: HarperCollins, 1999.

———. *The Picture of Dorian Gray*. *Collin's Complete Works of Oscar Wilde*. Centenary ed. Glasgow: HarperCollins, 1999.

Yeoman, Ann. *Now or Neverland*. Toronto: Inner City Books, 1998.

3

Babes in Boy-Land: J. M. Barrie and the Edwardian Girl

Christine Roth

> I courted the fair Alice W—n; and, as much as children could understand, I explained to them what coyness, and difficulty, and denial meant in maidens—when suddenly, turning to Alice, the soul of the first Alice looked out at her eyes with such a reality of representment, that I became in doubt which of them stood there before me.
>
> —Charles Lamb, "Dream Children"

> As you look at Wendy you may see her hair becoming white, and her figure little again, for all this happened long ago. Jane [Wendy's daughter] is now a common grown-up, with a daughter called Margaret. . . . When Margaret grows up she will have a daughter, who is to be Peter's mother in turn; and thus it will go on, so long as children are gay and innocent and heartless.
>
> —J. M. Barrie, *Peter and Wendy*

In "Dream Children," part of Charles Lamb's 1822 collection *Essays of Elia*, James Elia has a dream in which he confronts the children of his fantasy marriage to Alice W—n, the girl he loved and lost. Recalling the end of the dream, he describes the above scene, in which Alice (the dream mother and wife) seems to look at him through the eyes of her daughter (one of the dream children), who is also named Alice. The dream mother and the dream child exist simultaneously in the body of

47

a fantastical little girl figure. In the eighty years following the publication of Lamb's story, the nostalgia and allure surrounding a double image such as this one fueled a cultural, artistic, and literary phenomenon, as nineteenth-century writers and artists carefully negotiated a
fragile balance in their own "Alices."

Inheriting this tradition at the turn of the century, J. M. Barrie carefully negotiates in *Peter Pan* a similar fragile balance in his most famous young heroine, Wendy Darling, and works to hold two simultaneous images—child and woman, dream and reality, chaste and
fallen—in constant tandem. For despite the arguments put forth in almost every critical review and reading of the play, the anxiety in *Peter
Pan* does not revolve exclusively around the end of boyhood. A cultural fascination with the bounds of girlhood drives this text. While
readers are always able to see a former child in Wendy, they are also
haunted and thrilled by the ever-lurking image of a woman behind the
eyes of the little girl, and the eternal boy simply provides a new space
for old fantasies and tensions that previously flourished around female
children.

THE CULT OF THE LITTLE GIRL IN BRITAIN

Such a fascination with the dual nature of the girl can be explained by
what nineteenth-century writers and artists referred to as the Cult of the
Little Girl. Indeed, English female children were constructed and obsessively worshipped as *amie-enfants* between 1860 and 1911, a period of time spanning from the heyday of music hall through the cultish
interest in girls at Oxford in the 1860s to the publication of *Peter Pan*.
Whether inspiring Oxford undergraduates to place little girl "mascots"
on the sidelines at sporting matches or fueling John Ruskin's madden-
ing pursuit of his favorite Winnington school girl, the startling intensity
of the Cult of the Little Girl is most evident in its cultural manifestations.
Yet its literary, historical, and theoretical implications are best mea-
sured in texts that reveal paradoxical constructions of the nineteenth-
century girl as simultaneously worldly and ethereal, scandalous and
blessed. For artists and writers like John Everett Millais, John Ruskin,
Lewis Carroll (Charles Dodgson), Ernest Dowson, and Barrie, this ambiguity supported a titillating paradoxical construction of little girls that
relies on a tension created by the irreconcilable schism between the
fantastical and the mundane—a schism created and sustained by girls

who exist within a space that constantly negotiates two equally important ends of a spectrum. At one end of the spectrum, the girl figures as a corruptible (and corrupting) agent of adult desire and transgression. At the other, she possesses an invulnerable chastity that aligns her with domesticity and a sense of moral duty. In short, the ideal girl for these writers and artists embodies a fundamental duality and is able to keep that duality in tension so that the child and the woman become contending sides of the same girl figure. Neither side can complete the formula without the other: if they are isolated, the girl-child becomes distant, and the girl-woman becomes fallen and utterly forgettable.

This bifurcated view of girls is entirely unsurprising when considered in connection with the seemingly capricious constructions of the little girl at the turn of the century as chaste/innocent in some cases and sexual/worldly in others, based largely on markers of class. As Deborah Gorham demonstrates in *The Victorian Girl and the Feminine Ideal*, the middle class epitomized its privileged social position in its daughters and in its childlike wives—figures of saintly feminine purity who existed exclusively within the private sphere of domesticity. By safeguarding and sequestering the girls within a domestic sphere that denied any overt or accessible sexuality in the children, the middle class could reassure itself that its wives and daughters embodied, both physically and spiritually, the feminine ideals of innocence and purity more successfully than their working-class counterparts. Thus, says Gorham, middle-class daughters, unlike working girls in the public sphere of business, remained childlike (if not legally "children") longer. The daughters symbolized spiritual and sexual purity—a sanctified "place of renewal" for men (4)—and, within middle-class households, they remained "girls" until they became "girlish" wives and mothers.

On the other hand, when a working-class counterpart entered service within that same middle-class household, she was legally recognized as a sexual person and responsible for her own sexual conduct. Once a girl entered the middle-class home as an agent of the professional public sphere (as a domestic servant), she became a commodity, no longer worshipped and protected as an icon. As Claudia Nelson points out in her discussion of legal definitions of girlhood, "[I]f upper-class girls were supposed to be the embodiment of purity, their working-class counterparts were acknowledged to be sexual beings at puberty" (3). Working-class girls were defined and considered sexually available (or unavailable) according to the shifting age of consent.[1] Their sexuality and sexual availability were negotiable legal issues that fell outside the unspoken spiritual and cultural restraints sheltering their middle-class counterparts from physical "corruption."

Even William Stead in "Maiden Tribute of Modern Babylon," his famous 1885 *Pall Mall Gazette* exposé, used to his benefit the class-determined distinctions between sexual working-class girls and asexual middle-class daughters. In his series of articles, Stead proclaimed that working-class children—the "daughters of the people"—were forced into London brothels. Indeed, it was only Stead's reference to the girls as "daughters" that identified them as children at all. Essentially, he reconstructed child prostitutes as middle-class daughters suffering sexual abuse. Wishing to focus on the youth and innocence of his subjects, Stead manipulated the prevailing understanding of girlhood in order to situate working-class girls within a national story (child prostitution). The girls sold into prostitution were, in fact, almost always working-class girls older than thirteen, the legal age of consent at the time.

If Stead wanted to incite public outrage against "child" prostitution, he had little choice but to try to align working-class prostitutes with middle-class daughters because the ruling assumptions held that working-class girls were *naturally* more sexual and promiscuous, which would have undermined his efforts to characterize the girls as innocent victims. William Acton's famous 1870 study of the moral, social, and sanitary aspects of urban prostitution had claimed that working-class girls were sexually corrupt by nature: "[The girls'] seduction—if seduction it can be called—has been effected, with their own consent, by boys no older than themselves, and is all but a natural consequence of promiscuous herding, that mainspring of corruption among our lower orders" (207). In Acton's view (and in the view of most other Victorian "scientists"), working-class girls were not debauched by older men or men of higher classes, as Stead argued; instead, they willingly engaged in sexual activity with "boys no older than themselves."[2] Thus, sexual promiscuity and prostitution were seen as a "natural consequence" of an inherited degeneracy in the lower orders, the unquestioned outcome being what Benjamin Jowett called "a class of sinners" (54). This construction portrayed lower-class girls as essentially less innocent than their middle-class counterparts—an economically based construction that enabled men to see one girl as worldly and the other as ethereal, based almost solely on markers of class.

Given the inclination of Victorian social (and medical) science to portray girls as potential agents of degenerate sexuality, even as crusaders like Stead depicted them as innocent victims of criminal sexual

assault, the hyper-sensitivity and sensationalism surrounding such ex-
posés as the "Maiden Tribute" series encouraged most Victorian readers to consider the possibility that all thirteen- to sixteen-year-old
"daughters," working-class and middle-class alike, might somehow be
both ethereal children and sexually active young women. Even the
conventional fragile distinction between sexual and non-sexual girls
did not erase the implicit sexuality of the "virtuous child"; indeed, by
focusing on her innocence, Stead had only underscored the potential
for her corruption. Just as working-class girls could be reconstituted as
innocent victims, so seemingly innocent daughters could become incipient sex objects in waiting. The slippage between the sexual and innocent identities of girls provided endless titillation, always suggesting
the possibility of both identities.

At the turn of the century, this subtle hint of impending womanhood
in every little girl—the very ambiguity that the Victorian Cult of the Little Girl found so titillating—was the source of intense anxiety, even
loathing, for those who valued unsullied youthful vigor and innocence
above all else. So they looked to children in whom no such spectre appeared, resulting in what historian Peter Coveney marks as a shift from
a sexually morbid obsession with female children, as we see in the
works of Lewis Carroll, to the "cult of J. M. Barrie" (249). Without exception, scholars discuss this cultural and artistic shift from girl-worship
to boy-worship as if it were an abrupt change with no overlap of any
kind between the two phenomena:

> Between Alice [referring here to Carroll's *Alice's Adventures in Wonder-
> land*] and Peter Pan, something like a revolution in the perception of chil-
> dren occurred. The idealization of childhood remains in these years cen-
> tral to English culture, but a shift is marked around 1880, from an
> emphasis on the child as moral icon, emblem of purity, to a craze for the
> child as fun-loving playboy hero. (Wullschläger 109)

The Edwardian empire craved youths who would never grow old:
Rudyard Kipling's Kim, A. E. Housman's spectral Shropshire lad,
Robert Baden-Powell's rugged boy-men, and the many doomed public
school–trained youths of World War I—characters who would never
outgrow the fantasy of youth and adventure that was constructed
around them. The little boy so excluded from Victorian images of childhood in England was made to embody the desires of a new century.

Yet the transition was not sudden and complete. To argue that the
shift from girl-worship to boy-worship was immediate, complete, and

tidy is both inaccurate and unrealistic. Of course, if girl-worship were merely a symptom of particular aberrant personalities—Ruskin's or Carroll's often-cited aversion to adult women, for example—the obsession with female children would die with the personalities who celebrated them. However, the Cult of the Little Girl was not merely the product of a few individual obsessions; it was a force of culture in nineteenth-century and early-twentieth-century England, and the fervor surrounding little boys is intricately connected to it. In fact, Barrie, the author most often cited to mark the shift towards boy-worship, is a man whose corpus of work actually reflects a consistent obsession with the little girl figure. *Peter Pan*, his most popular play and a hallmark of Edwardian boy-worship, begins and ends as the story of a little girl who is tormented by the loss of her youth and innocence. In this play, as in many of his other texts, Barrie continues the practice of embodying two opposing images or roles in a single female character (invariably the role of mother and daughter, mirroring the split-image of Lamb's Alices in "Dream Children"), but only as a sort of female diptych. The two identities are incompatible, so they emerge in turns—a duality that most often punishes girls for becoming women by forcing them into painful masquerade and self-deception.

J. M. BARRIE AND THE CULT OF THE LITTLE GIRL

Barrie moved to London in 1884—the epicenter and heyday of little girls' cultish popularity in Victorian England—and many of his novels and plays reflect and negotiate constructions of the paradoxical girl figure at the center of this force of culture. In truth, he writes more about little girls than he does about little boys. *The Little Minister* (1891), the book that made Barrie a rich man, focuses on a gypsy girl named Babbie. In *Quality Street* (1913), a young woman named Phoebe agrees to be faithful to her sweetheart, Dr. Valentine Brown, when he marches off to war. He returns several years later to discover that Phoebe, who is almost thirty years old, has been transformed into a prudish old maid. To win back Dr. Brown's love, Phoebe pretends to be her own teen-aged niece. Similarly, the play *Rosalind* (1912) features an actress who is tired of always pretending to be twenty-nine (already fairly mature for Barrie's female characters). She occasionally takes a holiday that allows her to be comfortably middle-aged by posing as her own mother. During one of these trips, one of her ardent young lovers pursues her and she is forced to disillusion him. Finally, *The Little Minis-*

ter (1917) and *Dear Brutus* (1922) recall the spectral, redemptive little girls of so many Cult-of-the-Little-Girl narratives in their inclusion of "dream children"—daughters, of course—who approach life-weary men in enchanted woods.

Barrie often borrowed prototypical characters and dilemmas from texts associated with the Cult of the Little Girl, especially Carroll's iconic *Alice's Adventures in Wonderland.* Barrie's play *Alice Sit-by-the-Fire* (first performed in 1905 and published in 1918), for example, features an Alice who is driven by a nostalgia for her lost girlhood. Alice is a middle-aged mother who imagines she is a young girl; her daughter, Amy, is a teen-aged girl who deludes herself into believing she is an experienced woman of the world. In the stage directions, girlhood is idealized as a uniquely pristine condition. Indeed, the play opens as the narrative voice behind the directions considers looking at Amy's diary but warns that "we cannot be sure our hands are clean enough to turn the pages of a young girl's thoughts" (2). Any physical contact and potential physical corruption of the little girl are transferred to a surrogated, metonymical object associated with her. Recalling Carroll's preface to *Alice's Adventures in Wonderland,* in which a child's story is metonymy for the child herself, Barrie's text suggests that any defilement or invasion of Amy's thoughts or Amy's story is synonymous with defilement or invasion of the girl herself.

As the play progresses, the narrator explains that Alice (the mother) has been living as a colonel's wife in India. After her children are sent home to be raised in England, she is able to play (to masquerade in) the role of innocent sweetheart to the young British soldiers. Upon returning to England, Alice mistakenly assumes that Amy (her daughter) is having an affair with a young soldier from the Punjab. Ironically, Amy entertains similar suspicions about her mother. In a series of confusing scenes, mother and daughter play opposing and contending sides—youth/age, innocence/knowing—of a single sweetheart. Alice enjoys the game, but she must finally acknowledge her proper role in the drama: the heroine's mother. Any illusions of herself as a young sweetheart dissolve away. Alice recognizes her own past in her daughter's present, and she states that she can now see the world only through Amy's eyes. Alice and her daughter are never completely independent of each other; instead, as Alice explains, they constitute two halves of a single image:

> It's summer done, autumn begun. Farewell, summer, we don't know you any more. My girl and I are like the little figures in the weather-house;

when Amy comes out, Alice goes in. Alice Sit-by-the-Fire henceforth.
(138)

The familiar paradoxical diptych of femininity—the "summer" of virginal girlhood and the "autumn" of mature womanhood—holds the
opposing roles in balance, side by side in the weatherhouse. Both
woman and child are still embodied together, but the daughter is always replacing the mother: "when Amy comes out, Alice goes in."
    In Barrie's most famous play, *Peter Pan* (1911), mothers and daugh-
ters again negotiate the loss associated with adulthood. In fact, the
novel, renamed *Peter and Wendy* (1911), adds a final chapter titled
"When Wendy Grew Up." In this way, Barrie emphasizes the story's
primary lament for little girls' inevitable maturation and degeneration
from daughters into mothers. Daughters again continually replace
mothers throughout the story: Mrs. Darling is replaced by Wendy in the
first chapter; Wendy is then replaced by her daughter, Jane; and, finally,
Jane is replaced by Wendy's granddaughter. The girl figure is always
part woman and part child, which, for Barrie, means that she is never
completely a child. Just as class dictated who was a girl and who was
a woman in nineteenth-century England, a character's role, not age,
dictates who is a child and who is an adult in Neverland.
    So it is that *Peter Pan* ushers in the age of the boy with a sort of nod
and obeisance to the long-revered paradigm of the dualistic little girl
figure. As much as Peter is a celebration of the ever-youthful and ever-
fearless boy-man, he is equally a testament to a cultural disappointment that all girls must mature into wives and mothers. Barrie casts Peter in the traditionally female paradoxical role, and the influence and
endurance of the Cult of the Little Girl is unmistakable. Peter, as incarnation of the Greek god Pan, is both immortal spirit and fleshy boy; he
embodies sexual passion and unsullied youthfulness. He is nature incarnate and a symbol of *fin de siècle* Decadence, and the narrator
teases and torments a specifically adult audience as Peter tenuously
balances the extremes of life and death, childhood and adulthood, innocence and eroticism.[3] For Barrie, as for so many Edwardian lovers of
youth[s], males could remain boyish forever; the identities of father and
son, man and boy, civilized and savage existed simultaneously and
harmoniously. Females, on the other hand, were divided between two
generations in whom these paradoxical identities waged a constant
war. Yet the little girl provided the prototype for the eternal boy figures,
and men like Barrie continued to focus on these girl figures. Unfortunately, in these Edwardian stories, little girl figures always outgrow any

fantasy worlds around them—a tragic fate, or flaw even, that inevitably leads to the deep sense of loss that motivates most of Barrie's stories.

WENDY DARLING: BARRIE'S NEVER-GIRL

Peter and Wendy begins and ends with a mother and daughter (not a father and son) and a nostalgia for lost girlhood. The first scene, indeed the first lines, show Wendy and her mother discussing her inevitable maturation and degeneration:

> All children, except one, grow up. They soon know that they will grow up, and the way Wendy knew was this. One day when she was two years old she was playing in a garden, and she plucked another flower and ran with it to her mother. I suppose she must have looked rather delightful, for Mrs. Darling put her hand to her heart and cried, "Oh, why can't you remain like this for ever!" (1)

If the story stopped at this point or the focus moved entirely to the boy characters, readers could assume that Mrs. Darling is making this wish as a mother who wants to keep her children close, but there is an immediate link between the plucked flower and the fading girl, and the mother is more likely speaking these lines as a woman who longs for her own lost girlhood. In fact, the narrator goes on to explain that "until Wendy came her mother was the chief one" (1). Although "the chief one" is never defined, Wendy has clearly taken over a preferred position of some kind that her mother once held. Like Alice in *Alice Sit-by-the Fire*, the mother represents the little girl's loss, and the little girl represents the mother's former allure, and Barrie plays with the two female roles, intermingling and manipulating them to reveal the bifurcated duality of his heroine. Wendy begins the story as both prototypical middle-class girl and "every inch a woman, though there were not many inches" simultaneously (40). She is taken away and transformed into a mother of savages, and she returns to London as a middle-class daughter but is transformed immediately again into a mother (and wife to one of the former savages), and the story closes as Wendy's daughter and granddaughter take her place in the recurring cycle. Each Darling girl is removed from the nursery and transformed from English daughter to Neverland mother. The two opposing poles of each girl's duality cannot appear simultaneously; she is always either daughter or mother, never both and never neither. Once again, when one identity comes out, the other must go in. In fact, the Peter Pan stories provide a matrilinear chain of mother-daughter figures.

In each mother-daughter pairing, the mothers are targets of harsh aggression and resentment, punished for growing into adult women, while the father figures continue to live as part boys and part men. Both Mrs. Darling and Wendy are rejected and "forgotten" by Peter when he realizes that they are grown-ups. In *Peter and Wendy*, Peter "gnashe[s] the little pearls [his teeth]" at Mrs. Darling (16), and he gives a "cry of pain" and "dr[aws] back sharply" when he sees that Wendy is an adult in the final chapter (264). Even the narrator berates the story's adult women and seems bitter that they are no longer girlish. Mrs. Darling is criticized for her lack of "proper spirit" (236)—a sense of fair play and adventure that is closely associated with the male youths of the story. The narrator "despise[s] her" and refuses to say anything nice about her (236), and by the end of the story, Wendy's mother is dismissed as "dead and forgotten" (258). When Wendy grows up, the narrator again shows little care for adult women and encourages us to forget her, explaining, "You need not be sorry for her. She was one of the kind that likes to grow up" (257). On the contrary, while Mr. Darling is "one of those deep ones who know about stocks and shares," he is also boyish, rebellious, and always looking for a game (2). Indeed, "he might have passed for a boy again if he had been able to take his baldness off" (237). When Mr. Darling and his son Michael must take their medicine, for example, the father behaves like one of the children. Wendy counts to three and Michael takes his dose, but Mr. Darling slips his medicine behind his back. When the family notices, he retorts, "I meant to take mine, but I—I missed it" (28). He then tries to feed it to the dog and becomes pouty and frustrated when she gets coddled instead of him. Furthermore, in the dramatic version, because the same actor usually plays both Mr. Darling and Captain Hook, the character seems able to travel back and forth between London and Neverland, even though he is an adult—always somewhere between the two worlds.

Yet even though Barrie's individual female characters cannot exhibit both paradoxical identities simultaneously in one body, Barrie does maintain a paradigm for feminine duality. As a Victorian little girl, Wendy is, of course, the ultimate insider, commanding a decisive role in the invention of middle-class English identity and national character. For Barrie, however, this same middle-class girl is also a liminal figure who, in some ways, marks the boundaries between the various landscapes and tempestuous borderlands—"neverlands"—in each version of the Peter Pan story. He removes her to a distant quasi-imperial setting that builds layers of conflict, both internal and external to the child.[4] So Wendy is not only both daughter and mother, but she is also civilized English middle-class daughter and mother of primitive island "savages." She seems innocent and childlike when compared to Tinker Bell and Tiger Lily, but she seems ladylike and knowing when she interacts with Peter and the boys. By juggling these two identities in one little girl, Barrie is able to further explore the subtle boundaries that balance child and adult, innocent and knowing, civilized and savage without collapsing them, and girls like Wendy are able to simultaneously embody and distinguish between the exotic and familiar territories prevalent in an era of imperial expansion and cultural exchange.

Wendy—domestic, middle-class, and English—battles against two girls who are foreign in both character and nationality: the erotic(ized), working-class Irish Tinker Bell and the savage, coquettish Native-American princess, Tiger Lily. Each girl is able to switch back and forth between paradoxical identities, but she is always one or the other. Tinker Bell is a young girl; she is "still growing" (35). However, when she first arrives on the scene, she is "exquisitely gowned in a skeleton leaf, cut low and square, through which her figure could be seen to the best advantage. She was slightly inclined to *embonpoint*" (35). She also uses foul language and is characterized as "an abandoned little creature" (159). She can play two opposing roles; even her social class is negotiable. By name, she is a working-class girl: "She is quite a common fairy. . . . [S]he is called Tinker Bell because she mends the pots and kettles" (45). She associates with "street fairies" and walks around her "boudoir" in the boys' house in a "*negligée*" (121, 113, 171). Yet at some points, she seems to be cast as middle-class, as when Peter explains, "You know you can't be my fairy, Tink, because I am a gentleman and you are a lady" (45).

Similarly, Tiger Lily is both a chief's daughter and a "wayward thing," "cold" and "amorous" (82). The narrator repeatedly refers to her as a "daughter," but his introduction reveals a familiar Barrie diptych: "Tiger Lily, proudly erect, a princess in her own right. She is the most beautiful of dusky Dianas and the belle of the Piccaninnies, coquettish, cold and amorous by turns; there is not a brave who would not have the wayward thing to wife, but she staves off the altar with a hatchet" (82). She possesses two opposing identities, but she reveals them only "by turns," not simultaneously. She is most often illustrated as a little girl and she refers to Peter as her "father,"[5] but she is also an erotic femme fatale who keeps men away with a hatchet. Like the mermaids in the Neverland lagoon, Tiger Lily is exotic and foreign, insinuating libertinism in late-Victorian England—both alluringly physical and discouragingly distant "by turns." Together, the various girl figures create a paradoxical construction of femininity: corrupted and corrupting, victims of vicious attack and agents of degenerative (and violent) adulthood.

Whereas the battle between paradoxical female identities was previously waged in the body of individual little girls like Lamb's, Carroll's, and Barrie's various Alices, it is now waged by opposing girls—opposing generations, even—who embody one identity or the other. The battle is externalized, and the female prototypes contend with each other. Tinker Bell and some "street fairies" place Wendy on a great floating leaf in hopes of banishing her to the mainland (121), and the mermaids try to drown her. Wendy regrets "that all the time she was on the island she never had a civil word from one of [the mermaids]" (123), and as the narrator explains, "a mermaid caught Wendy by the feet, and began pulling her softly into the water. Peter, feeling her slip from him, woke with a start, and was just in time to draw her back" (141). Yet the most significant and symbolic attack comes early on, when Tinker Bell is responsible for Wendy's fall—both her fall to earth and her fall from middle-class girlhood. Tinker Bell "hate[s]" Wendy with the fierce hatred of a very woman" and "lure[s]" her "to her destruction" (74, 73). Wendy tries to fly, but as the narrator informs us, the "jealous fairy had now cast off all disguise of friendship, and was darting at her victim from every direction, pinching savagely each time she touched" (93). Tinker Bell then says to the Lost Boys, "Peter wants you to shoot the Wendy" (93). At the fairy's urging, the boys shoot "Wendy in the heavens" through the heart (92), causing her lifeless body to fall to earth. After this "fall," Peter frequently refers to Wendy as "old lady."

Of course, for Peter, the idea of death is not threatening; in fact, as the narrator of *Peter and Wendy* explains, "when children died, [Peter Pan] went part of the way with them, so that they should not be frightened" (11), and after Peter rescues Wendy from the mermaids, "a drum beating within him" even says, "To die will be an awfully big adventure" (143). Peter is not endangered by the same figurative deaths that Wendy suffers or by the literal deaths that she eludes throughout the story. Peter Pan is able to exist somewhere between life and death without being affected by either. He is both angel and boy, phantasm and flesh, but never completely either one. Barrie's little girl, however, maintains her duality by always taking one role or the other—child or adult, living or dead. In this way, Barrie commingles the figurative death of a particular girl with the death of girlhood. Wendy is taken out of her home during her last night in the nursery—her last night as a little girl. She is killed and transformed into a mother figure for the boys who will never grow up. As a result, Wendy becomes a virgin mother—a role that invokes a history of paradoxical girl figures caught between heaven and earth, including earlier Barrie characters like Babbie in *The Little Minister* and Grizel in *Tommy and Grizel*. Barrie finds a way to literally shoot the angelic girl out of the sky and bring her down to earth. Thus, Wendy ceases to be a child when she falls out of the sky. As the boys gather around her, Slightly (Wendy's future husband, according to the 1908 version of the epilogue, *When Wendy Grew Up: An Afterthought*) recognizes her as a mature "lady" (suggesting both age and social class) and mother figure. He says, "I think it must be a lady," and Tootles follows, "When ladies used to come to me in dreams, I said, 'Pretty mother, pretty mother'" (94–95). Here Wendy becomes both a reflection of her mother, recalling Barrie's recurring mother-daughter combinations, and a "fallen" girl who is no longer herself childlike.

This unnatural maturity—unnatural, at least, in Neverland—prevents Wendy from immediately living in the children's home (although Wendy's adventure later takes her underground to the cave hideout). As a daughter, she could live with boys, as she had done with John and Michael. However, the boys are unable to carry Wendy into their house because touching her "would not be sufficiently respectful" (99). The boys therefore build a house around the little girl—an activity that Barrie likens to wedding preparations by writing that "they were as busy as tailors the night before a wedding" (100).[6] Thus, as the boys build around her, Wendy is transformed into a wife and mother figure, and as she passes from death back into life, she mimics Carroll's Alice by recovering from her fantastical fall to find herself a young woman. Without opening her eyes, Wendy begins to sing as the boys build around her: "I wish I had a pretty house, / The littlest ever seen, / With funny little red walls / And roof of mossy green. . . . / Gay windows all about, / With roses peeping in, you know, / And babies peeping out" (104). Wendy the little girl has died; Wendy the mother awakens. She comes back to life only as a mother figure to all the boys, even her brothers. Michael, in fact, is placed in a basket and forced to play the role of the baby "peeping out." Though many of the boys are close to

Wendy's age and Wendy is supposedly in a place where children never grow up, she is forced into her mother's role while the boys remain un-questionably, even exaggeratedly, childlike. Gathering around her, they plead for her to "play along," saying, "Wendy lady . . . we are your children. . . . O Wendy lady, be our mother" (107). The scene is both domestic and quasi-religious, reflecting in the little girl the familiar dual image of holy Virgin Mother and secular virginal mother. Even so, she does not accept the role immediately. Like so many of Barrie's female characters, she is unaware of her own transformation. She insists to the boys gathered around her, "Of course it's frightfully fascinating, but you see I am only a little girl" (107).

Interestingly, despite their insistence that Wendy play a maternal role, both Peter and the Lost Boys seem to favor little girls. They want a mother to help them defeat Captain Hook, but girls are still revered over adult women. The narrator explains that the boys "knew in what they called their hearts that one can get on quite well without a mother and that it is only mothers who think you can't" (168). As for Peter, "Not only had he no mother, but he had not the slightest desire to have one" (38). Little girls, however, are different. According to Peter, girls are more clever than boys, and "one girl is more use than twenty boys" (40). Even Captain Hook, to whom Wendy is clearly a child, treats her deferentially:

> A different treatment was accorded to Wendy. . . . With ironical politeness Hook raised his hat to her, and, offering her his arm, escorted her to the spot where the others were being gagged. He did it with such an air, he was so frightfully distingué, that she was too fascinated to cry out. She was only a little girl. (185–86)

Nevertheless, as a mother to the boys, Wendy is ultimately an in-truder and "disturber of the peace and play" of Neverland (Kincaid 285). Because girls are more clever, she gives the Lost Boys an unfair advantage. Many of the pirate schemes to trap the boys rely on the ab-sence of a mother and the resulting vulnerability of the boys. Once Wendy arrives, Hook laments, "The game's up. . . . [T]hose boys have found a mother" (*Peter and Wendy* 131). She also sets up a school, ask-ing the boys questions about home, beginning with "What was the colour of Mother's eyes?" and ending with "Describe Mother's Party Dress" (116). The Lost Boys are even forced to behave like English gen-tlemen towards her—the very role they sought to escape. Tootles is inspired to "blood" anyone "who does not behave to Wendy like an English gentleman" (170), and when the boys are preparing to walk the Jolly Roger plank, Wendy says, "I feel that I have a message to you from your mothers, and it is this: 'We hope our sons will die like English gentlemen'" (211).

As a "lady," Wendy, in a sense, also intrudes into the game by interrupting the innocent, even naïve, homosociality of Neverland with a more "grown-up" English heterosexuality. In the clearest example, Wendy wishes to exchange "kisses" with Peter, but Peter is unaware of what a kiss is or how it is exchanged. Wendy is able to trick Peter into thinking that acorn buttons and thimbles are "kisses," so he is able to exchange kisses with Wendy without being overtly romantic or adult-like. As the narrator explains, Wendy "said she would give him a kiss if he liked, but Peter did not know what she meant, and he held out his hand expectantly" (41). Wendy is surprised and proclaims, "Surely you know what a kiss is?" to which Peter replies, "I shall know when you give it to me" (41) Wendy gives him a thimble. Of course, Wendy is aware of what a kiss really involves, and Barrie reminds us that this knowledge "cheapens" the little girl: when Peter offers to give Wendy a kiss, "[s]he made herself rather cheap by inclining her face toward him, but he merely dropped an acorn button in her hand; so she slowly returned her face to where it had been before" (41).

This mock courtship becomes a child's game for Wendy and Peter. Any potential sensuality is diffused by substituting innocuous objects for the kisses. The exchange is full of suggestion and paradox, but the tension remains in balance. When Wendy finally kisses Peter, she tells him that the kiss is a thimble. Wendy, of course, knows that the kiss is real and again makes herself "rather cheap." Peter "thimbles" her in return, which begins Wendy's descent or "fall" to maturity and motherhood:

> She kissed him.
> "Funny!" said Peter gravely. "Now shall I give you a thimble?"
> "If you wish to," said Wendy, keeping her head erect this time.
> Peter thimbled her, and almost immediately she screeched. "What is it, Wendy?"
> "It was exactly as if someone were pulling my hair."
> "That must have been Tink. I never knew her so naughty before."
> And indeed Tink was darting about again, using offensive language.
> "She says she will do that to you, Wendy, every time I give you a thimble." (47–48)

After they kiss, Wendy is immediately tormented by the jealous fairy-fatale—the story's clearest and most constant symbol of threatening female sexuality. And, of course, it is Tink's rage over the girl's affection for Peter that inspires her to have Wendy shot down to earth. Peter, who is unaware of the romantic meaning behind the "thimbling," treats the exchange as a game, but Wendy wants the boy to return her affections as a suitor or even a husband might.

Wendy assumes, presumably due to their similarity in ages, that Peter is her male counterpart and partner in the Neverland games. If she is going to act as female guardian to the boys, it seems only logical to her that he will be their male guardian. She sees Peter and herself as parents to the Lost Boys; if she is their "mother," she assumes that he is their "father." Peter does play with a fatherly role, but, like Mr. Darling, he always maintains a balance between child and adult, son and father. He proudly states his famous lines, "I don't want ever to be a man. . . . I want always to be a little boy and to have fun," but Wendy (the "loyal housewife") defers to him because "Father knows best" (151). The Piccaninnies call Peter "the Great White Father" (150), and the boy occasionally slips into reveries in which he imagines himself as the Lost Boys' father: "'Ah, old lady,' Peter said aside to Wendy, warming himself by the fire and looking down at her as she sat turning a heel, 'there is nothing more pleasant of an evening for you and me when the day's toil is over than to rest by the fire with the little ones near by'" (157).

In these reveries, Wendy must always return to her place as mother figure—a relatively "old lady" who will resume her filial role only after she returns to her own mother. Peter, on the other hand, is able to play with a paternal role while sustaining his boyish character as well. He is only titillated (and titillating) while he is able to move swiftly between opposing identities, flirting with a fall from childhood but moving away just in time to keep the game alive. For him and his admirers, once the danger or tension is gone, the fun is over.

In the clearest example of this playful dynamic, Peter and Wendy talk as if the Lost Boys are their biological children. Wendy even imagines that she is actually an "old lady" without any value:

> "Peter, I think Curly has your nose."
>   "Michael takes after you."
>   She went over to him and put her hand on his shoulder.
>   "Dear Peter," she said, "with such a large family, of course, I have now passed my best, but you don't want to change me, do you?"
>   "No, Wendy." (157–58)

Both Wendy and Peter seem to be adult figures here. Wendy's brothers are now her sons and Peter is her husband. But with the suggestion of change, Peter becomes a child again, leaving Wendy alone in her parental role:

> "Peter, what is it?"
> "I was just thinking," he said, a little scared. "It is only make-believe, isn't it, that I am their father?"
> "Oh yes," said Wendy primly.
> "You see," he continued apologetically, "it would make me seem so old to be their real father."
> "But they are ours, Peter, yours and mine."
> "But not really, Wendy?" he asked anxiously.
> "Not if you don't wish it," she replied; and she distinctly heard his sigh of relief. "Peter," she asked, trying to speak firmly, "what are your exact feelings for me?"
> "Those of a devoted son, Wendy."
> "I thought so," she said, and went and sat by herself at the extreme end of the room. (158–59)

Throughout the story, the narrator reminds readers that Peter is often unable to distinguish make-believe from reality.[7] One role is just as real as the other. The lines between childhood and adulthood blur completely, and he is both father to the boys and "devoted son." He is completely polymorphous, while the girl figures remain incarnations of two extremes between which Barrie constantly negotiates Peter's paradoxical boy/man image. From this privileged position, Peter regards Wendy (and Tiger Lily—the other girl in the story) as "queer" for playing a game he abandoned only a few lines earlier:

> "You are so queer," he said, frankly puzzled, "and Tiger Lily is just the same. There is something she wants to be to me, but she says it is not my mother."
> "No, indeed, it is not," Wendy replied with frightful emphasis. (159)

With this exchange, Peter is naïve and absolutely childlike/innocent again; he seems to have no knowledge of the husband or father role he had previously played for these girls. Thus the iconic boy begins to find his place in England's cultish obsession with the paradoxical duality of children's physical, mental, and social character.

When the children return to their home in London and Mrs. Darling takes over the role of mother to the Lost Boys, Wendy reminds us of her own duality as a little girl by immediately resuming her place as a middle-class daughter. The Lost Boys are adopted by the Darlings and Wendy becomes their sister, until, in one version, she becomes Slightly's wife. Before it was incorporated into the novel *Peter and Wendy* in 1911, the chapter describing Wendy's final transition into womanhood (*When Wendy Grew Up: An Afterthought,* performed in 1908 and published separately in 1957) was written as an epilogue to the play. Here Peter comes back to the nursery twenty years later, rejects the weeping grown-up Wendy, and flies off to Neverland with her daughter, Jane. Not surprisingly, Barrie focuses not on Peter's life after Wendy but only on Wendy's life after Peter and the loss that she feels:

> For a little longer she tried for [Peter's] sake not to have growing pains . . . and when they met again Wendy was a married woman, and Peter was no more to her than a little dust in the box in which she had kept her toys. Wendy was grown up. (257)

In the 1908 version of *When Wendy Grew Up,* Wendy is Slightly's wife at this point, and the Baby Mermaid is her daughter, Jane.[8] She is an "excessively matron[ly]" grown-up woman, who repeatedly reminds us that she is "no longer young and innocent" (*When Wendy Grew Up* 15). Dressed in the familiar white nightgown from *Peter Pan,* Jane must take her mother's place in Neverland, while Wendy can experience the adventure only through her daughter. Peter remains childlike, but Wendy has lost the two qualities that he still possesses: "I can't come with you Peter—because I'm no longer young and innocent," she laments (27).

As the story closes, Barrie does not focus on the fact that all of the Lost Boys, including John and Michael Darling, grew up. He writes, "All the boys were grown up and done for by this time; so it is scarcely worth while saying anything more about them" (*Peter and Wendy* 257). The anxiety in *Peter Pan* revolves around the end of girlhood, not the end of boyhood. The eternal boy sequestered away from the real world is merely a new, seemingly less fragile, space for old fantasies and fears that were previously associated with little girls.

In the original epilogue, Wendy ends the play by imagining that her own lost youth and innocence will live on through her daughter and granddaughter—mothers and daughters forever changing roles, one emerging in place of the other. The final lines of the play close with Wendy's voice and Wendy's perspective on the future of Neverland:

This is how I planned it if he ever came back. Every Spring Cleaning, except when he forgets, I'll let Jane fly away with him to the darling Never Never Land, and when she grows up I will hope she will have a little daughter, who will fly away with him in turn—and in this way may I go on for ever and ever, dear Nana, so long as children are young and innocent. (*When Wendy Grew Up* 31–32)

The "darling Never Never Land" seems to exist for the Darling daughters only; once again, there is no mention of sons. The play closes just as it opens—with the image and perspective of a rapidly aging Victorian little girl. Wendy fades into the background and loses her voice altogether, and thus the girl with a small arrow's hole in her heart is almost completely forgotten. Wendy Darling, one of the kind who fell to earth and grew up, becomes just one link in Barrie's chain of girlish mothers punished and dismissed for the reluctant but inevitable loss of their youth:

As you look at Wendy you may see her hair becoming white, and her figure little again, for all this happened long ago. Jane is now a common grown-up, with a daughter called Margaret; and every spring cleaning time, except when he forgets, Peter comes for Margaret and takes her to the Neverland, where she tells him stories about himself, to which he listens eagerly. When Margaret grows up she will have a daughter, who is to be Peter's mother in turn; and thus it will go on, so long as children are gay and innocent and heartless. (*Peter and Wendy* 267)

NOTES

1. The age of consent was raised from ten to twelve in 1861, to thirteen in 1875, and to sixteen in 1885, after Stead's exposé (and the resulting Criminal Law Amendment Act).

2. See also William Tait's *Magdalenism: An Inquiry into the Extent, Cause, and Consequences of Prostitution* (1840), which lists "Licentious Inclination—Pride and Love of Dress—Dishonesty and Desire of Property—Indolence" as innate weaknesses in prostitutes; Richard von Krafft-Ebing's *Psychopathia Sexualis* (1893), which implies that prostitutes had a distorted sexual drive; and *The Female Offender* (1893) by William Ferrero and Cesare Lombroso, which maintains that criminals and prostitutes were identical from a physiological and psychological point of view.

3. Barrie's narrator addresses a specifically adult audience, whom he characterizes as former children, in the description of Neverland: "On these magic shores children at play are for ever beaching their coracles. We too have been

there; we can still hear the sound of the surf, though we shall land no more" (*Peter Pan* 7).

4. Neverland is designed as an amalgam of exotic locations associated with Western imperialism. The children hide and play amidst lagoons, flamingoes, palms, brushwood, sugarcane, and other plants with leaves that "did not come from any tree that grew in England" (*Peter Pan* 9). The island is populated with dark pirates, "redskins" (Delawares, Hurons, "Piccaninnies"), mermaids, and fairies.

5. Peter saved Tiger Lily from a "dreadful fate, and now there was nothing she and her braves would not do for him. . . . They called Peter the Great White Father, prostrating themselves before him; and he liked this tremendously" (*Peter Pan* 107).

6. This scene, in which the boys build a house around Wendy, recalls a scene from a later prose iteration, *Peter Pan in Kensington Gardens* (1906). In this later text, Peter comes upon a little girl named Maimie, who has remained in Kensington Gardens after lockout time. Maimie is affectionate toward Peter, but she must return home to her mother where, Barrie suggests, she, as a girl, belongs. When the fairies find her, they build a fairy house around her, tailored exactly to her size. Yet when she wakes, she knocks her head against the roof, and her house shrinks slowly away when she becomes too large. In a scene charged with remorse and nostalgia, Maimie stands aside to watch her fairy house disappear, and she bursts into tears as it vanishes into nothingness. At the precise moment it completely disappears, a naked Peter Pan arrives to comfort her, making the boy the paradoxical figure of sequestered and sanctifying childhood—the redemptive dream-child—for the weary and disillusioned little girl.

7. When Slightly pretends to be a doctor, the narrator explains that the Lost Boys recognize the difference between make-believe and reality, but make-believe and reality are the same for Peter: "The difference between [Peter] and the other boys at such a time was that they knew it was make-believe, while to him make-believe and true were exactly the same thing. This sometimes troubled them, as when they had to make believe that they had had their dinners" (*Peter Pan* 71).

8. In *Peter and Wendy* (1911), Slightly marries "a lady of title, and so he became a lord" (257).

WORKS CITED

Acton, William. *Prostitution: Considered in Its Moral, Social, and Sanitary Aspects in London and Other Large Cities and Garrison Towns, with Proposals for the Control and Prevention of Its Attendant Evils.* London: J. Churchill, 1857.

Barrie, J. M. *Alice Sit-by-the-Fire.* New York: Scribner's, 1923.

———. *Peter Pan.* 1911. New York: New American Library, 1987.

———. *Peter and Wendy.* New York: Scribner's, 1911.

———. *When Wendy Grew Up: An Afterthought.* New York: Dutton, 1957.

Coveney, Peter. *The Image of Childhood: The Individual and Society: A Study of the Theme in English Literature.* Baltimore: Penguin, 1967.

Ferrero, William, and Cesare Lombroso. *The Female Offender.* London, T. F. Unwin, 1895.

Gorham, Deborah. *The Victorian Girl and the Feminine Ideal.* London: Croom Helm, 1982.

Jowett, Benjamin. *The Letters of Benjamin Jowett, M.A., Master of Balliol College, Oxford.* London: J. Murray, 1899.

Kincaid, James. *Child-Loving: The Erotic Child and Victorian Culture.* New York: Routledge, 1992.

Lamb, Charles. *Essays of Elia.* New York: Macmillan, 1927.

Nelson, Claudia. Introduction. *The Girl's Own: Cultural Histories of the Anglo-American Girl, 1830–1915.* Ed. Claudia Nelson and Lynne Vallone. Athens: U of Georgia P, 1994.

Stead, William Thomas. "The Maiden Tribute of Modern Babylon." *The Pall Mall Gazette* 4–13 July 1995 <http://www.attackingthedevil.co.uk/pmg/tribute/ mt1.php>.

Tait, William. *Magdalenism: An Inquiry into the Extent, Cause, and Consequences of Prostitution.* Edinburgh: P. Rickard, 1842.

Von Kraft-Ebing, Richard. *Psychopathia Sexualis: A Medico-Forensic Study.* Trans. Harry E. Wedeck. New York: Putnam's, 1965.

Wullschläger, Jackie. *Inventing Wonderland: The Lives and Fantasies of Lewis Carroll, Edward Lear, J.M. Barrie, Kenneth Grahame, and A.A. Milne.* New York: Free Press, 1995.

4

James Barrie's Pirates: *Peter Pan*'s Place in Pirate History and Lore

Jill P. May

> Oh, better far to live and die
> Under the brave black flag I fly,
> Than play a sanctimonious part,
> With a pirate head and a pirate heart.
> Away to the cheating world go you,
> Where pirates all are well-to-do;
> But I'll be true to the song I sing,
> And live and die a Pirate King.
>
> —Gilbert and Sullivan, *The Pirates of Penzance*

Critics have long asserted that James Barrie's *Peter Pan* is an autobiographical play about his deep attachment to his mother, his fantasy adventures with the Llewelyn Davies boys, and particularly his childhood reading while growing up in Scotland. LaRue Scott states that Barrie and his mother read books together from the time of his brother's death when the young James was three years old, and that these are the stories he used for his writing. Barrie himself continually alluded to his childhood reading in his public speeches and writings, referring to *Robinson Crusoe, Pilgrim's Progress, The Coral Island,* and *Sunshine Magazine,* which was "full of stories about pirates and desert islands, besides the gallimaufry of fairytales and romance (qtd. in Blow 3). *The Stage* review for the London opening night of *Peter Pan* in 1904 pinpoints this connection to his childhood reading, commenting that

Barrie "peopled his newest fantasy with the choicest personages from the pages of [Frederick] Marryat or [James Fenimore] Cooper, side by side with the heroes of our youth . . . and the blend of humor and pretty sentiment constitutes a piece that no one, old or young, should resist" (qtd. in Wilson 149).

Indeed, a large part of *Peter Pan*'s popularity when it was first produced in London was due to its use of legendary characters from the high seas and the ideals of high adventure that had long been associated with pirates. As James William Kelly has pointed out, pirate adventures had been common reading since Daniel Defoe's *Captain Singleton* was published in 1720. Defoe's *A New Voyage round the World*, first published in 1725, was released in a new edited version in 1895, demonstrating the lasting interest in these adventure stories, mainly because these characters reflected the British colonialist vision of white male explorers and conquerors, heroes to young boys who acted out the adventures in their play both in England and in America. Boys were allowed to roam the countryside, playing games of Robin Hood or enacting life on a desert island. Literature contained numerous male adventurers and women who nurtured their places in their homeland. When Mark Twain's youthful Tom Sawyer and his male companions take leave of civilization, Twain's description of the life they expect to live shows the popularity of stories about pirates, shipwrecks, and adventures on deserted islands. Tom explains that pirates "have just a bully time . . . and kill everybody in the ships—make 'em walk a plank" (93).

However, Barrie's characters also were undoubtedly influenced by the portrayal of pirates that he saw on the stage as an adult, particularly Gilbert and Sullivan's *The Pirates of Penzance*, an operatta that premiered in New York City on New Year's Eve, 1879, and later in London on 3 April 1880. Like Gilbert and Sullivan's, Barrie's pirates rely on the popular image of pirates as gentlemen at their core, parodying the iconic pirate as much as they emulate him. Barrie's pirates are more fanciful than factual and more joke than actual, yet his characters are as memorable as any of those found in history.

Historical pirates did indeed live by a code of honor, surprisingly. The pirates' lives aboard ship were governed by a set of laws they all agreed to before sailing, which prohibited stealing from one another as well as fighting one another, mandated regular weapon cleaning, protected a "prudent" woman's honor, and divided up all their shares of booty somewhat equally (Feder 27). Such a code is dramatized in Daniel Defoe's *The Four Years Voyages of Capt. George Roberts; Being*

a Series of Uncommon Events Which Befell Him (1726), which gives a
first-person account of a sea captain's encounter with a pirate ship:

> I had been once taken by Pirates before, coming from *Newfoundland*,
> when I was a youth, but I did not then think it proper to take notice of it
> to them, but the Reverse; and thought it the safest Course at present, to
> pretend ignorance. . . .
>   *No, damn you*, said he, *now it is too late: What Cloaths we took you in,
> you shall keep; But your Sloop. And what is in her, is ours.* I told him, *I
> perceived it was, but still hoped, as I wholly lay at his Mercy, he would be
> so generous as to take only what they had Occasion for, and leave me the
> rest.* He answered, *As to that, he could say nothing as yet, that being a
> Company-business to decide*, and withal demanded of me, an Account of
> every Thing that was on board of the sloop, particularly of the Cargo, and
> what money I had, or knew to be on board, and if I did not give a true and
> exact Account, and discover they would set the Sloop on fire, and me in
> her . . . for it was their Manner to punish Liars and Concealers, especially
> of those Things they had now mentioned in a very severe Manner. (32)

The irony of a pirate abhoring liars, expecting to be treated like a
gentleman, was clear to Defoe's readers, but such behavior reinforces
the idea of the pirate as both feared and admired. In a history of pirates
written in 1874, John S. C. Abbott claims that pirates in the Americas
were much like "the robber knights and barons of the feudal ages, from
whom the haughtiest nobles of Europe are proud to claim their lineage" (19). He calls their adventures "chivalric exploits" (19). Abbott describes their attire, commenting on their "gorgeous and extravagant
dresses." He notes, "Their favorite ornament was a broad crimson sash,
of bright scarlet, passing round the waist, and fastened on the shoulder
and hip with colored ribbons" (19). In *The Rose of Paradise* (1887),
Howard Pyle, who did much to popularize pirate lore in the late nineteenth century, describes—like Defoe, in first person—Captain
Mackra's fearful encounter with a pirate ship in 1742: "I knew as well
as anything in all of my life that it was the 'Black Roger,' and that the
white that I could see among the folds was the wicked sign of the 'skull
and crossbones,' which those bloody and cruel wretches are please to
adapt as the ensign of their trade" (41–42). Concerning the "pirate
king," he observes, "his apparel was better than the others" and "he
wore what appeared to be a crimson scarf tied about his body" (76).
    This aspect of gentlemanliness is highlighted by Barrie when Wendy
is told by Captain Hook that all of her boys will die, and she says, "Dear

Boys, I feel that I have a message to you from your real mothers, and it is this, 'We hope our sons will die like English gentlemen'" (120). In *Les Brigands* (1869), a French play translated by W. S. Gilbert in 1871, the thieving hero Falscappa leads his band against the equally thieving royalty, and the audience learns from the Duke of Mantua that "[o]ne must steal according to the position one occupies in society" (qtd. in Traubner 65). In *The Pirates of Penzance*, the pirates are allowed to marry the daughters of the Major General when it is revealed that they are peers who love their queen: "They are no members of the common throng; / They are all noblemen who have gone wrong!" (Gilbert 99). Pyle also suggested that pirates were akin to the upper class when he turned to the idea of having a lawyer or a magistrate as a hero in *The Buccaneers and Marooners of America* and asserted, "[W]ould not every boy, for instance—that is every boy of any account—rather be a pirate captain than a Member of Parliament?" (15).

Barrie was most certainly influenced by the pirates created in Robert Louis Stevenson's famous pirate story, *Treasure Island* (1883). Kevin Carpenter has argued that *Treasure Island* influenced boys' pirate literature more than any other book. He comments, "Stevenson's popularity in his day helped to make children's fiction without an underlying moral purpose widely acceptable to parents, critics and teachers" and calls it "a book that is quite modern in its emphasis on psychological realism" (90). Both writers created adventures based on their experiences with adolescent boys: Stevenson wrote his famous sea story for his stepson, and Barrie wrote *Peter Pan* for the Llewelyn Davies boys (and himself). Both were creating stories full of action with youthful male protagonists. Barrie had read and liked *Treasure Island* and found Stevenson's life on the secluded island of Samoa intriguing; and when Stevenson read Barrie's early works, he recognized a kindred spirit. Stevenson and Barrie began a correspondence in February 1892, with Stevenson writing to Barrie, commenting, "[I]t may please you to hear that the continuation of *Kidnapped* is under way. I have not yet got to Alan, so I do not know if he is still alive, but David seems to have a kick or two in his shanks" (*Letters* 296). Within his correspondence to Barrie, Stevenson continually invited Barrie to visit him at his island home. When a volume of reminiscences was proposed after Stevenson's death, Barrie wrote Rosaline Masson that he felt he should be included. Barrie acknowledged, "It is not necessarily that he was the greatest, I don't think he was the greatest, but of the men we might have seen he is the one we would like best to come back. Had he lived another year I should have seen him" (250).

Barrie's interest in Stevenson, as a fellow Scot who wrote about ship-wrecked men, was genuine, and it affected his creation of Hook and all the pirates. Yet Barrie's pirate king seems less fearsome than Stevenson's and his action is more playful. Like Gilbert and Sullivan, Barrie creatively parodies pirates. Stevenson's Long John Silver is both a sympathetic character and a cunning and ruthless pirate. Jim goes aboard the ship with Silver of his own volition, but soon he begins to regret his decision. When some of the crew is planning mutiny, Long John Silver says, "I'm an easy man—I'm quite the gentleman, says you; but this time it's serious. Dooty is dooty, mates. I give my vote—death" (95). Like Gilbert and Sullivan, Stevenson ties English gentlemen to pirate imagery: "When I'm in Parlyment, and riding in my coach, I don't want none of these sea-lawyers in the cabin a-coming home, unlooked for, like the devil at prayers" (95). Barrie makes a direct reference to *Treasure Island* when he states in the novel that Hook is "the only man that the Sea-Cook feared" (67)—the Sea-Cook being Long John Silver. Hook, though, acts like an adolescent most of the time. He is reckless and headstrong. Furthermore, he longs to have a mother who will take care of him. Hook, like Silver, is a ruthless murderer, yet because of his sophisticated dress and demeanor, we do not take him too seriously, or perhaps we are more likely to excuse him. In the novel, Barrie describes an encounter in which a fellow pirate "lurches clumsily against [Hook], ruffling his lace collar; the hook shoots forth, there is a tearing sound and one screech, then the body is kicked aside, and the pirates pass on. He has not even taken the cigar from his mouth" (68). Despite such callous and bloodthirsty behavior, Hook's ruthlessness is softened because he is afraid of his own blood, imitates the fancy costumes of Charles II, and is so concerned with having "good form."

Like Hook, real life pirates were generally depicted as attractive creatures even when they were violent. Pyle had asserted in the late 1800s that "the history of Captain Sir Henry Morgan has, at least in the past few generations, been very dear to English-speaking people" (*Buccaneers* 31). He noted that the story of Morgan's life had evolved from its first publication in 1684, with more and more seafaring heroes being introduced in each new edition (31–32), and he argued that pirates were largely imaginative figures. Little "actual data" concerning pirates existed, but they were heroes in chapbooks long before they entered other literature. Pyle observes, "[I]t is only in popular romance and fiction that their name and fame is embalmed and preserved" (39), and he writes,

> Who has not heard of Black-beard? Who does not know the name of the renowned Captain Kid? Who has not heard of the famous ballad which tells of his deeds of wickedness?—a rhythmical chant such as has from the beginning of time been most taking to the popular ear:—
> "Oh! My name is Captain Kid,
> As I sailed,
> As I sailed,
> Oh! My name is Captain Kid,
> As I sailed,
> Oh! My name is Captain Kid,
> And God's laws I did forbid,
> And right wickedly I did
> As I sailed." (34–35)

Barrie places Pyle's observations in his drama while Peter is still in the nursery teaching the boys and Wendy to fly. Peter tells the boys, "There are pirates," and John answers, "Pirates! Let us go at once!" (57). Barrie's pirates first enter the stage singing, "Yo ho, yo ho, the pirate life / The flag of skull and bones, / A merry hour, a hempen rope, / And hey for Davy Jones!" (63). In one swift scene, Barrie has combined two literary elements commonly found in his contemporary culture—a swaggering hero and legendary pirates who sing when they enter the landscape. Yet Barrie's stage pirates are not replications of those usually found in earlier literature. Instead, based on childlike visions, they emerge as less threatening characters than the renegades found in Stevenson's *Treasure Island* or Pyle's *Within the Capes* (1885).

Pyle's depiction of pirates is harsh and unyielding. Written for an American adult audience just five years prior to the release of his famous *The Buccaneers and Marooners of America*, Pyle cast his main character in *Within the Capes* as a young American Quaker who has determined to make his fortune at sea. When he is encouraged to join a ship of privateers, Pyle's hero, young Tom, replies, "I don't see, sir, that they are so very much better than pirates, except they don't do so much murder" (45). When the privateer ship is in danger, Tom finds himself to be right. These men are faced with a captain who will not tolerate disloyalty. And he can swear oaths with the best of the pirates:

Tom saw that there was no prospect of Captain Knight's giving the order to have the boats cleared away, so he went aft to the poop, where the captain stood, and touched his hat to him very respectfully.

"Captain Knight," said he, "the ship's sinking, and I can't keep the men at their work any longer. Shall I get the boats cleared away?"

"They won't work, you say?"

"No, sir."

The captain took a pinch of snuff. "Then let 'em drown, and be d——d to 'em—the mutinous dogs," said he. And he shut his snuff-box with a snap. (89–90)

By the early 1900s, many of the adventure stories American and British boys read were based on the journals and earlier fictional accounts of men conquering the elements and people of "virgin lands." In many respects, these men were rogues. Frank Stockton claims that even Christopher Columbus was a pirate:

Robbery, murder, and the destruction of property, by the commanders of naval expeditions, who have no warrant or commission for their conduct, is the same as piracy, and when Columbus ceased to be a legalized explorer, and when, against the expressed wishes, and even the prohibitions, of the royal personages who had sent him out on this expedition, he began to devastate the countries he had discovered, and to enslave and exterminate their peaceable natives, then he became a master in piracy. (9)

As an American who lived in the coastal areas where pirates had once roamed, Pyle acknowledged the strength of mystery and outrageousness found in the legendary tales of American expeditions in *The Buccaneers and Marooners of America*: "Even to this day it is safe to say that nowhere along the Atlantic coast of the whole United States, from Maine to Florida, are their names unknown, and that in all that stretch of sea-board there is hardly a lonesome sandy beach but is reputed to have held treasure hidden by one or the other of them" (36).

Barrie's Captain Hook, too, is a representation of man's natural need to explore new places and desire to dominate others, as Barrie acknowledges in his dedication to *Peter Pan*. Explaining to "The Five" (the Llewelyn Davies boys) his indebtedness to the earlier privately written accounts of their imaginative play in *The Boy Castaways*, Barrie ties Hook to Captain James Cook, who was killed by Hawaiian natives in 1778, when he writes that Captain Hook arrived as he and they embarked on their "Antarctic exploits when we reached the pole in advance of our friend Captain Scott" (16). There, Captain Hook fought with the boys; each claimed to kill him, "though you never, I think, got his right arm" (17). In the play, though Peter indirectly causes Hook's demise, it is Hook who determines to give up his life since he is no longer the "captain of the ship."

At the end of Scene One, Act V, Peter becomes Hook. In his stage notes, Barrie writes,

> *Where is* PETER? *The incredible boy has apparently forgotten the recent doings, and is sitting on a barrel playing upon his pipes. This may surprise others but does not surprise* HOOK. *Lifting a blunderbuss he strikes forlornly not at the boy but at the barrel, which is hurled across the deck.* PETER *remains sitting in the air still playing upon his pipes. At this sight the great heart of* HOOK *breaks. That not wholly unheroic figure climbs the bulwarks murmuring* 'Floreat Etona,' *and prostrates himself into the water, where the crocodile is waiting for him open-mouthed.* HOOK *knows the purpose of this yawning cavity, but after what he has gone through he enters it like one greeting a friend.*
>
> *The curtain rises to show* PETER *a very Napoleon on his ship. It must not rise again lest we see him on the poop deck in* HOOK's *hat and cigars, and with a small iron claw.* (132)

Barrie returns to Peter's new role as a pirate captain in *When Wendy Grew Up*:

WENDY: Oh! Peter, when Captain Hook carried us away ?
    PETER: Who's Captain Hook? Is it a story? Tell it [to] me.
    WENDY [*aghast*]: Do you mean to say you've even forgotten Captain Hook, and how you killed him and saved all our lives?
    PETER [*fidgeting*]: I forget them after I kill them.
    WENDY: Oh, Peter, you forget everything!
    PETER: everything except mother Wendy. [*Hugs her.*]
. . . .
WENDY: You sweet.
    PETER: So come on. [*Pulling her*] I'm Captain. (26–27)

Barrie's *Peter Pan* fit with the contemporary literature written for children, both in America and in England. The characterization alluded to the British Colonial stereotypes of "native heathens" in the Americas and the Caribbean. It was driven by a hero's journey from innocence to maturity. Interestingly, the pirates are forever frozen in the scenes of Neverland, destined to fight and to forget. Peter Pan, as captain of Neverland, will never need to grow up and marry anyone, not even Wendy. As the archetypal boy, he is a proverbial character who, though he forgets his adventures and conquests, cannot be easily forgotten. As William Lyon Phelps observes,

> The play, supposedly written by a child, is a child's world; the tick-tock crocodile; the pirate smoking cigarettes like a candelabra, the fairies and the flying are all romantically true to life. Yet . . . it is not a series of pretty pictures, it is emphatically a play, and no one but a great dramatist could have produced it. (32)

More than a child's play in a London garden was being produced on the London stage when *Peter Pan* opened in 1904. *Peter Pan* was a tour de force that played on popular contemporary adventure literature and the Victorian ideals of British colonialism. It was a representation of early American exploitation by British men who wanted to rule, either in the new world or at home. At the same time, with its seemingly straightforward plot and stock characterization, *Peter Pan* was an immediate success because it filled a theatrical void; it arrived on the scene when all the stage productions for children featured "tedious so-called fairy-plays or pantomimes with red-nosed comedians and principal 'boys' of a type hardly credible twenty years later" (Moult 188).

Peter Pan was American history just as much as it was British romanticism, and it was equally popular when it arrived in America. It has continued to enthrall its audiences in both countries with Neverland, a place where boys battle pirates, a landscape where boys crow and strut as they engage fairies, mermaids, Indians, and pirates in battles for physical and verbal supremacy. Barrie could not have created such a successful play about childhood and egotism had he not been a reader of pirate literature, a man who was aware of stage productions earlier created for adult audiences that featured pirates as kings.

Believing in Wonderland has always been essential for the pirates and Lost Boys who want to have a dreamland that is both wild with exotic beasts and frightening fights and safe because women manage their households and keep their stories safe. When the lights come up once the performance has ended, all the pirates in our twenty-first-century homes should ponder Barrie's dreamland, a subtle rewriting of the nineteenth century man's dreamland that could allow men to become captains of their pirate ships or, perhaps, Lords of London.

WORKS CITED

Abbott, John S. C. *Captain Kidd.* New York: Dodd, Mead, 1874.

Barrie, J. M. *Peter Pan.* 1911. New York: HarperFestival, 2003.

———. *Peter Pan and Other Plays.* New York: Scribner's, 1930.

———. "To Miss Rosaline Masson." *Letters of J. M. Barrie.* London: Peter Davies, 1942. 250.

———. *When Wendy Grew Up: An Afterthought.* New York: Dutton, 1957.

Blow, Sydney. Foreword. *When Wendy Grew Up: An Afterthought.* By J. M. Barrie. New York: Dutton, 1957. 1–11.

Carpenter, Kevin. *Desert Isles & Pirate Islands: The Island Theme in Nineteenth-Century English Juvenile Fiction.* Frankfurt, Germany: Peter Lang, 1984.

Defoe, Daniel. *The Four Years Voyages of Capt. George Roberts: Being a Series of Uncommon Events Which Befell Him.* London: A Bettesworth, 1726.

Feder, Joshua B. *Pirates.* New York: Friedman Group, 1992.

Gilbert, W. S. *Book and Lyrics of the Best-Known Gilbert & Sullivan Operas; and the Bab Ballads.* New York: Three Sirens, 1932.

Kelly, James William. "Buccaneer Narratives." *Literature of Travel and Exploration: An Encyclopedia.* Ed. Jennifer Speak. Vol. 1. New York: Fitzroy Dearborn, 2003. 136–38.

Moult, Thomas. *Barrie.* New York: Scribner's, 1928.

Phelps, William Lyon. *Essays on Modern Drama.* New York: Macmillan, 1929.

Pyle, Howard. Introduction. (signed 1890). *The Buccaneers and Marooners of America: Being an Account of the Famous Adventures and Daring Deeds of Certain Notorious Freebooters of the Spanish Main.* Ed. Howard Pyle. New York: Macmillan, 1891. 15–41.

———. *The Rose of Paradise.* New York: Harper, 1887.

———. *Within the Capes.* New York: Scribner's, 1885.

Scott, LaRue. "Small Museums." *British Heritage* March 2004: 56–57.

Stevenson, Robert Louis. "To James Barrie." February 1893. *Letters of Robert Louis Stevenson to His Family and Friends.* Ed. Sidney Colvin. Vol. 2. New York: Scribner's, 1899. 295–96.

———. *Treasure Island.* 1883. New York: Puffin Books, 1994.

Stockton, Frank R. *Buccaneers and Pirates of Our Coasts.* 1897–1898. New York: Macmillan, 1934.

Traubner, Richard. *Operetta: A Theatrical History.* Garden City, NY: Doubleday, 1983.

Twain, Mark. *The Adventures of Tom Sawyer.* 1876. New York: New American Library, 1980.

Wilson, A. E. *Edwardian Theatre.* London: Arthur Barker, 1951.

5

More Darkly down the Left Arm: The Duplicity of Fairyland in the Plays of J. M. Barrie

Kayla McKinney Wiggins

Steven Spielberg's *Hook* and P. J. Hogan's *Peter Pan* continue a tradition begun a hundred years ago in the writings of J. M. Barrie, a tradition that in the guise of children's literature explores such adult themes as death, sexuality, and the duplicity of existence. Critics and scholars through the years have analyzed Barrie and his audiences, looking for answers to his popularity and his particular breed of charm. As R. D. S. Jack has demonstrated in *The Road to the Never Land*, Barrie, once the most popular playwright of his day, has been the victim of a new critical age, which in its more prescriptive view of reality has reduced Barrie's status "from a position above criticism to one below it" (6). The critical attention accorded Barrie since his death has been primarily biographical or psychological, focusing on his relationship with his mother, his failed marriage, and his complex friendship with Sylvia and Arthur Llewelyn Davies and their five sons, the boys whose childhoods provided the fertile soil for the growth of associations that would evolve into Barrie's most famous play, *Peter Pan*. There is no denying the fascination of Barrie's complex psyche or the evocative power of his successful and yet deeply tragic life, but the real answer to the enduring popularity of his plays lies in his ability to tap into a deeper consciousness, to invite his audience to join with him in the process of creation and the making of meaning that lie at the heart of myth, folklore, and fantasy. While Barrie's fairie plays *Peter Pan*, *Dear Brutus*, and *Mary Rose* are certainly the products of the author's personal relationships and his consummate skills as a theater practitioner, they are also the products of his childhood in Scotland, nurtured and shaped by folk traditions growing out of the Celtic world.

While some scholars and educators may doubt the value of fantasy to the modern world, writers and readers the world over recognize the valuable role of fantasy and the traditional literature from which it derives. Fantasy is timeless and essential to the creation and understanding of reality. Dealing as it does with the great conflicts of the human condition, it can often speak to us on a more fundamental level than literature that is slavishly tied to the modern, "realistic" world. "Fantasy," says Charlotte Huck, "consistently asks the universal questions concerning the struggle of good versus evil, the humanity of humankind, and the meaning of life and death" (308). The range of responses to fantasy, from deploring what is perceived as its negation of reality to celebrating what is considered its essential truth, is evident in the criticism of Barrie. David Holbrook notes what he considers "the astonishing appeal of Barrie's plays . . . despite their embarrassing and even rather mad episodes" (74):

> What is so fascinating about *Peter Pan* is that such unusual explorations of schizoid existence anxiety, of death, and of "nonbeing," should be dealt with in such a way that adults and children in the theater take it all in their stride and allow themselves (in a sense) to go mad and to perceive the play's surrealistic fantasy as quite acceptable. (77)

At the opposite extreme, Jack discusses *Peter Pan* as a creation myth that encourages the audience to "continue the process of creation" (15) and locates the value of fantasy in part in its "capacity to transcend time" (13).

In defending his love of writing—and reading—fairy tale and fantasy, C. S. Lewis argues not only that there is a comfort in the fundamental truths of traditional literature and fantasy, but that those truths are not the exclusive property of children since an adult understanding elicits even more meaning: "When I became a man I put away childish things, including the fear of childishness and the desire to be very grown up" (1076). Lewis argues further that human beings have a basic indefinable urge toward fairyland, that while the average person doesn't really want the dangers and trials of fairyland in the contemporary world,

> fairyland arouses a longing for he knows not what. It stirs and troubles him (to his lifelong enrichment) with the dim sense of something beyond

his reach and, far from dulling or emptying the actual world, gives it a new dimension of depth. He does not despise real woods because he has read of enchanted woods: the reading makes all real woods a little enchanted. (1078)

J. R. R. Tolkien, Lewis's contemporary and friend, had said something similar in his seminal essay "On Fairy-Stories." In writing of his own youthful passion for the tales of Celtic and Norse lore, Tolkien says, "Fantasy, the making or glimpsing of Other-worlds, was the heart of the desire of Faerie. I desired dragons with a profound desire" (64). Tolkien argues that traditional literature carries such essential purpose for humanity because as naturally creative beings, we each long for a role in the process of creation, to be what Tolkien calls a "sub-creator" (49). This desire is fulfilled as we write or tell stories, as we make meaning from the chaos of existence. As we tap into the timelessness of traditional literature, we escape death and discover the "sudden joyous turn" of the "good catastrophe" that might be called a happy ending, except that fairy tales never truly end (Tolkien 85–86).

The optimism of Lewis and Tolkien is perhaps ironic, coming as it does from authors writing in the darker days of the mid-twentieth century. Barrie, on the other hand, living, writing, and working in the friendly glare of the Edwardian sun, tended toward abandoned joy shading toward despair. While Lewis saw adulthood as the fruition of childish understanding, Barrie saw it as the loss of eternal youth. The folklore of Barrie's fairy plays, nevertheless, offers a species of Tolkien's escape from death and Lewis' affirmation of childhood.

Victorian and Edwardian England—in ironic conjunction with a growing emphasis on science, psychology, and progress—enjoyed a Romantic cult of childhood that pictured "children as good, innocent and in some way connected with spirituality and imagination" (Wullschläger 12). According to Jackie Wullschläger, "the child came to be seen as a symbol, in a prosperous, progressive society, of hope and optimism" (12). However, there is another side to this cultural and literary atmosphere, as Wullschläger also indicates:

> The settings of the Victorian and Edwardian children's classics themselves suggest the mood of a golden age, of a secure, prosperous, optimistic country. Yet Wonderland, the Neverland of Peter Pan, the river bank of *The Wind in the Willows*, the idyll of a country station in *The Railway Children*, the enchanted rose garden in *The Secret Garden*, all also celebrate escape, the flight into an unreal dream world. They point to one of

the strongest influences on the Victorian and Edwardian cult of childhood
and on children's books: the regressive desire for a pre-industrial, rural
world and the identification of the child with purity, a pre-sexual life,
moral simplicity. (17)

At the same time that Victorian and Edwardian England was re-
visioning the role of childhood, they were also reshaping their traditional lore to include a whimsical, yet tentatively hopeful, portrait of
the denizens of the fairy realms. While there is ample evidence that the
country people tended to believe in fairies and to pay them a grudg-
ing, cautious respect well into the twentieth century, intellectuals and
writers tended to use this sort of popular lore for their own ends. Writing in 1967, the noted folklorist Katherine Briggs commented on the
range of responses:

> There are still, as we have seen, real believers in fairies—if anything they
> are perhaps on the increase—but the general incredulity among poets
> and writers dates from early times, and the accompaniments of fairy be-
> liefs are so picturesque as to make the temptation to use them as a pretty
> trimming almost irresistible. This is particularly so with the small fairies.
> The passion for the miniature which is so strong in England rendered
> them less and less formidable. When they were given butterfly and drag-
> onfly wings they were reduced to almost the status of insects, and in the
> sheltered days of the early twentieth century every care was taken to ren-
> der them unalarming. (*Fairies* 197–98)

Perhaps the same wistful backward glance which caused the Edwardians to romanticize childhood also caused them to believe in the possibility of magic, mysticism, and the unseen. Many people, including
some famous ones like Arthur Conan Doyle, were apparently willing to
believe when three little girls in Cottingley claimed to have pho-
tographed fairies on several occasions. Several experts in photography
concluded that the photographs were not faked, at least through pho-
tographic means, even though the fairies in question "seem the very
model of the butterfly-winged, gauze-clad fairies of the children's magazine illustrations" (Briggs, *Fairies* 238–40).

J. M. Barrie definitely fits the model of the sophisticated Edwardian
writer who romanticized the past even while he lived and worked in
the progressive present. There is no question that Barrie had a strong
affinity for the possibilities of fantasy or that he idealized childhood.
For a man who never had children of his own, Barrie seems to have

had a remarkable affinity for them, particularly for the five sons of
Sylvia and Arthur Llewelyn Davies. The character of Peter Pan originated in stories Barrie told to and with the Llewelyn Davies children. In
his preface to the published version of the play, Barrie dedicates the
work to them, implying that the story was created as a group effort and
presenting himself as a peer to the boys. According to Barrie biographers, however, the genesis of the character lies much further back in
Barrie's life, in the death of his brother David when Barrie was six and
David was thirteen, an event that caused great grief for Barrie's mother,
Margaret Ogilvy, and much sorrow for Barrie:

> If Margaret Ogilvy drew a measure of comfort from the notion that David,
> in dying a boy, would remain a boy forever, Barrie drew inspiration. It
> would be another thirty-three years before that inspiration emerged in the
> shape of Peter Pan, but here was the germ, rooted in his mind and soul
> from the age of six. (Birkin 5)

In much the same way, stories of his mother's childhood led to the
creation of Wendy. At age eight, Margaret Ogilvy became the mistress
of her family household as a result of her mother's death. As Birkin
notes, "it was the image of the substitute mother that was to take the
deepest root: the memory of his own mother as a little girl, refashioned
and remoulded into numerous heroines, epitomized as Wendy mothering the Lost Boys and Peter Pan in the Neverland" (6).

If Barrie understood children—their single-mindedness and egocen-
tricity, their essential heartlessness and inability to believe in the reality of death and danger—this awareness, coupled with his admiration
for and jealousy of the missing David and his image of his mother taking on adult responsibilities at the tender age of eight, led to a picture
of children in his works that is decidedly ambiguous, far from the
sweet innocents of other Victorian writers (Lurie 11). Peter in particular takes on a kind of sinister charm often associated with the fairies
themselves. While Barrie employs the fairy whimsy of the Victorian
and Edwardian worlds—depicting Tinker Bell as a tiny winged creature, for example—he also remains true to more traditional lore in a
number of ways, including presenting Peter as a powerful, larger-than-
life immortal. Barrie utilized elements of fairy lore in three major plays:
Peter Pan, Dear Brutus, and *Mary Rose.* His fullest treatment of fairy
lore and Celtic tradition is, of course, his depiction of Neverland in
Peter Pan.

THE NATURE OF THE CELTIC OTHERWORLD, FAIRYLAND, AND THE FAIRIES

In the folklore of the British Isles, fairyland seems to exist in parallel to the mortal world, a kind of alternate reality that can be entered in a number of ways. In some tales, the careless interruption of a fairy dance or stepping into a fairy ring will transport the mortal into the alternate realm. In other stories, mortals are lured into fairyland by immortals, or they enter through the side of the hill, through an underground passage, or even through water. Some, like Jamie Freel of Donegal, are attracted by the sound of fairy music and willingly venture into hills or ruined forts and castles to try their fortunes (Briggs, *Vanishing* 105). According to Briggs, "The fairy people in the British Isles, not to say all over the world, vary so much in character, size, appearance and powers, that it is not surprising to find that they inhabit all kinds of places on land and in water, under the earth and above it" (*Vanishing* 81). The Celtic Otherworld, too, exists in parallel with the mortal world. The Otherworld is also an alternate reality, a realm of the dead that can be entered by the living at various times and in various ways, through a "cave, a fissure in rock or earth, a burial place" (Rutherford 42). The Celtic New Year, Samhain, in particular is a time when the barrier between the mortal and immortal worlds is weak and mortals are at greatest risk of being lured into the Otherworld (Rutherford 95–96).

Although the origin of the fairies is a complex question, with views ranging from fallen angels to aboriginal ancestors to the guardians of the dead or the dead themselves, one prevalent view of at least the heroic fairies of the British Isles is that they are descended from the dethroned gods of the Celts (Briggs, *Vanishing* 30–36). The heroic fairies are the elite of the fairy world, and perhaps the closest to humankind. As Briggs notes,

> The heroic fairies are of human or more than human height. They are the aristocrats among fairy people, and pass their time in aristocratic pursuits, hunting, hawking, riding in procession on white horses hung with silver bells, and feasting in their palaces, which are either beneath the hollow hills or under or across water. It is a generally accepted belief that the Irish fairies are dethroned gods, euphemerized into an extinct race and supernaturalized again into fairies. (*Anatomy* 13–14)

These dethroned gods sought "refuge in a paradise over-seas" (Squire 133), the blessed isle common in Celtic myth, or retired to *sidhe*, "barrows, or hillocks, each being the door to an underground realm of in-exhaustible splendour and delight" (Squire 135–36). It is easy to see how concepts of the Celtic Otherworld could evolve into fairyland and how the Celtic gods themselves could become the fairies, powerful el-ementals, dangerous and marvelous neighbors, euphemistically called the Good People to guard against their whims and powers.

In conceiving Neverland, Barrie created a kind of child's view of the warriors' afterlife of which the Celtic Otherworld is one incarnation. In Neverland, the Lost Boys can fight Indians and pirates as often and as long as they like. They can feast—even if the food is pretense—and play, and sleep as long as they want, free of the rules and restrictions of the adult world. Of the three otherworlds common in European tradition—heaven, hell, and "Fairyland (the land of magic where the fairies live, and where logic like that of dreams governs everything)" (Leach 836)—Peter's island to the west encompasses at least two of them. It is a youthful heaven, even to the extent of being located in the sky: "Second to the right and then straight on until morning" (*Peter Pan* 98). However, it also encompasses the illogic of fairyland and, perhaps, the regrets of hell.

In both Fairyland and the Otherworld, time moves at a different rate, and even space operates according to different laws, with "movement from one location to another, even the most distant one," taking place in a moment (Rutherford 43). Briggs suggests that the "strong feeling of the relativity of time" in fairyland might be founded "on the experi-ences of a dream or a state of trance" (*Fairies* 11). While it is possible to find stories in which almost no time passes in the mortal world dur-ing a lengthy sojourn in fairyland, it is much more common to find tales in which mortals visit the fairy realms for what seems a very brief time, only to find that hundreds of years have passed upon their return to the mortal world. One of the best known of these stories is that of King Herla, a legendary Celtic king who visited the fairy realms to pay his re-spects at the wedding of a fairy king only to find upon his return that what had seemed a visit of three days was in reality three hundred years. Warned by his host not to dismount until a bloodhound given to him by the fairy king jumped down from his arms, Herla is riding yet (Briggs, *Fairies* 12, 15–17).

While the passage of time in fairyland is arbitrary at best, there does seem to be some awareness in the fairy realms of the seasons of the mortal world. Briggs suggests that the fairies may be able to ignore time but be bound to seasons (*Fairies* 106). In much the same way, time in the Otherworld is not so much linear as it is perpetual and cyclical. "Hence, the great festivals are not the commemorative enactment of a past mythological event, they are that event itself, a point to which we regularly and constantly return" (Rutherford 43).

Barrie envisioned each successive season of the performance of *Peter Pan* as just this sort of perpetual creation, each not a revival but a part of a larger successive whole (Jack 186–87). In much the same way, Peter's story exists in an evolving sequence of writings by Barrie, taking root in stories and play with the Llewelyn Davies boys, the Five to whom the play is dedicated; written initially as a section of the novel *The Little White Bird*, which would be published later as *Peter Pan In Kensington Gardens*; dramatized in the frequently revised play and its epilogue *When Wendy Grew Up: An Afterthought*; and even reproduced as a novel, *Peter and Wendy*.

Like the Otherworld, time and space are fluid in Neverland. The island can encompass all four seasons at once and is "very compact, not large and sprawly with tedious distances between one adventure and another" (*Peter Pan* 106, 105). The question of the passage of time in Neverland is a complex one. On at least one level, time seems to pass more quickly there than in the mortal world, instead of more slowly. While we are never told exactly how long Wendy and her brothers are away, the settled routine of their life on the island implies a much greater passage of time than that endured by their grieving parents, almost as if the time equation between the mortal and fairy world had been inverted. Peter seems to enjoy no such restriction. While he acknowledges the seasons in planning to come for Wendy each spring cleaning, he is so unaware of time that he almost never remembers to return and is blind to the passage of time when he does show up, even to the passage of many years.

As fairyland, the Otherworld is a danger to mortals who sojourn there, lured away from the mortal world for a variety of reasons. Mortals might be lured into fairyland to fulfill a need—for example, to serve as musicians for the fairy dances, as Peter does in *Peter Pan in Kensington Gardens*, or to serve as midwives to fairy children, in much the same way that Wendy becomes a surrogate mother to the Lost Boys. The more common cause of mortals being lured into fairyland, however, is that they are desired as lovers, a dangerous and chancy relationship. While the fairies are very alluring, it is dangerous to act on desire. There are many stories of humans who have taken fairy lovers—or who have been taken in turn—wasting away, unable to resume their normal life. One good example comes from Barrie's native Scotland, where a young girl told her sister of her fairy lover only to be abandoned by him when the sister revealed the secret: "After the loss of her lover Margaret never more came into a human house; she wandered about among the hills, and shepherds saw her sometimes, and heard her crooning a lament for her loneliness, without father or mother, and with a sister who had betrayed her" (Briggs, *Fairies* 127). Perhaps the most famous mortal to take a fairy lover was the thirteenth-century poet and prophet, Thomas the Rhymer. Beloved of the fairy queen, he was blessed (or cursed) by her with the gift of absolute truth and was granted the rare opportunity to visit fairyland and return unharmed to the mortal world (Briggs, *Encyclopedia* 394–95).

The passage of time during the stay with a fairy lover is also an issue. Because time passes at a different rate in fairyland, what seems one day—or one night—can be much longer in the mortal world; sometimes "a year is really nine hundred years, sometimes a night is twenty years, sometimes a few minutes' play . . . takes a hundred years or more" (Briggs, *Fairies* 105). Return generally spells disaster, with the mortal crumbling to dust upon contact with earthly soil, human food, or Christian symbols after wandering lost and desperately alone in a foreign landscape. As Peter himself discovered when he flew back to his window and found it locked, to delay return is to be lost to the mortal world. In *Peter Pan*, return to the mortal world does not result in death as it does in most other tales of visits to the fairy realm, but it does result in becoming an adult, a fate, the play implies, which is worse than death.

In most of the stories of mortals lured into fairyland, the mortals are accommodated in luxurious surroundings full of treasure, wonderful food and drink, glorious song and dance. A good example is the English story "The Fairy Widower," in which a vain young girl is hired to be a nursery maid for a widower. After her eyes are brushed with a handful of leaves, she finds herself in a marvelous kingdom and fulfills her year and a day contract in a beautiful mansion full of silver and gold and precious stones before returning home, discontentedly, to her mortal life (Briggs, *Encyclopedia* 161–64). In many of these stories, the fabulous surroundings turn out to be glamour, an illusion revealed when the mortal's eyes are inadvertently anointed with fairy ointment. Much the same can be said of Neverland, where the Lost Boys live a life of danger and adventure—a treasure to boys—but the reality is void of comfort, family, or love.

For many mortals visiting fairyland, food is the key to their inability to return to their own realm: if they eat or drink of the delectable delicacies of the fairy realm, they are eternally trapped. This idea is ancient in myth and lore, echoed in the traditions of many cultures, particularly in regard to fertility goddesses like the Greek Persephone, who must spend a season of each year in the realm of the dead because she partook of the food of that realm. A prime example of this motif in British lore comes in the story "The Fairy Dwelling on Selena Moor," the tale of a prosperous merchant lost one night on the moors who finds himself among a company of dancers in an orchard. Decoyed by a woman who has been playing music for the dancers, he realizes that she is none other than his former lover, supposedly dead for several years. She warns him not to eat the fruit of the orchard or drink the cider of the dancers lest he, like she, be lost to fairyland (Briggs, *Encyclopedia* 141–43).

The question of food in Neverland is a problematic one. The meals, much to Wendy's surprise, are often pretend ones, and apparently were always pretend before her arrival on the island since before that time "Peter knew of no other kind, and she is not absolutely certain even now that he does eat the other kind, though no one appears to do it more heartily" (*Peter Pan* 127). Thus it is Wendy who introduces the idea of food to Neverland, potentially trapping herself there forever, figuratively if not literally.

PETER PAN AS FERTILITY GOD AND FAIRY LOVER

If Peter Pan's Neverland is a version of the Celtic Otherworld in its incarnation as fairyland, who (and what) is Peter Pan himself? The stage directions introducing the island in Act II of the play seem to indicate clearly that Peter is both the author and the master of Neverland:

> The whole island, in short, which has been having a slack time in Peter's absence, is now in a ferment because the tidings has [*sic*] leaked out that he is on his way back; and everybody and everything know that they will catch it from him if they don't give satisfaction. While you have been told this, the sun (another of his servants) has been bestirring himself. (105)

While Peter claims to be a boy who has run away from home in order to avoid growing up, he is clearly something more, and less, than an ordinary child. He is master of his own world, even to controlling the operations of nature, and yet he is oblivious even to the details of his own adventures. He is omnipotent but so far from omniscient that he is forgetful even of himself. In *Peter Pan in Kensington Gardens*, he is still an infant, so close to the pre-mortal identity of the child as bird that he is neither human nor animal, a "[p]oor little half-and half" (28). Yet he is also Pan, named for the goat-god of classical lore, who had become "a natural and pervasive Edwardian god" (Wullschläger 111). As a pastoral god, Pan was associated with fertility and the pipes, with life-giving forces, but, as so often in myth, the two halves of the human equation are embodied in the same entity, and so he was also associated with death and the panic that bested enemies in war. "His name, derived from the root *pa* means 'guardian of flocks'" and he is the "personification of all natural wild things" (Harris and Platzner 210). A weather god, in time "etymological amplification of his myth made Pan the god of all (*pan*) nature" (Leach 841). Peter Pan shares some of these characteristics and hints at others in a paradoxical way. Like his namesake, Peter Pan is a fierce enemy, besting all in combat, but forgetting his enemies as soon as he has killed them. To Peter, all warfare is a game; he will even change sides if the competition proves too uneven. He certainly has a powerful influence on nature, down to waking the sun. His role as a weather god is played up in the latest film version of the play, P. J. Hogan's *Peter Pan*. When he returns to Neverland, his arrival introduces a premature spring thaw, freeing the pirate ship from its ice-bound stasis; when Tink dies, his grief erupts in chaotic weather—thunder, lightning, and snow.

As a fertility figure, Peter Pan is ambiguous at best. As many scholars have noted, the evolution of *Peter Pan* as dramatic text downplayed an earlier sexuality, until the 1928 version finally made Peter untouchable (MacKail 611). Clearly an untouchable immortal could not fulfill a sexual function, but more than his physical limitations separates Peter Pan from his function as a fertility god. While Peter cheerfully falls in with Wendy's plan to come to Neverland as storyteller, he is seemingly oblivious to her interest in him as a male, not knowing even what a kiss is. In much the same way, he is puzzled over the attraction Tinker Bell (and, in an earlier version, Tiger Lily) feels for him, and while he plays along with the make believe of Wendy as mother and himself as father, he is genuinely troubled by even the possibility of their roles being anything other than pretend. In essence, Peter becomes both the fairy lover and the antithesis of the fairy lover, drawing Wendy virtually unresisting into his realm but then failing, indeed unable, to answer the dynamics of the relationship even when coaxed to do so.

Steven Spielberg's *Hook* continues the traditions begun by Barrie by speculating on the events set in motion by the closing lines of both *When Wendy Grew Up* and *Peter and Wendy*. At the end of the epilogue *When Wendy Grew Up*, Peter flies off with Wendy's daughter for spring cleaning, and Wendy tells Nana, the dog nurse, that she planned it that way:

> Every Spring Cleaning, except when he forgets, I'll let Jane fly away with him to the darling Never Never Land, and when she grows up I will hope she will have a little daughter, who will fly away with him in turn—and in this way may I go on for ever and ever, dear Nana, so long as children are young and innocent. (163)

The ending of the novelized version of the tale, *Peter and Wendy*, takes the progression one step further and is even truer to the ambiguity Barrie saw in life and in childhood:

> Jane is now a common grown-up, with a daughter called Margaret, and every spring-cleaning time, except when he forgets, Peter comes for Margaret and takes her to the Never Land, where she tells him stories about himself to which he listens eagerly. When Margaret grows up she will have a daughter, who is to be Peter's mother in turn; and thus it will go on, so long as children are gay and innocent and heartless. (242)

In *Hook*, Margaret has become Moira, and instead of Peter taking her away for spring cleaning, she has won him so that he stays in the mortal world and becomes a man; thus the story of *Hook* becomes "When Peter Grew Up." The Peter of Barrie's works would never have been caught this way; he is determinedly pre-adolescent, single-mindedly untouchable. However much he may at times desire a normal life, he remains, as the subtitle of the play tells us, the boy who would not grow up. For Peter, make believe is real, and adventures are better than mothers. In the play, he tells Mrs. Darling that he doesn't "want to go to school and learn solemn things. No one is going to catch me, lady, and make me a man. I want always to be a little boy and to have fun" (151). But like all ambiguities of Barrie's Neverland, remaining a child, despite its joy and abandon, may not be such a good thing. Peter is not even sure of his own identity. When he tells Hook, "I'm youth, I'm joy, I'm a little bird that has broken out of the egg," he makes the comment, according to the stage directions, "*at a venture*" (*Peter Pan* 145). His is a brave, a bold guess, but it is a thin disguise for his tragic uncertainty. His unending childhood, like his lack of selfhood, is a hollow triumph. When the other children return to the Darling home in *Peter and Wendy*, Peter, who has "ecstasies innumerable that other children can never know," is left outside the window, looking in at the family experiencing "the one joy from which he must be for ever barred" (224).

Awakening sexuality brings Peter back to the mortal world in *Hook*, and the action of the film revolves around the paradoxes that exist between Peter's two worlds. Peter finally grows up when he visits Wendy on one of his spring cleaning jaunts and meets a grandmotherly Wendy and her sleeping granddaughter Moira. An unexpected urge to kiss the sleeping girl "as he had seen others kiss" results in the window closing and, with it, the close of Peter's unending childhood. Grown, Peter Banning is the ideal of late-twentiethth century responsible adulthood, but he is ruthless in business and boring in his personal life, incapable of having fun and unable to hold his children's affection. When he is transported to Neverland to rescue his kidnapped children, he is unequal to either the task or the reputation of Peter Pan until he can learn to be young and carefree again. When he finally finds the happy thought that enables him to fly again, it comes from memories of his family, but ironically, learning to fly returns him to youth, the heartless youth of Barrie's Peter Pan, which makes him forget his family and his duty. Tink's kiss brings him back to himself by reminding him of those adolescent stirrings which made him grow up, but, again paradoxically, his rediscovered passion is for his wife, not Tink, and she is left alone, just as Wendy was long before. Loving Peter Pan, in any of his incarnations, is a risky venture, as is any relationship with a fairy lover.

In Hogan's film, Peter is more overtly sexual and more overtly a fertility figure. He is capable of sexual attraction and of love: when the captured Wendy tells Hook that Peter needs her stories—stories of Cinderella, Snow White, and Sleeping Beauty—he points out that they are all love stories, each ending in a kiss, despite her contention that they are adventures. And when Hook almost defeats Peter by taunting him with the fact that Wendy was going to leave him, that he would be replaced in her life by a husband, Wendy gives Peter her hidden kiss, the symbol (according to her aunt) of her adult sexuality, and he erupts into virile new life. Echoing Peter Banning in *Hook* and the wistful, wishful closing stage directions in the play *Peter Pan*, he announces, "To live would be an awfully big adventure," the antithesis of his cry in the play, "to die will be an awfully big adventure" (*Peter Pan* 125).

MORTALS AND IMMORTALS IN FAIRYLAND AND NEVERLAND

In addition to stories of fairy lovers, the traditional lore of the British Isles is replete with tales of children stolen away into fairyland and replaced by wizened fairy changelings, with stories of young mothers captured and taken into fairyland to serve as midwives and nurses to fairy children, dying, to all appearances, in the mortal world. Nursing mothers who had not yet been churched—a ceremony of cleansing that generally took place three days after the delivery of a baby—were at the most risk, second only to unchristened children (Briggs, *Fairies* 119). For centuries, these tales served as a razor-edged comfort in a world of high infant mortality rates, frequent birth defects, and ever-present death in childbirth. In essence, then, and ironically, Peter and his world become the symbols not of fertility but of death. Wendy, John, and Michael, like the Lost Boys before them, are lost to the mortal world, dying to even their memories of the past. At storytelling in the evening when she is mother and Peter is father, even Wendy falters over her former family history, and at mention of their parents' names, John speaks of them in the past tense, "I knew them!" while Michael says "I think I knew them" (*Peter Pan* 130–31).

While it may be true that on some level the story of Wendy's sojourn in fairyland and her return for spring cleanings is Barrie's version of the Persephone myth (Geduld 158), it is also the traditional story of a mortal lured into fairyland to care for fairy children. Fairies all over the world are concerned with mortal things and close in kind with humans, as evidenced by the recurring tales of fairy lovers and changelings left in place of stolen human children, "as if the fairies needed human blood to reinforce their stock" or as if they needed humans to care for human captives in fairyland (Briggs, *Fairies* 95, 97). While the Lost Boys are not captives but children who have fallen out of their prams and remained unclaimed for seven days—always boys because girls, according to Peter, "are much too clever to fall out of their prams" (*Peter Pan* 101)—Wendy functions as a surrogate mother "captured" to care for them. Even the pirates long to steal her away to be their mother.

Although unpredictable and sometimes dangerous, fairies in traditional lore are both helpful to humans and dependent on them. "They bring luck and increase on the farm, they can give presents of silver money, and they keep a jealous eye on the order of the house and the farmstead" (Briggs, *Fairies* 102). They also live lives in imitation of hu-

mans: "They work and play and fight and dance and hunt, but it sometimes seems doubtful if they are doing more than acting over what they
have seen humans do, or anticipating human happenings or disasters"
(Briggs, *Fairies* 103). Barrie expresses this idea in *Peter Pan in Kensington Gardens*, though perhaps not in a very positive way, commenting that fairies "are frightfully ignorant, and everything they do is make
believe" (60). Again, while some of Barrie's use of fairy lore is clearly
whimsy, much of it is accurate and true to tradition. In *Peter Pan In
Kensington Gardens* the fairies hold balls in the open air in a fairy ring
and "mischief" humans, stabbing them, compelling them to nurse their
children, or turning them into something tedious (63, 90). Fairies are traditionally very fond of dancing, and they often hold their celebrations
in fairy rings. They are equally fond of pinching and otherwise tor-
menting humans, particularly those who are lazy, dishonest, or unclean.

Another bit of legitimate lore in *Peter Pan* concerns mermaids. In traditional lore, all water spirits are dangerous to humans, longing to drag
them down to death, though mermaids tend to be ambiguous creatures, at times aiding and even loving mortals (Briggs, *Fairies* 42).
Barrie utilizes both qualities of mermaid nature in *Peter Pan*. Although
Peter has lured Wendy to Neverland, in part, with stories of seeing mermaids, when they are actually in the Lagoon, he warns her against
them, saying, "They are such cruel creatures, Wendy, that they try to
pull boys and girls like you into the water and drown them" (*Peter Pan*
118). The mermaids of Neverland seem as enamored of Peter as the
other females in the story, even letting him join in their games, but
when he tries to catch one with the other children, she slips away,
warned by the "crow of a cock" (*Peter Pan* 118).

This is ironic and perhaps indicative of Peter's avoidance of female
contact, since crowing is Peter's own particular accomplishment,
which he uses to terrify the superstitious pirates when he boards their
ship to rescue the captured children. The sailors worry that the
"doodle-doo" has bewitched the ship, saying that "the surest sign a
ship's accurst is when there is one aboard more than can be accounted
for" and implying that the extra, the "doodle-doo," is the devil (*Peter
Pan* 143). Barrie employs a twist to tradition by associating Peter with
both the devil and the cockcrow since fairies were often associated
with the devil but were supposed to be driven away by the "crowing
of the cock" (Briggs, *Fairies* 55, 74).

In all of Barrie's works, those creatures explicitly identified as fairies
are very small, and in *Peter Pan in Kensington Gardens*, they disguise

themselves as flowers when people come too near (56). In traditional lore, the size of the fairies varies with time and locale, from the heroic fairies, the "aristocrats among fairy people" who "pass their time in aristocratic pursuits, hunting, hawking, riding in procession on white horses hung with silver bells (Briggs, *Anatomy* 13), to the small flower fairies utilized by Barrie. The heroic fairies as dethroned gods "are of human or more than human height" (Briggs, *Anatomy* 13). The small flower fairies, immortalized by Shakespeare as tiny but extremely powerful beings, are the more familiar. In utilizing these fairies, Barrie was drawing not on his native Scottish tradition (which in the Highlands presented the fairies as "diminished, in glamour if not in size, homelier, shyer, and often more grotesque" and in the Lowlands as "very beautiful, about half the size of mortal men") but on the English Midland fairies who "are gentler and less formidable than those on the Celtic fringe . . . generally small and beautiful, lovers like the rest of music and dancing, nearer to being flower spirits than spirits of the dead" (Briggs, *Fairies* 88, 89, 91–92).

According to Briggs, the problem with the prevalence of the tradition of the small flower fairies in England is that "the prettiness of these fairies and their lack of power makes it difficult to test the belief in them; it is apt to evaporate into whimsy" (*Fairies* 148). While, as Briggs notes, this whimsy is evident in Barrie's writings (*Fairies* 199), he was clearly aware of the actual traditions even if he sometimes chose to emphasize affected prettiness over the darker folk beliefs. This kind of literary affectation occurs in the more sentimental moments of the play, such as when Peter tells Wendy that fairies are born from the laughs of babies and when Wendy tells her mother that fairy babies are dropped by their mothers into Never birds' nests and "the mauve fairies are boys and the white ones are girls, and there are some colours who don't know what they are" (*Peter Pan* 152). It is possible that the whimsy is not just affectation but, from Peter, the product of his tall tales and poor memory, since according to the stage directions, he delivers the story of the babies' laughs "*Baldly*" (*Peter Pan* 99), as if everyone should know this, or as if he is making it up. With her story of the colored fairies, Wendy may be making a pretense to knowledge that she could not have acquired since the fairies in Neverland avoid contact with humans, except for Peter who is their particular favorite and the only one of the children they don't mischief even though they can touch him (*Peter Pan* 117).

Barrie's whimsy is more obvious, and more obnoxious, in *Peter Pan in Kensington Gardens* with his tale of babies coming from birds, but even here he employs an effective twist to traditional fairy lore. Barrie argues the idea that there is a period of time in which children are at risk of being lost to fairyland, not because the fairies steal them, but because they can't control the urge to return to the freedom and wild nature of a world they are nearer to than the human world. Able to remember his time as a bird, Peter can fly, and he flies first to Kensington Gardens and from there to the island in the Serpentine where babies are born as birds. He is neither a human nor a bird, but a "Betwixt-and-Between" who loses his ability to fly along with his faith that he can (*Kensington* 29). While this is clearly whimsy of a particularly sticky kind, it does have some foundation in the beliefs of traditional lore: fairies can take animal form, and in the English tradition, "what appear to be birds may really be disguised fairies" (Briggs, *Fairies* 72). Returning to the Gardens in a specially made thrush nest, Peter lives with the fairies, piping for them, and is granted wishes in return, but when he uses a wish to try to return home, he is too late; the window is barred and another baby is in his place (*Kensington* 66–76).

One obviously inaccurate use of fairy lore in Barrie's writings about Peter Pan occurs in the novel *Peter and Wendy* when Peter tells Wendy upon her return for spring cleaning that Tink is gone because fairies have short life spans (232). In reality, fairies live very long lives because of the arbitrary passage of time in fairyland. Closer, then, to true fairy lore is the reappearance of Tinkerbell in the film *Hook* and her final message to Peter: "You know that place between asleep and awake? That place where you still remember dreaming? That's where I'll always love you, Peter Pan. And that's where I'll wait for you to come back."

Life itself has ambiguous meaning for Peter. His cry during one of his adventures—"to die will be an awfully big adventure" (*Peter Pan* 125)—echoes an identical comment made by George Llewelyn Davies in response to Barrie's description of the afterlife as a child's paradise, the Never Never Land, a "haven of the Lost Boys, abounding in pleasures designed to gratify a boy's appetite for blood" (Birkin 69). This sounds surprisingly like a child's version of the Celtic warrior afterlife recounted in the story of Ossian, a Fenian warrior, himself a wanderer in fairyland, who, when he returns to find his world transformed to a Christian reality, refuses conversion to Christianity if it means an eternity "where there is no hunting, or wooing fair women, or listening to the songs and tales of bards" (Squire 226). The stage directions at the end of *Peter Pan* indicate that if Peter could just understand what Wendy means by her regret at not being able to hug him, "his cry might become 'To live would be an awfully big adventure!'" (94). However, "he can never quite get the hang of it, and so no one is as gay as he. With rapturous face he produces his pipes" and "plays on and on till we wake up" (94). Thus life is equated with love and adulthood, and Peter, for all the joy and abandon of his existence, is really not alive because he will never grow up.

FAIRY LORE IN *DEAR BRUTUS*

Barrie's other two fairy plays, *Dear Brutus* (first performed in 1917) and *Mary Rose* (1920), use less fairy lore but are dependent for their impact on certain beliefs about the power of fairies and the nature of fairyland. *Dear Brutus* concerns a party of people who have been invited for a holiday in an English country house. They have been invited specifically for midsummer week by their host, a small, elderly man named Lob. In questioning the butler about him, the ladies in the party discover that Lob claims to be "all that is left of Merry England" (482). Comparing notes, they realize that Merry England is a reference to the Elizabethan period and Lob is another name for Robin Goodfellow or Puck. In popular lore, Brownies, Hobgoblins, Hobs, Lobs, or Pucks—the names vary with time and locale—are creatures of ambiguous nature: "small, wizened, and shaggy," often "grotesque to look at" who, while they do favors for mortals, working around houses and barns, also create mischief, spilling and breaking and leading travelers astray (Briggs, *Fairies* 38). They are often connected with the dead, are "almost always solitary," and "can be really dangerous" (Briggs, *Fairies* 38, 39). The most famous of the Hobgoblins is Robin Goodfellow, or Puck, immortalized as an individual by Shakespeare's *Midsummer Night's Dream.*

"The Life of Robin Goodfellow," originally published in 1628 under the title of "Robin Goodfellow; his mad prankes, and merry Jests," relates the adventures of this merry sprite, enumerating many of the activities commonly associated with Brownies and echoed by Lob in Barrie's play. In the 1628 tract, Robin is presented as the half-mortal son of the fairy king, Oberon. He is granted certain powers by his fairy father, among them the ability to change his shape, but along with the powers come certain responsibilities:

See none thou harm'st but knaves and queanes;
But love thou those that honest be,
And helpe them in necessity.
Do thus, and all the world shall know
The prankes of Robin Good-fellow . . . (Halliwell 126)

Robin travels around having a fine time but also punishing wickedness and dishonesty. Among his other kindnesses, he aids a pair of misused lovers, punishes a dishonest tapster, and saves a young woman from rape. Of course, he also has an affair with a weaver's wife, leads travelers astray, and mischiefs guests at a wedding. Lob in *Dear Brutus* also aids his guests, although, like Robin, he often seems more sinister than kind.

Barrie, like Shakespeare, chose midsummer for his story of lovers' lives turned upside down. Midsummer has long had a mystical significance, with the Romans observing a "Midsummer Saturnalia" and the Celts of Gaul apparently observing a major festival at that time of the year (Frazer 153, 656). Sir James Frazer suggests "that the midsummer festival must on the whole have been the most widely diffused and the most solemn of all the yearly festivals celebrated by the primitive Aryans in Europe" (656). "In modern Europe," says Frazer, "the great Midsummer festival has been above all a festival of lovers and fire; one of its principal features is the pairing of sweethearts, who leap over the bonfires hand in hand or throw flowers across the flames to each other" (153). Thus, midsummer is associated with lovers, Puck is concerned with lovers, and *Dear Brutus* revolves around love in its many stages from fledgling to staid to mature.

Dear Brutus concerns fate and the turnings people take in life. All of the characters are unhappy in one way or another, thinking that they made a wrong choice somewhere in their lives. Early in the play, one of the characters, a drunken, failed artist named Dearth, tells his wife, "Three things they say come not back to man nor women—the spoken word, the past life, and the neglected opportunity" (498). Through the intervention of Lob, they are all given the chance to find out what would have happened if they could live over their neglected opportunities. A mysterious wood appears in the backyard, and despite the fact that they have been warned against it by the butler, they almost all rush into it, including the butler. Once inside the wood, their lives alter; they have the opportunity to live, for a brief time, in a different way. The blessing is a mixed one because, on returning to the house, most of them realize that they would not have been any better off no matter what choice they made, that fate doesn't orchestrate human destiny or human personality, that people themselves do. In its allusion to *Julius Caesar*, *Dear Brutus* evokes its theme of personal accountability, in essence the negation of fate: "The fault, dear Brutus, is not in our stars, / But in ourselves, that we are underlings" (*Dear Brutus* 527).

As with his namesake, Lob seems to have turned the lives of humans upside down in part out of mischief, in part out of an attempt to reward the good and at least expose the not-so-good. Again, lovers are his target, but in a paradoxical way. The womanizer Purdie, who excuses his womanizing by believing that he is unfaithful because he is married to the wrong woman, discovers when his wife and mistress reverse roles that he would be a womanizer regardless. The older couple, settled in their relationship, still choose each other. The butler has a brief fling with the socialite and discovers that no matter their paths in life, he would still be a thief and she would still be a snob. And the failed artist and his bitter wife learn that a daughter would have been their redemption, but they are left the saddest of all, aware of what they have lost but unable to redeem it. In the end, the characters' lives have not changed, but if there is any consolation despite the pain they have endured, they at least know themselves better. Perhaps Lob's intervention has been beneficial after all, though like all fairy gifts it is a little left-handed. Briggs calls Lob

> the best conceived and carried out of Barrie's fairy people. He has the great age of the fairy changelings, who have seen the acorn before the oak. He is more convincing than Peter Pan in having an old age that has never been manhood. He has the fairy tricksiness and the fairy insights. The appearing and disappearing wood is true enough to folk tradition, and so is the granted wish, and the way in which destiny conforms to character. (*Fairies* 199–200)

Like the mortals in *Peter Pan*, the characters of *Dear Brutus* have enjoyed a sojourn in fairyland, in this instance in its incarnation as a wood. They have been, in essence, out of time, in an altered temporal and spatial reality. While they are allowed to return to the mortal world without a loss of present time, they do not return unchanged. At least for a brief time, they are given the dubious gift of self-awareness and the opportunity, fleeting though it might be, of changing their lives and themselves.

MARY ROSE AND FAIRYLAND

There are certain similarities between *Dear Brutus* and *Mary Rose* beyond the use of fairy tale conventions and the ambiguity of contact with fairyland. Harry M. Geduld says that the true similarity between the two plays is in atmosphere:

> Both plays are essentially supernatural tales in which the usual horrific element has been replaced by wistfulness and pathos. That eeriness tempered with sadness, so evident in Barrie's treatment of the ghost of what-can-never-be and the dreams of what-might-have-been arises out of a yearning after the fantasy rather than the recoil from it that is so much more characteristic of the ghost story. (163)

With *Mary Rose,* Barrie returns to fairyland proper and to the theme of the un-aging mortal in fairyland. Again there is both ambiguity and charm in the story, with the result somehow more sinister and more hopeful than *Peter Pan,* as Barrie looks to heaven for comfort.

Like *Dear Brutus, Mary Rose* was written late in Barrie's career, after much personal grief and suffering, and it is in many ways the darkest and most convincing of his fairy plays. In it, Barrie uses a real folk legend to treat "with some subtlety the theme that he had already used in *Peter Pan,* of a child who had been in contact with Fairyland and had been checked in her growth, so that she could never come to womanhood" (Briggs, *Fairies* 199). The child in question is Mary Rose, who comes into contact with fairyland not once but twice in her life.

The play opens not with Mary Rose but with her son Harry, who ran away to Australia at the age of twelve. He returns many years later to the ghost of his family home, vacant and long up for sale, and whether he knows it or not, to the ghost of his mother. Mary Rose haunts the house in search of her lost youth and her lost boy, not lost to her when he ran away but years before when she herself disappeared. Left alone outside his mother's old room, Harry flashes back to the past and relives her story, beginning with her engagement day when her fiancé Simon learns from her parents that as a girl Mary Rose visited an island in the Outer Hebrides while on vacation and disappeared there, only to return twenty days later with no knowledge that she had ever been missing. When Simon and Mary Rose visit the island themselves as a young married couple with a baby, Mary Rose disappears again, this time for years. When she does finally return, Simon and her parents are middle-aged and elderly, respectively, and Harry has long since run away. In time, all but Harry die, and Mary Rose returns to her home in search of her lost little boy, unable to rest until she finds him.

This idea had long interested Barrie. Based "on old Scottish legends Barrie heard as a child, in which mortals are stolen away to fairyland and return days or years later with no memory of where they have been" (Lurie 14), it was refined by a fishing trip with the Llewelyn Davies boys in 1912:

> [T]he Ghost Mother, who had first appeared in Barrie's notebook for 1886, was still a long way from being named; but it was here in the Outer Hebrides, while fishing near the Castle on Loch Voshimid, that he pointed out to Nico a tiny island in the middle as being "the island that likes to be visited." People had been known to vanish on such islands, he told Nico. Years went by, and then suddenly they came back; the rest of the world had grown old, but they were as young as the day they disappeared. The story began to combine with his earlier notion about ghosts, which he had written in the *Little White Bird*: "The only ghosts, I believe, who creep into this world, are dead young mothers, returned to see how their children fare." (Birkin 205)

In 1919, after he had begun to have problems with his right hand and had been forced to write with his left, claiming "that he thought more darkly down his left arm," Barrie finally began to turn his ideas into *Mary Rose* (Birkin 284).

Barrie draws on a number of fairy traditions in developing the story of Mary Rose, with his primary emphasis on the duplicity of fairyland. As we have seen, mortals who visit fairyland do not age, at least not until they return to their mortal lives, but the world and the people they leave behind change significantly. The rowan tree that occupies Mary Rose's island is a traditional protection against "fairy enchantments and witchcraft" (Briggs, *Encyclopedia* 344), but it seems to have failed, as has the fir, a symbol of fertility (Guiley 344), which cannot protect Mary Rose from the spell that keeps her always young but stunts her growth. When first telling Simon about Mary Rose's childhood experience, her mother equates Mary's unusual youthfulness with a chilling frost: "I have often thought that our girl is curiously young for her age—as if— you know how just a touch of frost may stop the growth of a plant and yet leave it blooming—it has sometimes seemed to me as if a cold finger had once touched my Mary Rose" (567).

Mary Rose seems content on the island, as many mortals are while in fairyland, smiling as she sleeps, and the island seems a blessed spot until one realizes that the trees have "their arms outstretched for ever southward, as if they had been struck while in full flight and could no longer pray to their gods to carry them away from this island" (*Mary Rose* 572). The island has a sinister reputation among the native people; they believe that it resents being landed on and that it has the power to move. In keeping with the need to speak well of fairy things so as to prevent retribution, its name means "The Island that Likes to be Visited" in Gaelic (*Mary Rose* 580). The island's call comes for Mary Rose first in softness and then with rising storms, and a sweet sound of music fighting it, trying to protect her (588). Harry says later that there were "two kinds of dogs out hunting" her, "the good and the bad," and that the good won (608). When he asks her if there are any ghosts on the island, she emphatically says "no" (608), implying, if he is right about the good dogs, that the fairies in their more positive incarnation and not in their presence as the dead were her hosts for the years she was missing on the island.

Briggs suggests that the evil and good fairies may have been hunting "in rivalry for the soul of Mary Rose" (*Fairies* 109). No matter who won the contest, however, Mary Rose lost. Staying young forever comes at a high price. Despite the apparent pleasure of her visit to fairyland, it took her mortal life in more ways than one. First, it separated her from her loved ones. When she returns to them years later, she is overtly unchanged, but slightly faded, as if they can see through her. They, on the other hand, have gone on with their lives, have become different people than those she knew. When the news comes about her rescue, "many unseen devils steal into the room," and they chuckle when Simon doesn't recognize his long-lost wife (*Mary Rose* 598, 600). Second, the stay on the island robbed Mary Rose of her proper adulthood and sexuality. However, it may have done even more. She may, in fact, be a ghost throughout the play, even in the flashback segment. In this segment, when she returns from hiding away while Simon asks for her hand in marriage, Mary Rose mentions seeing an old woman on the stairs who reminded her of her beloved island, which she had forgotten. Who is this mysterious old woman so curiously alluded to and then passed over? Is she a fairy creature, Mary Rose herself in a later incarnation, or even the aged caretaker who opens the play? Framed by the desolation of the long-empty house that opens and closes the play, the cozy home life of the flashback scenes may be, in fact, an illusion, the glamour of fairyland, recreated not so much in the mind of the witness Harry, but in the soul of the rootless ghost, Mary Rose. In the end, it is the return of Harry that saves her. She does not recognize in the grown man the beloved little boy she lost. Indeed, she has forgotten the object of her search. She is a sad and lonely ghost whose life was stolen away by eternal youth. In the end, her son must make her hear the call again in order to send her home. He equates the island with Heaven and speculates that God has not called her sooner because she "broke some law, just to come back for the sake of—of that Harry" (610). He concludes that it is time the breach was overlooked and something, or someone, must have agreed. This time the call, when it comes, is not unholy but beautiful and celestial, presumably because it comes from God. The play closes with stage directions: "*The smallest star shoots down for her, and with her arms stretched forth to it trustingly she walks out through the window into the empyrean. The music passes with her. Harry hears nothing, but he knows that somehow a prayer has been answered*" (611).

This ending must have been in many ways a comfort to Barrie himself, who by this time had seen much of death. Since the death of his brother David, there had been many others, including his parents. He had lost Arthur and Sylvia Llewelyn Davies to illness, George Llewelyn Davies to war, and—perhaps the most bitter of all—Michael Llewelyn Davies to drowning. In dreaming that Michael returned to him year after year only to be have to go and drown on the same day again and again, Barrie finally realized, he said, the true meaning of Peter Pan: "Desperate attempt to grow up but can't" (Birkin 297). In a speech delivered at St. Andrews University in 1922, Barrie read a sonnet Michael had written during his last summer and referred to Michael simply as "the lad that will never be old" (Birkin 300). Fairyland is a dangerous place indeed, offering us magic and mystery, youth and adventure, but at the terrible price of mortal life and human love.

Although J. M. Barrie may have traveled far geographically and socially from the Scottish soil of his childhood, living his life among the elite of Edwardian London, his heart and mind remained always in the world of childhood, rooted deep in his Celtic heritage. A natural storyteller, Barrie drew on the tales and traditions of his childhood to inform and shape his novels and his plays, recognizing that this literature speaks to the deepest parts of the human soul, offering insights on the most profound questions of the human condition. In a life shaped equally by success and failure, triumph and tragedy, Barrie knew that not all the questions were easy ones or all of the answers comforting. But he knew, too, that if we could hold onto that part of ourselves that still believed in mystery, in magic, in dreaming, and in adventure, there would be at least hope for the journey.

WORKS CITED

Barrie, J. M. *Dear Brutus. The Plays of J. M. Barrie.* New York: Scribner's, 1950. 473–542.

———. *Mary Rose. The Plays of J. M. Barrie.* New York: Scribner's, 1950. 543–611.

———. *Peter and Wendy.* 1911. New York: Barnes and Noble, 1995.

———. *Peter Pan. Peter Pan and Other Plays.* Ed. Peter Hollindale. Oxford: Oxford UP, 1995. 73–154.

———. *Peter Pan in Kensington Gardens.* 1906. New York: Weathervane, 1975.

———. *When Wendy Grew Up. Peter Pan and Other Plays.* Ed. Peter Hollindale. Oxford: Oxford UP, 1995. 154–63.

Birkin, Andrew. *J. M. Barrie and the Lost Boys: The Love Story that Gave Birth to Peter Pan.* New York: Clarkson N. Potter, 1979.

Briggs, K[atharine]. M[ary]. *The Anatomy of Puck: An Examination of Fairy Beliefs among Shakespeare's Contemporaries and Successors.* London: Routledge & Kegan Paul, 1959.

———. *An Encyclopedia of Fairies.* New York: Pantheon, 1976.

———. *The Fairies in Tradition and Literature.* London: Routledge & Kegan Paul, 1967.

———. *The Vanishing People: Fairy Lore and Legends.* New York: Pantheon, 1978.

Frazer, Sir James. *The Golden Bough: A History of Myth and Religion.* Abr. ed. 1922. London: Chancellor, 2000.

Geduld, Harry M. *Sir James Barrie.* New York: Twayne, 1971.

Guiley, Rosemary Ellen. *The Encyclopedia of Witches and Witchcraft.* New York: Facts on File, 1989.

Halliwell, James Orchard. *Illustrations of the Fairy Mythology of A Midsummer Night's Dream.* London: Shakespeare Society, 1845.

Harris, Stephen L., and Gloria Platzner. *Classical Mythology: Images and Insights.* 4th ed. Boston: McGraw-Hill, 2004.

Holbrook, David. *Images of Woman in Literature.* New York: New York UP, 1989.

Hook. Dir. Steve Spielberg. Perf. Dustin Hoffman, Robin Williams, and Julia Roberts. Tri-Star, 1992.

Huck, Charlotte S., et al. *Children's Literature in the Elementary School.* 8th ed. Boston: McGraw-Hill, 2004.

Jack, R. D. S. *The Road to the Never Land: A Reassessment of J. M. Barrie's Dramatic Art.* Aberdeen: Aberdeen UP, 1991.

Leach, Maria, ed. *Funk & Wagnall's Standard Dictionary of Folklore, Mythology, and Legend.* San Francisco: Harper & Row, 1972.

Lewis, C. S. "On Three Ways of Writing for Children." *The Riverside Anthology of Children's Literature.* Boston: Houghton Mifflin, 1985. 1075–81.

Lurie, Alison. "The Boy Who Couldn't Grow Up." *New York Review of Books* (6 Feb. 1975): 11–15.

MacKail, Denis. *Barrie: The Story of J. M. B.* New York: Scribner's, 1951.

Peter Pan. Dir. P. J. Hogan. Perf. Jason Isaacs, Jeremy Sumpter, and Richard Briers. Universal Studios, 2003.

Rutherford, Ward. *Celtic Lore: The History of the Druids and Their Timeless Traditions.* London: Thorsons, 1995.

Squire, Charles. *Celtic Myth and Legend.* 1905. n. p.: New Castle, 1975.

Tolkien, J. R. R. "On Fairy-Stories." *The Tolkien Reader.* New York: Ballantine, 1966. 33–99.

Wullschläger, Jackie. *Inventing Wonderland: The Lives and Fantasies of Lewis Carroll, Edward Lear, J. M. Barrie, Kenneth Grahame, and A. A. Milne.* New York: Free Press, 1995.

II

IN AND OUT OF TIME
PETER PAN IN AMERICA

6

Problematizing Piccaninnies, or How J. M. Barrie Uses Graphemes to Counter Racism in *Peter Pan*

Clay Kinchen Smith

Piccaninnies. Why Piccaninnies? Why not the Great Big Little Panthers? Or some other "Indian"-sounding name? Anything but such a racialized term. Anyone who has read J M. Barrie's *Peter Pan* critically may have asked these sorts of questions. However, critics have ignored these questions when discussing Barrie's work, preferring to celebrate the complexity of its metatextuality while remaining silent on the term "Piccaninnies."[1] Perhaps a sense of embarrassment over his use of this overtly prejudicial term prevents critics from discussing it in their otherwise exuberant explorations of Barrie's work. Perhaps, they reason, if we don't talk about it, we can avoid any controversy that might arise from addressing it. Yet such controversy is precisely what he intended to elicit by choosing this term, as Barrie reiterates throughout this and his other works. There, he crafts a pedagogy that problematizes hegemonic categories, often through strategies that parallel those formalized by postcolonial and other deconstructive theorists (like Jacques Derrida, Lata Mani, Edward Said, and Gayatri Spivak). In short, he names the native Neverlanders "Piccaninnies" to foreground and prevent the sorts of erasure that critics have too often enacted.

To understand Barrie's pedagogical use of such a prejudicial term, we must first understand his methodology. This requires us to chart the evolution of the native Neverlanders throughout the development of the play, the context in which Barrie originated the characters, and his final efforts to problematize categorizations (racial and other forms of

identity) through publishing the play. Once we have completed this aspect of our analysis, we need to locate Barrie's pedagogy relative to
similar pedagogies. Finally, we should contrast Barrie's pedagogy with
those who have sought to adapt and otherwise appropriate it. Then we
can appreciate the extent of Barrie's pedagogy to counter racism and
the commitment to it that he exerted throughout his career.

Throughout his work, Barrie uses a sophisticated strategy to foreground those categories that he seeks to problematize. Most often, he
employs a form of metatextual play of differences that he formalized in
"Neil and Tintinabalum." There, he divides readers into two categories:
those who cannot read and those who can "read that human document" (87). The latter "enquire into its hidden meaning," while "the ordinary reader[s]" allow "the surface" to "suffice." As Barrie further explains,

> the digger would ask, what is the philosophy of life advanced by the au-
> thor, is the whole thing an allegory and if so what is . . . [the author's] Mes-
> sage; in short, is he, like the commoner writers, merely saying what he
> says, or like the big chaps, something quite different. (87)

Throughout the play *Peter Pan*, Barrie uses both explicit and implicit
gestures to signal his pedagogy. For example, he employs a visible/
invisible trope throughout his (re)articulations of the play to reinforce
critical reading of the text; most often he uses it with reference to the native Neverlanders as when he addresses the simultaneity of the audience's view above and below ground in Act IV or our ability to "watch
the carnage that is invisible to the children" (*Plays* 71). In short, Barrie
asks/shows readers/audiences to read/watch his (and others') texts
critically—deeply—unlike those who mistake surface for substance.

Here, as in many of his other works, he articulates his pedagogy: a direct undercutting of hegemonic categorizations through verbal
difference—the play of difference that parallels in form and intent de-
constructivist pedagogies like those of Derrida, which open a space
"between different things [where] one can think difference" (168). And
just as Derrida enacts his pedagogy through stylistic devices such as
graphemes, Barrie enacts his pedagogy through similar metatextual emphasis. As the following analysis will show, he does so to avoid "merely
saying what he says" and instead to "say something quite different."

When he published the play in 1928, Barrie crafted his final, definitive statement about Neverland and its inhabitants. Throughout the

many (re)articulations of the play undertaken by Barrie, he designated the native Neverlanders as "Piccaninnies."[2] Given such extensive revision, this designation cannot simply be an oversight on Barrie's part. Moreover, as these (re)articulations and certain of his other works reveal, Barrie actively promotes a pedagogy designed to empower his audiences to read critically by sensitizing them to the interplay of ideology and identity. In fact, these works demonstrate how such a negative term as "Piccaninnies" can function to problematize reductive categorization and reductive erasure. Evidence for this term's function within Barrie's larger pedagogy occurs with the first versions of the play.

In addition to engaging the specific categorization of Native-American peoples, his use of "Piccaninnies" as an identity category also directly engages the comparable categorization of African-American peoples. Throughout the time that Barrie crafted the play, racialist attacks against peoples of color were abhorrently ubiquitous. The "Piccaninny" as a determinative identity category achieved a degree of hegemony that is undeniable: it appeared literally on everything from postcards to toys to numerous films, including *Ten Pickaninnies* (1904) and the comedy shorts of Hal Roach's Our Gang series in the 1920s and 1930s.[3] The violence promoted by and promoting such images was manifest from the razing of Rosewood, Florida, to the innumerable lynchings of African-Americans throughout the U. S. Similar sorts of racialist categories, including the use of "Piccaninny" as a derogatory term, occurred throughout the British Empire, particularly in Australia, during this time as well.[4] Given the extent of "Piccaninny" as a racialist term, Barrie's choice to use it foregrounds a wide range of hegemonic forces—much more so than if he had named the native Neverlanders something like "The Great Big Little Panthers." It also indicates his active engagement of such forces in an attempt to subvert them.

By making racial categories so manifestly prominent and "overcharged" (to use his term), Barrie emphasizes their constructedness in order to deconstruct them. His specific productions and his pointed use of the term "Piccaninny" collapse categories of racial, spatial, and national difference (red/black/African American/Aboriginal peoples) as well as the larger productions of such categories. In short, he makes race (and class and gender) sites of struggle as part of an extensive pedagogical effort that he exerted throughout his career.

Such contestation illustrates Homi Bhabha's notion of "interstititial perspective." Bhabha argues that such a perspective replaces "the polarity of a prefigurative self-generating nation 'in itself' and extrinsic other nations" with "cultural liminality *within the nation*" by "split[ting 'the agency of a people'] in the discursive ambivalence that emerges in the contest of narrative authority between the pedagogical and the performative" (148). The consequence of such an agenda is to problematize the "fixed horizontal nation-space" through mimicry, hybridity, liminality, and "interrogatory, interstitial space" (142, 3). As close readings of *Peter Pan* and certain of his other works will show, Barrie engages in exactly this sort of pedagogy—especially mimickry and hybridity—throughout his various (re)articulations of *Peter Pan*.

Barrie's pedagogy reveals itself in virtually every aspect of the play, especially his continuous revision of its scenes to more effectively articulate his pedagogy of problematization. Evidence of this revisionist intent begins with the play's titular evolution. Before it was *Peter Pan*, it was *Peter and Wendy*; but before that, it was *The Great White Father* (Hammerton 351). Barrie's decision to revise his original title, with its invocation of colonial authority, informs his desire to move away from conventional reinscription of colonial authority (*The Great White Father*) toward mutuality, then finally to indeterminacy as he shifts the play's title to focus exclusively on the character embodying such problematization—an encoded gesture that informs Barrie's pedagogy.

However, Barrie does not include anything as sophisticated in his original formulation of the play—if we accept his claim to have extrapolated *Peter Pan* from *Peter Pan in Kensington Gardens*. There, Barrie designates "the island in the Serpentine" as simply a rookery forbidden to humans upon which Solomon Caw instructs Peter (27). Subsequently, May Byron extends this anonymity in her adaptation of the story when she defines the island as "dull" "because it wasn't a desert island, a treasure island, a pirate island, or anything but a hatching-place for birds who would become real boys and girls" (Byron 18). Notably absent are any native peoples.

Absence also informs Barrie's other (re)created geneses, as in his dedication to the final printed version of the play *Peter Pan* (1928). There, he painstakingly correlates events in both *The Boy Castaways* and *Peter Pan*, noting the origin of each character (*Plays* 11–12). Despite this intricate genealogy, he makes no references to native peoples, Redskins, or Piccaninnies on the island. In marked contrast to such stated origins, Barrie's play abounds with tribal people who enact a variety of encoding. This contrast also informs Barrie's growing commitment to use the Piccaninnies to problematize what would otherwise have been simply a transcription of earlier play/s. However, such is not the case in subsequent versions of the play (staged or printed), in which presence, not absence, defines the native Neverlanders. By over-charging their presence, Barrie redefines their apparent identity so that they perform a graphematic function to problematize the very categories that they seem to (re)present—a strategy that he will continue throughout his different versions of the play.

When he began producing the play for the stage, Barrie had visibly determined the centrality of native peoples to his pedagogy in *Peter Pan*. However, that centrality is not immediately noteworthy, especially in their staged appearance.[5] For example, the photograph of Miriam Nesbit portraying Tiger Lily in the original version performed at the Duke of York's Theatre (1904–1905) reveals a costume and character design that is indistinguishable from conventional images of native women.[6] Such conventionality (re)appears in William Nicholson's designs for the costumes and scenes for Nesbit and the other Redskins as well as the pen-and-ink drawings for the second London production of the play in 1905.[7] But such images are only the apparent articulation of the native Neverlanders' identity; as such they exemplify the ways in which Barrie frustrates such conventional appearances by overloading them with deconstructive meaning. To do so, he invokes and then deconstructs conventional identity through a complex interplay of stage directions and intertextual commentary. In other words, he encodes the native Neverlanders with deconstructive meaning, articulating them as graphemes within a pedagogy designed to problematize racialist categories.

Comparison of the original play (1904) and the final published version (1928) reveals how determined Barrie was to distance his play from contemporary stereotypes through such graphemes. Although the final version maintains much of the original's structure, Barrie constantly revised the sequence of scenes to (re)formulate his pedagogy. To accomplish this goal, Barrie often edited or excised entire scenes. For example, initially he had Tiger Lily capture, bind, and leave Peter for dead because he will not marry her even though she has spent several scenes trying to seduce him (Green 48–51).

In subsequent versions, Barrie either modified or completely deleted such scenes. By doing so, he also deconstructed the negative conventions associated with captivity narratives and the violence that they invoke as he did when he refused to publish the Ship Scene that opens Act V in the original versions. This scene consists of Great Big Little Panther's threatening Starkey, who is the natives' captive, if he does not change his concertina lament from "Oh miserable Starkey" to "Oh happy Starkey" (Green 76–77). He also edited this scene and the entire Indian Encampment for the American production in July 1905 (Green 103–4). As these edits illustrate, Barrie invoked and then denied hegemonic categories, thus (re)inscribing native identity. As these original scenes also vividly reveal, he was actively constructing his pedagogy to counter racism from the first staging of the play.

To make his pedagogy more accessible, Barrie also encoded metatextual commentary that emphasizes identity as an imposed construct. For example, as the Pirates prepare to smoke out the Lost Boys from their home in the original version, the Redskins shoot Starkey in the side with an arrow. In his stage direction, Barrie notes the origin of this apparently gratuitous gesture of violence: "*The effect got as in* [Stephen Philips's contemporary play] *Ulysses*" (Green 47). In so doing, he reveals that the Redskins' identity depends less upon "authentic" sources and more on contemporary stagings/constructs.

To emphasize this aspect of his pedagogy, Barrie repeated this gesture during the exchange between Tiger Lily and Great Big Little Panther that next occurs. There, he first has the "*Indians reappear stealing to house threateningly with tomahawks and knives*," but then abandon their murderous intent to listen to Wendy's stories (Green 47). This shift dramatically reveals their essential equality with the Lost Boys, a direct contrast with the Pirates. In so doing, he engages the reductivism of previous and contemporary sources, like captivity narratives, James Fenimore Cooper's novels, and other racialist rhetorics.

However, his pedagogy assumes its greatest dimensions when he invokes the term "Piccaninny" in the printed versions of the play. Initially, he used the terms "Indians," "Red Indians," and/or "Redskins" to designate the native Neverlanders and problematized their identity through over-charging. For example, *The Peter Pan Picture Book* (1907) uses all three terms, but *Peter and Wendy* (1911) introduces and establishes the term "Piccaninny" as the native Neverlanders' tribal name. Some later editions avoid that term, but Barrie has obviously introduced it as part of his larger pedagogy of problematization at the initial printed version of the play. Since this version forms the basis for all subsequent narrative versions of *Peter Pan*, Barrie has formulated a definitive statement meant to counter such reductionism. To emphasize his pedagogy, Barrie chose to write this grapheme in blood by having the Pirates massacre the Piccaninnies.

Before this climactic statement, he carefully orchestrates scenes to invoke and establish the Piccaninnies' identity as constructions informing determinism. For example, Barrie describes the Piccaninnies as "*mute but picturesque*" as they stand guard over the Lost Boys' home (*Plays* 63–65). Similarly, Barrie overdetermines the "brush with the redskins at Slightly Gulch" to emphasize the relativity and constructiveness of identity (by having Peter and the Lost Boys and the Piccaninnies freely exchange identities during the "sanguinary affair"). Such examples sensitize audiences to the performative nature of the characters (and their attendant identities) that they see upon the stage.

In addition to these stagings, Barrie also articulates his pedagogy more directly through the sorts of metatextual stage directions examined above (e.g., Starkey's arrow-in-the-side scene). There, he had used such stage directions to form graphemes of racialist categories and the reductive identity that they seek to impose on native peoples, but he had used the device sparingly. Here in the final version, he crafts several scenes that rely on the problematization possible through metatextual commentary, and in doing so more explicitly deconstructs such racialist rhetoric.

One of his most important constructions occurs in the scene when the Piccaninnies are guarding the Lost Boys. There, Barrie has Peter define the guards, including Tiger Lily, as "Piccaninny braves." After having the Piccaninnies voice their abject servitude to Peter, Barrie has Peter declare,

> It is well. The Great White Father has spoken. (*This has a note of finality about it, with the implied "And now shut up," which is never far from the courteous receptions of well-meaning inferiors by born leaders of men . . .*). (*Plays* 65)

Barrie's stage direction here redefines this display as a problematization of the offensive colonial fantasy that it seems to enact.[8]

This direction could simply serve as another example in the list of Barrie's metatextuality. However, it assumes a greater function than a qualification of Peter's authority through its context: because it directly confronts colonial authority at the moment of its absolute invocation, this stage direction clearly reveals Barrie's intent to problematize such authority. By extension, it resonates with Barrie's deconstruction of such authority that he had enacted much earlier when he had changed the play's original title from *The Great White Father*. Moreover, it plainly indicates that Barrie has a pedagogy that he wishes to communicate to his audiences. Finally, his inclusion of this stage direction in the final printed version of the play informs his desire to actively promote and continue such problematizing features in subsequent (re)productions of the play.

In contrast to such explicitly graphematic instances, Barrie also uses more implicit devices. He strategically frames the Piccaninnies' entrance and exit in rhetoric literally and figuratively taken from the sensationalist language of racialist texts. The first instance occurs when he introduces audiences to the tribe; the second, when he has the Indians massacred. Both passages warrant extended quoting to reveal the subtlety of Barrie's pedagogy. In the play, Barrie introduces the tribe rather succinctly: "none can see or hear [them] because they are on the warpath" (*Plays* 38). However, in the novel, he elaborates this introduction:

> On the trail of the pirates, stealing noiselessly down the war-path, which is not visible to inexperienced eyes, come the redskins, every one of them with his eyes peeled. They carry tomahawks and knives, and their naked bodies gleam with paint and oil. Strung around them are scalps, of boys as well as of pirates, for these are the Piccaninny tribe, and not to be confused with the softer-hearted Delawares or the Hurons. In the van, on all fours, is Great Big Little Panther, a brave of so many scalps that in his present position they somewhat impede his progress. Bringing up the rear, the place of greatest danger, comes Tiger Lily, proudly erect, a princess in her own right. She is the most beautiful of dusky Dianas and the belle of the Piccaninnies, coquettish, cold and amorous by turns; there is not a brave who would not have the wayward thing to wife, but she staves off the altar with a hatchet. (77)[9]

His language here defines the native Neverlanders in terms of excessiveness: Great Big Little Panther's excessive scalps, the tribe's excessive violence, Tiger Lily's excessive beauty and virginity. By overcharging their identities, Barrie foregrounds the rhetorical construction of such categorization—the excess striking through those categorical terms as effectively as any Derridean grapheme. By doing so, he also exploits the textual advantages inherent in the fictionalized version's format, thus demonstrating his ability and desire to craft his pedagogy to fit the media in which it appears.

After this explicit indictment, Barrie completes his bracketing of the Neverlanders' identity with a more implicit construction in both play and novel versions. While more dramatic than the above introductory passage, his account of the Piccaninnies' massacre functions in precisely the same graphematic ways that he employed above—using excess to strike through reductive categorization. In both versions, he defines the Piccaninnies as fatefully abiding by the codes of honor promoted by Cooper's novels, conventional penny dreadfuls, and other contemporary adventure fiction. In the novelized version, he crafts the scene this way:

> By all the unwritten laws of savage warfare it is always the redskin who attacks, and with the wiliness of his race he does it just before the dawn, at which time he knows the courage of the whites to be at its lowest ebb. The white men have in the meantime made a rude stockade on the summit of yonder undulating ground, at the foot of which a stream runs, for it is destruction to be too far from water. There they await the onslaught, the inexperienced ones clutching their revolvers and treading on twigs, but the old hands sleeping tranquilly until just before dawn. Through the long black night the savage scouts wriggle, snake-like, among the grass without stirring a blade. The brushwood closes behind them, as silently as sand into which a mole has dived. Not a sound is to be heard, save when they give vent to a wonderful imitation of the lonely call of the coyote. The cry is answered by other braves; and some of them do it even better than the coyotes, who are not very good at it. So the chill hours wear on, and the long suspense is horribly trying to the paleface who has to live through it for the first time; but to the trained hand those ghastly calls and still ghastlier silences are but an intimation of how the night its marching. (91)

This invocation requires readers who are sensitive to Barrie's pedagogy to note how this scene elides into virtually every other prefatory scene in such conventionalized rhetoric. In other words, since this scene and its language are virtually indistinguishable from any other comparable scene found in conventional genres, Barrie has crafted a situation to test his audience's awareness of his pedagogy—a grapheme that informs his pedagogy through its invisibility. For those audience members who can see the grapheme in this scene, Barrie articulates an extreme comment on the devastation inherent in that rhetoric. For those audience members who cannot see the grapheme, this scene functions merely as an extended passage prior to the Piccaninnies' massacre. By having the Piccaninnies fall victim to their blind adherence to convention, Barrie over-charges this scene to deconstruct its authority and correspondingly other similar scenes outside the play.

Similarly, in the final play version, Barrie foregrounds the constitutive elements determining the Piccaninnies' massacre. However, here he more directly and explicitly confronts the audience's complicity in the violence:

> We can watch the carnage that is invisible to the children. HOOK has basely broken the laws of Indian warfare, which are that the redskins should attack first, and that it should be at dawn. . . . [A]las, [the Piccaninnies] have trusted in the pale-face's honour to await an attack at dawn, when his courage is known to be at the lowest ebb. . . . If the braves would rise quickly they might still have time to scalp, but this they are forbidden to do by the traditions of their race, for it is written that they must never express surprise in the presence of the pale-face. For a brief space they remain recumbent, not a muscle moving, as if the foe were here by invitation. Thus perish the flower of the Piccaninnies. . . . (*Plays* 71)

As these passages illustrate, Barrie employs a strategy designed to foreground the massacre as a product of conventional ideology. In other words, he has convention, not the pirates, massacre the Piccaninnies.

Confirmation of this strategy also comes from Barrie's earlier versions of this scene. For example, in *Peter and Wendy* (1911), Barrie composes the massacre scene in virtually the same terms, but then adds the following lines after the massacre has concluded: "No more would they torture at the stake. For them the Happy Hunting-Grounds now" (179). Barrie obviously chose to delete these lines from his final play version. The contrast between these two versions informs the depth and dedication of Barrie's pedagogy to counter reductive categorization as well as his decisive move away from such reinscriptions.

After this elaborate (re)articulation of his pedagogy, Barrie adds a final grapheme through Starkey's captivity. By doing so, he engages the excessive violence found in conventional captivity narratives. When Peter and the Lost Boys massacre the pirates on their ship, Starkey, the lone survivor, is taken captive by the Piccaninnies, who make him a nanny to their children. Barrie uses another apparently innocuous instance to transform convention. He simultaneously invokes the (usually negative and racist) conventions of Indian captivity narratives and redefines them. To accomplish this grapheme, he has the Piccaninnies impose a feminized subjectivity onto Starkey, while highlighting the tribe's continued existence outside biological and textual confines. Such encoding also privileges those readers/audience members who are able to (mis)read those codes.

The depth and complexity of Barrie's pedagogy becomes more apparent when compared to story and picture book adaptations of the play and to Barrie's film adaptation of *Peter Pan* (1924) and his short fiction piece "Neil and Tintinabalum" (1925). Since most of the story and picture book versions either reproduce or extend the published version of the play or the text of the 1911 novel, they are noteworthy for the contrast that they provide with Barrie's organic play versions. Most of these adaptations either radically condense or erase Barrie's carefully formulated rhetoric. For example, Phoebe Wilson's 1956 adaptation strips the Massacre Scene to the following summary: "The pirates had attacked the Indians! . . . Then the noise of the struggle ended as quickly as it had begun" (32). Others oversimplify this scene, as in Cathy Dubowski's recent version (1991): "The air filled with the battle cry of pirates and Indians! . . . But the battle above ground was over quickly. Hook and his pirates had cheated. They had surprised the Indians. They had attacked in the dark! And they had won. Hook had Peter cornered" (62–63).

Similar erasure occurs in other key scenes that Barrie developed to problematize such erasure. For example, the story and picture book adaptations and versions of *Peter Pan* are much more succinct in their introductions of the islanders. Several versions feature paintings on their endpapers depicting the introductory circle, for example Ruth Woods's paintings for Wilson's 1956 adaptation. Gwynedd M. Hudson extends this circular hierarchy, but in a much more blatantly racist way, throughout *J. M. Barrie's Peter Pan and Wendy* (1931): there Hudson includes numerous illustrations of its constituent groups as in "The Piccaninny Tribe" (a line of war-bonneted braves in stylized dance poses and wielding knives) trailed by "Princess Tiger Lily" (90–91). Even more extreme is *Walt Disney's Peter Pan and the Pirates* (1952), adapted by Bob Moore, which shows a map of the island with the location of the "Indian Camp" indicated but no Indians either on the map or in the story. Other versions edit this circle within the text itself, as does Wilson when she eliminates the circle and has only pirates looking for Peter Pan and the Lost Boys (18).

Such revisions and erasure create a textual body devoid of the pedagogy that Barrie so carefully crafted prior to the final printed version of the play and which he insisted upon in that version. In the process, they reinscribe native peoples within conventions that Barrie intentionally sought to destabilize. Moreover, they create a body of textual identity for Peter Pan against which Barrie's authorized version must struggle.

While Barrie's pedagogy continues to struggle today against forces that would align it with binary determinism, its origins are somewhat surprising: his legendary fascination with adventure-oriented fiction.[10] Biographers have most often portrayed this drive by recounting similar or the same anecdotes, many supplied by Barrie or his classmates. However problematic such anecdotes may be, they provide crucial insight into Barrie's pedagogy of race.

While at Dumfries, Barrie maintained and shared his interest in adventure fiction with several of his classmates, most notably by recounting and enacting fantasies inspired by adventure-oriented fiction and penny dreadfuls that they had read. Evidence also emerges of Barrie's particular intimacy with two opposing authors (Cooper and Captain Mayne Reid). His familiarity with Cooper manifests itself in the earlier, close readings of his play's deconstruction of racialist categories. His familiarity with Reid is less explicit but equally central to his pedagogy. James Hammerton claims that "these boyhood days in Dumfries were the great days of Red Indians and pirate fiction. Mayne Reid with his *Scalp Hunters* and *Rifle Rangers* had long been a favorite" (560). This last point indicates an intriguing inspiration for Barrie's later deconstructive pedagogy.

For all of his categorization as a boys' adventure author (and all of the assumptions that attend to such a category), Reid problematizes as much as he confirms stereotypes of race, class, and gender. One of his most telling examples occurs in *The Scalp Hunters* (1851), when Reid problematizes conventional codes by juxtaposing them with revisionist counters. Primarily, he contrasts the standard image of the victimized white female captive (Adele) with the excessive barbaric captivity of the Navahos that Sequin's party takes while trying to rescue Adele (355, 444–45). However, Reid saves his final and most effective transcoding for the novel's end, where he destabilizes conventional images of female captivity by explicitly labeling Adele's rescue as captivity: "She was returning to the home of her childhood; not voluntarily, but as a captive; captive to her own kindred, her father and mother!" (446–47). Reid performs similar sorts of transcoding in some of his other novels, such as *The White Chief* (1872). Given the ubiquity and influence of Reid's work in general, and specifically for Barrie, this connection supplies an intriguing causal element to Barrie's pedagogy.

Barrie also sought to promote his pedagogy through other media—most notably film. Critics such as Donald Crafton have addressed Barrie's dissatisfaction with the 1924 Paramount film version of *Peter Pan*. Of these critics, R. D. S. Jack formulates most fully the complexity of Barrie's desire and disgust with the film version. In his analysis, Jack reveals that Barrie's frustration derives from Paramount's simplistic (re)creation of his play through a medium that allows (and from his perspective demands) innovation. The difference between Barrie's film proposal and Paramount's actual film is manifest in a movie promotional poster in which Peter prominently leads the pirates in the attack against the Indians.[11]

Barrie's proposed film scenario closely parallels the final published play version, but it also significantly reveals his pedagogy immediately prior to the final version of the play (only four years later). As in the play, Barrie first invokes and then deconstructs conventional stereotypes, here through an explicit reference to Cooper: "The redskins, in the Fenimore Cooper story manner, torturing a [pirate] prisoner who is tied to a tree" (Green 183). Then he has Tiger Lily dispatch a suitor with her hatchet. His reference to Cooper seeks to establish this scene as a continuity of Cooper's original reductivism. At this initial node, Barrie's characterization of the native islanders lacks any distinction from the predecessor to which he refers. But just as he has done in the play, he will subvert this continuity through graphemes.

However, he first continues this referential chain to Cooper and such contemporaries when he next introduces the "redskins" "on the warpath following the pirates in single file" "to the redskin music" (Green 186). Subsequent scenes, such as the redskins smoking a pipe in front of their wigwams (197), do not introduce any revisionary imagery. However, just as he does in the play, Barrie saves his most dramatic problematization for the massacre scene:

> Now the scene changes to above ground. The pirate music is heard. The redskins start up into fighting positions, and at the same moment the pirates are upon them. Now takes place the great fight between pirates and redskins, which should be a much more realistic and grim affair than in the play. There it has to be more pretence, but here we should see real redskin warfare that will be recognized as such by all readers of Fenimore Cooper, etc. (Green 201)

His commentary juxtaposing "reality" (pointedly based on fiction) and fiction problematizes the "realistic and grim affair." This parallel with the play further illustrates the extent of Barrie's commitment to his pedagogy: despite changes in media and an explicit desire to create a different version of the play for film, Barrie retains the pedagogy that he performs in his play.

As the above examples reveal, Barrie advances a pedagogy that disrupts drives toward normalizing conventional racial categories as prediscursive and natural by emphasizing their rhetorical and artificial origins. By so qualifying the apparently stereotypical native Neverlanders, Barrie creates and deploys a hybrid that challenges the racist, ethnocentric, and nationalistic forces that this tribe seems to validate. In doing so, Barrie creates "an intermediate concept, between the local and the global," to borrow from Paul Gilroy, that can "break the dogmatic focus on *national* cultures and traditions which has characterized so much Euro-American cultural thought" (188).[12] Through such means, Barrie also promotes revisionism, a goal he shares with critics like Derrida, Said, and Spivak as well as a wider range of critics like Meaghan Morris, Michelle Wallace, and Cornel West.

Ascribing such a radically revisionist pedagogy to Barrie runs the risk of replicating the sorts of disingenuous appropriations of "otherness" and "difference" in the name of justifying exclusionary postmodern theories—the sorts of appropriation against which bell hooks warns (23–31). However, Barrie escapes such a charge through his concerted graphemes. Such a charge is applicable to many of those agencies that have adapted Barrie's play to reinscribe such categories, most notably Walt Disney Studios.

Numerous critics have explored the evolution and development of Disney Studios' racism as it manifests itself in animated films. For example, Eleanor Byrne and Martin McQuillan trace the uninterrupted (re)presentation of an "essentially bellicose nature of 'Red Indian' identity" from *Peter Pan* to *Pocahontas* (122). But in doing so, such critics often conflate the stabilizing hegemony of the culture industry with the heterogeneity of the original. Furthermore, such conflations enact the same sorts of erasure of specific identity in the service of production that these critics accuse Disney of performing. Absent from their analyses are the permutations created by Barrie in his versions of *Peter Pan*. Such oversight is understandable given the context into which the Disney film emerges.

Disney's racism in the 1950s is legendary. Frontierland represented Native-Americans as violent antagonists and African-Americans as servile slaves, thereby codifying racial identity within categories that stabilize racial otherness as part of a hierarchical, essentialist, and atemporal ordering of peoples and identity. Such ubiquitous formulas also devalue people of color for an Anglicized ideal by erasing any complexity for characters of color. Disney's 1953 animated version of

Peter Pan performs the same sorts of reductivism, radically erasing Barrie's (de)constructive categories in two major ways: overtly by obscuring Barrie's problematizing construction with a veneer of "play" and covertly by erasing the tribe's specificity and replacing it with a more invidious history of erasure. This erasure is the result of concentrated effort.

Disney's version of *Peter Pan* evolved over several decades and involved numerous authors. Disney first considered producing an animated version of *Peter Pan* in the mid-1930s and then invested extraordinary time and talent in revising the work until it released the final animated version in 1953. Walt Disney's comments at storyboard sessions for *Peter Pan* reveal his primary concerns with the film's editing: he was particularly concerned about developing the relationship between Hook and the crocodile; his comments do not address Neverland's tribe in any way (Thomas 221–22). Instead of (re)creating a polyphonous, organic (re)articulation of Barrie's productions, this lengthy effort by Disney represents a determined effort to control and authorize Barrie's play of differences. As Donald Crafton insightfully argues, Disney Studios "engaged in a systematic rewriting of the original text to reflect attitudes and assumptions that prevailed during the project's development in the 1940s, modifying it for a new pertinence" (34). This new pertinence manifests itself in overtly racist films like *Dumbo* (1941) and *Song of the South* (1946). As evidenced by its erasure of Barrie's problematizing elements, Disney's animated version of *Peter Pan* promotes racist and sexist perspectives.

Book versions of the Disney movie repeat this rhetoric. For example, Annie North Bedford's picture book adaptation of the Disney movie (1952), complete with illustrations by the Walt Disney Studios, collapses violence and play when it represents the Piccaninnies. That same year, another Little Golden Book version, *Walt Disney's Peter Pan,* emphasizes the violence of Disney's adaptation when it has Foxy and Cubby counter John's claims that he is "familiar with all the known tribes" of Indians: they pointedly explain to him that "these ain't tribe Injuns . . . these are scalpin' Injuns" (76). Such determinism and erasure of identity by Disney continues to this day, though often not as explicitly, as Monique Peterson's adaptation for Disney (2001) demonstrates by reproducing the animated version's plotline. Thanks to such Disneyfication, Michael, John, and the Lost Boys continue to "hunt" the Injuns and thereby perpetuate the racism so intentionally manifest in Disney's versions of Barrie's play.

More recent versions have avoided issues of identity generated by Barrie through the Piccaninnies. When famed fantasy author Terry Brooks adapted the screenplay of *Hook* into a novel (1991), he included only a passing reference to native Neverlanders: Peter Pan "lived in a world of pirates and Indians, of magical happenings, of time suspended and dreams come true" (94). Gerry Gravel's junior novelization of the movie (1991) also uses the Neverlanders only as a modifier of the Nevertree: "Taller than any redwood, the mighty tree reached toward the sky from its own small islet, safe from irate Indians and pillaging pirates alike" (35). Succinct though they may be, these references equate the island's tribal people and pirates—two groups that Barrie pointedly· distinguished from each other. By doing so, Brooks and Gravel enact the same sorts of erasure promoted by Disney's reauthorized version and perpetuate the same sorts of reductivism. Such erasure serves to promote the image of Barrie as racist. Only by returning to the Neverland that Barrie author(iz)ed can readers realize their critical mistake.

As we have seen, Barrie's works reveal how carefully and consistently he (re)articulates prior categories of racial, ethnic, and national identity to problematize their authority. To do so, he crafts graphemes—most dramatically in *Peter Pan*—to deconstruct such racialist binaries. Given the complexity and continuity of Barrie's pedagogy, we can no longer deny its centrality to his works. Rather than serving as an embarrassment to a classic of children's literature, the Piccaninnies in *Peter Pan* function as main characters in Barrie's play of differences. Through them he is able to say "something quite different."

NOTES

1. Typically, critics fall into the two categories that Jacqueline Rose so succinctly articulates when she writes "*Peter Pan* is sometimes scoffed at today for the excessive and cloying nature of its innocence. It is in fact one of the most fragmented and troubled works in the history of children's fiction" (10–11).

2. My use of terms here and throughout this paper reflects the sorts of counter-hegemonic constructions that Barrie promotes. With reference to Native-American peoples, I adopt Gerald Vizenor's injunctions about defining native identity in *Fugitive Poses* by my use of the term "native." To further emphasize its constructive nature, I also use the term "Neverlander(s)." Vizenor's quote below informs both my position and Barrie's (re)articulation of native peoples in his play: "The *indian* is a mundane romance, the advertisement of

the other in the narratives. Natives are elusive, the traces of presence are unnameable in literature; the origins are deferred, and the acts of reading native stories are the *différance*, a *postindian* 'fragmentary insight.' The tricky native, not the racialist simulation of the *indian*, is an invitation to a 'pleasurable misreading'" (35).

3. See David Pilgrim's website for a thorough survey of such images.

4. As the extensive research of Ross Woodrow chronicles, prejudicial images of Aboriginal peoples coincide with increased colonization of Australia and its native peoples by Anglo Australians.

5. Their invisibility becomes apparent, for example, in George Henry Payne's review of one of the play's first London productions, in which he defines them only in terms of the massacre: "Then the Indians fight the pirates, but are defeated in a terrible battle" (Hammerton 352). Payne avoids any negative terms like "Piccaninny" and casts them as the victims of pirate violence, but his conventional rhetoric reduces their importance.

6. Roger Lancelyn Green reproduces this photograph between pages 66 and 67.

7. Green reproduces Nicholson's designs in the section of illustrations after page 146, and Susan Aller reproduces the pen-and-ink drawings for the second London production (91).

8. Significantly, in the first versions Barrie had defined Peter's patriarchy in less overt terms, merely calling him "cocky" and "like a king to his subjects" (Green 199). Here, in his final, definitive statement, he foregrounds the silencing inherent in colonial relations with subalterns.

9. All references to the novelized version of *Peter Pan* come from the 2000 edition illustrated by Raquel Jamarillo.

10. All of Barrie's writings emphasize the centrality of adventure fiction to his youth. From his first articulation of it in *Margaret Ogilvy* (1897), he continued such claims throughout his career. For example, in 1924 he summarized his early reading as comprised of "magazines containing exclusively sanguinary matter" (Hammerton 55).

11. The movie poster can be accessed online through moviegoods.com or mysci-fi.com.

12. This reference comes from Gilroy's argument about the black Atlantic world and the ethics of cultural studies, but it is applicable to Barrie's pedagogy.

WORKS CITED

Aller, Susan Bivin. *J. M. Barrie: The Magic Behind Peter Pan.* Minneapolis: Lerner, 1994.

Barrie, James Matthew. *J. M. Barrie's Peter Pan and Wendy.* Illus. Gwynedd M. Hudson. London: Hodder & Stoughton, 1931.

———. "Neil and Tintinabalum." *The Flying Carpet.* Ed. Cynthia Asquith. New York: Scribner's, 1925. 65–95.

———. *Peter and Wendy.* 1911. New York: Scribner's, 1926.

———. *Peter Pan.* 1911. Illus. Raquel Jaramillo. New York: Simon & Schuster, 2000.

———. *Peter Pan in Kensington Gardens.* Illus. Arthur Rackham. New York: Weathervane Books, 1975.

———. *The Plays.* 1928. New York: Scribner's, 1956.

Bedford, Annie North. *Peter Pan and Wendy.* Racine, WI: Western Publishing, 1952.

Bhabha, Homi. "The Other Question: Stereotype, Discrimination and the Discourse of Colonialism." *The Location of Culture.* London: Routledge, 1994.

Brooks, Terry. *Hook.* New York: Ballantine, 1991.

Byrne, Eleanor, and Martin McQuillan. *Deconstructing Disney.* London: Pluto, 1999.

Byron, May, adapt. *J. M. Barrie's Peter Pan in Kensington Gardens.* New York: Scribner's, 1930.

Crafton, Donald. "The Last Night in the Nursery: Walt Disney's *Peter Pan.*" *The Velvet Light Trap* 24 (Fall 1989): 33–52.

Derrida, Jacques. "Genesis and Structure of the Essay on the Origin of Languages." *Of Grammatology.* Trans. Gayatri Chakravorty Spivak. Baltimore: Johns Hopkins UP, 1974. 165–268.

Dubowski, Cathy East, adapt. *Peter Pan.* 1991. New York: Random House, 1994.

Gilroy, Paul. "Cultural Studies and Ethnic Absolutism." *Cultural Studies.* Ed. Lawrence Grossberg, Cary Nelson, and Paula Treichner. New York: Routledge, 1992. 187–98.

Gravel, Geary. *Hook.* New York: Fawcett Columbine, 1991.

Green, Roger Lancelyn. *Fifty Years of Peter Pan.* London: Peter Davies, 1954.

Hammerton, Sir James Alexander. *Barrie: The Story of a Genius.* New York: Dodd, Mead, 1929.

hooks, bell. "Postmodern Blackness." *Yearning: Race, Gender and Cultural Politics.* Boston: South End Press, 1990. 23–31.

Jack, R. D. S. "From Drama to Silent Film: The Case of Sir James Barrie." *International Journal of Scottish Theatre* 2.2 (Dec. 2001). Online. 2 Sept. 2004 <http://arts.qmuc.ac.uk/ijost/Volume2_no2/2_jack_rds.htm>.

Moore, Bob, adapt. *Walt Disney's Peter Pan and the Pirates.* New York: Simon & Schuster, 1952.

Peterson, Monique, adapt. *Peter Pan.* By J. M. Barrie. New York: Disney, 2001.

Pilgrim, David. "Jim Crow Museum of Racist Memorabilia." Oct. 2000. Online. 2 Sept. 2004 <www.ferris.edu/news/jimcrow/picaninny/>.

Reid, Captain Mayne. *The Scalp Hunters: A Thrilling Tale of Adventure and Romance in Northern Mexico.* 1851. New York: Hurst, 1899.

———. *The White Chief: A Legend of North Mexico.* New York: Carleton, 1872.

Rose, Jacqueline. *The Case of Peter Pan; Or, the Impossibility of Children's Fiction.* New York: MacMillan, 1984.

Thomas, Bob. *Walt Disney.* 1976. New York: Disney, 1994.

Vizenor, Gerald. *Fugitive Poses: Native American Indian Scenes of Absence and Presence.* Lincoln: U of Nebraska P, 1998.

Walt Disney's Peter Pan. Racine, WI: Whitman, 1952.

Wilson, Phoebe, adapt. *Peter Pan.* Illus. Ruth Wood. New York: Grossett and Dunlap, 1956.

Woodrow, Ross. "Images of Race & Image Archive: Relations Between Paintings and Words." Online. 2 Sept. 2004 <www.worldartcelebritiesjournal3 .netfirms.com/analysis.htm>.

7

The Birth of a Lost Boy: Traces of J. M. Barrie's *Peter Pan* in Willa Cather's *The Professor's House*

Rosanna West Walker

> Peter was not quite like other boys; but he was afraid at last. A tremor ran through him, like a shudder passing over the sea. . . . Next moment he was standing erect on the rock again, with that smile on his face and a drum beating within him. It was saying, "To die will be an awfully big adventure."
>
> —J. M. Barrie, *Peter and Wendy*

> St. Peter could remember a time when the loneliness of death had terrified him. . . . He set off down the street, sniffing the lake-cooled morning air and trying to overcome a feeling of nervous dread. . . . Yet when he was confronted by accidental extinction, he had felt no will to resist.
>
> —Willa Cather, *The Professor's House*

The reader who is familiar with J. M. Barrie's story of Peter Pan and Wendy can more fully understand the essential and fascinating chain of events in Willa Cather's *The Professor's House* (1925). What story could be more important than *Peter and Wendy* to a writer like Cather, who frequently wrote about adolescence and growing up in her novels? Susan J. Rosowski notes that "adolescence is one of the most important subjects of Willa Cather's fiction, one she treated far more extensively than she did subjects with which she is most identified" ("Writing Against Silences" 60). While Cather deals with female development in much of her writing (*Lucy Gayheart, My Ántonia, The Song of the Lark*), *The Professor's House* considers male growth and progression. Barrie's ideas about sex, romance, growing up, sense of place, and the importance of story—especially oral narrative—fit very well with Cather's. Both Barrie and Cather designed a character—Peter Pan and Tom Outland, respectively—who seems to suddenly pop into existence, surprising the other characters in the novels as well as the readers. Barrie fostered this ability in the character of Peter Pan, who not only appears magically in the Darling nursery, but whose bronze statue suddenly showed up in the middle of London in a corner of Kensington Gardens. It was erected behind screens during the night, so that on the morning of the first day in May, 1912, passersby might think it appeared magically.

As one of Barrie's fans, Cather was pleased when, later in her life, he wanted autographed copies of *her* books (Woodress 502). She was familiar with his works; indeed, as my analysis will show, she drew upon motifs, imagery, symbols, metaphors, and characters from *Peter and Wendy* for *The Professor's House*. In addition, she drew on the overly publicized events she knew about in Barrie's personal life to portray aspects of the professor's relationship with Tom Outland, the boy who appears suddenly in Professor St. Peter's garden. Of course, Cather's plot outlines and characters are not exactly like Barrie's, but it is possible to approach her novel and ferret out the similarities to his famous work, and thus better understand Cather's cryptic story.

In *The Professor's House*, the protagonist, Godfrey St. Peter, is a professor of history at a university in the Midwest. The professor has lived all of his married life in the antiquated house from which his family has just moved. He decides he cannot bear to work in the new house just yet and arranges to continue renting the aged but familiar dwelling in which he has lived, so that he can work in his study until his current writing project is completed. Resolved to create a written composition resembling a musical arrangement, Cather divided *The Professor's House* into three segments (Books I, II, and III) similar to the three movements of a sonata (Woodress 370). In Book I, Professor Godfrey St. Peter is in conflict with his family, their conventionalism, avarice, and cosmopolitan affairs—things that are in opposition to his profound sense of loss at the death of his young heroic friend and student, Tom Outland. Tom Outland's inventions were left to one of St. Peter's daughters, Rosamond (Tom's fiancée), and sudden wealth has fostered an attitude of materialism and created discord between his two daughters. Book II is a long personal narrative by the deceased Tom Outland. It takes the reader back in time, and it is here that Cather shifts her focus from St. Peter and his family to Tom Outland and his past. Book III is about Professor St. Peter and his near brush with death and subsequent rescue by Augusta, the family sewing woman.

Scholars have analyzed *The Professor's House* as a well-formed work without realizing that Barrie inspired Cather. Those who have attempted to comprehend and explicate the formal basis of Cather's artistry specific to *The Professor's House* have had little to go on, not only because this work is difficult, but also because, as a review of the literature will show, Cather was intentionally obscure when discussing it. An understanding of the significance of the Peter Pan motifs sheds light not only on Cather's structure, but also on meaning in *The Professor's House*. Why "Tom Outland's Story" was written stylistically to be a story-within-a-story has prompted endless speculation, but a comparison with some of Barrie's themes, and with the idea of Neverland itself, reveals so much about Cather's linkage of adventure, change, death, and loss that it is as if cobwebs obscuring the light had suddenly been swept away. As critics have noted, this is a novel of life passages, but it is also about a sense of childhood place and about treachery, piracy, and greed. Barrie wove all of these themes together in *Peter Pan*, in which he clearly aims the level of irony at adults. An examination of how Cather drew upon the motifs present in the most famous play in the United States in her time reveals much about how she viewed aging and death.

Both of Cather's central male characters share attributes with Peter Pan, but Tom Outland, the deceased boy with the "strange" past who came through St. Peter's garden gate one day, remains the quintessential Peter Pan–like child—forever a dream in the minds of those who loved him. Professor Godfrey St. Peter, despite his name, is more like one of the Lost Boys because, unlike Peter Pan or Tom Outland, he ultimately chooses to grow up. Conversely, the women in the novel accept maturity without reservation, just like Wendy.

Barrie's Wendy and Cather's Augusta are strong female protagonists who function and perform as surrogate mothers, seamstresses, storytellers, and spiritual midwives. The vision that informs both novels is created from the concerns of these women as mothers and healers. Cather's Augusta is "a reliable methodical spinster, a German Catholic and very devout" (17). Readers do not meet Peter Pan's Wendy as an old woman until the end of *Peter and Wendy*, but throughout the story—even as a child—she tends to the needs of her family: sewing, putting on bandages, and mothering. The signs of Wendy's maternal reliability can be felt early on when Peter Pan entices her to go with him to Neverland because he wants her to tell stories to him:

> "Wendy," he said, the sly one, "you could tuck us in at night."
> "Oo!"
> "None of us has ever been tucked in at night."
> "Oo,"and her arms went out to him.
> "And you could darn our clothes, and make pockets for us. None of us has any pockets."
> How could she resist? (49)

How characters mirror each other in the two works is interesting and important, but Cather's reading of Barrie also directly influences the main themes at play in *The Professor's House*: the chasm between dreams and reality; the connection between death and rebirth; and the male longing to return to a maternal presence. Not only did Cather feel directly inspired by Barrie, but she was also, like many others in American and European culture, influenced by the idea of *The Boy Who Would Not Grow Up* (the original title of *Peter Pan*)—a symbol that had begun to permeate modern Western culture by 1915, by which time millions had seen the play or read the book.

Since its publication in 1925, critics have asked many questions about *The Professor's House*. Cather's biographers have offered various explanations for the unusual story, which Cather called "a nasty, grim little tale" (Woodress 367). By her own admission, the work is an experiment in form—"the device often used by the early French and Spanish novelists; that of inserting the *Nouvelle* into the *Roman*" ("On *The Professor's House*," reprinted in the scholarly edition of *The Professor's House* 335). Indeed, "Tom Outland's Story" can stand on its own and has often been published separately, but the question remains: were there other reasons for the use of this device—reasons that Cather, who was quite secretive about her methodology (particularly with this book), chose not to tell? She mentions seeing Dutch paintings of interiors with windows "through which one saw the masts of ships, or a stretch of grey sea" (336). In Professor St. Peter's "stuffy" and "overcrowded" house, she installed one of these open windows to "let in the fresh air that blew off the Blue Mesa, and the fine disregard of trivialities which was in Tom Outland's face and in his behaviour" (336).

These comments were in the form of a letter to Pat Knopf, her publisher's son, and they were among the few explanatory words Cather ever offered about the writing of *The Professor's House*. She reiterated this story in an interview with Alice Booth, emphasizing one painting in particular, which showed

> through an open window a sunlit wharf with fishing boats ready to set off for all the magic ports of the seven seas—brighter and more alluring for the very grayness of medium surrounding that open window into all the possibilities and all the promise of a rainbow future. (Cather, *Willa Cather in Person* 125)

Because she remained mostly silent about her writing process, particularly about *The Professor's House*, these words are quoted in almost every critical analysis of the novel. In *Willa Cather: Double Lives*, Hermione Lee says that "Tom Outland's story derives from the raw material of Cather's own past" (229). Cather's friend Edith Lewis agreed that *The Professor's House* is "the most personal" of Cather's novels (137). Some critics see the book as hopeful; some see it as tragic. Rosowski discusses the fact that Cather used settings that "have only the slightest concern with circumstantial reality" (*Voyage Perilous* 131–39). Stephen Tennant, in his preface to *Willa Cather on Writing*, believes that Cather brought to the story "something beyond the story itself—the unseen vision, the unheard echo, which attend all experience" (vii). Dorothy McFarland, in her biography of Cather, proposes,

> The emergence of [Professor St. Peter's] boyhood self and his seeming drift toward death are puzzling and difficult to deal with if taken literally; they seem to suggest a kind of Freudian regression to childhood or prenatal unconsciousness in the face of insoluble difficulties in adult life. (82)

McFarland views the emergence of his boyhood self, however, as a rebirth, citing Jung's idea that the archetype of the child has a redemptive significance: "as the child archetype symbolizes the whole nature of man, it reaches back to the preconscious life of early childhood and forward to 'an anticipation by analogy of life after death'" (82).

E. K. Brown thinks that *The Professor's House* reveals Cather's "desolate" feelings about aging. David Stouck says that the novel has "puzzled literary critics" more than any other of Cather's books (96). In fact, *The Professor's House* continues to be one of Cather's most debated books. On the other hand, as Stephen L. Tanner rather humorously puts it:

> The professor's house has been thoroughly searched. It is as though search warrants had been issued wholesale. The attic study has been exhaustively examined for clues. The dress forms in particular have been subjected to minute laboratory analysis by a variety of forensic experts. Even the garden has been combed for the slightest intimation of evidence. The result is a substantial and surprisingly disparate body of testimony. (qtd. in Stouck 109)

The fact is, however, that this flowering of criticism is recent; in the 1960s, *The Professor's House* was not very well known (Schroeter 368). Besides the often-quoted remarks in her letter to Knopf, Cather, who made few comments about any of her works, did say a few things to her friends. She told Elizabeth Shepley Sergeant that the deep theme of *The Professor's House* "was the connection between youth and age, and the way they mutually stirred one another" (Sergeant 204). Sergeant says that Tom Outland is a "meteor" who draws "St. Peter's routine and inner life out of focus." Many critics have tried to make a decision regarding whether Tom Outland is a caricature of someone Cather knew. Sergeant says, "We have heard of this earth boy before" (Sergeant 214).

Earlier critics, Lillian and Edward Bloom, noted that Cather's work "depends for its essential meaning upon a secondary level of interpretation" (14). According to Joseph R. Urgo, this places Cather "in the allegorist tradition of Dante and Kafka" (qtd. in Lee 23). Upon what raw material did Cather draw? What is "the wider connection with her whole writing life," to which Hermione Lee alludes (204)? Lee says the book's "'massive dislocation' was very much in keeping with [Cather's] persistent interest in doubleness" (233). She draws on a statement Cather made once, that "the primitive real self is pre-sexual" (241). Cather also said that *The Professor's House* was written in "a middle-aged mood" (qtd. in Robinson 240). These statements focus on the critical confusion about *The Professor's House* while at the same time recognizing its nostalgic look at childhood.

Scholars say that Cather was inspired by other artists: Richard Dillman reads Tom Outland "as an American archetype," and he analyzes Tom in light of his "Emersonian qualities" (375); Alice Hall Petry agrees with Barbara Wild that Cather draws heavily upon the relationship between Christ and St. Peter in the Christian Bible (29); Thomas Strychacz suggests that "the echoes of 'The Pit and the Pendulum' are a tribute to her fascination with Poe" (57); Missy Dehn Kubitschek states that the "underlying myth capable of uniting these disparate issues [the social/personal split of St. Peter] . . . is surely that of *Paradise Lost*" (13); and Rosowski and Bernice Slote show that "the major source for 'Tom Outland's Story' is, of course, the account of Richard Wetherill," an early explorer of Mesa Verde (85). Merrill Skaggs discusses the fact that scholars have found literary sources for *The Professor's House* in such disparate works as Thomas Carlyle's *Sartor Resartus*, Washington Irving's *Rip Van Winkle*, Anatole France Thibault's *Le Mannequin D'Osier*, Milton's *Paradise Lost*, and Brahms' *Requiem*. Skaggs agrees that all of this information adds to our understanding of Cather's work:

> In fact, the first problem when we consider *The Professor's House* is to keep lungs breathing and eyes focused while the scholarly facts swirl around us. But all these facts have not yet added up to an inclusive and coherent reading of the book. It is therefore time to ask again (and in asking, identify) the most basic questions which are crucial here: what is the primary thing Cather is doing in this novel? Why does she shape this story this way? (422)

There is one source that has not been discussed. Concerning *The Professor's House*, Cather said, "Desire is the magical element" in the creative process (qtd. in Bloom 18). Desire is also the magical element that threads through *Peter and Wendy*: desire to make dreams come true, to find a mother, and to stay in the realm of the pre-sexual self. Could it be that we all have, as Sergeant said, "heard of this earth boy before"? Barrie's Peter Pan is the character upon which both Professor St. Peter and Tom Outland are based. Tennant's idea of "the unseen vision, the unheard echo" and McFarland's claim that Professor St. Peter's boyhood self and his apparent impulse toward ending his life hint at a kind of Freudian regression to childhood are actually both part of the connection to Peter Pan and Neverland. Why, as Rosowski asks, does *The Professor's House* "strain against the logic of the everyday world?" (*Voyage Perilous* 133). If Cather was an allegorist, then it makes sense that she would have seen how the Peter Pan stories were so integral to her vision. In fact, Cather invoked Barrie's famous motifs (to a lesser degree) in some of her other works as well.[1]

The real proof of Cather's interest in Barrie's themes lies within the text of *The Professor's House*, but it is useful to situate both writers within their social and working circles—circles that, after they were both established authors, overlapped constantly. Pulitzer Prize–winning author Cather (1876–1947) began her career as a journalist before writing the novels that would make her famous. In a curious foreshadowing of her later work, Cather said, "[T]he Scotch fiction of this decade is the cry of the new childhood in us" ("Passing Show" 13). In a letter to William Lyon Phelps, Cather said that she "[h]ad little direct contact with Barrie because of his shyness" (qtd. in Stout 253). She traveled to Europe many time and belonged to the same trans-Atlantic social circles Barrie did. They had mutual friends—George Meredith, William Archer, H. G. Wells, and others. Archer took her to Meredith's funeral, which Barrie attended. As biographers James Woodress and Janice Stout note, Barrie and Cather read each other's works and discussed them in letters to friends.

Barrie introduced Peter Pan to the world in *The Little White Bird* (1902), which was a colossal best seller. The theme was popular in America: Peter Pan escapes from his nursery to live on an island in the Serpentine River. He resolves to return home, dreams that his mother is crying, and flies straight to the nursery window, only to find it barred. Upon peering in, he sees that his mother has given birth to another little boy and therefore does not need him anymore. The publication of the *Little White Bird* and the production of *Peter Pan* (1904) occurred while Cather was sitting squarely in the middle of the world of art, first as a drama critic, and then as an executive at *McClure's Magazine*.

The American version of the play *Peter Pan* opened in New York on November 6, 1905. Mark Twain said, "The next best play is a long way behind it" (Robinson 90–91). As Andrew Birkin writes, "The American public embraced *Peter Pan* with a fervour that made its London success seem almost trivial. It became the topic of much earnest analysis and intellectual vivisection among adults" (126). Audiences suddenly became "nursery-conscious, fairy-conscious, pirate-conscious, and . . . Redskin-conscious" (Mackail 379).

By 1907, Barrie was regarded as "the most praised and successful dramatist alive" (Peter Davies, qtd. in Birkin 148), and Willa Cather, from Red Cloud, Nebraska, had made it to the publishing capital of the United States and to the staff of a great national magazine, *McClure's*. Scottish writers, like Barrie, intrigued Cather, who felt that the world was "jaded" and that people wanted to "begin anew"; these writers fulfilled this hope. She said "Barrie, Crockett, and Watson have taken the sentiment and quiet pathos that have lain for years in the old Scotch ballads . . . and given it to the world when the world most needed it" ("Passing Show" 13).

Cather was steeped in the world of literature and drama and ready to give her public a unique reading experience. She emulated no one. Rather, she took the images that mattered to her the most and gave them the benefit of her own contradictions, her own impasses, her own transcendent passions. Like the tracings of veins in a skeleton leaf from Neverland, the imprint of *Peter Pan* begins to assert itself in Cather's first novel (often considered the prototype of *The Professor's House*), *Alexander's Bridge* (1911), which has a male protagonist who cannot face growing older and a female who refuses to embrace youth. James Woodress says that the protagonist, Bartley, remembers his missing youth and "yearns and seeks for something he cannot find . . . [which is] a *leitmotif* through Cather's fiction" (220), and of course, in the *Peter Pan* play and stories.

Critics often say that Barrie's work has strong autobiographical elements. Most of the criticism about Cather says the same and that her work often yearns backward "to a vanished youth, a vanished era" (McFarland 1–2). Barrie himself has often been labeled "the boy who couldn't grow up" or the real "Lost Boy." Historical interpretations of their lives and art show that, without a doubt, both Barrie and Cather drew upon real events for their stories, but some presumptions based upon comparisons have the potential to trivialize their work. The truth is that both Barrie and Cather used themes that invoked metaphors of growing up, growing older, rebirth, and dying because they knew how to do it better than just about anyone else. There was, according to Denis Mackail, no attitude in America that *Peter Pan* "was only or essentially a play for children—as it most certainly isn't" (379). The fact that Barrie appeals equally to adults as to children and that Cather relocated themes often found in children's books to adult literature with such consistency defies explanations from critics who belong to the "she/he never grew up school"; both Barrie and Cather knew full well that the reflection of the self marks a discursive space wherein all may enter. Barrie hated the label "whimsical," a term often applied to his work by critics. A tour of *The Professor's House* shows that Cather conceived and wrote it in such a way that she could use Barrie's famous characters and motifs and no one would think *it* whimsical. When the novel is examined against the backdrop of the Peter Pan stories, it is not difficult to see the characters' actions and settings in terms of Barrie's themes.

In *The Professor's House*, the protagonist, Napoleon Godfrey St. Peter, as a professor of history, has for over twenty years worked in a sort of attic-study on the third floor of his old home—a study he has shared with Augusta, the woman who sews all of the clothes for his family. His life's work is an eight-volume history of the Spanish adventurers in North America, which won him the Oxford prize that enables his "fair, pink and gold" wife, Lillian, to build a new home (37). St. Peter watches the negative effects more wealth has on his family, especially since Rosamond, his "brilliantly beautiful" eldest daughter, has inherited a huge fortune from her late fiancé, Tom Outland (who remains the most beloved person in the professor's life) but is now happily married to the energetic Louie Marsellus. Kathleen, his artistic younger daughter, is married to Scott McGregor, who writes editorials for the local paper. Rosamond's inheritance seems to have brought out the worst in the two sisters. When talking about the ways in which Rosamond and Louie have marketed Tom's invention, the Outland engine, Kathleen remarks to her father, "Now he's all turned out chemicals and dollars and cents, hasn't he? But not for you and me! Our Tom is much nicer than theirs" (130).

The story opens with Professor St. Peter working in his old office—the only room with any furniture left, since they have moved everything to the new house. St. Peter's conflict involves confusion about aging, doubt regarding the loyalty of loved ones, and repugnance toward marriage and women. He tries to find ways to endure an emotional emergency that he cannot accept; the loss of Tom Outland devastated him. Like the Lost Boys in Neverland, Professor St. Peter lives in a mental Neverland devoid of enduring female companionship, and he has had no adventures of his own since Tom died. He lives in the past now and feels estranged from his materialistic wife and daughters. When Augusta comes to move her sewing belongings from the empty house, especially some dress forms, he protests vehemently: "I can't have this room changed if I'm going to work here. . . . [P]ut her [the dress form] back on the chest where she belongs, please. She does very well there. . . . You shan't take away my ladies. I never heard of such a thing!" (22). Augusta wonders how she will work without them and reminds him that he has always complained of them in the past. The professor replies, "I never complained, Augusta. Perhaps of certain disappointments they recalled, or of cruel biological necessities they imply—but of them individually, never. . . . Go buy, but you can't have my women" (22). With that, he offers to purchase new ones, and the old dressmaking forms become his. The professor's women include "[t]he bust," which belongs in the "darkest corner of the room" on top of "a high wooden chest" (18). It is "a headless, armless female torso, covered with strong black cotton, and so richly developed" that the professor used to make risqué jokes about it:

It is also ample and billowy (as if you might lay your head upon its deep-breathing softness and rest safe forever) . . . but if you touched it you suffered a severe shock. . . . [I]t presented the most unsympathetic surface imaginable. (18)

The other form looks like

a full-length female figure in a smart wire skirt with a trim metal waist line. . . . [I]t ha[s] no legs . . . and no viscera behind its glistening ribs. . . . [I]ts bosom resemble[s] a strong wire bird-cage. But St. Peter contended that it had a nervous system. . . . At times the wire lady was most convincing in her pose as a woman of light behaviour, but she never fooled St. Peter. (19)

Therefore, St. Peter's "women," the ones he cannot live without, are voiceless, mutilated, and docile, while at the same time they evoke images of maternity and whoredom. Out of what particularized view do the professor's statements emerge? Like the Lost Boys who long for a mother, St. Peter wants to lay his head on a "safe" bosom. His surrogate mother—the black-clothed bust—is always "fooling" him by behaving other than a mother should. In like manner, the "wire-lady" promises sex but cannot deliver. These dressmaker's busts remain permanently on the dresser unable to speak, like Tinker Bell, locked up in a drawer the night Peter Pan meets Wendy. Tinker Bell is "slightly inclined to *embonpoint*" and uses offensive language and gestures. She wears a gown "cut low and square, through which her figure can be seen to the best advantage" (Barrie, *Peter and Wendy* 35). She promises but cannot deliver and is jealous that Wendy will be Peter's mother now. The scene between Augusta (surrogate mother), Professor St. Peter, and the mute busts, which the professor infuses with life, mirrors the scene in *Peter Pan* in which the busty Tinker Bell is relegated to the dresser drawer.

Professor St. Peter knows he must face life as it really is. He has rented the old house for a year but realizes he cannot stave off change forever. He must go and take up his rightful place in the new house and participate in the family life he has been evading. This avoidance of participating in real family life is the hallmark of Peter Pan. When, in *Peter and Wendy*, the Lost Boys are preparing to leave Neverland forever, Peter Pan says, "If you find your mothers, I hope you will like them," and the Lost Boys "look rather doubtful" at what they were about to do though they knew they must (158). Peter Pan toys with the idea of barring the nursery window so that when all the children return, they cannot gain admittance. Nevertheless, he knows, as Professor St. Peter knows, that some things are inevitable, and he flies away without barring it (222).

The seeds of St. Peter's ultimate transformation are sown in his feeling that he cannot "evade the unpleasant effects of change by tarrying among his autumn flowers. . . . He must plunge in like a man" (16). The implication here is that change means accepting the past and moving into the future, which means growing older, facing death, and owning up to his grown-up role: a man who cannot run off anymore with Tom Outland to exotic places. He must return to the realization that part of his life is over; he must take up conventional living. In the end, he realizes that Tom Outland is never coming through the garden door again ("as he had so often done in dreams"): "This boy and he had meant, back in those far-away days, to live some sort of life together . . . [but] they were unevenly matched" (263). In this same way, ultimately, the Lost Boys cannot stay with Peter Pan. It is clear, by the nature of the name, that a Lost Boy wants to be found. The Lost Boys are present and vocal throughout *Peter and Wendy*, and Professor St. Peter's voice is central to *The Professor's House*. He is lost in the past and longs to find a way to face the future—to grow up.

Why is it that Peter Pan has no interest in being discovered or recovered? He is a mysterious personage. If he, more than any other character in the story, longs for a return to a female presence, then why does he evade one? It is an interesting predicament that Peter Pan, in *Peter and Wendy*, and Tom Outland, in *The Professor's House*, do a mediocre job of representing themselves. We may know Peter Pan a little better than Tom Outland, but neither is present in the day-to-day lives of those who have chosen to grow up. Rather, they live in the minds and dreams of others and their representations must be, by nature, shadowy and vague.

Even more than St. Peter, Tom—Cather's young genius, who, at the age of twenty, suddenly appears one day in the garden—is a model of Peter Pan. Recognizing this is important in understanding the novel. Cather describes St. Peter as a middle-aged man who is disgruntled about the way his life has turned out, and Tom Outland enters his life just when "the morning brightness of the world was wearing off for him," bringing him "a kind of second youth" (258).

After the meeting in the garden, Tom stays with Professor St. Peter's family on and off for years. He goes to college, and "before he dashes off to the front [of World War I]," develops a unique aviation device

called the "Outland engine" that he patents (42). True to Tom's im-
petuousness, he never takes the time to see his brilliant discovery
through the manufacturing and sales process; like Peter Pan, who tires
readily of an adventure or actually forgets that he agreed to a promise,
Tom has great vision but finds it hard to sustain it. Before meeting the
professor and his family for the first time, the adolescent Tom lived ad-
venturously on an obscure mesa in the southwest. He left his diary
there and later goes on a trip to the mesa with the professor to retrieve
it. Soon after, Tom dies in World War I, and Louie Marsellus, Rosamond's new husband, finds the wherewithal to market Tom's Outland
engine.

Though the professor wishes for eternal youth, Tom seems to be the
quintessential boy who never grows up. Many details give away his Peter Pan qualities. First, he is a sort of super-human character who lives
outside of real time, as evidenced by an outburst from Kathleen, the
professor's daughter, one evening at dinner: "Mother, what do you
think! Tom hasn't any birthday" (121). He does not have a birthday because, like Peter Pan, he does not need one for his character to function.
He seems, like Peter Pan, to live outside of real time. When Wendy asks
Peter how old he is, he tells her he doesn't know because he ran away
when he was born. When the professor asks Tom how old he is, Tom
blushes, and St. Peter finds that he really has no idea. Tom also seems a
bit like a runaway. He worked as "a call boy" for "train men," and he is
not used to a regularly ordered household (114). Peter Pan's ageless-
ness manifests itself by the fact that he still has his baby teeth; likewise,
Tom's age when he was adopted was determined by his new mother:
"They thought he must be a year and a half, because he was so big, but
Mrs. O'Brien always said he didn't have enough teeth for that," Kathleen
tells her parents (121). Peter Pan states that he has no mother and no address; Tom Outland's parents died when he was a baby while they were
moving west in a prairie schooner, and he worked on a freight train as
an adolescent; therefore, he has no address either.

Book I and Book III are about the professor and his family, but Book
II is a long personal narrative told by Tom, and it is a bold digression
into his past on the Blue Mesa. Later, St. Peter and Tom recover Tom's
diary from its hiding place there, but as the professor reveals, the diary
is a "plain account," with an "austerity" of words, and recounts things
like the weather (262). So if "Tom Outland's Story" is not the diary of
which the professor speaks, whose voice is the narrative voice of "Tom
Outland's Story"? It is here that Cather shifts her focus from St. Peter

and his family to Tom and his past. Besides recounting Tom's adventures on the mesa, she changes the fabric of time, presenting the young genius as an active presence in the book instead of a shadowy ghost. Tom narrates the tale of his ramblings, his discovery of the Indian artifacts, and his pent-up desire to interest the government in preserving them. Like the adventure stories Tom tells St. Peter's little girls, there are pirates, landscapes like Neverland, and Indian ruins. The professor lives in his imagination with Tom Outland on the mesa. Tom "had been a stroke of chance he couldn't possibly have imagined; his strange coming, his strange story, his devotion, his early death and posthumous fame—it was all fantastic" (257–58).

Inexplicably, upon meeting Tom for the first time, St. Peter feels fear, like the fear he feels when he knows the seamstress, Augusta, may come to his room the night he almost dies. It seems that, of all the people he knew, these two were unusually astute. He knows that "the unusual becomes commonplace by a natural law" (120). Like Peter Pan, who comes to the nursery window without prior announcement to hear Wendy's stories, Tom shows up at unexpected moments to tell the professor's little girls stories "when there [is] no one by to listen" (121). Like his life, the stories he relates of his adventures often do not seem to happen in real time, and they lack consistency just like Peter Pan's. For instance, when relating facts about his trip to Washington, D.C., to Mrs. St. Peter, Tom gets the time wrong. The girls, who have memorized the details of his life from his stories, correct him: "But, Tom, you were on the section gang that year! Why do you mix us all up?" asks Kathleen (170–71, 172). Lillian (Mrs. St. Peter) begins to worry:

> In personal relations, he was exaggerated and quixotic. . . . Tom, Lillian reminded her husband, was far from frank, though he had such an open manner. He had been consistently reserved about his own affairs, and she could not believe the facts he withheld were altogether creditable. . . . [I]n the stories he told the children, there were "no shadows." (169–70)

The concern Mrs. St. Peter feels matches the way Mrs. Darling worries at her children's accounts of Peter Pan's visits: "My child," she cries to Wendy, "Why did you not tell me of this before?" (17). One day, Mrs. Darling tries to catch him, "but his shadow had not had time to get out; slam went the window and snapped it off" (21). She "put it away carefully in a drawer" (22).

"Tom Outland's Story" makes it is clear that Tom, like Peter Pan, is adventurous, lives dangerously, and is unafraid of death. The summer before meeting the professor's family, Tom and his friend, Blake, have taken a job driving cattle in the Southwest. Tom is fascinated by a canyon behind a high cliff. "Nobody has ever got into it yet," says the foreman, Rapp, speaking of the Blue Mesa, because the way into it is "through that deep canyon that opens on the water level, just where the river makes the bend. You can't get in by that, because the river's too deep to ford and too swift to swim" (188–89). Before the foreman leaves, he forbids Tom and Blake to climb the high rock fortress—the only way to enter the Blue Mesa, making it increasingly "tantalizing" (189).

Tom's Neverland is very like Peter Pan's. "Second to the right, and straight on till morning" are the directions that Peter uses to guide the Darling children to Neverland (56). After several days' journey, "a million golden arrows" from the sun direct them (61). The children see a lagoon, caves, and the Mysterious River winding through a landscape with "astonishing splashes of colour here and there . . . that become so vivid . . . they go on fire" (13, 114). The children and the Lost Boys live in an underground cave of a house with a recess in the wall, "no larger than a bird-cage," which is the private apartment of Tinker Bell (106). Their adventures happen at places with names like "Slightly Gulch" or the "Mermaid's Lagoon." Similarly, as Tom and Blake approach the Blue Mesa, they see that it is "no longer a blue, featureless lump" but ringed with trees, and the river, which is "invisible at a distance," is "fringed with beautiful growth . . . like the hanging gardens of Babylon" (189–90). The mesa tempts Tom because, like the Neverland, it is "always changing. . . . The mesa top would be red with sunrise [and] . . . the rocks would be gold . . . like a blazing volcanic mountain . . . against a sky on fire" (190–91). He and Blake decide to spend the summer exploring it. The mesa is full of "deep caverns," and when they finally figure a way to get into the box canyon on the other side, Tom finds a city of "immortal repose" preserved in "almost perpetual sunlight like a fly in amber" in an ancient site of cliff-dwelling Indians in a cavern of "perpetual twilight" (200, 207). The "town hung like a bird's nest in the cliff," and Tom regards it as a sacred place where "the arc of sky over the canyon [is] silvery blue . . . and stars shiver" (211, 220, 249). After this idyllic summer, Tom leaves for Washington, D.C., to convince the Smithsonian, albeit unsuccessfully due to lack of interest and funding, to save the ruins (222). The history of Tom's adventures on the Blue Mesa would have been largely lost had he not stuffed his diary into a stone cupboard in the Eagle's Nest, one of the Indian dwellings. Cather does not present this novel chronologically; the time shifts and narrative shifts are meant to be jarring. Tom's adventures on the mesa occur before he meets the professor and his family. He and St. Peter later return to retrieve his diary from the ruins. Tom invents his famous aviation engine, and then, without marketing it, goes off to fight in World War I and dies, leaving behind his invention, his diary, and his legacy of fantasy.

Like Peter, who often forgets what he was doing, Tom gets side-tracked. The adventure on the mesa begins with a poker game and "a string of accidents" (177). At the Blue Mesa, time is strange; not only do the men feel that they have gone back in history, but there is also a feeling of awe—of the perpetual. In *Peter Pan* the lagoon in Neverland is described in magical terms: "If you shut your eyes . . . you may see at times a shapeless pool of lovely pale colours suspended in the dark-ness; then if you squeeze your eyes tighter, the pool begins to take shape" (114). Of the Blue Mesa, Tom says, "By closing my eyes I could see it against the dark, like a magic-lantern slide" (202).

When Mrs. Darling is dreaming one day, "the Neverland come[s] too near," and she sees Peter Pan. It does not alarm her, though, because she has "seen him before in the faces of many women who have no children. Perhaps he is to be found in the faces of some mothers also" (18). This could imply several things, among them that grown-ups never get over a longing to return to childhood or at least to retain the powerful images from tales of that time, and that women are not ful-filled unless they have children, or conversely, children must have mothers. When Peter Pan sees Mrs. Darling looking at him in her dream, he (who has all of his first teeth), "gnash[es] the little pearls at her" because he sees she is a grown-up (20). This is ironic because the one thing he wants, more than anything in the world, is a mother, even though he affirms the opposite to Wendy when she thinks he is crying because he has not got one. He begins to show a different side of him-self, however, when he tells Wendy that he and the Lost Boys are "rather lonely" and need someone to tuck them in and sew for them— clearly motherly duties (44, 49). When Tootles, one of the Lost Boys, thinks Wendy is a bird and shoots her, the others realize that Peter Pan was bringing them "a lady to take care of us at last" (89). That Wendy was to be a surrogate mother is confirmed when Peter arrives and says, "I have brought at last a mother for you all" (91).

Profoundly, Tootles reflects: "When ladies used to come to me in dreams, I said, 'Pretty mother, pretty mother.' But when at last she re-ally came, I shot her" (91). This statement echoes the leitmotif of lost maternal benefits in Tom Outland's life. The mummy of a female Indian, named "Mother Eve" by Tom and his workers, is lost while the workers are transporting all of the Indian ruins out of the mesa in Tom's absence. And very tellingly, "Hook" is the name of the local man who provides the mules to steal the ruins in "Tom Outland's Story"; as most people know, the leader of the pirates in *Peter and Wendy* is Captain Hook—a name that has become synonymous with the idea of the pirate in popular culture. Cather's Hook relates to Tom, in pirate language, how he and some other thieves removed the Indian artifacts while Tom was in Washington: "My mules were busy three weeks packing the stuff out of there on their backs, and I held the Dutchman up for a fancy price" (237).

Tom's supposed friend, Hook, has a mule that accidentally throws Mother Eve into the abyss of Black Canyon. According to Susan Rosowski, the attempted removal of Mother Eve from the mesa "suggests a would-be delivery" because the removal of the mummy from her "womb-like resting place" among the Indian ruins represents the loss of "a surrogate mother" for Tom ("Writing Against Silences" 62). This idea of longing for the lost mother is more blatant in *Peter and Wendy* but runs all throughout *The Professor's House*.

The loss of Tom's mother and of Mother Eve both represent the loss of security and sustenance. Peter Pan fails to keep Wendy, his own surrogate mother, because he will not allow himself to be adopted by the Darlings. While Peter is smug, thinking that the Darling siblings and the Lost Boys are perfectly happy staying children forever in Neverland, they have actually grown weary of make-believe and plot to return home. Peter has enjoyed Wendy's pretend mothering and cannot believe he will lose her. He fails at convincing her and the Lost Boys to stay and avoid the pitfalls of growing up. Before the Lost Boys decide to go with Wendy and her siblings, they are "panic-stricken at the thought of losing [her]" and actually advance on her violently (154–55). Peter, however pained he is at the thought of losing Wendy, is devastated at the idea of growing up—which going home with her would mean—and he is "bitter" and sarcastic, but stoic: "Peter . . . was not the kind that breaks down before people" (159).

In an earlier version of the Peter Pan story (*The Little White Bird*), the reader sees Peter desperately knocking at the nursery window of his own babyhood home. His mother ignores him as she contentedly nurses a new baby, thinking Peter is dead. In like manner, Professor St. Peter is a man longing to recover his boyhood self. Tom Outland, however, is the real motherless boy of Cather's story, even though he tries to find surrogates like the friends who accompany him to the mesa, the mummified body of the woman found there, and later, the professor to take care of him. By dying young, he remains a youth, while the professor cannot. His sincerity when he tells Blake, "I'd have sold any living woman first [before losing Mother Eve]" (244), speaks about his outrage over the loss and makes it clear that his relationship to the history of the mesa goes beyond other earthly feelings, confirming his longing for a maternal presence, just as Peter Pan's connection to Neverland and his nurturing of the Lost Boys keep him somewhat centered through time and space in the middle of a continual search for the maternal (he returns "except when he forgets" [242] every spring to the female progeny of Wendy). That Tom invests these feelings in a mummy, or that he would be willing to "sell any living woman" rather than give up the dead one, makes him more like Peter Pan than ever. He does not want a real mother and would probably gnash his teeth at one just as Peter Pan did. This also contributes to his otherworldliness, more than anything else does.[2]

Writing about the structure of *The Professor's House*, Marilyn Arnold notes that the book focuses on a movement from society to solitude. She states that it "is the ideal represented in Tom Outland and the mesa" that really separates St. Peter from his family. This ideal includes "non-materialism, solitude, and primitive oneness with the landscape" (170). Tom refuses to stay at the St. Peters' after he completes work on his invention. Behaving impetuously like Peter Pan, he "simply [bolts] to the front and [leaves] the most important discovery of his time to take care of itself" (42). He even leaves behind his rainbow-striped Mexican blanket, of which Kathleen says, "It was like his skin" (128). The professor—possibly Tom's last surrogate mother—keeps it locked up in a chest just as Wendy's mother kept Peter Pan's shadow in the nursery drawer. This idea of the shadow-self that remains behind speaks of lost longing as clearly as the words Peter and Tom speak before leaving their shadows.

Peter seems to think that by empowering the Darling children, especially Wendy, to fly, they will stay with him. This ever-present concept of flying is also a central, though subtle theme in Cather's novel that does allow another important comparison between Tom Outland and Peter Pan. Tom's invention revolutionizes aviation and is pressed into development soon enough to be used before the war ends. The Outland engine not only enables people to fly by breaking new ground in the aeronautics industry, but it also enables Tom to be a hero who saves lives, just as Peter Pan, obliviously and at the last moment, manages to save all of the Indians, the Lost Boys, and Wendy's family from Hook's pirates. The fact that the Outland engine saves domestic lives also means it kills enemies, another talent of Peter Pan's. Tom dies bravely fighting with the Foreign Legion in Flanders during the second year of World War I, but he leaves Rosamond a fortune from the patent. Like Peter, he is prepared to die alone. Perhaps in some way this aloof, renegade quality makes Peter Pan and Tom Outland seem both heroic and ethereal. Later, Wendy wonders if she dreamed Peter Pan up, and the professor's younger daughter, Kathleen, feels the same about Tom.

Tom Outland seems like a dream in the minds of those who knew him, but he is also historicized in a false way. Louie Marsellus, Rosamond's husband, gives a luncheon for visiting engineers at the Country Club. Later, Louie and Scott, Kathleen's husband, take their guests to visit "Outland"—the name they have given to their magnificent estate, and a sort of museum set up by Louis and Rosamond, Tom's heir. Scott tells the professor about it later:

> We had poor Tom served up again. It was all right, of course—the scientific men were interested, didn't know much about him. Louie called on me for personal recollections; he was very polite about it. I didn't express myself very well. . . . You know, Tom isn't very real to me any more. Sometimes I think he was just a–a glittering idea. (109–10)

Both Peter Pan and Tom remain in legacy and legend. Like Neverland, the mesa remains largely unattainable as it requires mountaineering or flying skills to enter. Professor St. Peter, like one of the Lost Boys, must return home from the ethereal mesa. He must be content with only the memory of Tom Outland as he prepares to take up residence with his real family in their new house. Neverland and the blue mesa must remain primal places in the minds of those who have heard about them. Outland, the glittering estate that testifies to Tom's genius, is a travesty to the professor because it embodies exactly the opposite of the mesa (Neverland). It flourishes because of materialistic greed and represents Tom as a technological wizard, an idea that does not represent the real Tom to Professor St. Peter—the Tom who, with no thought of material gain, attempted to save the Indians' culture by rescuing their artifacts.

"Tom Outland's Story" is not as separate and disjointed from the rest of the novel as some critics think. It is a performance—a play within a play. Like Neverland, which is an escape from all of the concerns of the adult, care-ridden, civilized world, Tom Outland's mesa is a stylized departure from the professor's anxiety-ridden home. The Darling children's lengthier adventures in Neverland work the same for Peter Pan and the Lost Boys as Tom's adventures work for him and the professor. The stories of these other worlds are the aesthetic centers of the narratives, and it is in these departures from home base that readers suspend belief for a moment. Both "Outland" and "Neverland" are otherworld systems that have a certain order but ultimately fail to meet expectations. Before the coming of Tom Outland and Peter Pan, both the Darlings and the St. Peters function (at least outwardly) in a seemingly ordered way.

The word "Outland" seems to describe a place where one could escape daily life, go away, be absent from something, be outside, or even be disqualified from a modern household or business life. "Outland" also connotes a land of unconsciousness that is distant or even disappearing. Thus the Blue Mesa, the estate named "Outland," and the island of Neverland have much in common. Of course, this is Tom's surname, but Outland becomes a real place, a museum to Tom's discovery when Tom dies. It does not describe Tom to people who loved him, and they deny the industry that has sprung up around him.

In comparison, "Neverland" describes somewhere that does not exist ever, or exists outside of time, or is a place that cannot exist ever again, or the opposite—a place that is never-ending, or simply a place where one can "never land." Yet in Barrie's novel and play, Wendy and her siblings go there once, and Wendy revisits for spring cleaning (as long as Peter remembers to come and get her) until she begins to age. It is only as an adult that Wendy questions whether it really exists. Unlike Neverland, the mesa exists, but it can never be seen again in the same way Tom saw it, especially since the workers carted out and sold the Indian ruins, representing the loss of an entire civilization. Peter Pan and Tom Outland are escapists, adventurers who come out of nowhere, do not stay long in one place, and decline, in a sense, to participate in human daily life that involves growing up and belonging to systems that require maturity and the endurance to master everyday, boring, working life.

So Tom Outland is Cather's version of Peter Pan; but Wendy has a counterpart too: Augusta. Like all good healers, Augusta and Wendy are both used to sitting up all night with babies or taking care of the sick. Wendy passes out bandages to the Lost Boys, sits up all night when anyone is ill, and soothes Peter when he has bad dreams. In *The Professor's House*, Augusta does the same: "You do a good deal of this sort of thing—watching and sitting up with people, don't you?" the Professor asks (279).

Like Augusta, Wendy is a seamstress. She sews all of the clothing for Peter and the Lost Boys. Before they go to Neverland, she sews Peter's shadow back on. In Neverland, she is always busy stitching—an occupation important to Barrie both for its metaphorical and concrete importance in his life. Barrie was born in Kirriemuir, Scotland—a weaving town. His father was a weaver, and by the time Barrie was ten, the technological takeover of traditional weaving in Kirriemuir was almost complete. Barrie witnessed and later wrote about these changes: "Where had been formerly but the click of the shuttle was soon the roar of 'power,' and hand-looms were rushed into a corner as a room is cleared for a dance" (*Margaret Ogilvy* 238). He explains in *Margaret Ogilvy*, the biography of his mother, that he did not think the power looms necessarily bad, but he felt that family structure was weakening because so many poor people went off to work in factories. His mother was always sewing, and Barrie saw sewing as a metaphor for creating honest work, done by hand with honor.

Both Wendy and Augusta are instructors when it comes to matters of life and death. After one of Augusta's visits, St. Peter returns to his old study to write, and there is a change in his mood. Like Mary after the visit of Elizabeth in the Magnificat ("the babe leaped in her womb for joy"), St. Peter feels creative and warmed, as though Augusta ("his handmaiden") had "been there and brightened it up for him" (99). Wendy functions in like manner for Peter Pan, finishing a story about her mother with comments about "our sublime faith in a mother's love" (152). Augusta brings a sense of the holy into the professor's house; she tells him about church doctrines and about the true meaning of Christmas. She feels omniscient as her words are on the professor's mind even when she is not present. Unlike Peter Pan's Wendy, her presence in the book is confined to very few occasions, though the reader is always aware of her behind the scenes. Just as Peter Pan relies on the mermaids' bells to signal the end of the day, the bells from "Augusta's church" tell Professor St. Peter when to quit working; the dressmaker forms he insists she leave in his study are a reminder of her constancy.

Wendy is the first female to exert influence over Peter Pan because he despises all mothers except her. She settles into stories whose themes relate to returning home. Strangely, they seem to have the same overtones regarding a mother's love as Augusta's stories of the Virgin Mary. Wendy reminds her brothers that their mother will always be there waiting: "There is the window still standing open. Ah, now we are rewarded for our sublime faith in a mother's love" (152). Like the professor, Peter is skeptical: "Long ago, I thought like you that my mother would always keep the window open for me; so I stayed away . . . and then flew back; but the window was barred" (153).

Wendy fails to convince Peter Pan to grow up; Augusta fares better in the sense that Professor St. Peter decides to face life after his brush with death. When St. Peter's gas stove malfunctions, rendering him unconscious, Augusta opens the windows at the head of the stairs and drags him out of the room. However, he still does not participate fully in the life he decides to live. The professor, reflecting that Augusta has always been a good influence, finds the courage to let the past go. But his apathy toward his family is still present. In *Peter and Wendy*, Peter Pan predicts repeatedly that the Lost Boys will not find growing up and assuming responsibility to be fun at all. Like the Lost Boys in Neverland, who ultimately choose to go home with Wendy, be adopted, and grow up, Professor St. Peter ultimately chooses to face real life, even if it means learning to "live without delight" (282). Cather begins the conclusion to *The Professor's House* with this somewhat mysterious phrase. Many critics have quoted the professor's comment; some see it as hopeful, but most see it as tragic. Throughout her letters Cather makes it clear that she liked to create mixed feelings in her readers. She did not like her earlier novels as well as her later ones because they had definite plots and neat conclusions. The ending to *The Professor's House* is intentionally ambiguous. The professor's resignation and failure to find joy in his life seem somewhat mitigated by the fact that, unlike Tom Outland, he does live. Only Tom succeeds in retaining his Peter Pan qualities, remaining forever in legacy and legend by refusing to live in real time and grow up.

When Augusta has rescued Professor St. Peter from the fumes of his gas stove, it is a time for enormous self-reflection as he tells himself that

he had no more thought of suicide than he had thought of embezzling . . . . [I]t [was] a grave social misdemeanour—except when it occurred in very evil times, as a form of protest. Yet when he was confronted by accidental extinction, he had felt no will to resist, but had let chance take its way. (282)

He decides that he will "have to learn to live without delight, without joy, without passionate griefs," especially since his wife Lillian "had had the best years of his life" (281–82). Thus, the conclusion is harsh—just as it is in *Peter Pan* when Peter chooses to remain a boy forever—a decision that means he must continually seek (and lose) a mother.

In the conclusion, it is night in the professor's study, and Augusta sits by the light of her lamp, sewing. The fact of her presence seems magical: "Just when did you come in, Augusta?" he asks (277). She relates how she saved him from death. He watches her, "regarding in her humankind, as if after a definite absence from the world of men and women" (279). Wendy tries to help Peter Pan; Augusta tries to ease the professor's transition into the world he must face. He still thinks of himself, however, realizing that "he didn't, on being quite honest with himself, feel any obligations toward his family" (281). His is not an awakening of acceptance; it is an awakening of transcendence. It is hard to face the real world:

> Augusta was like the taste of bitter herbs; she was the bloomless side of life that he had always run away from—yet when he had to face it, he found that it wasn't altogether repugnant. . . . And when you admitted that a thing was real that was enough—now. (280–81)

Professor St. Peter seems selfish, childish, removed from the daily concerns of his family, and dissatisfied with his world. Before the night when Augusta saves his life, he feels unsafe and he "dreads" her coming. She saves him from dying, but by representing the "bloomless" side of life, she enables him to face reality—leaving the reader feeling hopeful that St. Peter's future may grow to seem cheerier to him.

At the end of Barrie's story, Peter Pan comes at night to take Wendy to Neverland: "'Hullo, Wendy,' he said, not noticing any difference [that she has grown old], for he was thinking chiefly of himself" (238). Wendy sits by the light of her lamp, sewing, and tells Peter that she has grown up in his absence:

> "I will turn up the light," she said, "and then you can see for yourself."
> For almost the only time in his life that I know of, Peter was afraid. "Don't turn up the light," he cried. . . Then she turned up the light, and Peter saw. He gave a cry of pain. (239)

James Woodress, in his biography of Cather, says that she was pleased later in her life when Barrie wanted autographed copies of her books, but other accounts say Cather was "puzzled when he requested an autographed copy of one of her books" (Woodress 502; Cather, *Willa Cather in Person* xxvii). Perhaps she knew that he would recognize and applaud her unique treatment of "The Boy Who Would Not Grow Up." Cather is said to have remarked that her autograph was on every page.

Barrie was an avid reader of American literature and a close friend to many authors on both sides of the Atlantic. His fascination with the American frontier is the force that shapes Neverland. Cather's *The Professor's House* is but one example of the influence of the *Peter Pan* play and novels on early-twentieth-century American fiction. The figures of the innocent, escapist, immature male, and his maternal, mature female companion became more complicated after Barrie's stories offered new insights about maternity, gender, and aging. His works, like L. Frank Baum's, were later relegated to the children's shelves (especially after Walt Disney's rendition of *Peter Pan*), but they were popular among adults at the turn of the century. His psychological probing of a boy's relationship with his mother and his fear of growing up continues to fascinate literary critics, feminists, mental health experts, filmmakers, philosophers, and historians. They draw upon his metaphors, settings, and characters to amplify and give meaning to their own rhetorical situations, which, in an increasingly technological, war-torn world, call for ways to talk about love, growing up, and dying. Peter Pan and Wendy are important to the history of fiction in America after 1910. Barrie created characters who grapple with problems that are difficult to read about, but his subtlety and wit (often mislabeled as "whimsicality") allowed him to make social statements that American readers rejected in some other works (like *Maggie, A Girl of the Streets*, which, because it was so dire, was not widely admired when it was published). In a January 14, 1904, review of the play in *The King*, a critic echoes the idea that *Peter Pan* is for everyone: "Dear Mr. Barrie, You have the secret of making us grownup people feel like the children for whom you wrote *Peter Pan*" (qtd. in Hanson 49).

This need in adults to locate and retain a sense of childhood may hold the secret of why Barrie's work is continually trotted forth and reframed. Critics are always asking why our culture has a fascination with Neverland and its characters. The actors (almost always female) who have created the role of Peter Pan over the years have recognized that complicated social issues are at stake. Nina Boucicault, the first actor to play Peter Pan, said,

To me *Peter Pan* has always been much more than a fairy play for children. The fairy trappings are only a setting for the development of a serious idea. From beginning to end the story is a rather wistful commentary on human nature, taking as its theme the supreme selfishness of man and the supreme unselfishness of woman. (qtd. in Hanson 31)

One result was that other authors—whether realistic, naturalistic, or romantic—wrote Peter, the immature male, and Wendy, the mature girl, into the American script in new, illuminating ways. Cather's brilliant revamping of *Peter Pan* is just the tip of the iceberg.

NOTES

1. I claim in my master's thesis (1998) that "Tommy the Unsentimental" (August 1896), an early Cather story that first appeared in the *Home Monthly*, has a title that certainly seems to be a play on the title of Barrie's book *Sentimental Tommy*. Although Barrie's book was not published in England and America until October 1896, *Sentimental Tommy* first appeared in *Scribner's Magazine* as a serial beginning in January 1896. The narrator of Barrie's *Tommy* claims, "Oh, who by striving could make himself a boy again as Tommy could! I tell you he was always irresistible then. What is genius? It is the power to be a boy again at will" (vii). Tommy Sandys is a man who cannot grow up. On the other hand, Cather's *Tommy* is a woman who can ride faster than anyone on her bike to save a run on the bank. She hangs out with local businessmen, drinks cocktails, and has a logical mind. In short, she is totally capable of anything a man can do. Tommy has a friend, Jessica, who is demure and feminine and so much the opposite of Tommy that Tommy ends up telling her bumbling boyfriend, Jay, to marry Jessica, who is more like what a stereotypical man would want. This Tommy grows up and is very much the opposite of Barrie's Tommy, who declines responsibility repeatedly. It is amusing to think that perhaps Cather, who probably read the serialized version because she was a literary columnist at the time, decided to rebel against Barrie's inept but lovable Tommy, and write about a woman who could and would grow up.

2. The additional meaning behind the pun "Mommy/Mummy" gives new meaning to the idea of longing for a maternal presence.

WORKS CITED

Arnold, Marilyn. "The Function of Structure in Cather's *The Professor's House*." *Colby Library Quarterly* 11 (1975): 169–78.

Barrie, J. M. *Margaret Ogilvy*. New York: Scribner's, 1927.

———. *Peter and Wendy*. 1911. London: Penguin, 1994.

———. *Sentimental Tommy.* New York: Scribner's, 1932.

Birkin, Andrew. *J. M. Barrie and the Lost Boys: The Love Story That Gave Birth to Peter Pan.* New York: Potter, 1979.

Bloom, Edward. *Willa Cather's Gift of Sympathy.* Carbondale: Southern Illinois UP, 1962.

Brown, E. K. *Willa Cather.* Completed by Leon Edel. Lincoln: U of Nebraska P, 1987.

Cather, Willa. *Alexander's Bridge.* Lincoln: U of Nebraska P, 1977.

———. "The Passing Show." *Nebraska State Journal* 24 May 1896: 13.

———. *The Professor's House.* Willa Cather Scholarly Edition. Lincoln: U of Nebraska P, 2002.

———. "Tommy the Unsentimental." *Home Monthly* 6 (Aug. 1896): 6–7.

———. *Willa Cather in Person.* Ed. Brent L. Bohlke. Lincoln: U of Nebraska P, 1986.

Dillman, Richard. "Tom Outland: Emerson's American Scholar in *The Professor's House.*" *The Midwest Quarterly* 25 (1984): 375–85.

Hanson, Bruce K. *The Peter Pan Chronicles: The Nearly 100 Year History of "The Boy Who Wouldn't Grow Up."* New York: Birch Lane, 1993.

Kubitschek, Missy Dehn. "St. Peter and the World All Before Him." *Western American Literature* 17.3 (1982): 13–20.

Lee, Hermione. *Willa Cather: Double Lives.* New York: Pantheon, 1989.

Lewis, Edith. *Willa Cather Living.* New York: Knopf, 1953.

Mackail, Denis. *Barrie: The Story of J. M. B.* New York: Scribner's, 1941.

McFarland, Dorothy Tuck. *Willa Cather.* New York: Ungar, 1972.

Petry, Alice Hall. "In the Name of the Self: Cather's *The Professor's House.*" *Colby Library Quarterly* 23 (Mar. 1987): 26–31.

Robinson, Phyllis C. *The Life of Willa Cather.* New York: Holt, 1983.

Rosowski, Susan J. *The Voyage Perilous: Willa Cather's Romanticism.* Lincoln: U of Nebraska P, 1986.

———. "Writing Against Silences: Female Adolescent Development in the Novels of Willa Cather." *Studies in the Novel* 21.1 (1989): 60–77.

Rosowski, Susan J., and Bernice Slote. "Willa Cather's 1916 Mesa Verde Essay: The Genesis of *The Professor's House.*" *Prairie Schooner* 58.4 (1984): 81–93.

Schroeter, James, ed. *Willa Cather and Her Critics.* Ithaca: Cornell UP, 1967.

Sergeant, Elizabeth Shepley. *Willa Cather: A Memoir.* Philadelphia: Lippincott, 1953.

Skaggs, Merrill Maquire. "A Glance into *The Professor's House:* Inward and Outward Bound." *Renascence* 39 (1987): 422–29.

Stouck, David. *Willa Cather's Imagination.* Lincoln: U of Nebraska P, 1975.

Strychacz, Thomas. "A Note about Willa Cather's Use of Edgar Allan Poe's *The Pit and the Pendulum* in *The Professor's House.*" *Modern Fiction Studies* 36.1 (1990): 57.

Tennant, Stephen. Introduction. *Willa Cather on Writing.* By Willa Cather. New York: Knopf, 1949. 1–18.

Woodress, James. *Willa Cather: A Literary Life.* Lincoln: U of Nebraska P, 1987.

III

TIMELESSNESS AND TIMELINESS OF *PETER PAN*

8

The Pang of Stone Words

Irene Hsiao

"What do you want to be when you grow up?" is a question as often posed by one child to another as it is by inquisitive adults. Rarely will a child protest to declare that there is no need of future becoming because one already *is*. The response, "a fireman," "a dancer," "an intellectual properties lawyer," tacitly acknowledges that the child defies definition and categorization while adulthood demands it or, in other words, is defined by definition. Similar to how Geoffrey Hartman describes Freud's *Interpretation of Dreams*, my allegedly interpretive essay is actually a confession, a confession of a fear that I am starkly aware of. As Toys R Us commercials plainly state, "I don't wanna grow up." And indeed, as a student, I have had the luxury of prolonging my childhood years beyond their legal boundaries. But who can remain a child forever? Ah . . . that is the secret of print. Consulting J. M. Barrie's *Peter Pan*, I am spellbound by the immediate, the obvious, the first line of the novel, "All children, except one, grow up" (1). Although apparently unsubtle, the line yet manages to equivocate. One of the main features of childhood is its transience; Wendy learns that she must grow up when Mrs. Darling cries in aching counterpoint to that first line, "Oh, why can't you remain like this forever!" (1). Perhaps this transience is the root of all those insistent inquiries of being, the inevitably fleeing childhood subordinated to the "reality" of adult existence, itself an illusion before the true inertia of death (though I suppose that grown-ups do ask themselves what they will be when they die—that is the question of fame). So in refusing to grow up, has Peter Pan already, mayhap by some undisclosed shortcut, attained the imagined fixity of adulthood? In other words, does he not grow up because he has already grown up? Perhaps what he lacks is the final shift of the constantly shifting identity of indefinition to permanent identity. Perhaps I should simply believe him when he says, "I'm youth, I'm joy, I'm a little bird that has broken out of the egg" (158).

One thing I do know about Peter Pan is that he is a stranger to letters, "the only boy on the island who could neither write nor spell; not the smallest word" (81). Of course, all children enter the world unable to read. Illiteracy, as I know from reading advertisements regarding the sorry state of reading in this country, is a severe debility. It isolates a person from the wonders of print, certainly, but furthermore isolates him or her from the reading community. In an age beyond the immediate circle of oral tradition, illiteracy is therefore also isolation from a set of collective knowledge. This isolation is echoed in the construction of Neverland, which is "always more or less an island" (6). Even as Peter is an object of admiration for the other children, he is similarly always set apart by the simple fact of his illiteracy, the illiteracy that is the result of never having had any education, formal or otherwise. The words that Peter says cannot have been filtered through the drilled tongue of elementary primers—his words are thus the words of instinct, not instruction.

As a literary character who cannot read, Peter Pan presents the reader with a conundrum, that of assessing him in a medium he cannot himself access. Walter J. Ong suggests that writing or print dramatically reforms the consciousness of the literate. Briefly we might say that the shift in representation of the word from transient oral/aural event to fixed visual presence frees perception from monomaniacal devotion to the direct experience of the present and the straitjacket of personal memory, permitting abstract thought and observation of recorded phenomena from a removed perspective. In other words, the invention of writing also invents scientific thought. In *Peter Pan*, the interplay of orality and literacy elucidates the implications of illiteracy in a print culture. The illiterate character of Peter centralizes the trope of the child's primarily oral usage of language, while his nemesis, Hook, is presented as an obsessively literate character. The other children and adults of the novel occupy the middle range between literacy and illiteracy, childhood and immaturity, demonstrating a social order that defines adulthood by facility with language.

In *The Case of Peter Pan; Or, The Impossibility of Children's Fiction*, Jacqueline Rose employs *Peter Pan* as the primary model to posit that the gulf between childhood and adulthood is reinforced by the concept of children's literature—that is, that special genre of writing that is created by adults ostensibly for the child reader. "Children's fiction sets up a world in which the adult comes first (author, maker, giver) and the child comes after (reader, product, receiver)" (1–2), she writes, exposing a certain social hierarchy that establishes a literary, "adult" language as a taught normative. Rose complicates her ideas by referencing Rousseauean hypotheses about the child's relationship to language, which establish the child as closer to a pure language "uncontaminated by the intrusion of the verbal sign" (Rose 46). But the child's tenuously "natural" condition must be guarded, cultivated, and restored by education. Literature for and about the child thus takes upon itself the precarious role of inducting the child reader into adult language even as it attempts to reach the pure, natural elements of child language by ventriloquizing its child characters.

As an illiterate character, Peter Pan eludes both halves of this cycle of destruction and regeneration: he is resistant to the decay of natural language generated by cultural exposure as well as to the restorative effects of literary education. He is therefore no model for the child reader, being always in a state both behind and beyond the reader's grasp. Yet even if Peter the illiterate is as lost to readers as innocence to Eden, readers are those for whom representation consciously supplants presence,[1] and thus Peter-the-absence is perhaps best known through the always-departed nature of writing. Rose writes, "If children's fiction builds an image of the child inside the book, it does so in order to secure the child who is outside the book, the one who does not come so easily within its grasp" (2). In the situation of *Peter Pan*, on the other hand, Peter's intangibility comes closest to the evasive child outside of the text as a direct result of the marked absence that characterizes text. The painful half-presence of text is Peter's milieu, the agonistic realm that must always be his native land.

Peter Pan's knowledge correspondingly takes the form of that which cannot be explained in words. When asked about flight, "instead of troubling to answer . . . Peter flew around the room" (36). Flight isn't something that could be believed by hearsay, anyway—the assertion of flight to the earthbound human requires empirical substantiation; the only possible answer to John's "I say, Peter, can you really fly?" (36) is flight, not "yes." On the other hand, "no," as a verbal response, would be understood without necessary elaboration or proof. John's "practical" request to know the method is met with a similar non-answer. Peter first gives the fanciful reply, "You just think lovely wonderful thoughts, and they lift you up in the air" (36), suggesting that flight is actually a matter of thinking the right way, but no, "Of course Peter had been trifling with them, for no one can fly unless the fairy dust has been blown on him" (37), a solution that cannot be intellectualized at all. Flight via fairy dust cannot even be willed. The dust must be "blown" on you; it must be attained by a chance application of breath and direction, more of an infection than an acquisition.

Still, there is a certain internal environment required for the dust to take hold. Flight is inversely correlated with education. A clear example of this is when, after being sent to school, the Lost Boys lose their power of flight and explain it as "want of practice." This rationalization implies that their conception of flying has shifted to an attribution to skill—that is, a product of instruction and repetition—when it "really meant that they no longer believed" (176). Their inability to fly is not really a forgetting of something they knew as much as it is a loss of an instinctive faith in flying, a kind of ignorance of process and progress that the logic behind schooling obliterates. More interesting, perhaps, is the example of the Darling children's discovery of flight. While we are reminded that, at first, "Not one of them could fly an inch, though even Michael was in words of two syllables, and Peter did not know A from Z," Michael, the first to lift off, "not quite mean[ing] to let go," responds with an immediate, agrammatical, "I flewed!" (37), an interjectional exclamation that describes, more than the unutterable fact of flight, a breach with the accepted patterns of language. Although it is widely believed that language acquisition is a natural (that is, an untaught) process, Michael's "I flewed!" is an example of the language-learning child's creative use of language, producing a sentence he has never heard before out of a misconjugation that he has certainly not experienced in the surrounding adult speech, the very kind of creative use of language that Noam Chomsky employs as an example against the idea that language is learned through imitation,[2] the kind of creative use of language that a teacher or listening adult would correct to the standard, "I flew." Michael's "I flewed!" is actually a sort of double-conjugation, first a correct shift from "fly" to "flew" and then an addition of the "-ed" that signifies pastness in most English verbs, making a statement of regression that goes beyond the physical flight of just a moment before into a wormhole to a state of incipient understanding of language, that is, to a stage where the child is deciding through his use of speech his relationship to adult conceptions of the world. What I mean by this is that after a period of observation, one would become conscious of the pattern of adding "-ed" as a common way to mark an action in past tense and would hence extrapolate the usage to other verbs in an effort to adopt the norms of the language. However, recognizing that "flewed" is incorrect is akin to recognizing idiomatic speech, which either requires further exposure to the language or instruction by an outside party. "Flewed" is a chimerical combination of both the idiomatic "flew" and the logical, but incorrect, "-ed," an implementation of actual "adult" speech with the retention of something that seems to the child like it should be adult speech.

Michael's creative speech, however, is in contrast to the kind of speech that the Lost Boys and even Peter Pan exhibit. The Lost Boys, for example, often speak in chorus or canon and are completely indistinguishable in an episode of tattling around the afternoon tea table:

> "Slightly is coughing on the table."
> "The twins began with mammee-apples."
> "Curly is taking both tappa rolls and yams."
> "Nibs is speaking with his mouth full."
> "I complain of the twins."
> "I complain of Curly."
> "I complain of Nibs." (108)

What begins as Wendy's way of settling "matter[s] of dispute" (107) is subverted into a futile cycle of speech, one that does not move the issue closer to resolution as much as it amplifies the conscious existence of conflict. Their cacophonous objections lose the power of speech to go beyond the ability to declare—it is as though each exclamation only becomes a name for speaking. In the "I complain of" exclamation, action itself is irrelevant; no result is intended except noise, noise that is a reflex, not a product of reflection, an end in itself, not a means of communication. In fact, what each complaint reveals is nothing more than what should already be known by every member in the party. The statement that is really being made is, "I am noticing —," or really, object of note being previously known, "I am." While the unsaid bid for attention comes as no surprise to anyone who has ever spent an hour or two with a child, the corollary, "See that I am," that springs from the spoken complaint causes the burden of identification to fall upon the recognizing adult, in this case, as the mother-figure, Wendy.

Like Michael's conjugation of "to fly," the Lost Boys use the speech devised by the adult (figure) at cross-purposes to its original intent, but the appropriated pattern is not so much an expression of a developing mind as it is a request that a self be defined by external acknowledgement. Ironically, these individually made demands have the quality of choral speech; no single boy is distinguishable in the clamor. In fact, unlike Michael's self-defining reinvention of adult speech, the Lost Boys' adoption of the vehicle of adult convention without the corresponding comprehension of its function or occasion serves to parodize their imitation of maturity. Rather than illuminate their emerging personalities, each utterance, though expressed individually, only regresses them further into a similitude that begs an outside agency to sort them out.

On the other hand, when the Lost Boys interact verbally with Peter, the impulse is quite the opposite:

[Peter] called out, "I'm redskin to-day; what are you, Tootles?" And Tootles answered, "Redskin; what are you, Nibs?" and Nibs said, "Redskin; what are you, Twin?" and so on, until they were all redskin . . . (82)

These lines, presented without paragraph breaks between speakers, emphatically demonstrate the Lost Boys' desire to abandon their own potentially awkward identities and huddle in the assurance of a communal entity created by echoing Peter's words. However, at the same time that they are squeezing into the shelter of the same name ("redskin" and, by extension, "Peter"), they are each in turn calling each other by name and then responding by renaming themselves; each Lost Boy is recognized by the others as a decision-making entity whose acquiescence strengthens the community and, as a consequence, the power of its name. As opposed to an undifferentiated mass, community is dependent on recognizing the individuals that compose it, and here, especially, each Lost Boy gets his say one at a time. Importantly in this situation, the Lost Boys are speaking to each other, establishing a language of peers in each exchange of interrogation and response and furthermore acknowledging themselves as entities with the power to choose a name by which to define themselves, as well as the power of identifying others by it.

On the subject of the name, it should be noted that the Lost Boys' names are epithets—Curly, Tootles, Nibs, Slightly, the Twins—Peter is the only one with a "real" name. Under ordinary circumstances, the epithet differs from the name in that the former is a word that encompasses a person by amplifying a single characteristic, a verbal caricaturization of a person achieved by limiting him to the extent of the word, whereas the name is a word that indicates the person, reserving the definition of itself for the person inhabiting it. In the above situation, Peter becomes almost a Lost Boy in taking on the name of "redskin," making an epithet on the contrary a desirable characteristic, an affectation of choice, an extra badge on the sash, rather than a diminution or objectification. This conversion of the epithet from all-defining to merely semi-descriptive takes place by still summoning each boy by his other appellation; just as Peter is always Peter even when he is redskin Peter, each Lost Boy is first called by his Lost Boy name before joining the redskin association. Being "forbidden by Peter to look in the least like him" (52) becomes less a quashing of the Lost Boys' individuality than a possibility to achieve personality.

Although I refer to Wendy as the adult-figure in the Lost Boys' community, Wendy is actually also depicted as a child adopting adult speech. When Wendy and the others arrive on the island, she is called upon to be the mother of the Lost Boys, resulting in a game that attempts to mimic adult domestic patterns. Cooking and cleaning and chores and rules are the very activities one would expect a child to want to escape (although that's perhaps more of an adult fantasy, especially considering children "playing house"), but these things are transposed in whole to the "happy home" in Neverland. However, the re-creation of adult behaviors is just that: recreation. As in any game, there are rules and a bit of sweat or tedium, but these elements are necessary: they inform the player that the activity is fully willed. Wendy's departure from the Darling home only to attempt to recreate a similar domestic dynamic in Neverland is not a disguised longing for home, which cannot exist for one who harbors a "sublime faith in a mother's love" (116), the belief of Wendy's that crystallizes the Darling home into an ageless, immutable sanctuary to which she may always return. Nor can her domestic game be fully explained by a latent maternal instinct. Instead, the desire is to engage in labor that may at any moment end, labor that is at once familiar and yet the scene of a reassignation of power, the transformation of subordinate child to authority figure. At the same time, there is a certain unconsciousness to a child pretending to be an adult. Because no narrative background exists for the choice of adult words—that is, the speakers haven't grown into the scenes they are enacting—Wendy's saying, "Oh, dear, I am sure I sometimes think spinsters are to be envied" can express pleasure instead of dissatisfaction: "Her face beamed when she exclaimed this" (79). The reasoning is simple; Wendy isn't even at a stage in her life when "spinster" and "matron" really begin to have meaning. She is only a girl pretending to be a matron, a spinster by qualification, co-habiting so many roles that she is bound to none. She has the freedom to experiment and reject, and in doing so, she can discover what she likes and doesn't like. More than just playacting, the game teaches Wendy how to become an adult and, specifically, what kind of adult she might want to become.

The game evidently does not work the same way for the Lost Boys, Michael, John, and Peter. The Lost Boys, Michael and John, assume the roles of Wendy's children. Of course, they are already children, so the stretch of the imagination is lessened considerably. However, Barrie depicts men as being even more childish than children; Mr. Darling, for example, struts and frets, worries that his dog doesn't "admire" him ("'I know she admires you tremendously, George,' Mrs. Darling would assure him, and then she would sign to the children to be specially nice to father" [5]), argues pettishly with his son ("So are you a cowardy custard" [19]), hides his "nasty, sticky, sweet" medicine to avoid his dose (18), has "no real mastery of his tie" and "yells" at its exasperating unmanageability (16–17), grumbles that "nobody coddles" him (20), and plays unhumorous practical jokes on the faithful nurse/dog. Addressing Mrs. Darling as "mother" (16) is only another symptom of his insufferable immaturity, and she does soothe and "coddle" him more than an adult rightfully deserves. The portrait of manhood that Barrie makes with Mr. Darling indicates that boys never really have to grow up as long as they have wives to manage them, and they only need a bit of strategy, a bit of superior game-playing, to get a wife—Mr. Darling got his by having "took a cab and nipped in first," ahead of all the other men who "discovered simultaneously that they loved her" (2), rather than by any merit of his individuality. As Mr. Darling demonstrates, having children of one's own does nothing to promote adult behavior, so long as one is careful to occupy the position of father. Even when Wendy and John enact the parts of their parents in a make-believe of the scenes of their own births, John only says in the role of Mr. Darling, "'I am happy to inform you, Mrs. Darling, that you are now a mother,' in just such a tone as Mr. Darling himself may have used on the real occasion" (15), essentially present to announce, ever so helpfully, the obvious. Thus, Peter playing father to the Lost Boys has no effect on his maturation, or lack thereof, and when Wendy asks Peter,

"What are your exact feelings for me?", Peter's reply, "Those of a devoted son, Wendy" (111), is not strange as much as it is a sad awakening for Wendy about the nature of relationships.

When I said that illiteracy isolates a person from a set of collective knowledge, certain obvious threads were left dangling. For example, does this assertion mean that all children are isolate beings up to that fantastical point when words congeal on the page? Anyone would say, Certainly not—what about the body of knowledge that is passed down through speech? And even before the acquisition of speech, is the preverbal child truly closed off from the world? Humans being what they are—that is, helpless products of mammalian birth—cannot reach adulthood in isolation. Humans being what they are—that is, sensate organisms—cannot seclude themselves from the world at large and survive biologically. Perhaps I have gone too far. Let us step back and look briefly at orality. Peter Pan's original attraction to the Darlings' nursery window is "not to see [Wendy], but to listen to stories." "You see," he explains, "I don't know any stories. None of the Lost Boys know any stories" (32). Stories, like children's make-believe games, are disjointed from the continuity of real life, but exist, like the games, as whole narratives unto themselves. Unlike the acted out children's games, stories are acted through the transference of words; the acting-out retreats from the body to the mind. Peter Pan does not understand stories. His excitement at learning "that was Cinderella, and he found her, and they lived happily ever after" (33) from Wendy comes from not knowing that a story is make-believe and therefore not realizing that any answer will do, even one that he invents. Captain Hook, on the other hand, is immediately described to the reader as "a *raconteur* of repute" (55), and this skill, rather than simply a disparity of age, is the chief dissimilarity between Hook and Peter.

Why is it that storytelling should be first and foremost an adult pleasure? One reason might be that the ability to recognize narratives is also the ability to recognize beginnings and ends. Peter is astonishingly inept at this kind of distinction, most likely because of his extraordinary power of forgetfulness: "He would come down laughing over something fearfully funny he had been saying to a star, but he had already forgotten what it was, or he would come up with mermaid scales still sticking to him, and yet not be able to say for certain what had been happening" (42). This fey quality, this mind that cannot determine where his body has wandered and why, separates even what should be the unbroken experience of living into discrete events—not even events, impressions, perhaps—that shatter the logic of causality and temporality into unrelated, disordered sensations. To Peter, actions are not taken to achieve particular ends; particular ends just happen to accompany actions. For example, during the Darlings' flight to Neverland, Peter's method of finding food is to "pursue birds who had food in their mouths suitable for humans and snatch it from them; then the birds would follow and snatch it back; and they would all go chasing each other gaily for miles, parting at last with mutual expressions of good-will" (40), the act of play having greater importance than the meal. Similarly, when one of the Darlings would succumb to sleep midflight, dropping precipitately,

> [e]ventually Peter would dive through the air, and catch Michael just before he could strike the sea, and it was lovely the way he did it; but he always waited till the last moment, and you felt it was his cleverness that interested him and not the saving of human life. Also he was fond of variety, and the sport that engrossed him one moment would suddenly cease to engage him, so there was always the possibility that the next time you fell he would let you go. (40)

Peter's inconsistency is the essence of caprice; he is ungoverned by any recognizable rationale. The incoherence of his character is exactly that indefinite potential that I postulated earlier as the fundamental nature of childhood.

On the other hand, forgetting is an essential component of growing up. As mentioned earlier, the Lost Boys' forgetting how to fly is associated with their attendance at school, the commencement of an itinerary that leads to "an office" and, finally, manhood, as even Peter knows (174). However, this forgetting distinguishes itself from the kind of forgetting that possesses Peter by belonging to a memory that operates on a verbal system. As demonstrated by Mr. and Mrs. Darling's obsessive recounting of the children's escape on that "never-to-be-forgotten Friday," adult memory is formed at least in part by storytelling:

> "I ought to have been specially careful on a Friday," she used to say afterwards to her husband, while perhaps Nana was on the other side of her, holding her hand.
>
> "No, no," Mr. Darling always said, "I am responsible for it all. I, George Darling, did it. *Mea culpa, mea culpa.*" He had had a classical education.
>
> They sat thus night after night recalling that fatal Friday, till every detail of it was stamped on their brains and came through on the other side like the faces on a bad coinage. (13)

Mr. Darling's "classical education" notably manifests itself in an expression of Latinate guilt, whose emphasis only reverberates the sentiments of the preceding English, as if at some phase of practicing conjugation, he had acquired a notion of agency that permits a fuller understanding of the parts of speech in the declaration, "I, George Darling, did it"—as if the product of education could be summarized as a comprehension of grammar, the skeleton of discrete ideational units that build the mosaic of generative power determined by language itself. The repetitious recalling of the events that surround the children's departure plays like a recitation before a schoolmaster, and the litany of "if only"s that follows—"If only I had not accepted the invitation to dine at 27," "If only I had not poured my medicine into Nana's bowl," "If only I had pretended to like the medicine" (13–14)—reflects the wish that a single cause could be responsible for the event and that the responsibility for the event could be taken by a single "I," in accordance with the structure of the sentence, "I did it."

In addition, the way the scene presents the adult memory indicates that it is by no means a rigid object but rather a malleable material upon which the grammatical image of the past is impressed. Wendy, whose transition to adulthood is accelerated instead of suspended in her sojourn in Neverland, shows that she is beginning to understand this aspect of the adult mind when she "trie[s] to fix the old life in their minds by setting them examination papers on it, as like as possible to the ones she used to do at school" (80). This imitation of school assignments reveals itself as an impulse to petrify the past by finding the right words for it. Wendy, of course, knows both the questions and the answers, although she "had been forgetting too" (81); in fact, what really distinguishes her from the other children is her compulsion to ask the questions, to erect a scaffold of terms for remembrance.

In contrast, "Peter" means "stone," and, correspondingly, his mind does not take up impressions so easily:

> He often went out alone, and when he came back you were never absolutely certain whether he had had an adventure or not. He might have forgotten it so completely that he never said anything about it; and then when you went out you found the body; and, on the other hand, he might say a great deal about it, and yet you could not find the body. (80)

Just as he forgets his repartee with the stars or his games with the mermaids, his adventures, which are the promise of a book titled after his name, are irretrievable to even himself. In fact, what is narratable is completely disconnected from what has truly occurred, throwing the whole nature of how we acquire truth into question. If what is presented to the mind is different from what is presented to the body, or rather if signs presented to the reason differ from death presented to the senses, the function of narration is compromised. We cannot rely on reports of action to reveal Peter's character, since his activities apparently do not affect his memory in a way that can be externalized in words.

James Hook, of the "forget-me-not blue eyes," on the other hand, suffers from just the opposite: he is all legend and refuses to forget a minute of his own story. In reputation, he is known immediately to John as "Blackbeard's bo'sun," "the worst of them all," "the only man of whom Barbecue was afraid" (46), his name inalienable from his legends. In dress, he imitates "the attire associated with the name of Charles II, having heard it said in some earlier period of his career that he bore a strange resemblance to the ill-fated Stuarts" (42), a historicization and additional literal contextualization of his person. Furthermore, Hook broods. He dreams of revenge on Peter, because, he says, "[T]was he cut off my arm. . . . I've waited long to shake his hand with this. Oh, I'll tear him," he resolves; however, he adds, "'[I]f I was a mother I would pray to have my children born with this instead of that,' and he cast a look of pride upon his iron hand and one of scorn upon the other" (59). The hook's "homely uses" upon which Smee remarks and Hook concurs, the hook that gives him his name and raises the bar of terror associated with the dread pirate, are subordinated to the ruthless haunting of its particular history and Hook's unremitting shame and fury at having his severed hand "flung . . . to a crocodile that happened to be passing by" (60). The incessant ticking of that same crocodile, who by fortune swallowed a clock, gives ominous warning of what Hook knows too well, that "[s]ome day . . . the clock will run down, and then he'll get you" (60), a transparent reference to the grave fear of the ultimate end-of-narrative, the divination of mortality that lies in wait for every cohesive identity.

Of course, storytelling is also dependent on a facility with words. While certainly literacy is hardly necessary to make a good storyteller, it is a useful metaphor for the claim I wish to put forward. Literacy is an obliging figure because it enables the reader to make the word itself physical, visible, and tangible on the page. For the illiterate, on the contrary, the word goes straight from breath to ear without solidifying along the way. We can see this best in Peter Pan's dearth of metaphorical speech, the curious corollary to his perfect imagination. One example of this is when Wendy, shot down by the luckless Tootles, causes Peter to order that a doctor be fetched. Slightly agrees and, knowing no doctors on Neverland, returns in costume, and Peter, not playing in the least, asks earnestly, "Please, sir, are you a doctor?" (70). Aside from being unable to read, the reader is informed that the "difference between [Peter] and the other boys at such a time was that they knew it was make-believe, while to him make-believe and true were exactly the same thing" (70). But it isn't all so illusory as the incident with the doctor, where a faulty perception may be blamed for Peter's belief. In fact, "[m]ake believe was so real to him that during a meal of it you could see him getting rounder" (79). If pretending that eating has occurred is tantamount to physical consumption, little explanation is needed for the very real fear that Peter has of returning to his mother: "perhaps she would say I was old, and I just want always to be a little boy and to have fun" (121)—her saying he was old would truly make it so for Peter.

Again, we turn to the pirates to observe the antithesis. The pirates are introduced to us as "Robt. Mullins and Alf Mason," "Bill Jukes" (54), "Geo. Scourie," and "Chas. Turley" (126) in addition to "Starkey," "Cecco," "Cookson," and "Smee." Hook himself signs as "Jas. Hook" (54). Unlike the Lost Boys' epithets, these are abbreviations, alterations of the names into symbols intended to indicate something fuller. Abbreviations are constructed in a way that only the literate would understand because the symbolization takes place via a visual shortening of the physical word; they are not symbols in an imagistic sense, except in the sense that the written word is an image for the idea of words. The pirates' names being short for a literate relationship with words additionally exhibits what a literate relationship with words consists of. Words, to the literate, become objects. Objects can be manipulated. Some would call this storytelling; others might say it was deception. The word can be trimmed, twisted, spun, made to fit a purpose. In fact, though, we are told straight out, "Hook was not his true name"—but a careful reader, one who "read[s] between the lines must have already guessed" it (141). A good reader, then, is one who can trace the myriad modifications of the word and read the unwritten.

The problem of this treatment of language is for those who cannot read. We might examine first the benign scene where Wendy offers Peter a kiss: "Peter did not know what she meant, and he held out his hand expectantly" (27). Akin to Michael's "flewed," Peter's actions imply an unfamiliarity with an idiomatic phrase—a kiss, though usually a noun, is an object only when it is a word; otherwise, it ought more logically to be a transitive verb. Quite counter to instinct, then, illiteracy actually creates a more literal relationship to words. While the solidity of letters marks the ethereality of words, without the existence of paper currency, one can only trade through barter, whose main stipulation is unconcealed presence. Although the kiss incident results in only a gentle misunderstanding, greater consequences lie in verbal contracts. When Michael refuses to take his medicine, Mr. Darling first chides him to "be a man" (17). Then, when presented with his own medicine, Mr. Darling agrees that Michael will take his medicine if he swallows his simultaneously: "Wendy gave the words, one, two, three, and Michael took his medicine, but Mr. Darling slipped his behind his back" (19). Mr. Darling's dishonorable behavior isn't so hard to understand to the literate adult; after all, he was bound only by the insubstantiality of spoken words. However, to a child, for whom the word is equivalent to action, Mr. Darling's failure to keep to his word is a betrayal that disrupts the child's entire grounding of belief.

Hook effects a similar betrayal when he leads a pirate siege on the redskins. "By all the unwritten laws of savage warfare it is always the redskin who attacks, and with the wiliness of his race he does it just before dawn, at which time he knows the courage of the whites to be at its lowest ebb" (123); thus begins a passage detailing the rules of proper Neverland combat, and we are assured that Hook "cannot be excused on the plea of ignorance" (124) regarding these rules. While his "fell genius" is to be praised or looked upon with contempt for his violation of Neverland convention—convention that can only be trusted, it would seem, to be adhered to by the illiterate, for whom no distinction exists between written and unwritten laws—his worst betrayal is yet to come:

> "If the redskins have won," [Peter] said, "they will beat the tom-tom; it is always their sign of victory."
>
> Now Smee had found the tom-tom, and was at that moment sitting on it. "You will never hear the tom-tom again," he muttered, but inaudibly of course, for strict silence had been enjoined. To his amazement Hook signed him to beat the tom-tom. (128)

This usurpation of the sign is the diabolical shrewdness that only a "raconteur of repute" could imagine—it is the absence of the "good form" that is, as Hook will later admit to himself, "all that really matters" (142), a transparency of form that results when words are exactly as they give the impression of being.

Yet it would be careless to discuss Hook's exploitation of the tom-tom beat without addressing the two instances in which Peter effects a similar turn; that is, when he pretends to be Hook to free Tiger Lily from the pirates, and when he pretends to be the crocodile when tracking the Lost Boys and Wendy to the pirate ship. Like Hook's manipulation of the tom-tom beat, Peter's successful imitation depends upon a replication of auditory signs that would seem to stand in for a different presence. However, whereas the sound of the tom-tom is the "sign of victory"—that is, the sign of an idea—Peter's imitation of Hook's voice at the lagoon and his imitation of the crocodile while boarding the ship are not meant to represent ideas but identities. While the concept of communication implies that ideas can be transferred without deterioration, identities are the fixed points they pass through, the dangerous sites where deformation of ideas can occur. However, identities are also slippery things. Peter and the pirates know that they are delineated by their relationships to ideas, which are made visible through idiosyncrasies of language usage. Thus, when Peter intones "in Hook's voice" Hook's own peculiar phrase, "Odds, bobs, hammer and tongs," and pronounces the man before him "a codfish, only a codfish" (93), the pirates "draw back" from the person formerly known as James Hook, muttering, "Have we been captained all this time by a codfish?" (94). The pirates' disregard of Hook's bodily presence when his verbal signature is taken up by Peter indicates that identity is bound up in the voice more than the body. Peter's imitation is truly an impersonation, a sounding-through, of the verbal equation that constitutes Hook's identity.

In a more roundabout fashion, when Peter takes the tick of the crocodile, he still impersonates Hook. A common device of fairy tale magicians is to hide their mortality in an object, to remove the life from their bodies and leave the evil behind. In order to vanquish his antagonist, the hero must find and destroy the object hiding the displaced life. An example which comes to mind is "The Firebird," in which the sorcerer, Kostchei, conceals his mortal life in the head of a pin in an egg in a box high on a mountaintop, which Prince Ivan, led by the Firebird, breaks to free his beloved and the other imprisoned dwellers of Kostchei's enchanted garden. In *Peter Pan*, the tick, whose termination means Hook's death, is internalized in Peter himself and structures a collapse of hero, quest object, and villain. In other words, Hook's identity, as that of any villain, is dependent on an opposition with that of the hero—the terms by which the hero and villain are recognized and quantified are the same in each. Indeed, as Peter creeps, ticking, through the forest and then onto the ship, "he had but one thought:

'Hook or me this time'" (150). Following his defeat of Hook, Peter takes his impersonation a step further, wearing a suit made "out of some of Hook's wickedest garments," "with Hook's cigar-holder in his mouth and one hand clenched, all but the forefinger, which he bent and held threateningly aloft like a hook" (162). However, this masquerade reveals itself as only a game in the end: Peter, whose essence lies in indefinition, proves that he has neither need of Hook nor, more important, the story of his defeat in order to persist in his curious role. "I forget them after I kill them," he says "carelessly" when he returns a year later to take Wendy for spring cleaning. "New adventures had crowded the old ones from his mind" (177). His forgetfulness draws him further away from us. We realize we cannot know him from stories about him—the things about him that are narratable are only traces in water for the boy himself.

While all I have said would seem to place the child's imagination into the realm of the literal and the adult's lack of imaginative belief in the realm of the metaphorical or symbolic, there still remains one item to be considered: Peter's crow. His crowing is mentioned throughout the book—mentioned, but unheard, as there is no way to represent it in text. The crow identifies Peter. "I can't help crowing . . . when I'm pleased with myself" (27), he tells Wendy; it is the noise he makes in recognition of himself, and thus it is the only evidence we have that there is a self to be recognized, that such a self has criteria for self-identification. The crow is his exulting cry of triumph; it is the mystery that causes the pirates to wonder at the sound "more eerie" than a pirate's death screech, the "doodle-doo," the "curse." Yet what is frightening to the pirates is "well understood by the boys" (152)—it is the "sound that ma[kes] the heart of every one of them rise to his mouth" (66). The crow is some kind of language that cries directly to the core of the other boys, yet these hearts, once summoned, do not crow in return. They stick, somehow catching in the throat; "[t]hey opened their mouths, but the cheers would not come" (66). The reason for this is found in an episode we have previously touched. After Peter rescues Tiger Lily from the pirates in the lagoon, Wendy claps her hand over his mouth, seeing that he will "very likely crow and thus betray himself" (90). In other words, the crow as an identifying mark is a kind of self-betrayal, one that, in signing self-satisfaction, leaves the self vulnerable to injury—the same kind of injury that is the "first unfairness" that "no one ever gets over," except Peter, who "often met it" but "always forgot it" (97): the discovery of damage, cost, difference, and therefore, the border between the self and the other that weighs one inferior. The other boys cannot release their hearts from their mouths—they cannot crow—because they have already experienced the painful differentiation of unfairness and have learned to protect themselves with a silence that muffles the will to speak. Unlike the inarticulate, primal screeches that only count the death of each pirate finishing his life in a relapse into indistinguishability, Peter's crow characterizes him by being an utterance that expresses through its inimitability and irrepresentability his fearless self-celebration, one that cannot be subverted by objectification or contained in valuation—it is the fluid non-word that keeps him the boy that will never grow up.

NOTES

1. See Jacques Derrida.
2. That is to say that the child actively produces never before heard language rather than simply parroting known phrases.

WORKS CITED

Barrie, J. M. *Peter Pan.* 1911. London: Penguin, 1995.

Chomsky, Noam. "A Review of B. F. Skinner's Verbal Behavior." *Language* 35 (1959): 26–58.

Derrida, Jacques. "Signature Event Context." *Margins of Philosophy.* Trans. Alan Bass. Chicago: U of Chicago P, 1984. 307–30.

Hartman, Geoffrey. "The Interpreter's Freud." *Modern Criticism and Theory: A Reader.* Ed. David Lodge. London: Longman, 1988. 412–24.

Ong, Walter J. *Orality and Literacy: The Technologizing of the Word.* London: Methuen, 1982.

Rose, Jacqueline. *The Case of Peter Pan; Or, The Impossibility of Children's Fiction.* London: Macmillan, 1984.

9

Playing in Neverland: *Peter Pan* Video Game Revisions

Cathlena Martin and Laurie Taylor

It should come as no surprise that the story structure of J. M. Barrie's *Peter Pan* proves easily portable to digital media, and video games in particular. While video game scholar Janet Murray in *Hamlet on the Holodeck* has briefly addressed Vladimir Propp's *Morphology of the Folk Tale* in relation to video games, our study presents an in-depth analysis of the story structure of *Peter Pan* in relation to video games. Our essay also studies *Peter Pan* as a story developed and told through various media within oral and literary traditions, which aid the story in its transfer to digital media. This includes an examination of *Peter Pan* in video games, from the less advanced games to the elaborate game world of *Kingdom Hearts*. Most video games rely on a single hero or a group of heroes working with several outside donors and helpers against a villain or group of villains to save someone in need of rescue. Barrie's *Peter Pan* story excels in presenting these basic criteria, while also existing within a multitude of revisions. As such, the story becomes part of cultural knowledge, which makes it more immediately accessible for video game-players. Because of the probable prior knowledge of the text *Peter Pan*, some players are comfortable reading new versions, such as are found in new media.

Different versions of the story in different media share many elements, each of which revises *Peter Pan* for continued use and relevance. Catherine Storr argues that *Peter Pan* has become outdated and is in need of retirement because of its disconnect with today's children.

Storr states that, as of her writing in 1992, Peter Pan, both as a character and as a story, has become obsolete. Storr argues that the tale could remain viable,

> [i]f we can forget some of the whimsy, the fairies, the eternal boyishness, and the harping on mothers. . . . But Peter has not changed and our world has moved on. It was Robin, twenty years ago, who flew with Batman; now it's space invaders who occupy the upper air and whatever is already succeeding Ninja Turtles. (25)

Yet while the novel and play versions may not connect as easily as they once did to today's children because of the form, it is not time for Peter's retirement. Instead, it is time for his story to take on a different medium. We all know that plays are not the entertainment media of today's children—video games are. Barrie's story retold in video game form helps modernize it to appeal to the twenty-first-century child. In turn, the video game form can inspire new revisions of the story in other media.

Barrie's *Peter Pan* has appeared in several video game versions, including *Peter Pan: Return to Neverland,* based on the 1953 Disney film of the same name, and *Peter Pan,* based on the film *Peter Pan* (2003). Other game versions include *Fox's Peter Pan and the Pirates* and *Disney Junior Games: Peter Pan Neverland Treasure Quest.* These versions are all more faithful to the video game form than to the story of Peter Pan because they generally follow Peter alone through an adventure in Neverland that most often involves treasure. As such, these games could use any existing adventure narrative rather than integrating the actual story of *Peter Pan.*

Multiple video game versions of *Peter Pan* appear partly because this work seems to fit closely with the established schemas for video games. Schemas or schemata are cognitive sets of expectations; for video games, these expectations most often relate to story themes, characters, narrative and spatial divisions, and expectations that derive from existing works. Perry Nodelman and Mavis Reimer devote a chapter of *The Pleasures of Children's Literature* to developing reading strategies and schemata within a literary text. The schemata used for literary texts include conceptual categories like stories of adventure and heroism, stories that include reader involvement or participation, and stories that are open for change. *Peter Pan* clearly fits the basic structure required for adventure and heroism, following a number of conventions and schemas from other works such as hero epics and Victorian adventure stories. As Chris Routh states, "Considered in its historical context, *Peter Pan* can be regarded as a progeny of Victorian adventure stories" (292). Using Joseph Campbell's model in *The Hero with a Thousand Faces*, we can link the structure of *Peter Pan* back to other hero epics from Greek mythology and fairy tales. Further, *Peter Pan* provides structural and character archetypes that are often used in video games, as well as in oral narratives, including the family unit and the emphasis on popular character types like fairies and adventurous young boys. However, *Peter Pan* also parallels video game sensibilities in that both video games and the *Peter Pan* play and novel versions fail to adequately address female characters even when the female characters are pivotal or when they offer new possibilities. This is especially true for video game versions of *Peter Pan* because many of the games rely heavily on video game schemas, which often use only one main male character. Although the multiple game versions could allow for versions with Tinker Bell or Wendy as the main character, major video games have not yet explored these possibilities from the story of *Peter Pan*.

While many of the video game versions of *Peter Pan* are fairly faithful to a limited version of Barrie's narrative because they focus solely on Peter Pan's story, the newest video game, *Kingdom Hearts*, incorporates Peter into a larger structure of children's stories at play with each other. For example, within the game, Disney's versions of characters such as the Little Mermaid and Winnie-the-Pooh are paired with *Final Fantasy* characters such as Sora and Riku to create dynamic team play and story-making. Just as Barrie's *Peter Pan* existed as a story within a play, so does the story of *Peter Pan* exist within a larger play of stories in *Kingdom Hearts*, which incorporates many characters specifically from *Peter Pan*, including the integral characters of Peter, Wendy, Tinker Bell, Captain Hook, Smee, and the Crocodile. Similarly, in the *Kingdom Hearts* revision of *Peter Pan*, themes from the earlier versions are continued. For instance, time serves a pivotal role both metaphorically and structurally, as it does in Barrie's originals, because of the fear of growing up, the Crocodile's alarm clock, London's Big Ben, and the technical time limits with the theatrical format.

REVISIONS OF THE STORY STRUCTURE

Peter Pan's story, structure, and history combine to lay a foundation for change and remediation. Barrie's *Peter Pan* originated in games of make-believe played with the Llewelyn Davies boys. From those early games, Barrie penned a play and several prose versions of the story, but no definitive first version exists. As such, Barrie's story begins within the oral tradition. Some of the plot draws on that tradition to create a tale based on oral narrative conventions, in which tales are retold and the audience plays a large part. In *You're Only Young Twice: Children's Literature and Film*, Tim Morris notes that, in addition to Barrie's multiple versions of the tale,

> Barrie also franchised out the writing of versions of *Peter Pan* to other writers, a practice that persists as the story is regenerated around the framework of Barrie's characters and settings. *Peter Pan* has been recreated in this way continually from its first appearance as an episode in Barrie's 1902 novel *The Little White Bird,* to the 1992 Steven Spielberg film *Hook* and beyond. (87–8)

As Morris mentions, the character of Peter Pan first appeared in the novel *The Little While Bird* (1902), but then quickly moved into the title role of the stage play *Peter Pan* (1904), morphing again in both form and content to expand Peter's character back into book form with *Peter Pan in Kensington Gardens* (1906). Barrie even wrote in novel form, *Peter and Wendy* (1911), basing his character descriptions on the actors' portrayals of certain characters (Tarr 64). Even in Barrie's own writing, the influence of one version of the story on the next illustrates the intertextual revisionist nature of the Peter Pan story. In more recent years, several textual, filmic, and video game versions have been released and have added to the cultural knowledge of the story, providing a familiar format for later revisions. While the first animated Disney film remains the best known, each iteration of the story opens new possibilities.

With its release of *Peter Pan* in 1953, Disney continued the tradition of revising Peter's story through several media with no definitive text; now the Disney repertoire of Peter Pan stories includes picture books, films, books based on the films, and video games. Once Disney adapted the story, it was no longer Barrie's *Peter Pan*, but instead *Walt Disney's Peter Pan* or *Walt Disney's Peter Pan and Wendy*. The story lost a clear authorial voice but gained cultural distribution through the mass-marketing efforts of Disney. After the release of the film, Disney published at least five different editions of the story (Routh 291). Even today, Disney helps to perpetuate new releases of *Peter Pan* by collaborating on the production of the recent video game *Kingdom*

Hearts. Each revision of *Peter Pan* strengthens its relationship to an oral tradition in regards to the adaptation of the story for the current time and telling.

IMAGINATION, ORALITY, AND STORYTELLING

With the multitude of versions, imagination as realized through oral tradition grounds the texts and links them together with Barrie's structure of storytelling. Barrie began working in the oral tradition, creating distant and make-believe worlds from an early age, including pirate adventures. These adventures impacted Barrie and continued to play a part in his adult life, his writing, and his characters' lives, thus creating a basis of oral storytelling within his games and fictional stories. With his childhood friend Stuart Gordon, Barrie imagined pirate trips, keeping log-books and journals of their adventures (Birkin 8). As an adult, he transferred these skills of and oral storytelling first into his interactions with children and then into his writings. Subsequently, his characters pretend by playing the same games that both he and his mother and he and the Llewelyn Davies boys played. The fluidity allowed by this original oral structure also allows the later textual versions to more immediately translate to the digital format because of the similarities in storytelling conventions and in the inclusion of play. Further, the playful nature of these tales and their emphasis on spatiality drawn from the locations of play, along with Barrie's sense for mappings (he often made maps of make-believe places), also aid their transfer to the spatial domains of digital media.

Barrie's characters not only play games of traveling to far-off places, chiefly Neverland, but they also participate in the oral tradition of storytelling. The catalyst for Peter meeting the Darling children is storytelling: driven by the need to hear stories, Peter Pan listens outside the Darlings' nursery window to hear the end of one specific fairy tale, "Cinderella." He, in turn, takes Mrs. Darling's stories back to the Lost Boys, thus continuing the strain of storytelling by passing down the tale to the next eager listener. In fact, it is Wendy's ability to tell stories that convinces her to join Peter in Neverland, where she can tell stories to the Lost Boys.

The history of *Peter Pan* provides a storytelling model by having Wendy as the impetus for action and the source of additional stories. This allows her to simultaneously act as narrator, as storyteller, or even as audience in video games. In both the novel and play, Peter's changing role as actor and as audience also allows for dynamic variation. In earlier versions of the text, not only does Peter want to hear fairy tales, but he also wants to hear stories about himself. The recent live action film version *Peter Pan* (2003), directed by P. J. Hogan, begins with a blending of these narratives: Wendy combines "Cinderella" with pirate adventures involving Peter Pan. In this version, Peter wants to hear tales, but narcissistically, he specifically wants to hear stories in which he is the hero. Morris heightens this quest for stories into a basic desire: "More than sex, more than touch, more than being held, we want to be told stories, preferably those long ritual storytellings during which we turn out to be the hero" (118). Peter's desire for stories connects to video game-players because games offer stories to the player—stories that change and allow the players to act as the characters. Peter does crave stories more than physical intimacies; most versions of *Peter Pan* eliminate any sexual inclinations from Peter, mainly because those actions and emotions fall into the realm of adults and because Peter allows no one to touch him. However, Hogan's film gives Peter opportunities to love, something Hook discovers when he asks Wendy what type of stories Peter listens to. When Wendy replies with a common list of fairy tales—"Cinderella," "Snow White," "Sleeping Beauty"—Hook announces that these are all love stories that end in a kiss, elucidating the fact that Peter can love and also foreshadowing the film's climax when Wendy kisses Peter, linking the movie to fairy tales through the action of a life-giving kiss. These linked stories also connect the film *Peter Pan* to the story frame with changing segments, as with *Kingdom Hearts*. Morris concludes, "Narrative itself is desire . . . the desire that drives Peter Pan" (118).

Having narrative as the driving desire for Peter makes the story easily translated to video games, which often reward players for successful game-play with additional narrative segments. In a similar vein, video game stories are combinations of individual stories oriented through a frame or storyteller, who can be either a narrator or a player-character. The player-character is the character through whom the player performs, like Mario from *Super Mario Brothers* or Peter Pan in *Fox's Peter Pan and the Pirates*. As such, the player-character often acts as a blend of narrator, storyteller, and primary character. Many games fail to adequately differentiate these roles, leading to confusing or bland game-play. By relying on the story of *Peter Pan,* game designers and players have multiple characters who, in multiple variations, fulfill these roles, which allows for dynamic and coherent game-play.

Like modern-day video game designers, Wendy, John, and Michael immediately recognize Neverland when they fly there with Peter because they have designed Neverland: the Darlings have created the landscape, drawn the borders, and named the animals. Neverland is an imaginary game to the children before they reach it; therefore, they know the layout and structure of the island when they physically arrive at the real Neverland. Routh notes, "In Disney's version, John and Michael believe Peter Pan is a real person and make him the 'hero' of their games even before he appears" (292). This demonstrates the interconnectedness of games and stories, as well as reality and make-believe. When today's children encounter a version of *Peter Pan* in video game format, the learning curve diminishes because they have heard the story (making it part of cultural knowledge), and have played other video games (the make-believe games of today's child). Just as Wendy, John, and Michael recognize the pirates as enemies, first-time game-players understand the directive of fighting Captain Hook to save the innocent victim. The logistics of controlling and manipulating the game interface may take some practice—just like Wendy, John, and Michael had to slowly learn to fly and maneuver in the air—but the basic strategy and structure of the game are understood.

The audience, or the reader, is then asked to participate in an imaginary storytelling session, whether listening to the text read out loud, reading the book alone, or playing the video game. The narrator as storyteller prompts the reader in the book version: "Let us pretend to lie here among the sugar-cane and watch them as they steal by in single file, each with his hand on his dagger" (258). The reader can watch the Lost Boys tramp by but cannot completely join them. The narrator keeps the reader at a distance by reminding the reader that he/she is not a character or actor in the story: "You or I, not being wild things of the woods, would have heard nothing, but they [the Lost Boys] heard it, and it was the grim song" (262). By linking the reader with the narrator, the narrator shows the reader-position as the next possible storyteller. The reader of *Peter Pan* is like the video game-player because the player continues the telling or creation of the story by playing the game. However, the reader or player does not become an actual character, serving instead only as a vehicle to further the story and game along.

Players perform as characters by controlling one central character or a group of characters in the video game using a game controller, joystick, or keyboard and mouse. The player is thus aligned with that central character through that control. In *Kingdom Hearts,* the central character is Sora, and Peter Pan is one of the other characters that the player can control. In video games, a player controls and performs from that character position within the game narrative. However, the player is also the catalyst by which the game continues, so he or she functions in some way as the narrator by continuing the story. The official narrator of the text retains a similar role as an official narrator within a video game. Like the book's narrator, the game narrator acts as a helper, directing players' and readers' attention to important story strains and giving clues. When the Lost Boys disappear to hide from the pirates, the novel's narrator tells the reader, "I will tell you where they are" (262). This is an unnecessary comment within the context of the book because the storyline could have proceeded to describe their location without explicitly pointing out that the narrator was doing so. But within the context of oral tradition and video games, this pause in narration provides a prompt to retain the reader's attention and further the action while giving the player valuable hints for his/her course of action.

DIGITAL MEDIA, VIDEO GAMES, AND *PETER PAN*

In order to be rewritten or regenerated from the initial story, *Peter Pan* had to be created as a collection of modular and mutable tales, as oral narratives are within the larger framework of the novel. Following the oral tradition, within which Barrie's *Peter Pan* begins, are digital works, which offer a literate return to oral narratives in their modular format, nonlinear structures, participatory requirements, and lack of one definitive version. Also within the oral tradition, each narrator changes, adds, and adapts each version as well as choosing which version or adventure to tell.

Digital works fall under the rubric of new media, which includes video games, Internet web pages, interactive software, hypertext, and other digital forms. In defining the key elements of new media in *The Language of New Media,* Lev Manovich notes the importance of modularity and variability. Manovich defines modularity in new media as being composed of various elements that can exist alone, or that "can be combined into even larger objects—again, without losing their independence" (30). The modularity of new media directly parallels the modular structure of oral narratives, in which one segment of a story may be added or removed based on audience or time constraints. For video games, modularity allows games to be played as one large story or as a larger set of stories; the player can choose to play all or just a few of the stories within the game. *Peter Pan* is inherently modular because the story can be told with or without various story elements, such as the Lost Boys, the Indians, the Mermaids, Nana as the nurse, and so on. In addition to exchanging characters, the manner in which the events take place changes with different characters, which connects to retellings of *Peter Pan* because various characters are exchanged for different stories; for example, some versions remove the Indians and Tiger Lily. This removal follows Propp's *Morphology of the Folk Tale,* in which he argues that not all of the elements of a tale need to be included for the tale to remain intact. Instead, the elements are interchangeable within and through multiple categories for those tales. This interchangeability of fairy tale elements relates to the modular structures of new media narratives like video games. Thus, multiple elements are required for the *Peter Pan* story, but these elements change based on the other elements in use, overall requiring only a core of elements to create a *Peter Pan* story.

Manovich defines new media in connection with variability: "A new media object is not something fixed once and for all, but something that can exist in different, potentially infinite versions" (36). Variability also holds true for *Peter Pan* because of its history as a retelling instead of a set story. As Jacqueline Rose notes in *The Case of Peter Pan; Or, the Impossibility of Children's Fiction,* "*Peter Pan* was both never written and, paradoxically, has never ceased to be written" (6). These revisions drew upon the modular structure to exchange the story segments for different retellings, as well as modifying those segments. For instance, the Indians and Tiger Lily have been removed from several *Peter Pan* retellings, but their removal has not devastated the story of *Peter Pan* or made it unrecognizable.[1] Part of this constant revision is due to the participatory nature of the story, as designed by Barrie and the Llewelyn Davies boys.

The participatory aspect of *Peter Pan* has already been noted by video game scholars like Murray who, in *Hamlet on the Holodeck,* cites the phenomenon of clapping for Tinker Bell in the play versions of *Peter Pan* as an experience akin to video game-play. She explains that such works call the reader/player to participate in some capacity, even if only to the limited degree of clapping (126). Video games require participation, as do oral narratives like the make-believe play within which *Peter Pan* began.

Despite these connections, the majority of *Peter Pan* video games serve as complements to the films instead of actual re-visionings or remediations of Barrie's work or the story of *Peter Pan* as it has evolved in its various incarnations. However, *Kingdom Hearts* provides a foil to these rather straightforward video game versions of *Peter Pan*. *Kingdom Hearts*, unlike other *Peter Pan* video games, was a major video game release that both included and remediated the story of *Peter Pan* by including story segments from *Peter Pan,* altering the overall story and these segments to operate specifically for video games, and using the format of the story to frame the larger game design. Rose notes that *Peter Pan* can only be rewritten; *Peter Pan* itself requires a major re-writing to fully translate into the form of video games as a story that can be *rewritten* in itself and repeatedly *rewritten* within the new medium, instead of existing as a simplified version of an existing version as the majority of *Peter Pan* video games are. Unlike the other video game versions, which are often linear revisions of existing tales, *Kingdom Hearts* explores *Peter Pan* by presenting the story within a frame that mirrors the modular structure of the original story. By using this modular structure, *Kingdom Hearts* serves to create a basic framework that can be used for subsequent versions in the same way that *Peter Pan's* modular structure lays the foundation for revisions. Because of these changes, *Kingdom Hearts* proves the best place to analyze the manner and means by which Barrie's *Peter Pan* translates into the digital form of video games.

Kingdom Hearts embeds the story of *Peter Pan* within a similar narrative about a boy named Sora who is fighting to save one of his friends from an evil group known as the Heartless. These Heartless are not just heartless adjectivally, as Peter is; instead, these characters are part of a group known as the Heartless. The game follows Sora through various adventures in multiple worlds, with the characters and worlds based on Disney films and Square Enix games.[2] In the *Peter Pan* segment of *Kingdom Hearts,* the player must subdue Sora's own shadow; defeat Hook, who is aligned with the Heartless; save Wendy from Hook; and reset Big Ben to the correct time—all to combat the overall enemy, the Heartless. Like Peter, Sora must grapple with his shadow, but unlike Peter, Sora must actually defeat his shadow rather than merge with it. Sora must do this in order to progress in the game. *Kingdom Hearts* also includes the Crocodile, complete with the clock in her belly. Significantly, these connections to the story are only part of the relationship of *Peter Pan* and *Kingdom Hearts,* with the larger connections present in the similar structure and theme of both narratives.[3]

Kingdom Hearts begins with the player manipulating only the character Sora. Disney's Goofy and Donald Duck join Sora after his early travels in Traverse Town, the nexus space for connecting game-play areas. Like the novel *Peter Pan*'s use of Peter as the main fighter aided by Tinker Bell, Wendy, and the boys, *Kingdom Hearts* shows Sora to be the main character, while also showing the significance of other heroes. Jiminy Cricket also joins the group as the scribe; he takes notes on all of the battles, the enemies, and the main characters. By retelling the events and acting as a convenient mnemonic device for players, Jiminy Cricket replaces Wendy as storyteller within the digital medium of video games, where events occur differently based on how the game is played, and so the stories are needed to tell what has happened and to provide direction for later play.

Kingdom Hearts begins with an initial character gathering, during which the player uses Sora for play and then adds other characters to the playing party so that the player is able to manipulate multiple characters simultaneously. By having several characters within the primary group, *Kingdom Hearts* is like *Peter Pan* in that Peter, Wendy, John, and Tinker Bell are all primary characters, unlike most video game versions of *Peter Pan*, which focus solely on Peter instead of including a group of characters. The player can also exchange members of the playing party of Sora, Donald, and Goofy for other characters in the various game worlds, including Peter Pan, when the game progresses into Neverland. Some of these players can be used for extensive periods of time and others only for selected battles or game areas. By being able to switch characters, participants can dictate the game-play and narrative. For instance, some of the additional characters cannot be accessed until they have been won by performing special tasks and earning special stones. Then the player must take these stones to Traverse Town to have the characters separated from the stones. This is done by the Fairy Godmother, who resides at Merlin's house in Traverse Town and who helps the players by drawing spirits out of the special stones so that the characters who were trapped in the stones can help in the fight against the evil Heartless.

Tinker Bell is one of the spirits that can be freed, and she acts by healing the entire group and by preventing Sora from being knocked out in battle. Here Tinker Bell, as opposed to mending pots and kettles as her name implies, mends her companion's health. Because of her healing powers and because she is added to the group rather than replacing one of the characters in the group, Tinker Bell proves very useful during game-play. Most characters must be exchanged ultimately so that the overall group does not grow too large, but Tinker Bell can be added to the group without forcing the removal of any of the other characters. Additionally, Tinker Bell serves as a supplemental character who alters the group dynamic by greatly adding to its effectiveness without taking up additional space. In the stage versions of *Peter Pan,* Tinker Bell is often portrayed as a point of light, as she is in the beginning of the Disney cartoon movie, but she is not a physically defined character. Likewise, she does not take up space in the game-play group, but she does change the game-play of a group when she is added to it.

Kingdom Hearts also mirrors *Peter Pan* in the method of travel used in the narrative, especially as it relates to the pacing of the narrative. Paralleling Peter Pan's flying ability, *Kingdom Hearts* uses an airship, called a Gummi Ship, for travel in the game. Airships in video games are generally depicted as either zeppelins or large sailing ships that fly. The airship provides players with the ability to have characters that they are manipulating fly together as a group without the confusion that flying in large areas would cause during game-play. Flying without an airship in *Kingdom Hearts* would be more difficult because the player would otherwise need to be able to navigate and to spend time manipulating his or her characters in flight over large and complicated areas. Further, the player would have to manipulate the controls for flying, which would be difficult to do between the large game areas like Neverland and Wonderland and which would be difficult to do for sustained periods of time with a group of characters. The airship creates a more simplistic mode of travel because the player can set the controls and then the airship makes travel instantaneous. The characters, by being able to fly, are able to move easily and quickly.

The use of an airship also connects thematically to *Peter Pan* and other adventure tales with pirate ships because the ship in *Kingdom Hearts* is based on the ships from other Square Enix games, especially the *Final Fantasy* game series. In the *Final Fantasy* games, travel is normally done with an airship, which looks like a traditional large sailing pirate ship. Airship travel also exists in many of the film versions of *Peter Pan,* in which the *Jolly Roger* pirate ship transports the children back to London, so that their mode of re-entering civilization is on a flying ship. Video game airships, like the Gummi Ship in *Kingdom Hearts,* can travel over the mapped-out world, making travel much faster and allowing players to reach areas that would otherwise be inaccessible. *Kingdom Hearts* actually presents one screen that shows a map of the multiple game worlds, which includes Traverse Town, Neverland, Wonderland, and many others. By using the map, the player only has to board the Gummi Ship to travel. The ship then takes the player to the map screen, where he or she can choose which world to travel to next. The ship thus acts as a narrative, rather than a literal, flying ship. The literal flying in the game occurs in Neverland with Peter Pan. By quickening the pace of spatial transitions via flight, the game relies on flying as both a game-play and a narrative component, just as *Peter Pan* relies on flying for a narrative and plot device. Flying acts as a plot device by transitioning locations quickly and a narrative device by providing a method that sparks adventures.

Further, the use of a map for traveling also relates to the significance of maps in *Peter Pan* because, in both *Peter Pan* and *Kingdom Hearts,* maps directly relate to and illustrate the intimate connection between space and narrative, just as the *Indiana Jones* films use maps to represent transition both for the narrative and spatial movement for the characters. The treasure maps in the *Peter Pan* narrative as well as the literal maps in the beginnings of many of the novels and the maps for travel in *Kingdom Hearts* also serve to spatially orient and organize the possible narratives. As digital media scholar Espen Aarseth has noted, space is the defining factor in video games (154). For video games like *Kingdom Hearts,* the space is represented modularly, with many worlds joined by the connecting node of Traverse Town. *Kingdom Hearts* uses Traverse Town as its nexus point for departure into other stories, including the specific *Peter Pan* tale, in the same way that *Peter Pan* begins and ends with London. This nodal structure easily affords side quests by allowing players to access some areas without having to access all and by allowing the sequence of access to vary. The nodal structure and sequence are similar to the reorganization of events in other retellings of *Peter Pan.* However, since the reorganization in *Kingdom Hearts* is participatory, it can change each time the player plays the game, just like an oral version of *Peter Pan.*

Peter Pan and *Kingdom Hearts* both rely on nodal structures based in the cities that spawn them—cities that allow for a multitude of stories, and cities that easily connect to other worlds. Yet within these expansive, open worlds of London and Neverland, the smaller spaces for the narrative or video game (such as the Darlings' house and the pirate ship) must be defined in some manner. Defining the space for most narratives means defining the place in which the narrative occurs, like a home in London; but for *Peter Pan* tales, it includes defining the spaces in multiple narratives for multiple alterations, like the multiple versions of London. For video games, the spaces must be completely defined by computer code in order to create playable spaces, so the island, town, ship, and other spaces help to limit the scope of the game. Because these spaces are completely defined, they can be used for multiple types of game-play, as with the Big Ben segment in *Kingdom Hearts* in which the player can fly around Big Ben and correct the time to progress in the game or simply fly around and look at London's cityscape. Because video games narrowly define spaces in this way, like having Big Ben represent London in *Kingdom Hearts,* other video games may approach the same narratives and spaces in new, though still limited, ways, as in Disney's *Peter Pan: Return to Neverland*, in which the video game depicts London as a city street. In presenting only certain spaces, but fully presenting them, video games open up the possibility for play in those spaces and possibilities for other games to construct other versions of play in those and other spaces.

As Joseph Bristow notes in *Empire Boys: Adventures in a Man's World,*

> In children's literature, the island regularly serves as an appropriately diminutive world in which dangers can be experienced within safe boundaries. . . . Islands provide an appositively "child-like" space which boys can easily circumnavigate without revealing any lack of manful maturity. (94)

Bristow's comments on adventure tales connect *Peter Pan* and *Kingdom Hearts* as adventure stories that rely on spatial limits for mastery and play. Further limiting the areas of these tales is the method of access for the island or fantastic spaces—methods such as pixie dust and keyblades in *Kingdom Hearts*. Pixie dust allows players to fly only within the Neverland game level instead of allowing players to fly from world to world or level to level. In order to travel to other worlds, the player must access keyblades, which are keys that open various doors and act as weapons against the Heartless. By providing a device that opens new areas, the narratives are controlled and constrained like the islands Bristow mentions. As such, the keyblades further reinforce the nodal structure of the game's spatial representation and the game's narrative. Like islands in children's literature, the spatial limits in video games allow for simpler, less confusing game-play by permitting the players to divide the spaces into areas for side quests and minor stories. Segmented spaces are also easier for game designers to program because each space acts as a separate, yet connecting area. Further, the modularized chunks allow players to save their game progress and return to it later with particular portions complete, like a bookmark at a chapter break. Given the benefits of nodal design for the narrative and game-play areas, *Kingdom Hearts* moves from an island to Traverse Town and then to the pirate ship for the *Peter Pan* game segment.

In addition to the spatial design within the game and narrative, both *Kingdom Hearts* and *Peter Pan* present multiple levels of reality in these spaces. Like the game-play control of *Kingdom Hearts,* where the player plays in the fantastic spaces while also learning to operate the game controls, Barrie divides Neverland into a make-believe Neverland and a physically real Neverland. The reader, although active in parts of the story, remains estranged from the actual action of the text, while the narrator destroys the illusion of reality by reminding the reader that he/she is not part of the real Neverland island: "Would that he could hear us, but we are not really on the island, and he passes by, biting his knuckles" (Barrie 258). Statements such as this show the self-reflexive construction of *Peter Pan.* Video games also jolt the player out of the artificial reality of the game at times, especially while the player is learning the game interface and the game tells the player which buttons to press. Yet both the text and the games attempt to convince the player of their reality and authenticity by language and interaction.

While attempting to present seemingly real spaces, both the game and the text manipulate time for different reasons. In most video games, time and space exist as tropes for exploration and conflict because many games have time limits that players must effectively battle in order to explore or to win the game. For instance, in many games players are encouraged to explore the game space and must accomplish certain specific goals along with that exploration within a time limit, which thus restricts the exploration while also acting as a force that the player must combat. Unlike many video games, *Kingdom Hearts* does not have time limits during the *Peter Pan* segment. However, if the players take too long to defeat the larger enemies, the enemies regain their health and are more difficult to defeat. In this way, time is not counted in exact increments as it would be with a clock or gamer timer; instead, time in the game is an underlying force that affects the game less directly. Additionally, time functions thematically and narratively because, as a puzzle in the game, the player must fix Big Ben so that all of the clock faces show the same time. In different versions of the *Peter Pan* story—novel, play, and film—time alters. In some versions, the trip to Neverland is a short journey, while in others it takes weeks for the children to get from London to Neverland. In the video game versions of *Peter Pan*, including *Kingdom Hearts*, the trip to Neverland is either very short or is instantaneous, as it is on the Gummi Ship. While the novel of *Peter Pan* focuses on time as it runs out—Hook being killed by the silent Crocodile whose clock has run down, Wendy growing old, and Peter refusing to grow up—*Kingdom Hearts* extends time and allows for time to replay and to loop. In the novel, play, and film versions, Peter returns sporadically for Wendy (or her daughter or granddaughter) to return to Neverland and start new adventures. In other words, the novel invites replay in the same manner as video games. If the player loses or "dies," then he or she is able to replay the game from the last saved area. Further, the player can restart the game at any point. But time is an investment because gameplay generally lasts around forty hours for one game completion.

Like time, memory also plays a prominent role in the story of *Peter Pan*, as evidenced by Peter's lack of memory: "Alas, he had already forgotten that he owed his bliss to Wendy. He thought he had attached the shadow himself" (Barrie 235). Several times in the novel Peter forgets adventures he has been on, forgets where he has been, and even forgets Wendy's name. She never knows whether to believe his tales or not because of his lack of memory. The recent *Kingdom Hearts: Chain of Memories* (Game Boy Advance 2004) capitalizes on the aspect of memory: like *Peter Pan*, video games must necessarily include a forgetting by the characters because the game characters cannot remember repeated segments if not programmed to do so by the game. In this way, games can have memory for saved events and for repeated events, but only if these are programmed into the game. Otherwise, the games cannot remember because they have not been programmed to do so. Despite forgetting, video games must also include an ability to remember saved events and to help the player in remembering those events. In *Kingdom Hearts,* this remembering is done through the game journal, just as it is done in *Peter Pan* through clues from Peter's adventures, like the mermaid scales left on his clothing after an adventure with the mermaids.

Time and memory function in video games and textual versions of *Peter Pan* to show the players or readers that the story will end, even if only to begin again. In the novel, the narrator assures the audience of a good ending: "If they [Mr. and Mrs. Darling] are not in time, I solemnly promise that it will all come right in the end" (Barrie 244). Players have that same assurance with the video game version. However, if a player plays long enough, he or she will beat the game, and everything will be right at the end. While the reality of the game and the text will come out all right, the make-believe game of Neverland may not. Neverland was a game that could be lost, because with the approach of night, "you lost the certainty that you would win" (252). The narrator also perpetuates uncertainty that Peter Pan will win: "Such is the terrible man [Hook] against whom Peter Pan is pitted. Which will win?" (260). This uncertainty in the novel is mirrored in the game, which offers continuous opportunity for better play and further completion of side goals. Like the oral tales of the Llewelyn Davies boys, these incomplete and uncertain versions of *Peter Pan* encourage readers and players to return, re-reading and re-playing to change the story as they go just as Wendy, her daughter, and her granddaughter do.

GIRLS, WOMEN, AND PETER PAN'S POSSIBILITIES

Because the matriarchal chain of replaying or retelling begun by Wendy carries through the play, novel, and film versions of *Peter Pan,* Wendy acts as the impetus for change and growth for both herself and Peter. As such, Wendy provides a potential for revolution because of her often understated significance in and to the story for all versions of *Peter Pan,* including video games. While Wendy may seem to function as only a helper to the boys, Wendy is actually the more pivotal character. As Carol Anita Tarr explains, "[T]he adventure is for Wendy. . . . Wendy is the center of the whole novel, around whom adventures revolve" (65). Tarr clearly shows that Wendy is the catalyst and the storyteller. Unlike Tarr, Catherine Storr misunderstands both Wendy as a character and Wendy's place in the story:

> Revolting as Wendy is as a character—self-satisfied, possessive, limited in outlook—she is nevertheless interesting in the light she throws on her creator. Apart from that occasion when she tries to persuade Peter to act as a potential husband, she is all mother; her longing to be grown up is centered on the idea of having babies. (23)

Wendy is far from centered on creating babies—she is centered on creating stories. As such, she is both the audience and the creator of these tales. Wendy's role cannot be truncated to her desires within the tale, but must be considered with her significance on the tale itself. For instance, Tarr describes Wendy as a mythic hero: "she leaves on a journey of adventure, through which she practices her mothering skills (much like Snow White), to return a more mature young woman" (64). Wendy does experience several stages of the hero journey described by Campbell, including his three main categories of departure, initiation, and return. Wendy is called to an adventure by Peter, and after a brief refusal of the call, departs into the unknown by first crossing the threshold of the windowsill through the use of flight, a magical agent. Her trials and adventures are many, but she returns and again crosses the threshold of the windowsill, this time as a changed, more mature Wendy. She has delved into two different cosmic worlds—the Neverland of make-believe within her own nursery and the real Neverland of adventures—and successfully mastered both with the aid of Peter and other Neverland helpers. In the video game, with Wendy as both the storyteller and the catalyst, gamers effectively become a Wendy character in the sense that the adventure is for them and that Peter or Sora is their guide. Like the oral narratives or plays that required an audience for the telling, *Peter Pan*'s newest form again requires someone like Wendy, not just within the story, but as an active participant in order for the story to be told. Wendy thus plays an important role for the story of *Peter Pan,* for video games, and for children because, as video games continue to gain popularity as the preferred storytelling medium for children, both genders need representation. Video games, like media before them, have tended to focus more heavily on male characters. As players manipulate and perform as their characters, representation becomes increasingly important.

Although Wendy presents an opening for new story types in video games, most games still rely on limited narratives. Focusing on what he considers the masculine nature of *Peter Pan*, Routh states, "Peter is the 'hero' of a typically masculine narrative which rejects women, marriage, work, and even death" (301–2). Video games also reject these by oppressing women and getting rid of death with replay. However, because more and more game players are female—a fact that the video game industry has acknowledged—video games need to address female players and provide innovative stories. Wendy presents one possibility for doing so. By removing the female characters, especially by attempting to reduce Wendy to a damsel in distress, video game versions of *Peter Pan* have only served to further limit the current versions while simultaneously opening the possibilities for new remediations of the story. As Tarr notes, "In the film [*Hook*], females are ever-loving and right-minded, but static. They are more representations than real" (68). This is also a flaw in the video game versions, in which the game's creators have chosen to keep the females as minor or non-player-characters (that is, a player cannot choose to become Wendy; she is not a character with agency). This proves odd given the fact that *Kingdom Hearts* draws on characters from both Disney and the game publisher Square Enix, including female characters from Square Enix's *Final Fantasy* games. The non-Disney characters in *Kingdom Hearts* are decidedly similar to the characters of the *Final Fantasy* games, which is important to note because Square Enix has recently released *Final Fantasy X-2*. This eleventh game in the series focuses on what once were minor female characters, thus responding to the demands of players of the previous game, *Final Fantasy X.* Yet the *X-2* denotes that this game is not a new version of the main storylines—which would actually be titled *Final Fantasy XI*—but rather a substory, an indication that female characters are still not implemented as the main characters in the main series.

Clearly, the most recent video game remediations of *Peter Pan* are still following other *Peter Pan* versions by neglecting female characters. Nevertheless, by virtue of including Wendy in such a pivotal position, even as a substory, we are hopeful that female characters will continue to evolve as the next logical step in the ever evolving tale of *Peter Pan.*

NOTES

1. Tiger Lily and the Indians are not included in the film *Hook,* the book *Walt Disney's Peter Pan and Wendy,* or the video game *Kingdom Hearts.*

2. Disney and Square Enix are the co-creators of *Kingdom Hearts.*

3. Because Square Enix is based in Japan and *Kingdom Hearts* was released in both the United States and Japan, *Kingdom Hearts* is a cross-cultural endeavor.

WORKS CITED

Aarseth, Espen J. "Allegories of Space: The Question of Spatiality in Computer Games." *CyberText Yearbook 2000.* Ed. Markku Eskelinen and Raine Koskimaa. Jyvaskyla, Finland: Research Centre for Contemporary Culture, 2001. 152–71.

Barrie, J. M. *Peter Pan*. 1911. New York: Smithmark, 1995.

Birkin, Andrew. *J. M. Barrie and the Lost Boys: The Real Story Behind Peter Pan*. New Haven: Yale UP, 2003.

Bristow, Joseph. *Empire Boys: Adventures in a Man's World*. London: Harper Collins, 1991.

Campbell, Joseph. *The Hero with a Thousand Faces*. 1949. Princeton: Princeton UP, 1973.

Disney Junior Games: Peter Pan Neverland Treasure Quest. Video game: PC. Prod. Disney Interactive. San Mateo, CA: Sony, 2002.

Fox's Peter Pan and the Pirates. Video game: Nintendo Entertainment System. Prod. THQ. Redmond, WA: Nintendo of America, 1991.

Hook. Dir. Steven Spielberg. Perf. Dustin Hoffman, Robin Williams, and Julia Roberts. Columbia Tristar, 1991.

Kingdom Hearts. Video game: Playstation 2. Prod. Square Enix. Los Angeles: Square Enix, 2002.

Kingdom Hearts: Chain of Memories. Video game: Game Boy Advance. Prod. Square Enix. Los Angeles: Square Enix, 2004.

Manovich, Lev. *The Language of New Media*. Cambridge: MIT Press, 2001.

Morris, Tim. *You're Only Young Twice: Children's Literature and Film*. Urbana, IL: U of Illinois P, 2000.

Murray, Janet. *Hamlet on the Holodeck: The Future of Narrative in Cyberspace*. Cambridge: MIT Press, 1998.

Nodelman, Perry, and Mavis Reimer. *The Pleasures of Children's Literature*. 3rd ed. Boston: Allyn and Bacon, 2003.

Peter Pan. Dir. Clyde Geronimi and Wilfred Jackson. Perf. Bobby Driscoll, Kathryn Beaumont, and Hans Conried. Disney, 1953.

Peter Pan. Dir. P. J. Hogan. Perf. Jason Issacs, Jeremy Sumpter, and Rachel Hurd-Ward. Universal Studios, 2003.

Peter Pan. Video game: Game Boy Advance. Prod. Atari. New York: Atari, 2003.

Peter Pan: Return to Neverland. Dir. Robin Budd and Donovan Cook. Perf. Harriet Owen, Blayne Weaver, and Corey Burton. Walt Disney Home Video, 2002.

Peter Pan: Return to Neverland. Video game: Game Boy Advance. Prod. Disney Interactive. Burbank, CA: Disney Interactive, 2002.

Propp, Vladimir. *Morphology of the Folktale*. 1968. Austin: U of Texas P, 1998.

Rose, Jacqueline. *The Case of Peter Pan; Or, the Impossibility of Children's Fiction*. Philadelphia: U of Pennsylvania P, 1992.

Routh, Chris. "Peter Pan: Flawed or Fledgling 'Hero'?" *A Necessary Fantasy: The Heroic Figure in Children's Popular Culture*. Ed. Dudley Jones and Tony Watkins. New York: Garland, 2000. 291–307.

Storr, Catherine. "Peter Pan." *Children's Literature in Education* 23.1 (1992): 15–26.

Tarr, Carol Anita. "Shifting Images of Adulthood: From Barrie's *Peter Pan* to Spielberg's *Hook.*" *The Antic Art: Enhancing Children's Literary Experiences Through Film and Video.* Ed. Lucy Rollin. Fort Atkinson, WI: Highsmith, 1993. 63–72.

Walt Disney Productions. *Walt Disney's Peter Pan and Wendy.* New York: Random House, 1981.

10

The Riddle of His Being: An Exploration of Peter Pan's Perpetually Altering State

Karen McGavock

Sir James Matthew Barrie defied being "fixed" by anyone, either emotionally or in print. In his dedication to the play *Peter Pan or the Boy Who Wouldn't Grow Up*, he insisted, "only he [No 4] and No 1 could touch me" (311).[1] Numbers one to five corresponded, in descending order of age, to the five Llewelyn Davies boys, whose games inspired *Peter Pan*. Michael and George were numbers four and one. It is ironic that they were the only two who could "touch" Barrie since they had both died by the time this dedication was written. By converting them into copy, Barrie attempted to hold on to the remaining boys who were growing up and away from him by the time the 1928 edition of the play was published. He thus perpetrates the practice that he defied and rebuked in others who attempted to fix him. The significance of Barrie's untouchable nature is reaffirmed in his inaugural address to the Incorporated Society of Authors, Playwrights and Composers, in which he remarked, "I suppose many of you have been reading the noble biography of which half has just appeared. There is a passage of two or three lines in it that may be more revealing than anything else in the book, that in which we are told how from his earliest years he disliked being touched by anyone" (*McConnachie* 158).[2] Barrie referred to himself in the second person when commenting on his work, possibly as a means of distancing himself from his creation. Using his tremendous capacity to occupy more than one space simultaneously, he avoided stagnancy and subverted convention.

Peter Pan, like his creator, claims to be untouchable. The only explanation Barrie offers in the play is that "it has something to do with the riddle of his being" (*Peter Pan* 153). Even Captain Hook cannot touch Peter Pan. He sets out to "cleave him to the brisket (but he has a sinking [feeling] that this boy has no brisket)" (144). Hook's claw "find[s] nothing to tear at" (145) when he attempts to strike out at his archrival. As with Barrie, any attempt made by Peter Pan to remain untouchable is undone. Our first and last encounters with Peter Pan find him sobbing, so others can touch Peter emotionally even though he prefers to withdraw for fear of being hurt. Further into the play we discover that only fairies "can touch him." They "tweak Peter's nose and pass on" (117). However, fairies can touch Peter only when he is asleep. A correlation can therefore be drawn between Barrie and his creation in that nothing can consciously touch either of them. Peter Pan can be touched only when asleep and only the dead can touch Barrie.

FLEXIBILITY OF CHARACTERS

The paradoxical and uneasy relationship between fixity and lack of fixity in *Peter Pan* is worth scrutinizing. Contrary to Holbrook Jackson's belief that "Peter Pan is a symbol of eternity, of that complete unchangeable spirit of the world" (113), I believe his ephemeral changing renders him unfixed. I also contest Jane Ellison, who suggests that Peter Pan does not change. In his perpetually altering state, he is in constant flux, always changing rather than not changing, thereby shirking fixity and remaining a vivifying force. Suspended animation occurs within and through *Peter Pan*, illustrated by the games on the rock, which "end so abruptly that several divers are checked in the air. There they hang waiting for the word of command from Peter" (119). Barrie describes Peter Pan as "betwixt and between" (*White Bird* 186), the symbol of process, as one who finds beginnings and endings problematic. Peter Pan has the capacity to start and stop, though he chooses to remain suspended between origin and terminus. However, the suspension does not last forever, and the magical fairy dust gradually dissipates. Barrie can hold moments in suspense only for a limited time in *Peter Pan*. He has enough power only to *defer*, but not to *deny* terminus. Neither Peter Pan nor Barrie is unchangeable; rather, each constantly changes in order to avoid being fixed. Peter Pan, text and character, can best be described as transient. As Peter Hollindale, the play's most recent editor, suggests, "Barrie's plays can be seen as explorations of the tension between change and changelessness" (*Peter Pan* x). Barrie actively rejects fixity, resolution, and certainty in his writing. Therefore, he occupies a space "in between" which provides an insight into his suspicion regarding fixity as a stagnant state of death. Through occupying a liminal space between childhood and adulthood and through *Peter Pan*, Barrie also allows readers the space to negotiate reflexivity and to explore the altered state of childhood.

Peter Pan is a tale of form and re-form, and perpetual change occurs both in and through Peter Pan as an atemporal entity. Hollindale acknowledges, "neither in time passing nor in time stilled do Barrie's people essentially change" (x). He believes that "in Barrie's thinking there was an unresolved contradiction between belief in the fixity of human personality and belief in the multiple possibilities opened up for every individual" (x). Yet this is difficult to reconcile with a comment made by Barrie in his autobiography, *The Greenwood Hat*. Here he assures us that "one remains the same person throughout" (78). By confirming his belief in the fixity of human personality, he ironically fixes himself in this statement, probably something he would have striven to avoid in hindsight. The debate between change and changelessness finds voice in Barrie's comment that "Wendy looks a little older, but Peter is just the same" (*Peter Pan* 153). Wendy is implicated in time whereas Peter Pan exists in a timeless domain. The difference between change and changelessness typifies their relationship (*Peter Pan* xiii).

Barrie repeatedly refers to Peter Pan as "that tragic boy." There is a strange but insightful connection between the origins of the term "tragic" and its association to Pan and the term "chimera," which best describes Peter Pan's propensity to perpetually change position and to shape-shift. The connection is the association between Peter Pan and goats. Indeed, in the earlier iteration of *Peter Pan*, *The Little White Bird*, Peter rides a goat and plays pipes, rendering the connection explicit. The etymology of "tragedy" is "he-goat song" (*OED* 1478). The pagan figure of Pan is definitely goatish, being half-man and half-goat, and the etymology of "chimera" is "she-goat" (*OED* 228). So it seems that Peter Pan contains both the he-goat and she-goat aspects. In representing Hook, who stereotypically fits the image of a dominant male, Barrie chooses to focus on his feminine side. He says, "there is a touch of the feminine in Hook, as in all the greatest pirates" (*Peter Pan* 122). This is not merely a flippant remark since he later refers to "Smee at his sewing machine [which] lends a touch of domesticity to the night" (139). In this way, Barrie emasculates the pirates. He also disrupts stereotypical associations of women with domesticity. Other such blur-rings between female and male characteristics are apparent in *Peter Pan*. Barrie refers to the co-existence of the masculine and the femi-nine in fairies, explaining, "the mauve fairies are boys and the white ones are girls, and there are some colours who don't know what they are" (152), which reveals some gender confusion in the narrative.

Peter Pan changes shape and position so often that he is uncertain about his identity. Wendy is the first to ask Peter Pan what he is but he cannot answer. His responses to Wendy's question are vague and ab-stract. Hook asks, "Pan, who and what art thou?" (*Peter Pan* 145), but he is not satisfied with a response. Peter Pan is suspended between the realms of subject (since he cannot indicate "who" he is) and object (since he cannot state "what" he is), so he remains uncategorized. Sev-eral references are made to Peter Pan's shape-shifting throughout the play. Barrie indicates, "Peter, who will be the determining factor in the end, has a perplexing way of changing sides" (123). Peter Pan is of am-biguous intent, changing position so often that neither the readers nor the characters within the text are ever certain where they are with him. Another example of Peter Pan as shape-shifter occur when he mimics Tiger Lily's war cry to the Indians "so naturally that even the lost boys are deceived" (120). The only insight Barrie offers us into Peter Pan's condition is through reference to the Llewelyn Davies boys, whom Bar-rie had used to form Peter and who "had changed from Lost Boys into pirates, which was probably also a tendency of Peter's" (81). Barrie re-quires his readers to remain alert when in the company of Peter Pan since nothing is ever certain and darkness lurks in his adventures, in his personality, and on every page.

Peter Pan exists in suspended animation and therefore his life is on hold, to the extent that nothing can be fully resolved. As an elusive character, Peter constantly moves so quickly that he cannot develop. Barrie comments that Peter Pan can "hardly ever stand still" (*Peter Pan* 100). The fairies and Peter Pan seem to lead an accelerated existence. Even the island itself appears to exist in a state of accelerated change or motion. When Wendy, Michael, and John first see Neverland, they perceive it gradually, but actually the island appears so quickly that its bang would shock them. This explains why Peter is the only character who instigates change but remains unchanged. Symbolizing the form of time itself, he remains unaffected by time and so cannot die, result-ing in his suspension.

Since Barrie actively rejects fixity, resolution, and certainty in his writing, he occupies a liminal space, providing an insight into his suspicion regarding fixity as a stagnant and deathlike state. Unlike Kurt Vonnegut's Billy Pilgrim in *Slaughterhouse-Five*, Peter Pan has not become *unstuck* in time but is, instead *stuck* in time. Time "fastens" as well as "quickens" in him in that it fixes and holds him. All time is continuously present for Peter, and indeed, time seems to exist entire in him. He embodies the form of time (as process) rather than being affected by time. Barrie explains that Peter "had no sense of time. He thought all the past was just yesterday. He spoke as if it was just yesterday that he and I had parted—and it was a whole year" (*Peter Pan* 159). Yesterday was as far back as Peter Pan could remember. He was not only "stuck" in time; he was "lodged" in time, which evokes the antithetical connotation that he not only passively *dwelt* in, but also actively *inhabited* time in his symbolic role as "process."

TEXTUAL FLEXIBILITY

Barrie had a problem with origins, and he also found resolution difficult. Consequently, his texts and the characters within them remain highly volatile and irresolute. He resisted closure, being reluctant to fix the play *Peter Pan* in print and taking years to agree on a version for publication. Humphrey Carpenter reveals the tremendous difficulty that Barrie had "in finding a satisfactory ending for the play, [because for Barrie] there can be no ending, only a return to the beginning" (180), and Roger Lancelyn Green also indicates Barrie's difficulty with conclusions in other works such as *The Admirable Crichton* (1918). Barrie rebels against being fixed by a canon, and he also simultaneously reinforces and undermines convention by desentimentalizing childhood in *Peter Pan*. Barrie recoils from completion, leaving his reader at the point of transition, a situation described by Edward Said as a "transitive beginning" (xiii). To resolve tensions would be to commit himself, rendering him fixed, which he is reluctant to do.

There are various kinds of problems in categorizing Barrie because of the many tales he spins about the origin of *Peter Pan*, his divided locus as an exiled Scot (having lived in London most of his adult life), and his claims that he had forgotten when he wrote *Peter Pan*. I believe the genre flexibility is due to the fact that Barrie had a problem with origins, linked with his desire to resist fixity and defer responsibility for his works. As postmodern critic David Jasper points out, "myths of origin abound . . . in literature. In every case, they are born of the fear of textuality" (xvi). Barrie's "fear of textuality" derives from the terror of committing himself in print. An example of this can be found in the many accounts he gave of the origin of *Peter Pan.*

Barrie was reluctant to "fix" his text in print because it was constantly changing, evolving. It took Barrie until 1928 to publish a version of the text after the 1904 performance. He does not explicitly state his reason for the delay, only remarking in the play's dedication to his "uncomfortable admission that I have no recollection of writing the play of *Peter Pan,* now being published for the first time so long after he made his bow upon the stage" (76). It is curious that nowhere in his autobiography does he mention *Peter Pan.* When he did offer commentary on *Peter Pan,* his remarks were whimsical and he was reluctant to elaborate on explanations. A speech delivered by Barrie to the Royal Literary Fund on May 9, 1904, resonates with *Peter Pan,* which he was drafting contemporaneously. In it he reflected,

> I suppose it comes of following this trade of imagining things, but, indeed, I am not certain whether we are really here or whether this is only a chapter in a book; and if it is a chapter in a book I wonder which of us all is writing it; and whoever is writing it, Heaven knows, I wish him well through the opening sentence. (*McConnachie* 13)

Barrie delayed publishing *Peter Pan* because he thought that publication of it would "spoil the nature of the play to pin it down forever: static" (Ferguson 11). Barrie's unending revisionism is the artistic projection of a philosophical stance that was sceptical of fixed and permanent truth and convinced of relativity or circumstantial change, seeing life and art alike as fluid and provisional (*Peter Pan* xi). Indeed, this is borne out in Barrie's interest in metaphysics and philosophical dilemmas, particularly those theories espoused by Bishop George Berkeley, who explored notions regarding the persistence of matter amid transience. Barrie was a compulsive reviser, and as a result, Heather Neill believes that "*Peter Pan* must be the most written and rewritten play ever" (3). Hollindale also recognizes that "the more obviously mobile texts including . . . *Peter Pan,* permit all manner of synthetic reconstructions. . . . All we can do is take a 'freeze-frame' of one stage in Barrie's thinking about a play" (*Peter Pan* xv).

Arguably the first incarnation of Peter Pan occurred in 1896 in the form of *Sentimental Tommy,* which tells the tale of Tommy Sandys, a young Scot who was born in London but who grows up in the village of Thrums. At the end of the book, Tommy becomes a writer. *Sentimental Tommy* basically documents Barrie's own rise to literary success. The year 1902 heralded the second incarnation of Peter Pan in *The Little White Bird*, a prose work marketed for adults and the first actual appearance of Peter Pan in print. At this stage, *Peter Pan* was not intended for a child audience. The change in audience must have occurred later on in *Peter Pan*'s history, since it was children this time, rather than adults, that were the afterthought. R. D. S. Jack believes that explicit changes were made to concur with the change in the audience which the play attracted (9). *Peter Pan* thus transgressed conventional boundaries and evolved to become a play predominantly targeted at child audiences.

The third incarnation of *Peter Pan* appeared in 1904 when the text had been freed from the constraints of an adult novel and had been transposed onto the stage. The first steps toward staging *Peter Pan* were tentative. Susan Aller writes that "the first producer he showed the script to was sure Barrie had lost his mind, and he told a few people so" (9). Never one to give up at the first hurdle, he tried another producer. Jacqueline Rose explains that "Barrie effectively blackmail[ed] his producer, Charles Frohman, into staging *Peter Pan* by offering him another play, *Alice Sit-By-The-Fire*, as a guaranteed financial investment, with Frohman immediately enamoured of *Peter Pan*" (90). So it appears that *Peter Pan* gained success by the back door. *Peter Pan* was staged for the first time on December 27, 1904, in the Duke of York's Theatre in London. Ironically, *Peter Pan* was to become more popular than its insurance guarantee of *Alice Sit-By-The-Fire*, which was published in 1905. The first published version of *Peter Pan* appeared in 1906 in *Peter Pan in Kensington Gardens*, and in 1908, another scene was added to the end of *Peter Pan*. On February 22, 1908, during the last night of the fourth London season of *Peter Pan*, "When Wendy Grew Up" made its first and last stage appearance in Barrie's lifetime (*Peter Pan* vii). Having begun life in a prose work, *The Little White Bird*, then been transformed into a play, *Peter Pan* once again made the transition from play to prose with the publication in 1911 of *Peter and Wendy*. In 1920, the final addition was made to *Peter Pan* when Barrie wrote his dedication to the play, in readiness for the most authoritative version of the play, published in 1928.

The evolution of texts from one genre to another was not unusual for Barrie, for he often "generically re-configured his own novels into plays" (Jack 3). *Peter Pan* is the most adapted work of Barrie's career, and has also been prolifically reproduced and adapted throughout its publication history. Barrie was also keen on modal differentiation. As a result, it is interesting to negotiate the tensions that occur both within and between the boundaries of prose and drama in *Peter Pan* and which result in a blurring between genres. Indeed, *Peter Pan* is re-garded as the first text to issue different versions simultaneously ("First Golden Age").³ Jack believes that *Peter Pan* epitomizes generic virtu-osity: "the basic plot is translated into nine different modes, as hypoth-esis within novel, photograph collection, episode in novel, full-length play, one-act play, ballet, short story, film and speech" (4).⁴ *Peter Pan* breaks the rules of literary representation for children as a result of Bar-rie's selective approach to amalgamating diverse elements of various types of narrative fairy tale and fantasy. He mixes genres, resulting in a loss of coherence and confusion at the level of character relationship, gender, and identity. Jasper believes that no "ontological surety" equals no "guarantee of sense and coherence" (111). The text remains unsta-ble and irresolute, and as a result of ambiguity between the text and character, manifold confusion occurs.

MULTIPLE ORIGINS OF PETER PAN

Complications in tracing the origin of Peter Pan are attributable to the multiple sources from which the texts and the eponymous character are derived. Contrary to Rose, Hollindale, and Carpenter's belief that Peter Pan was of singular origin,⁵ I argue that he was of multiple origin. Peter Pan arose out of a conglomeration rather than an amalgamation of factors, the strains of which are evident on closer inspection of the text. The factors that constitute Peter Pan's being are not melted down and homogenized; instead they continue to exist heterogeneously and are held in tension. There are several "Peters" in Peter Pan, just as there are several "Alices" in *Alice in Wonderland.* This is a magical, phan-tasmagoric act whereby objects interact with one another and merge to create the illusion of one from many component parts. Since Barrie's Peter Pan and Carroll's Alice appear as phantoms from their own lives, it is not surprising that they haunt the narratives of both writers. They are drawn from a deep source within and are brought together as one in the text to reconcile or make manageable their disparate parts. It is not simply the case of one part being addressed, perpetuated, and sustained. When asked to explain who he is, Peter Pan replies, "I'm youth, I'm joy, I'm a little bird that has broken out of the egg" (145). His answer is threefold; he cannot offer merely one response. He fails to categorize himself and avoids being categorized by others. Hollindale suggests that this avoidance behaviour is an indication of Barrie's mutability: "Barrie can be at once Scot and Englishman . . . Pan and Hook" (*Peter Pan* xx). In Chapter 8 of *Margaret Ogilvy*, Barrie culturally differentiates Scotland and England, accounting for dichotomies within his writing:

> I saw myself speaking English the long day through. You only know the shell of a Scot until you have entered his home circle; in his office, in clubs, at social gatherings where you and he seem to be getting on so well he is really a house with all the shutters closed and the door locked. I try to keep my shutters open and my foot in the door but they will bang to. (122)

Barrie is "trapped" by his Scottishness, yet finds himself "exposed" in England. He did not want, however, to be defined by anything or anybody, let alone by nationality. Carpenter indicates a difficulty in pinning Barrie down since when "one part of him is being horribly sentimental; the other part is standing back and mocking it" (186). In publishing his prose version of the text under the title *Peter and Wendy*, Barrie "speak[s] to two different children at once" (Rose 125), which suggests that the tale is of double or split origin—almost evocative of the biological process of cell replication and division or "mitosis" during reproduction.

There are several sources for Peter Pan: the Llewelyn Davies boys; Barrie's brother David, who died at age thirteen; the mythic Pan; and of course Barrie himself. Barrie's dedication to the play addresses his five child companions, the Llewelyn Davies boys. Although denying authorship of the play, he does claim to have made Peter Pan from a variety of elements. He writes in the Dedication, "I made Peter by rubbing the five of you violently together, as savages with two sticks produce a flame. That is all he is, the spark I got from you" (*Peter Pan* 75). Barrie refers to the tasteless process of sewing "some of the gory fragments together with a pen-nib" (76). He informs us that *Peter Pan* was "streaky" with the residue of the boys. The imagery is graphic. Streakiness can be likened to a blurring which permeates the text, indicating that tensions remain unresolved. It is symptomatic of Barrie's decision to heterogenize rather than homogenize the text or, in other words, to

retain the diversity of elements and hold them in tension rather than as-
similate them by reducing or forging them to a base amalgam in which
difference is lost and potential scope for enrichment is sacrificed. Barrie's most candid revelation about Peter Pan comes from a program
note written by Barrie for the 1908 Paris production of *Peter Pan*:

> [O]f Peter you must make what you will—perhaps he was a boy who died
> young and this is how the author perceives his subsequent adventures. Or
> perhaps he was a boy who was never born at all; a boy whom some peo-
> ple longed for but who never came—it may be that these people hear Pe-
> ter more clearly at the window than children do. (qtd. in Ferguson 11)

This insightful remark should be contrasted with Rose's argument
that Peter Pan was a child who was born, then died (28). Here Barrie
claims that Peter Pan did not die, because he was never born at all.

Although Barrie explains that Peter Pan began life in an egg, which
fell out of his mother's nest, he perplexes at every turn. In conversation
with Wendy, Peter claims that "I ran away the day I was born" (*Peter
Pan* 99). Though he returned when he was older, he found that the
window had been barred. His position within the family had been
usurped, or at least, he had relinquished his position by flying the nest.
He refers to the origin of fairies in vague and abstract terms: "when the
first baby laughed for the first time, the laugh broke into a thousand
pieces and they went skipping about and that was the beginning of
faeries" (99). It appears that, like Peter Pan, fairies are fragmented, so
they are highly volatile and tense. By denying knowledge of the exact
particulars of Peter Pan's conception, Barrie also denies the act of in-
tercourse having taken place, linking Barrie's problems with origins
and his impetus to shirk responsibility as an author. If there is no per-
ceptible origin, it is impossible to return to that fixed point or moment.
Indeed, Rose regards "conception as something which can only be
thought of . . . after" (36). Barrie has a peculiar regard toward conception. He refers to Peter Pan as "a sort of dead baby—he is the baby of
all the people who never had one" (qtd. in Ferguson 11). Rose explains
that

> Peter Pan's task in Kensington Gardens is to bury the dead children who
> break the rules by staying in the Gardens overnight. His own favourite
> birds are the house-swallows, which, unlike all the other birds, are not
> unborn children, but children who were born and then died. (27–28)

If this is the case, then once again it is possible to observe Peter Pan occupying two spaces at once. Barrie offers various counter-claims regarding the conception of Peter Pan, which further complicate our understanding of his origin. The ambiguity of positions in *Peter Pan* makes it easy for readers to form "misconceptions" about Barrie's work. It could also be that Barrie has more ontological concerns with "reproduction" since *Peter Pan* takes such a mutable form.

Another instance of Barrie's idiosyncratic attitude toward conception occurs in the scene in the Darlings' nursery when Michael asks, "[A]m I not to be born at all?" (*Peter Pan* 89). Quite obviously, this is a postnatal impossibility, yet this was not the first time Barrie had subverted the linearity of a sequence. A similar situation arises in *The Little White Bird* (1902), which, as Rose explains,

> starts with the narrator telling David the story of the child's own origins. . . . David is . . . implicated in the story at a number of different levels, each with their own form of ambiguity. The story is told to him, but since it goes back to before the beginning, he has to disappear in order for it to be told. . . . This child is produced inside the story and the story stands in for him when he leaves. (24)

The simultaneous appearance and disappearance, or the dissolution and resolution, of David mirrors the disappearance of the narrator and of the narrative voice. The result is an unmediated directness. It is not surprising that, as Carpenter argues, from "1910–21 Barrie slightly lost authorial control of the play; but dramatic tension was retained to the end" (176). This period of Barrie's life was particularly traumatic since his much cherished wards, George and Michael, died during this time: George on the Western Front in 1915 and Michael in a mysterious suicide pact at Oxford. These losses troubled Barrie immensely, and the trauma sent shockwaves through his writing, resonating at its very core.

Peter Pan's origin can be at least partly derived from the Greek god, Pan.[6] In the first scene of the play, Mrs. Darling thinks she sees "a strange little face" (89) peering in the window. When she leaves the room, the window blows open and Peter Pan flies into the room, "dressed in autumn leaves and cobwebs" (97). Barrie was able to draw on a history of legend, thus facilitating the cultural hold the text had on readers' imaginations. Pan meant different things to different historical periods. Pan's origins lie in Ovid's *Metamorphoses*. Ovid represents Pan as a rapist—a pre-civilized, brutal embodiment of masculinity. In *The Marble Faun: Or, The Romance of Monte Beni* (1860), Nathanial

Hawthorne depicts the faun as resembling Pan in its pagan, primitive. and goatish dimensions. Hawthorne refers to the figure as a raider, which suggests that Barrie's Peter Pan is much truer to the spirit of Pan as described by Ovid. Barrie is also true to the spirit of the original conception of Pan as a devilish raider of childhood, a plunderer or abductor of children. In *Peter Pan*, Barrie explains that Peter Pan does not benignly *find* children who have "fall[en] out of their perambulators when the nurse is looking the other way" (101); he *steals* them. In the Romantic period, Pan was regarded as a symbol of ruralism. In the late nineteenth century, Pan symbolized the youth and vitality of the age, as Patricia Merivale documents in *Pan the Goat-God: His Myth in Modern Times* (1969). Oscar Wilde referred to Pan in his writing, and Barrie must also have known W. B. Yeats's poem, "The Stolen Child" (1889), which draws on Celtic legends about children stolen by fairies and which provides a reworking of the Pan of antiquity while virtually summarizing the plot of *Peter Pan*. Yeats, on the other hand, idealizes Pan as a romantic figure. He consolidates the link between Pan and paganism in the way in which he traces the evolution of a mutable character. The third chapter of *Peter and Wendy* is entitled "Come Away, Come Away!" and refers to the lure of the Neverland, which seems to resonate with Yeats's lure of the faery world and the land of youth. The chorus of "The Stolen Child" is particularly evocative of Barrie's characterization of Pan:

Come away, O human child!
To the waters and the wild
With a faery, hand in hand
For the world's more full of weeping than you can understand.

Barrie must also have been aware of Maurice Hewlett's play, *Pan and the Young Shepherd* (1898). According to Andrew Birkin,

Peter Pan [was] named after the Greek god who symbolized nature, paganism, and the amoral world. Whether this was a deliberate joke to provoke Mary Hodgson's [the Llewelyn Davies boys' nurse] preferences for stories with a "moral application," or merely an allusion to Peter's gay and heartless character, or a multitude of other possibilities, is open to speculation. Cecco Hewlett sometimes accompanied them in the Gardens, and his father, Maurice Hewlett, had just published a play entitled *Pan and the Young Shepherd*, which opened with the line, "Boy, boy, wilt thou be a boy for ever?" This may have been a pure coincidence, but Barrie almost certainly knew of its existence, as he and Hewlett were close friends. (70)[7]

Peter Pan is not the only Pan-based figure, however, in literary culture. Angus Stewart explains that

the Jacobite Pan stood for the pre-Hanoverian golden age, the country virtues of loyal lairds, the hope of renewal. The original Greek Pan had been an ambivalent force, part goat, part man, delight and "panic" terror rolled into one, depicted either with the syrinx, his pipes, or with the lagobolon, a crook or hook for controlling flocks and hunting small game—or it may be Lost Boys. So Hook in more than once sense (though not in all) is Pan. And Pan is Hook. Barrie underlined the point in his 1920 film treatment: the pirate is killed and Peter actually turns into Hook complete with claw. (49)

Stewart therefore furthers the claim that Barrie doubles the characters of Pan and Hook. In one scene of the play, Peter mutates into Captain Hook, who was never originally intended for inclusion in the play. Hook came to be included merely because Barrie needed an additional act for a scene change to be made. In a documentary on Barrie, Birkin revealed that

from his later revision notes it's clear that he completed his first draft without any mention of Hook at all. He didn't need a villain for the simple reason that he already had one: Peter Pan. Captain Hook's inclusion only came about as a result of a technical necessity. The stagehands needed a front cloth scene to give them time to change the scenery. All Barrie now had to do was leaf through the pages of *The Boy Castaways* to find a startling discovery, that the island is the haunt of Captain Swarthy and his pirate crew. It seems to me that this afterthought of Hook's inclusion was one of Barrie's great strokes of good fortune. Had he conceived of Peter as the hero from the outset, he might well have emerged as a one-dimensional character not, in Tyrone Guthrie's words, "as delicate as a moth; as deadly as a bomb." Barrie rewrote it six times and in fact was still rewriting it on the eve of the opening night, trying to bridge gaps in the plot that had been deleted because of staging problems and so it was that in these inauspicious circumstances the curtain finally rose on J. M. Barrie's dream child. The audience consisted entirely of adults. ("Good Ideas")

The late addition of Hook also explains why we never discover the reason Hook is in Neverland: whether he arrived there through expulsion or choice.

Hook and Pan are strangely twinned, and the two divide and then double at the moment of conception. As Stewart notes, the association

with Hook and Peter in terms of their alignment with the Stuarts during Jacobite times was a strong one. Hook's first name is Jacobus,
evocative of the association between Hook and James the Old Pretender. Barrie explains that Hook "bore a strange resemblance to the
ill-fated Stuarts" (*Peter Pan* 108). This places Peter in the position of the
Young Pretender, Bonnie Prince Charlie. In this respect, Hook is regarded as the father of Peter. Hook, like Peter, declares his allegiance
to the Stuarts. He informs John Darling that a condition of being a pirate is "you would have to swear 'Down with King George'" (140).
Here, dual reference is made—to King George III but also to King
George V, who occupied the throne when Barrie drafted his 1928 version of the play for publication. As always with Barrie, ambiguity pre-
vails, and once again, one stands for all.

We may also look to Barrie himself as the origin of Hook. In the role-
play between Barrie and the Llewelyn Davies boys, Barrie always performed the part of the pirate captain. This arrangement was possibly
unavoidable since it appears nobody wanted to be Hook. As Barrie
points out: "they force the baby to be Hook. . . . They would rather be
a Twin than Hook" (*Peter Pan* 139). This is ironic given the obvious
doubling or "twinning" between Hook and Pan. Another indication
that Barrie is the image of Hook is revealed by the way in which he
gave up his Christian name of "James" to Hook. Captain Hook's evolution can be traced through the characters of Captain W and the headmaster Pilkington in *The Little White Bird* and Captain Swarthy (played
by Barrie) in *The Boy Castaways of Black Lake Island*, a private photograph album that recorded Barrie's games with the Llewelyn Davies
boys. Subsequently, the figure became Captain Stroke in *Sentimental
Tommy*. With each incarnation containing the germ of Hook, the character's development gathered momentum. Tracing the trajectory of
Hook, it seems he can be regarded as a malevolent headmaster or
more generally as a flawed adult.

Other insights into Hook's origin may be gleaned from a photograph, which I discovered in the local archive of Kirriemuir Library,
and which has since been transferred to the Kirriemuir Gateway to the
Glens Museum. A picture taken of a Masonic Lodge includes the image
of a local postman, who has a hook in place of his left hand. This Masonic postman may have inspired Hook. Barrie, who made frequent return visits to the small town of Kirriemuir to spend time with relatives,
may well have known of this local figure. Since Barrie relished converting local figures into copy, it is entirely possible that he chose to do
this once again in his characterization of Hook.[8]

Figure 10.1.   Kirriemuir postman and mason (circa 1900): extreme left, front row.[9]

Since prosthetic limbs had yet to be invented, hooks may have been a fairly common sight. It could also be said that in creating a character with a hook as a menacing hand-replacement, Barrie created a variation on the theme of Long John Silver, fashioned by his friend, Stevenson, in *Treasure Island* (1883).

GENRE BENDING

In its metatextuality, *Peter Pan* can be regarded as a mélange of genres (Rose 77). This text can therefore be regarded as seminal to the genre of children's fiction while simultaneously subverting it. It occupies a position both within and outside the genre. An example of this is that Wendy could quite plausibly be based on the figure of Snow White. She takes on the responsibility of nurturing seven Lost Boys as her own. Carpenter identifies the metatextuality and intertextuality of *Peter Pan*, acknowledging that "the Never Land . . . is visibly stuck together out of bits of well-known stories" (180). As most critics note,

Barrie experimented with different modes of writing. John Bayne states, "for no reason that is apparent he abandoned the novel for the drama" (188). I believe, however, that his reason for abandoning the novel form was that he felt restrained by prosaic convention. C. N. Manlove clearly believes that Barrie upheld the maxim that more authorial control could be had in plays than in prose. He remarks, "*Peter and Wendy* . . . being a prose story is not so clearly 'managed' as a play" (146). Christopher Harvie also believes that this change can be attributed to the coming of technology when "it was, he realised, beyond the power of the novel to describe an experience so amorphous and mutable. Neatness and finiteness meant going back in time to the society, now perished" (324). This perhaps explains why Barrie, in *The Little White Bird*, had to go back in time to tell David the story of his origin. He was not prepared to risk looking to the future, preferring to reflect on the past, which offered more scope for artistic manipulation.

Vadim Linetski refers to *Peter Pan* as a "pharmakon: a foreign body in the body of tradition, an entity which the tradition has tried but failed to expel" (2). Here he uses a Derridean phrase, originally from Plato's *Dialogues*, of the pharmakon as both poison and cure. Rose uses the related image of virus replication to describe the regeneration of *Peter Pan*. Barrie's text borrows enough material from previous sources to gain entry to the canon of children's fiction and then invades and injures its host by undermining the conventions of the genre. Rose believes that

> what *Peter Pan* seems . . . to demonstrate is a type of permanent oscillation. . . . It might be that we are witnessing the beginning of the end of *Peter Pan*; but to date *Peter Pan* has shown that uncanny ability . . . to absorb or take on board exactly what it needs in order to reproduce itself. (xiii–xiv)

Peter Pan reproduces itself like a virus and adapts to change. As a result, it is both symptom and cause, since it simultaneously expresses (as a symptom) and undermines (deconstructs) constructions and categorizations. This virus, however, could be regarded as a form of contamination, underlining Rose's assertion that what we may be witnessing is "the beginning of the end of *Peter Pan*." However, this inhabitation of the host is particularly devious since "*Peter Pan* plays itself out with all the innocence of the symptom . . . and exactly the opposite [i.e. the cause], at one and the same time" (Rose 38–39). *Peter Pan* takes on the appearance of its host and mutates so that it injures the body it has inhabited. Contrary to Rose, I believe that *Peter Pan* is neither beginning nor end; rather it is situated somewhere in between, symbolizing, as I've said before, "process."

The rebellious practice of inhabiting and subverting the genre of children's fiction suggests that Barrie is a renegade. Barrie is a Trojan horse; he dons the appearance of a sentimental children's writer but all the time undoes constructions. Rose protests, "it would not be going too far to say that *Peter and Wendy* constitutes something of an attack on, or at least an affront to, the very concept of children's literature with which it is most often linked" (86). *Peter Pan* masquerades as a simple and pure tale, yet this façade merely conceals the tools through which Barrie dismantles the enclosed and privileged genre it has entered. Barrie occupies two places simultaneously. He exists both within and outside categories. Linetski explains that this scenario arises because of "the simultaneous belonging and non-belonging of khora or gaps to the series which it coordinates [and] evaporates [in] the moment" (10). Linetski's use of the Derridean term "khora" shows how Barrie can undermine and be centrally connected to children's literature as a whole. *Peter Pan* is displaced from the genre just as children's fiction displaces the child. Peter Pan occupies a central yet tense position within the canon of children's fiction. He can be free but excluded or trapped but included: neither is an attractive alternative.

Hollindale describes "Barrie's contribution of detached amusement at absurd conventions, and simultaneous imaginative relish of them" (*Peter Pan* xx). Barrie's own particular approach was to draw "nostalgically on those very performance traditions from which [his] play was emancipating children's theatre" (xiii). It was by this process of confirming and undermining categories that he subverted convention and facilitated change within and between genres. H. M. Walbrook realized that Barrie "broke down finally the barriers which had so long and so disastrously stood between Literature and the Drama" (49). In this way, the barriers were "alternately broken down and re-established" (Jack 128–9). Barrie is able to deconstruct narratives to the point of authorial annihilation.

The writer's impetus to defy categorization and remain ineffable, like Peter Pan, continued into other aspects of his life. He was regarded as "a lad o' pairts" and transcended the boundaries of categorization from a young age. He also defied categorization in the recognitions he received, becoming first a baronet (an honorary award for "commoners"), then a knight (an award for "nobles").[10] There is such a close,

almost inextricable, connection between Barrie and his text that it may
be argued that they are coterminous. Earlier in this paper, I referred to
a speech Barrie delivered to the Royal Literary Fund on May 9, 1904,
made around the time he was drafting *Peter Pan*. In it, he remarked, "I
am not certain whether we are really here or whether this is only a
chapter in a book; and if it is a chapter in a book I wonder which of us
all is writing it" (*McConnachie* 13). Clearly, there is some blurring or
confusion between the writer and his work. The view is strengthened
because Barrie never settled in one place. His work also defied categorization after his death: *Peter Pan* is unique in being the only book
other than the Bible to have been given a special parliamentary dis-
pensation so that its copyright will never expire.[11]

Both the text and character of Peter Pan epitomize transformation,
crisis, reformation, and regeneration. Peter Pan's riddle may be explained, I am suggesting, by Barrie's lack of fixity: the desire to shirk
responsibility and remain untouchable. But it is also thanks to his perpetually altering state that generations continue to enjoy, and are enchanted by, Barrie's re-creation.

NOTES

1. Here Barrie may be teasing. This is an instance of the way in which Barrie causes confusion at the point of reference. He says, "No 1 could touch me,"
but "No 1," written in full, reads "No one." Barrie used wordplay here to slip
from accountability and the critics' grasp.

2. Barrie delivered his speech at Hyde Park Hotel on November 28, 1928.
He was appointed President of the Society on the death of the former office
bearer, Thomas Hardy.

3. David Buckingham refers to Peter Pan being the first wide-scale marketing venture: "The work of JMB reflected widespread fascination and longing
for childhood" (9). There were many spin-offs from the book which lucratively
commodified and exploited the package of a sentimentalized childhood.

4. I am grateful to R. D. S. Jack for providing the following information
about the production history of *Peter Pan* as a ballet. The ballet of Peter Pan
with music by Arnold Bax was discovered in the Berg collection, New York
Public Library. It was one of the many modal re-translations of the Peter Pan
theme and was a spin-off from a spin-off; that is, the cast off *Commedia del-
l'Arte* act of the *Peter Pan* manuscript became *Pantaloon* (1905), which in turn
became *The Origin of Harlequin* (1917). Jack believes this is related to the ontological concerns of all the Pan performances. In 2002, the Washington Ballet
staged performances of *Peter Pan* (Tampa Bay Performing Arts Center), and

City Ballet performed a version of *Peter Pan*, the ballet (City Ballet of San Diego).

5. Rose categorically states that "Barrie is Peter Pan" (6), Hollindale labels "David's [Barrie's brother's] death as undoubtedly the origin of Peter Pan" (xxiii), and Carpenter states that "Peter Pan is, of course, Barrie himself" (177).

6. For the history of Pan, see Wullschläger 111–12.

7. Indeed, perhaps because of his games in Kensington Gardens, Barrie mentions Cecco Hewlett in *The Little White Bird*, in which reference is made to "Cecco Hewlett's tree, that memorable spot where a boy called Cecco lost his penny, and, looking for it, found twopence. There has been a good deal of excavation going on there ever since" (112). Cecco also appears as a pirate in *Peter Pan*, described as "the handsome Cecco, who cut his name on the back of the governor of the prison at Gao" (107).

8. According to a descendant of the Darling family of Glen Prosen, Angus, "Barrie regularly visited" their home, so it may well have inspired the family name in the play ("Peter Pan Art"). Barrie sought inspiration for his characters and settings from multiple sources and preserved them in copy for posterity. Many of the locals in Kirriemuir resented Barrie's turning them into copy and portraying them negatively. They believed he violated the core of their community and cast a shadow over small town life.

9. A hook replaces his left hand. This photograph depicts members of Kirriemuir's Masonic Lodge.

10. Birkin explains that "Barrie rejected a simple knighthood in 1909, but was unable to resist a baronetcy" (214), which he was awarded in 1913. He became Rector of St. Andrews University in the same year. He was subsequently awarded the Order of Merit in 1922. Barrie received honorary degrees from Edinburgh (his alma mater), St. Andrews, Oxford, and Cambridge.

11. Lord Callaghan introduced this bill in Parliament in 1987 in order to ensure that Great Ormond Street Hospital (where Barrie had served on the Board of Trustees) continued to receive royalties from *Peter Pan* as stipulated in Barrie's will. In 1988 a special bill was instituted to reinstate copyright of *Peter Pan* in perpetuity.

WORKS CITED

Aller, Susan Bivin. *J. M. Barrie: The Magic Behind Peter Pan*. Minneapolis: Lerner, 1994.

Barrie, James Matthew. *The Greenwood Hat: A Memoir of James Anon 1885–1887*. London: Peter Davies, 1937.

———. *The Little White Bird*. Edinburgh: Constable, 1902.

———. *Margaret Ogilvy*. London: Hodder and Stoughton, 1896.

———. *McConnachie and J. M. B.: Speeches by J. M. Barrie*. London: Peter Davies, 1938.

———. *Peter Pan and Other Plays*. Ed. Peter Hollindale. Oxford: Oxford UP, 1995.

———. *Sentimental Tommy: The Story of His Boyhood*. London: Hodder and Stoughton, 1896.

Bayne, John. "Barrie—The Riddle of Genius." *The Scots Magazine* June 1960: 188.

Birkin, Andrew. *J. M. Barrie & the Lost Boys*. London: Constable, 1979.

Buckingham, David. *After the Death of Childhood: Growing Up in the Age of Electronic Media*. Cambridge: Polity Press, 2000.

Carpenter, Humphrey, *Secret Gardens: A Study of the Golden Age of Children's Literature*. Sydney: Allen and Unwin, 1987.

Ellison, Jane. "Tinkerbell Lives." *Evening Standard* 21 Dec. 1978.

Ferguson, Gillian. "On the Never Never." *The Scotsman* 27 Dec. 1994: 11.

"The First Golden Age: Sir James Barrie 1860–1937." *Masterpiece Theatre Online*. 2005. PBS. 28 Mar. 2005 <http://www.pbs.org/wgbh/masterpiece/railway/age/barrie_bio.html>.

"Good Ideas of the Twentieth Century: Peter Pan and Sir James Matthew Barrie." *Without* Walls. Channel 4 [UK]. 15 June 1995.

Green, Roger Lancelyn. *Fifty Years of Peter Pan*. London: Peter Davies, 1954.

Harvie, Christopher. "The Barrie Who Never Grew Up: An Apologia for *The Little Minister*." *Studies in Scottish Fiction: Nineteenth Century*. Ed. Horst W. Drescher and Joachim Schwend. New York: Peter Lang, 1985. 321–35.

Hawthorne, Nathaniel. *The Marble Faun: Or, The Romance of Monte Beni*. 1860. Ed. Richard H. Brodhead. London: Penguin, 1990.

Jack, R. D. S. "From Drama to Silent Film: The Case of Sir James Barrie." *International Journal of Scottish Theatre* 2.2 (Dec. 2001). *IJoST*. Mar. 2002. 28 Mar. 2005 <http://arts.qmuc.ac.uk/ijost/Volume2_no2/2_jack_rds.htm>.

Jackson, Holbrook. *Modern Essays*. London: The Kings Treasuries of Literature, 1928.

Jasper, David. *The Study of Literature and Religion: An Introduction*. London: Macmillan, 1992.

Linetski, Vadim. "The Promise of Expression to the 'Inexpressible child': Deleuze, Derrida and the Impossibility of Adult's Literature." *Other Voices* 1.3 (Jan. 1999). 28 Mar. 2005 <http://othervoices.org/1.3/vlinetski/child.html_>.

Manlove, C. N. *Scottish Fantasy Literature: A Critical Survey*. Edinburgh: Canongate, 1994.

Merivale, Patricia. *Pan the Goat-God: His Myth in Modern Times*. Studies in Comparative Literature 3. Cambridge: Harvard UP, 1969.

Neill, Heather. "Up, Up and Away." *Times Educational Supplement* 5 Dec. 1997.

Ovid. *The Metamorphoses of Ovid*. Trans. Mary Innes. London: Penguin, 1955.

"Peter Pan Art Makes Author's Birthplace." *The Courier and Advertiser* [Dundee, Scotland] 15 June 1999: 3.

Pick, John B. *The Great Shadow House: Essays on the Metaphysical Tradition in Scottish Fiction.* Edinburgh: Polygon, 1993.

Rose, Jacqueline. *The Case of Peter Pan: Or, The Impossibility of Children's Fiction.* Basingstoke: Macmillan, 1992.

Rustin, Michael. "A Defence of Children's Fiction: Another Reading of Peter Pan." *Free Associations* 2 (1985): 128–48.

Said, Edward William. *Beginnings: Intention and Method.* New York: Basic Books, 1975.

Stewart, Angus. "Captain Hook's Secret." *Scottish Literary Journal* 25 (May 1998): 45–53.

Walbrook, H. M. *J. M. Barrie and the Theatre.* London: F. V. White, 1922.

Wullschläger, Jackie. *Inventing Wonderland: The Lives and Fantasies of Lewis Carroll, Edward Lear, J. M. Barrie, Kenneth Grahame, and A. A. Milne.* London: Methuen, 1995.

Yeats, William Butler. *The Wanderings of Oisin and Other Poems.* London: Kegan Paul, 1889.

11

Getting Peter's Goat: Hybridity, Androgyny, and Terror in *Peter Pan*

Carrie Wasinger

The first theatrical trailer for Universal Studios' 2003 adaptation of J. M. Barrie's *Peter Pan* pauses momentarily on an image of Wendy in her nightgown as she stands behind a toy soldier, holding a sword to its throat. The soldier represents Napoleon; Wendy, playing at pirates with her younger brothers, pretends to sever its head. As the camera cuts to various scenes of chaos in the nursery, a voiceover resonates: "What if you could escape to a faraway world?" The film imagines the girl-child as a site of gender play and political power, a privilege it does not extend to boys; indeed, director P. J. Hogan cast an adolescent actor (Jeremy Sumpter) as Peter instead of the traditional adult woman. However, in locating gender play primarily in the character of Wendy, the film forecloses on the possibility that the boy-child, Peter, may also figure resistance to gender norms, and that anxieties about gender indeterminacy and the political power enabled by such ambiguity of identity are, in fact, written into Peter's literary history. My purpose here is to designate the figure of the child, and Peter Pan in particular, as a cultural trope for signifying resistance to narratives of heteronormativity and to suggest that the models of indeterminacy represented by Peter were as threatening to Victorian heterosexual adulthood as they were progressive.

In marketing its adaptation as an escapist fantasy, Universal Studios has voiced a popularly held belief about Peter Pan and children's fiction. From the moment of Peter's literary birth at the turn of the twentieth century, adults have characterized him as the pre-eminent example of childhood's spirited caprice and Barrie's story as the superlative vehicle for returning us to the promised land of juvenile innocence. Shortly after its London debut, for instance, a reviewer for the *Illustrated London News* wrote that in Neverland "all the romantic fancies of youthful brains . . . are thrillingly materialized" ("*Peter Pan*" 2), while Max Beerbohm of *The Saturday Review* insisted that since he could not "communicate the magic of a dream" to his readers, Londoners would have to "go to the Duke of York's, there to dream the dream for [themselves]" (14). At times contemporary scholarship rehearses this belief, as when Ann Wilson describes the play's transition to Neverland as a "regression" to a "world of childish adventure that is an escape from the pressures of adult life" (600).

Twentieth-century critical thought, spurred on by the assertion that our cherished idealizations of childhood screen the juvenile's not-so-innocent sexual appetites and anxieties, has done much to explode such popular mystifications. A number of psychoanalytically inflected readings of *Peter Pan* have investigated Peter's hostility toward femininity, anxieties about maternal abandonment, and fear of paternal tyranny. Claudia Nelson, for instance, has argued that Barrie's fantasy figures a destructive femininity that is fundamentally at odds with the escapist philosophy of Neverland and that must necessarily be "barred from the childish paradise" (150). Alison Lurie's characterization of the story as the "fulfillment of intense but contradictory childhood wishes," which "demonstrates graphically that parents are timid and hypocritical" (131), similarly juxtaposes the interests of childhood and adulthood, and James Kincaid attributes Peter's "alluring otherness" to "absolut[e] self-possess[ion]," lack of "interest in imitating the grown-up," and lack of "need of anyone outside himself" (279). These commentators, like most contemporary critics, view *Peter Pan* as emblematic of a psychoanalytic conception of socialization that exposes adult/child antagonism. These projects share the determination to see Peter Pan/ *Peter Pan* reflecting deficiencies in adult self-understanding more than the nature and experience of real children.

The strongest and most compelling of contemporary critical claims comes from Jacqueline Rose. In *The Case of Peter Pan; Or, the Impossibility of Children's Fiction*, Rose demonstrates that readers cannot assume an unproblematic relationship to children's fiction. In visiting the post-structuralist troubling of assumptions about the purity of language on our relationship to children's fiction, Rose problematizes the idea of critically reading such stories *as* stories intended for child audiences, by subverting the image of the child as "a pure point of origin" or "a pioneer who restores [utopic] worlds to us . . . with a facility or directness which ensures that our own relationship to them is, finally, safe" (8, 9). According to Rose, the idea that children's fiction accesses the so-called purity of childhood—a purity that is essentially different from the "fallen" adult world of experience—is a mystification. Instead, *Peter Pan* shows all too often how adult voices collapse into child voices, and vice versa. Our desire to construct children as "a group which is knowable and exists for the book" and to see children's fiction as "the book [which] exists for them" alone (1), masks the instability of the child's relationship to language and identity and, by extension, the instability of our adult relationship to language and identity. In other words, *Peter Pan* doesn't just offer a pleasing entertainment to children; nor does it really offer adult culture a picture of the primal, essential innocence that we have lost because we've aged. In consistently pointing to the collapse of narrative voices, *Peter Pan* shows us that we can never be sure of our relationship to language and identity, as adults or as children.

But *The Case of Peter Pan* is limited by its deconstructionist ethos. Because Rose does not look to instability, indeterminacy, or uncertainty as ways of imaging progressive or radical identities, her critique of *Peter Pan* cannot imagine that the instability of our relationship to language and to the child in/as language could demonstrate an alterity which is positive and powerful. It is the very instability of our relationship to the child in fiction or as fiction, I argue, which allows us to imagine the political power of gender indeterminacy through *Peter Pan*. The collapse of narrative voices, the hybridity of subject positions, and even indeterminacy itself make Peter a compelling hero, and allow us (adults and children alike) to identify with his agency.

To make this argument, I will draw on the theoretical frameworks offered by Judith Butler and Eve Sedgwick. To Butler, I owe the idea that gender is constituted through the repeated performance of certain behaviors, although my critique of the *Peter Pan* texts extends Butler's scope and asserts that gender performance can and does occur through the medium of text. Thus adults' repeated identifications with literary child-figures, I argue, can be and often are a means of constructing and performing gender(s). To Sedgwick, I owe the idea that gender indeterminacy may be a productive space which shapes belief systems: "The exact, contingent space of indeterminacy—the place of

shifting over time—of the mutual boundaries between the political and
the sexual is, in fact, the most fertile space of ideological formation"
(15). My argument looks to indeterminacy as productive in the sense
that it gives rise to ideologies, although the extent to which those
"products"—the ideologies themselves—are beneficial or repressive
remains to be established.

My goal is to chart a middle path between the popular mystification
of *Peter Pan* and Rose's critical analysis that neither masks the subversive power of children's literature with idealization nor reduces the text
to an exposition on the instability of language. Reading moments of
narrative indeterminacy alongside the story's thematic interest in hybridity, I contend that Peter, as an ambiguously gendered child-figure,
was a site for imagining political agency and gender transgression at
the beginning of the last century.[1] The models of indeterminacy that
Peter represents threatened the coherence and stability of heterosexual
adulthood. In identifying with Peter, late Victorian/Edwardian audiences confronted the terrifying experiences of hybridity—in particular,
the frighteningly dangerous potential for transgender—and the radical
political subjectivities they enabled. Thus while questioning the binary
distinctions of late Victorian/Edwardian heterosexuality, I contend that
Peter also troubled the popular view of the palliative function of nostalgic escapism.

Peter Pan has a complicated literary history. After 1911, there were
four versions of Peter Pan circulating simultaneously. Peter appeared
in 1902 in Barrie's novel for adults, *The Little White Bird,* as the protagonist of a series of episodes narrated by an adult to a child. In 1904,
Peter Pan, or the Boy Who Wouldn't Grow Up was first performed on
the London stage. Although children were undoubtedly present, the
audience consisted primarily of adults; the following year the play
opened in New York. In 1906 the sections of *The Little White Bird* that
focused on Peter were excerpted, attached to illustrations by Arthur
Rackham, and published in an art volume, called *Peter Pan in Kensington Gardens.* Barrie then rewrote the play as a short novel, *Peter
and Wendy,* which was published in 1911. This was the only manifestation of the Peter story that Barrie explicitly directed toward child-
readers.[2]

To be acceptable as children's literature rather than a fantasy *about*
children for adults, Rose argues, over time the Peter Pan story suffered
"an unmistakable act of censorship" which alleviated most "difficulties"
in the fairy tale's representation of adult/child relations (5). For *The*

Case of Peter Pan, such "difficult" moments as the following demonstrate the instability of adults' relationship to the child:

> All children, except one, grow up. They soon know that they will grow up, and the way Wendy knew was this. One day when she was two years old she was playing in a garden, and she plucked another flower and ran with it to her mother. I suppose she must have looked rather delightful, for Mrs. Darling put her hand to her heart and cried, "Oh, why can't you remain like this for ever!" This was all that passed between them on the subject, but henceforth Wendy knew that she must grow up. You always know after you are two. (*Peter and Wendy* 69)

According to Rose, this moment subverts our expectation of distinct narrative voices: "In the process of language, in the slippage from 'all' to 'they' to 'you,' J. M. Barrie's 1911 version of *Peter Pan* undermines the certainty which should properly distinguish the narrating adult from the child" (68). Barrie's textual revisions, she implies, progressively erased the adult audience's identification with the figure of the child, so that with successive iterations of *Peter Pan* Barrie reduced the "confusion of tongues" that pointed so strongly toward the unknowability of our relationship to language and to the child.

Such moments of narrative confusion, however, should not be seen as gaps or absences of knowledge but rather, as the texts themselves suggest, productive moments of confusion in which culture experiments with radical identities. In the example cited above, "you" stands in for Wendy as well as the implicitly adult male narrator, who thus occupies an ambiguous position in terms of both gender and age. The following incident from *Kensington Gardens*, an episode entirely neglected in *The Case of Peter Pan*, provides another example:

> If you ask your mother whether she knew about Peter Pan when she was a little girl, she will say, "Why, of course I did, child"; and if you ask her whether he rode on a goat in those days, she will say, "What a foolish question to ask; certainly he did." Then if you ask your grandmother whether she knew about Peter Pan when she was a girl, she also says, "Why, of course I did, child," but if you ask her whether he rode on a goat in those days, she says she never heard of his having a goat. Perhaps she has forgotten, just as she sometimes forgets your name and calls you Mildred, which is your mother's name. (12)

As in the passage from *Peter and Wendy*, the narrative confusion demonstrated in this passage from *Peter Pan in Kensington Gardens* enables gender slippage. The interaction of child and adult precipitates the experience of categorically *in*distinct genders. The very moment our anonymous narrator introduces Peter, he cites two storytellers who are alter egos for himself: David's mother and David's maternal grandmother. Further, David, the boy-child auditor, collapses into Mildred, the girl-child auditor. During this moment of narrative confusion in which identities collapse, the characters' Christian names, their previously stable markers of gender, come unfixed. This passage from *Peter Pan in Kensington Gardens* suggests that the moment of producing and consuming stories is the moment at which such markers begin to float freely. Thus David and Mildred become androgynous figures—figures playing freely amidst the categories of masculinity and femininity.

Barrie's thematization of gender indeterminacy becomes most insistent and compelling in such moments of narrative confusion, which are, not coincidentally, often instances of staged storytelling. Storytelling in *Peter Pan*, as Rose asserts, represents a kind of seduction: "talking to the child is . . . an act of love, but it is also a claim on the child, a demand made on the child as a means of holding it fast," making the narrator's vocation "anything but innocent" (23). But if storytelling represents a kind of seduction, and the narrator's presence threatens the virtue of the audience by instigating a narrative moment that may elide gender distinctions, then we must pay closer attention to the collapse of *narrative* distinctions as well. Mildred, who exists as both child and parent in the above passage (the daughter of the grandmother and the mother of the son), also represents a synthesis of narrator and audience; she tells the story of Peter Pan to her son just as she heard it from her mother. In addition, David, the auditor, appears remarkably similar to the narrated object, Peter Pan; like Peter, David inhabits Kensington Gardens; like Peter, David has privileged access to the world of the fairies; like Peter, David must be wary of an adult world that wants to appropriate him for potentially dangerous uses. But since David, who closely resembles Peter, can be mistaken for Mildred, we begin to see Peter occupying Mildred's synthetic role: a fantasized child-figure that is indistinctly gendered, that may be both auditor and narrator, and that is seduced at the same time that it seduces.

Indeed, *The Little White Bird* asserts that the seductive story is a collaborative production: "I ought to mention here that the following is our way with a story: First I tell it to [David], and then he tells it to me, the understanding being that it is quite a different story; and then I retell it with his additions, and so we go on until no one could say whether it is more his story or mine" (159). Because the text accounts for multi-generational composition, the category of "adult" cannot be mapped directly onto the category of "narrator" any more than "child" can be mapped directly on to "object of narration." Narrative seduction operates both ways, from adult to child and from child to adult; just as the narrator seduces his/her child-audience, the child seduces the narrator. If it is possible to read the adult storyteller as a threat to the virtue of his/her child-audience, then this reversal of narrative authority makes it possible to read the figure of the child (a figure whose gender the narration has deliberately confused) as a threat to the sexual integrity of the Victorian adult. In this episode, slippage between narrative categories encourages readers to identify with the child-figure's androgyny and thus imaginatively occupy alternative gender roles.

The collapse of distinct narrative categories around an indeterminately gendered child-figure may reveal how the text invites the reader into a fantasy of his/her *own* indeterminacy, but it is the story's thematic concern with hybridity that demonstrates just how active that indeterminacy can become. Pursuing the relationship among adult/child hybridity, gender indeterminacy, and sexual terror into the latter textual variants may reveal the child-figure's potential for symbolically revolutionary acts. But to uncover and understand these relationships we should first turn to *Peter Pan in Kensington Gardens*, the variant most replete with uneasy mergers between the categories of "child," "adult," and "gender," and then to an analysis of the play and novel.

The setting of *Peter Pan in Kensington Gardens* provides one source for the story's thematization of hybridity. Unlike Neverland, which resembles the distant locales of boys' adventure tales, Kensington Gardens embeds the exotic elements of fairyland in the familiarity of a London city park. During the day, people walk the peaceful paths of Kensington Gardens, but at night the fairies come out to play. While Peter Pan's map of the gardens places the island in the Serpentine (his birthplace) at the very edge of the illustration, maps of the city at large show that the island hovers between Hyde Park and Kensington Gardens. Indeed, the island lies in much closer proximity to the centers of government—Buckingham Palace and the Houses of Parliament—than Peter's illustration will concede. The space is at once a margin and a center, part arcadia and part politically inflected sphere.

Children, the narrator informs us, are the park's native hybrid inhabitants; infants are birds on the island until they fly away to their mothers' nurseries to become sons and daughters. Newborn Peter, however, forgetful "that he was now a little boy in a nightgown," flies directly out of his nursery window to the island, where his advent inspires the fairies with terror and causes the birds to shun him. Saddened and confused by his reception, he consults the wisest of wise old birds, Solomon Caw, who explodes Peter's belief in his ability to fly and dubs him "little half-and-half." Neither "exactly human," nor "exactly a bird," Peter becomes a "Betwixt-and-Between" (*Kensington Gardens* 17).

Peter's hybridity, though, isn't limited to species. As Solomon Caw states, disillusionment doesn't fix Peter in infancy; it makes him a "betwixt-and-between," neither child *nor* adult. Although disillusionment grounds Peter on the island, it *resists* fixing his psychological development, just as the narrative's collaborative production resists fixing the narrator's (narrators') gender and age. Indeed, Peter seems impossibly adept at slipping back and forth between the ignorance of childhood and intricate knowledge of the laws of fairyland. Although merely one week old, Peter has seemingly always been capable of walking, talking, dancing, piping, building boats, purchasing labor, distributing salaries, and officiating disputes between belligerent birds. Simply put, Peter is an infant with the abstract reasoning abilities of a bourgeois professional.

Such indeterminacy does not appear dangerous, however, until it distorts the narrative of heterosexual domesticity. Having survived a perilous journey from island to garden, Peter returns to the same nursery window from which he first escaped. Thrice hesitating on the sill, he belatedly decides to go back to his cradle, only to find himself excluded from the nursery; in his place, another infant boy sleeps soundly. When Peter encounters the barred window, he becomes permanently indeterminate, an infant who will never grow up nor ever quite be the brother who has displaced him. Further, the window's proximity to his mother's post-parturitional body suggests that Peter's self-inflicted exile separates him from the processes of heterosexual fertility that produced both himself and his parents' second child. Thus Peter's ambivalence irrevocably disrupts his maturation. More importantly, to the extent that the barred window keeps Peter's little brother *in*, it also keeps Peter *out*. When Peter's mother shuts the window, no doubt fearful of losing a second son, she transforms the sill from a site of indeterminacy to a marginalizing device. Peter can no longer enjoy his titillating oscillation between the maternal sphere of the nursery and the hybridity of Kensington Gardens. In *Kensington Gardens*, hybridity poses enough of a threat to domestic heterosexuality that it is, literally, locked out of the middle-class home.

Lock-out not only arrests Peter in time, but it also impedes his entry into the binary significations of late Victorian/Edwardian heterosexuality. Evidence suggests that nineteenth-century sumptuary customs for very young children did not discriminate as to gender. At the turn of the nineteenth century, it was as common for little girls to go bare-headed or to sport "boy-style" cropped hair as it was for their brothers, and in the 1880s, when the Fauntleroy suit was all the rage, boys and girls alike wore long, wavy ringlets. The fashion of indicating the youngest in the family by the term "baby," rather than by gender or name, continued well into the century.[3] Throughout the period, toddlers and infants were dressed alike, regardless of sex. Boys were not "breeched"—put into pants or trousers—until the age of four or five.[4] As an unbreeched infant boy, Peter would have been indistinguishable from a girl of the same age.

Biographical evidence indicates that even in adapting *Peter Pan in Kensington Gardens* to the stage, Barrie wanted Peter to be associated with gender indeterminacy. Producer Charles Frohman and Barrie agreed that a woman should play the title character. In April of 1904, shortly after finishing the play, Barrie wrote to actress Maude Adams in the United States: "I have written a play for children, which I don't suppose would be much use in America. She [Wendy] is rather a dear of a girl with ever so many children long before her hair is up and the boy is Peter Pan in a new world. I should like you to be the boy and the girl and most of the children and the pirate captain" (qtd. in Birkin 103). Accordingly, Maude Adams was cast in the title role in the original American production.

At this particular moment in theatre history, audiences were already witnessing a peculiar confluence of staged gender inversion and children's fantasy. When revising the original narrative into *Peter Pan, or the Boy Who Wouldn't Grow Up*, Barrie chose Christmas pantomime as his new vehicle. Rooted in the Italian tradition of the *Commedia dell' arte*, the "panto" form began appearing on British playbills in the early eighteenth century and quickly became associated with Drury Lane (Wilson, *Pantomime* 15–16). By the late nineteenth century, the typical pantomime was a comic manifestation of the fairy tale and contained a number of stock characters, including the Dame, the part of an adult woman played by a grown man, and the Principal Boy, the part of a juvenile hero played by an adult woman. Although gender inversion has been a long-standing tradition of English theater, the Principal Boy came into its most popular moment at the end of the nineteenth century.

As theater critic Peter Holland has argued, "the Principal Boy is a remarkable complex of gender markers," at once "emphatically boy not man, a figure who would like to be adult . . . but who occupies particularly in the case of a lower-class Principal Boy like Aladdin, a space of yearning for the adulthood of sexuality" (197, 198). Holland's statement is significant not only for its emphasis on panto's gender-blending, but also for its emphasis on panto's ability to represent multiple, interwoven crossings of age, gender, and class. David Mayer reminds us that in pantomime fantasy's voluptuous Principal Boys, audiences found a site of identification with all these hybrid subject positions: "by the late nineteenth century pantomime was one of the few genteel middle class entertainments . . . where the pleasing configurations of a woman's body, clothed in tunic and fleshings, could be observed by all the family without shame or guilt" (56). Panto's transvestism, writes Mayer, was primarily a response to new gender roles enabled by the Industrial Revolution (59). Through panto, one could encounter sexually and economically powerful others.

The extent to which such hybridized characters provided "safe" sites of identification, however, remains undetermined, as John Ruskin's 1867 account of viewing *Ali Baba and the Forty Thieves* demonstrates. Shocked by the knowledge that Ali's forty thieves are in fact women, Ruskin records: "there being no thieving to be presently done, and time hanging heavy on their hands, arms, and legs, the forty thief-girls proceeded to light forty cigars. Whereupon the British public gave them a round of applause. Whereupon I fell a-thinking; and saw little more of the piece, except as an ugly and disturbing dream" (28). Ruskin suggests that the identification with gender indeterminacy called for by pantomime was as disturbing as it was progressive. We might question if the same held true for *Peter Pan.* In inviting readers to identify with the indeterminate or androgynous child-figure, did Peter threaten the dominance of heterosexuality? Could identifying with Peter be terrifying at the same time that it was productive, and if so, how?

To suggest that there is something terrifying about the hybridity of the figure of the child is to suggest that, in identifying with Peter, Victorian adults encountered their own dangerous gender indeterminacies. As Martha Vicinus has argued, the androgynous boy, a marginal sexual object, was a point of *fear* as well as identification for nineteenth-century audiences. In positing a human/animal hybrid as the central character, *Peter Pan in Kensington Gardens* alludes to the tradition of representing monstrosity through hybridity. Classical discourses of morality often signified sexual transgression through beings manifesting both human and animal attributes.

Of course, our beloved betwixt and between is also Peter *Pan,* an avatar of the pipe-playing Grecian goat-god; certainly the pastoral setting of *Kensington Gardens* implies the Arcadian myth. But Pan wasn't all sweetness and light, being as closely associated with bacchanalia as he was with music. Sir James Frazer describes Pan in *The Golden Bough* as a demi-god of goatish appearance. Closely associated with Dionysus as well as "Satyrs, and Silenuses, all of whom are . . . represented more or less completely in the form of goats . . . Pan was regularly portrayed in sculpture and painting with the face and legs of a goat" (538). Any reader with the least bit of classical knowledge would have recognized Peter's satyr-like qualities. The hand-drawn map of Kensington Gardens that serves as frontispiece to *The Little White Bird* shows fairies dancing in the margins while Peter leads them, riding a goat and holding a long pipe to his lips. The goat-image returns in the text, of course, when the narrator opens chapter two of *Kensington Gardens* with the recollection of how Peter "most certainly" rode a goat (12).

Barrie wasn't the only turn-of-the-century children's author to turn to the image of Pan and to associate that image with gender transgression and the figure of the child. Kenneth Grahame's immensely popular *The Wind in the Willows,* first published in 1908, situates the story of a lost otter cub in the center of the wider, worldly adventures of Badger, Mole, Rat, and Toad. When Rat and Mole set out in search of the otter cub, they encounter the animal god. Although unimportant to the overall plot of the novel, the episode was thematically significant enough to provide the cover illustration for the first edition. I quote the passage at length below to preserve its eloquence as well as its emphasis on Pan's physicality:

> though the piping was now hushed, the call and the summons seemed still dominant and imperious. [Mole] might not refuse, were Death himself waiting to strike him instantly, once he had looked with mortal eye on things rightly kept hidden. Trembling he obeyed . . . and then, in that utter clearness of the imminent dawn[,] . . . he looked in the very eyes of the Friend and Helper; saw the backward sweep of the curved horns, gleaming in the growing daylight; saw the stern, hooked nose between the kindly eyes[,] . . . the bearded mouth[,] . . . the rippling muscles on the arm that lay across the broad chest, the long supple hand still holding the panpipes only just fallen away from the parted lips; saw the splendid curves of the shaggy limbs disposed in majestic ease on the sward; saw, last of

all, nestling between his very hooves, sleeping soundly[,] the little, round, podgy, childish form of the baby otter. (124)

Like Peter, who befriends children left in Kensington Gardens past lock-out time, the Pan of *The Wind in the Willows* acts as patron saint for lost children. Also like Peter, though benevolent, Pan inspires terror. When Mole inquires whether his friend feels fear, Rat replies: "Afraid! Of *Him?* O, never, never! And yet—and yet—O, Mole, I am afraid!" (125). This Pan's seductive masculinity evokes rapt attention: "the rippling muscles," "the long supple hand," and "the parted lips" sexualize the moment of terror. But Rat's fearful attention also focuses on a kind of birth, for "the little round, podgy, childish form of the baby otter . . . nestl[ed] between [Pan's] very hooves." There are, in fact, two types of gender transgression occurring in the passage: male-male attraction and male birth.

Although benign in *The Wind in the Willows*, Pan more often signaled fright. Defender of pastures, forests, and flocks, the Pan of antiquity is said to have inspired travelers with deadly terror when they met him in their rambles, especially when they met him at night. Medieval peoples used Pan's half-human, half-goat image to represent Satan, and from his name we've derived the English term "panic," a sudden and irrational fear. In one version of the myth, Pan's mother, horrified by her son's goatish appearance, abandons him immediately after birth (Grant and Hazel 254–55). This anxiety of maternal abandonment certainly invades *Kensington Gardens*, but with the implication that parental fear is justified by the child's monstrous hybridity and proximity to radical sexual practices. Frazer and Thomas Bulfinch both record that the ancients saw Pan as a giver of fertility; Pan caroused with nymphs and satyrs, and his various sexual exploits were, literally, the subject of myth (Bulfinch 155). Often signifying licentiousness as well as sudden fear, Pan's image associated hybridity with promiscuity and terror.

Other turn-of-the-century literary Pans tapped the vices of the ancient icon. A contemporary tale by E. M. Forster entitled "The Story of a Panic" (1904) chronicles the brief "career" of the boy Eustace who, along with a group of picnickers, encounters Pan in an Italian vale. Overcome by a sudden, unexplainable terror, the adults flee from their picnic site, only to return minutes later to find Eustace writhing in pleasure next to a set of goat prints (11). The boy's trademark lethargy then transforms into wild abandon: "He was getting too uproarious, I

thought; and we were all glad to leave the wood[,] . . . Eustace scurrying in front of us like a goat" (15). Thinking him mad, the adults curtail
Eustace's increasingly bacchanalian profligacy by confining him to the
house; eventually the bestialized Eustace escapes back to the vale,
thwarting all adult control.

In Arthur Machen's 1894 novella *The Great God Pan*, a young
woman, victim of a scientific experiment that forces her to "see the
Great God Pan," is impregnated by the deity, and later gives birth to incarnate evil in the guise of a little girl. That child, Helen Vaughn, ter-
rorizes a boy, Trevor, who catches her playing in the woods with a
strange naked man near a stone head "of grotesque appearance,"
which is later "pronounced by the most experienced archaeologists of
the district to be that of a faun or satyr" (25). The adult Helen's rapa-
cious sexuality drives several London men to suicide, for an encounter
with her promotes "knowledge of the most awful, most secret forces
which lie at the heart of all things" (92).

Fear accrues to the satyr in "The Story of a Panic" and *The Great God
Pan* partially because it embodies a kind of desire that exceeds the
strictures of heterosexual love. Although her adult promiscuity doesn't
admit of female lovers (as far as we know), Helen's promiscuous childhood is marked by bisexuality. The story of the boy Trevor, who discovers her in the woods and falls into idiocy, is balanced by the story
of the corruption of the girl Rachel, a "friend" of Helen's, who meets a
tragic end similar to that of Helen's adult male partners. Forster's Eustace pursues an ambiguous relationship with the Italian Gennaro,
who perishes during Eustace's escape. In the course of pursuing their
desires, both Helen and Eustace seriously threaten the stability of the
heterosexual adult communities that surround them.

Kensington Gardens incorporates Pan's association with hybridity
and panic into a philosophy of agential indeterminacy by which the
transgendered child-figure acquires power and autonomy through its
ambivalence. Peter's goat itself originates with a transgendered child.
Maimie Mannering, not unlike the barbarously sexualized Helen
Vaughn in her innate disregard for Victorian feminine passivity, is the
only other child to survive staying past lock-out time. Four years old,
"Maimie [has been] always rather a strange girl, and it [is] at night that
she [is] strange" (41). During the day, Maimie submits to her six-year-
old brother, Tony, but "with dark there [comes] into her face . . . a leary
look" (41). At night, Maimie threatens Tony with an imaginary goat: "'It
is coming nearer! . . . [I]t is feeling your bed with its horns—it is boring

for you, O Tony, oh!'" until he flees, screeching (42). Given that Tony's panic ensues at night, in the bedroom—literally on the bed itself—and that the goat refers to the satyr Pan, it is difficult to avoid interpreting the girl-child as a sexual predator. Maimie breaks taboo by threatening incest and inverts the conventional heterosexual gender dynamic by being the aggressor instead of the pursued.

Kensington Gardens eventually solves the problem of radical femininity, but not by eradicating sexual terror completely. Maimie meets Peter when she stays in the park past lock-out time, and he subsequently helps to save her from freezing to death. Their brief interaction ends with a proposal of marriage. Although the play union would seem to resolve the challenge the child-figure presents to heteronormativity by inscribing radical femininity in the hegemonic structure of marriage, significantly it never occurs; Maimie wants to return to her mother, and Peter (not quite sure what marriage is anyway) is haunted by the tragedy of his own exile. Returned home to domestic consolations Peter never achieves, Maimie desires to give him a gift. Her mother suggests the goat, which has in the meantime become "frightfully real" to Maimie. A mock incantation ensues, in which Maimie exiles her goat with the following rhyme: " *'I have a goat for* [Peter] *to ride, / Observe me cast it far and wide. . . . By dark or light I fondly swear / Never to see goats anywhere'"* (*Kensington Gardens* 63, italics original). That Maimie now finds something fearful in an image she first wielded to terrorize her brother suggests that her brush with death in Kensington Gardens has imbued her with a proper heteronormative mistrust of feminine sexual aggression. Tony's masculinity develops uninhibitedly, free to tyrannize his sister during day *and* night. But even now Maimie retains a sense of agency; she *chooses* not to "see" goats anymore. The threat of the satyr has only been evicted from the bourgeois bedroom to be relocated into the fantasy realm of Kensington Gardens, removed from one child-figure but attached to another.

Instead of marriage, the symbolic event ending conventional melodramas and romances, *Kensington Gardens* transfers the goat, the symbol of sexual transgression, from the household to fairyland and from little girl to androgyne. Although the resolution of the goat problem diffuses the gender tensions of the nursery, it metaphorically raises the potential for sexual exploits in Kensington Gardens; only through the goat can Peter become Peter *Pan*. If the goat is the symbolic threat Peter poses to the stability of late Victorian/Edwardian heterosexuality, it is also the symbolic difference between himself and Maimie. Either he has it, or she has it, but they cannot share it. The story doesn't deflate gender panic; it merely shifts it from one dangerous child-figure to another. Further, when *Kensington Gardens* relocates the goat, it transmits the sexual threat across genres, from the domestic to the fantastic, in part containing the dangerous figure of the child in an "escapist" literary form. The transference of the goat from the domestic sphere to Kensington Gardens mimics the ritualistic public expulsion of evil chronicled by Frazer's discussions of the scapegoat. According to Frazer, the medium of expulsion may be inanimate, animal, or human; when it is animal, goats or birds (equally applicable to *Peter Pan*) often figure as the vehicle (Frazer 626–27). Moreover, Frazer links "the custom of publicly expelling the accumulated evils of a village or town or country" to the rejuvenating principle of vegetation myths through the conduit of the divine man or dying god (665, 668). As such, the process of transferring evil to the scapegoat manifests (often yearly) as a recurring spiritual event that replicates, through public spectacle, the cycle of life and death.

Certainly Peter appears as both scapegoat and god; Neverland seems to sleep while Peter is away, but upon his return things are "all underway again" and "if you put your ear to the ground . . . you would hear the whole island seething with life" (*Peter and Wendy* 112).[5] If Maimie's gift of the goat expulses sexual terror from the domestic sphere, thereby allowing it free play in fantasy, Peter's literal acquisition of Maimie's "gift" makes him a metaphorical scapegoat. Bearing, even embodying, the weight of sexual terror, he carries it away with him to Kensington Gardens.

More important, the processes of identification embedded in *The Little White Bird*'s collapse of narrator and audience and replicated by the stage audience's imbrication in the production of the play (they are urged to clap to save Tinker Bell's life) serve as scapegoating operations. The Christmas pantomime, a yearly theatrical celebration of disorder and license (a tradition for London children and adults alike), coincided with the anniversary of the birth of a messiah whose very purpose was to assume and evacuate public sin. The Christmas pantomime, *Peter Pan* in particular, is nothing other than a melodramatic scapegoat. Just as readers could experience the transference of sexual terror from Maimie to Peter in *Kensington Gardens*, London playgoers could annually experience the transference of gender anxiety from self to Peter Pan. Universal Studios' December 2003 release of the latest version of *Peter Pan* is certainly not coincidental.

While the thrust of this essay up to this point has been to recuperate encryptions of gender indeterminacy and sexual terror in *Peter Pan*'s child-figures, in this concluding section, I want to briefly examine the relationship between the child-figure's androgyny and its political agency. In an analysis of Peter's revolutionary potential as it is articulated through the climax of the play and novel, I contend that the traces of hybridity and sexual terror that have persisted from his earlier incarnation in *The Little White Bird / Peter Pan in Kensington Gardens* enable Peter's defeat of Captain Hook in the later texts. Thus, Peter not only figures adult identifications with gender indeterminacy but also adult identifications with progressive political subjectivities.

When Barrie created Peter Pan, he drew on classical and contemporary traditions alike. As a child, Barrie was an avid reader of penny dreadfuls as well as adventure tales like *Robinson Crusoe* and *The Coral Island* (Birkin 6–12). The adventure tale, popularized by such authors as Frederick Marryat, R. S. Ballantyne, G. H. Henty, H. Rider Haggard, and Robert Louis Stevenson, incorporated a number of conventional elements that cannot all be adequately treated here; however, insofar as it placed earnest English juveniles in foreign locales and amidst exotic adventures, the genre invested in nation-building and its protagonists became symbolically charged political agents. As both Joseph Bristow and M. Daphne Kutzer record, to be an English boy in an adventure story was to be already constructed as subject to and representative of the crown. Yet in the play, Wendy's brothers, not Peter the hero, bear the weight of British nationalism. Tempted to piracy by Captain Hook, John asks, "Stop, should we still be respectful subjects of King George?" Hook replies, "You would have to swear 'Down with King George.'" John respectfully declines (*Peter Pan* 75). The offer is never made to Peter, whose indeterminacy would seem to most qualify him for a swashbuckling career.

While Hook's piracy would seem to undermine the ideology of constitutional monarchy in this scene, the text's allusions to Hook's blue-blooded ancestry demonstrate an even stricter will to power. Appropriately wrapped in quaint Restoration garb, Hook anachronistically emulates Charles II, "having heard it said in some earlier period of his career that he bore a strange resemblance to the ill-fated Stuarts" (*Peter and Wendy* 115). An Etonian "of a different caste" from his crew, even Hook's sinister politeness speaks "the truest test of breeding" (115). Hook captains a sailing vessel, symbol of Britain's military and economic proficiency on the high seas, but he is also a pirate, a villain, who kidnaps and assaults middle-class femininity (in the person of Wendy) and ravages the native land and the natives themselves (in the persons of Tiger Lily and her father). Hook is a tyrant who seems always waiting for his head to be cut off.

In the phantasmic political landscape of Neverland, Peter's relationship to political authority remains complicated to say the least. Peter cannot be read as the conventional hero of the adventure tale, standard of imperial manliness and bearer of Englishness abroad, for he detaches too often from sympathetic identifications. Nor is he the cultural Other; Neverland's Indians fulfill this role. Rather, Peter seems to have a remarkably malleable political agency. When the Lost Boys attack the Indians, for instance, Peter fights first on the side of the Boys and then on the side of their enemy. Peter would never swear allegiance to King George, but neither would he align himself with Hook's symbolic Charles II. Yet despite the number of individuals who have access to him (in the play, all of the Lost Boys are present for the final battle), the text leaves Hook's destruction to Peter alone, with the caveat that he may destroy merely to replace. When the battle is over and the "curtain rises to show Peter a very Napoleon on his ship," the stage notes caution that "it must not rise again lest we see him on the poop in Hook's hat and cigars, and with a small iron claw" (*Peter Pan* 82).

Thinking about Peter's political agency as enabled by gender indeterminacy is not out of the question. As A. J. L.Busst has demonstrated, the image of the androgyne in the early nineteenth century was "characterized above all by its important historical, social and even political associations," becoming a symbol of "social equality and of the emancipation of woman" (12, 22). Busst specifically cites the association of hermaphroditism with the social ideals of the French Revolution. By the later half of the nineteenth century, however, a more pessimistic image of the androgyne dominated cultural philosophy; this image gave in to "isolation, loneliness, self-sufficiency, independence, and despair in the future, in God and in man" (39). This second-order androgyne then became synonymous with sexual vice in the form of "demoniality, onanism, homosexuality, sadism and masochism" (39). Wendy Bashant has echoed Busst's thoughts in discussing Victorian hermaphroditism: the ambivalence of the double-sexed body, she argues, was woven deeply into the fabric of nineteenth-century Britain's social progressivism as well as its fears of cultural dissolution. Elements of both androgynes can be traced through Peter. Like Busst's early androgyne, Peter demonstrates political agency and emancipatory impulses by freeing Wendy, the Lost Boys, and Tiger Lily from Hook's tyranny. But like Busst's later androgyne, he experiences isolation in Neverland and despair in never really knowing a mother's love: "[Peter] had ecstasies innumerable that other children can never know; but he was looking through the window at the one joy from which he must be for ever barred" (*Peter and Wendy* 214).

Both play and novel suggest that Peter's rise to power depends strongly on his hybridity. Edwardian audiences witnessing the final battle would see a buxom Principal Boy abandon the fray to play pan pipes while Hook, heart breaking, throws himself to the jaws of a waiting crocodile. More important, during the final battle Hook repeatedly calls Peter by his mythic name: "So, *Pan* . . . this is all your doing" and "*Pan*, who and what art thou?" (*Peter and Wendy* 202–03, my emphasis). Hook has a moment of panic; seeing his own destruction, the classically educated Etonian perceives Peter as the satyr-like, ambiguously gendered god. The text's articulation of Peter's mythic name at the moment of insurrection signals a dynamic political agency that is enabled by gender indeterminacy—an indeterminacy that remains terrifying despite its power to upset absolutist regimes. The traces of androgyny which have accompanied Peter's transposition from *Kensington Gardens* to *Peter Pan* enable the revolutionary moment in which Peter defeats the tyrannical monarch in this latter text.

For Bashant, the Victorian poetic imagination evoked the androgyne precisely to stage such "play between desire and disease" only to end in sapping the figure's creative and political power (7). Certainly Peter's is a qualified androgynous agency; after sending Hook to his death, Peter sleeps unsoundly, spending much of the night weeping in Wendy's arms. But whatever the personal psychological cost to the androgynous agent, the fact remains that s/he performs a progressive function: Hook's tyranny ends, the Darling patriarch gets his comeuppance, and the Lost Boys find a home in a newly expanded and democratized domestic sphere. Indeed, the domestic byproduct of Peter's political maneuver is an alternative, non-nuclear family organized by affective rather than biological ties. If the hero of boys' adventure fiction is supposed to export heteronormative Englishness abroad, our androgynous Peter reverses the process, upsetting and redefining the Empire of home.

The burden of this essay has been to show that instead of an absence of identity, Peter Pan / *Peter Pan* represents a presence of indeterminacy, which is both terrifying and politically powerful. An androgynous figure, Peter gives to the cultural imagination a dynamic vehicle through which we may construct, fear, and contain non-normative, but socially progressive, agencies. So perhaps, as Universal Studios asserts, *Peter Pan* does give us a "far away world," a true "Neverland," but one in which we never can, nor ever should, feel entirely safe.

NOTES

1. For the purposes of this essay, I deploy "androgyny," "hermaphroditism," and "gender indeterminacy" as roughly synonymous categories.

2. See Andrew Birkin's biography *J. M. Barrie and the Lost Boys: The Real Story behind Peter Pan*, and R. D. S. Jack's *The Road to the Neverland*, as well as Rose, for more detailed discussions of *Peter Pan's* evolution from notes to play to novel.

3. In Edith Nesbit's *Five Children and It*, the children denote their youngest sibling "baby" or "lamb." For more on naming practices, see Lawrence Stone's *The Family, Sex and Marriage in England 1500–1800*.

4. For more on children's dress, see Anne Buck's *Clothes and the Child: A Handbook of Children's Dress in England 1500–1900* and Elizabeth Ewing's *History of Children's Costume*

5. The 2003 film is remarkable for its characterization of Peter as a vegeta tion god. When Peter returns to Neverland from London, gray plants become green, silence turns to the noise of the jungle, glaciers fracture and melt, and the fairies awake.

WORKS CITED

Barrie, J. M. *The Little White Bird*. New York: Scribner's, 1902.

———. "Peter Pan." *The Plays of J. M. Barrie*. London: Hodder and Stoughton, 1928. 1–90.

———. *Peter Pan in Kensington Gardens / Peter and Wendy*. Oxford: Oxford UP, 1991.

Bashant, Wendy. "Redressing Androgyny: Hermaphroditic Bodies in Victorian England." *Journal of Pre-Raphaelite Studies* 4 (1995): 5-23.

Beerbohm, Max. "The Child Barrie." *The Saturday Review* 7 Jan. 1905: 13–14.

Birkin, Andrew. *J. M. Barrie and the Lost Boys: The Real Story Behind Peter Pan*. New Haven: Yale UP, 2003.

Bristow, Joseph. *Empire Boys: Adventures in a Man's World*. London: Harper Collins, 1991.

Buck, Anne. *Clothes and the Child: A Handbook of Children's Dress in England 1500–1900*. New York: Holmes & Meier: 1996.

Bulfinch, Thomas. *Bulfinch's Mythology*. New York: Random House, 1998.

Busst, A. J. L. "The Image of the Androgyne in the Nineteenth Century." *Romantic Mythologies*. Ed. Ian Fletcher. London: Routledge & K. Paul, 1967. 1–95.

Butler, Judith. *Gender Trouble*. New York: Routledge, 1993.

Ewing, Elizabeth. *History of Children's Costume*. New York: Scribner's, 1977.

Forster, E. M. "The Story of a Panic." *Collected Short Stories*. London: Sidgwick and Jackson, 1947. 1–29.

Frazer, Sir James George. *The Golden Bough: A Study in Magic and Religion*. Vol. I. New York: Simon and Schuster, 1996.

Grahame, Kenneth. *The Wind in the Willows*. 1908. New York: Penguin, 1992.

Grant, Michael, and John Hazel. *Who's Who in Classical Mythology*. Oxford: Oxford UP, 1993.

Holland, Peter. "The Play of Eros: Paradoxes of Gender in English Pantomime." *New Theatre Quarterly* 13 (1997): 195–204.

Jack, R. D. S. *The Road to the Never Land*. Aberdeen: Aberdeen UP, 1991.

Kincaid, James. *Child-Loving: The Erotic Child and Victorian Culture*. New York: Routledge, 1992.

Kutzer, M. Daphne. *Empire's Children: Empire and Imperialism in Classic British Chidlren's Books*. New York: Garland, 2000.

Lurie, Alison. *Don't Tell the Grown-Ups: The Subversive Power of Children's Literature*. Boston: Little, Brown, 1990.

Machen, Arthur. *The Great God Pan and the Inmost Light*. London: John Lane, 1894.

Mayer, David. "The Sexuality of Pantomime." *Theatre Quarterly* 4 (1974): 55–64.

Nelson, Claudia. *Boys Will Be Girls: The Feminine Ethic and British Children's Fiction, 1857–1917*. New Brunswick, NJ: Rutgers UP, 1991.

Nesbit, E. *Five Children and It*. 1902. New York: Puffin, 1996.

Peter Pan. Dir. P. J. Hogan. Perf. Jason Isaacs and Jeremey Sumter. Universal Studies, 2003.

"*Peter Pan*, at the Duke of York's." *Illustrated London News* 7 Jan. 1905: 5.

Rose, Jacqueline. *The Case of Peter Pan; Or, the Impossibility of Children's Literature*. Philadelphia: U of Pennsylvania P, 1984.

Ruskin, John. *Time and Tide*. New York: John Wiley and Son, 1868.

Sedgwick, Eve. *Between Men: English Literature and Male Homosocial Desire*. New York: Columbia UP, 1985.

Stone, Lawrence. *The Family, Sex and Marriage in England 1500–1800*. New York: Harper, 1979.

Vicinus, Martha. "The Adolescent Boy: *Fin-de-Siècle* Femme Fatale?" *Victorian Sexual Dissidence*. Ed. Richard Dellamora. Chicago: U of Chicago P, 1999. 83–106.

Wilson, A. E. *Pantomime Pageant*. London: S. Paul, 1946.

Wilson, Ann. "Hauntings: Anxiety, Technology, and Gender in *Peter Pan*." *Modern Drama* (43) 2000: 595–611.

12

Peter Pan, Pullman, and Potter: Anxieties of Growing Up

John Pennington

"Like all fairy stories, mine begins in the shadows—with one particular shadow called Pan," says Wendy, the "fourth-generation Darling, the daughter of the daughter of the daughter of Wendy Darling, the original guide to the Other World" (Fox x). This statement cannot be found in any of J. M. Barrie's writings about Peter Pan; rather, a reader will find it in *The Lost Girls* (2004), a novel by Laurie Fox. Writing in a literary tradition that Geoff Ryman and Gregory Maguire have most recently tilled, Fox has created a contemporary response to a classic work of children's fantasy literature. Ryman in *Was* (1993) and Maguire in *Wicked* (1996)—a novel that has become a popular Broadway musical—returned to L. Frank Baum's Oz. In *The Lost Girls* Fox returns to Neverland and continues the Peter Pan saga by placing the fantasy in a Jungian and Freudian context filtered through feminism.[1] More particularly, Fox updates *Peter Pan* in the shadows of pop psychology, which has further contributed to the enduring legacy of the perpetual boy. In *The Peter Pan Syndrome: Men Who Have Never Grown Up* (1983), Dan Kiley coined the term "Peter Pan Syndrome," which has been embraced by the general populace as a legitimate psychological affliction, though the second edition of *Webster's New World Medical Dictionary* (2003) reports that the syndrome is not yet accepted as a clinical disorder by the medical establishment. And Ann Yeoman, in the exhaustively titled *Now or Neverland: Peter Pan and the Myth of Eternal Youth: A Psychological Perspective on a Cultural Icon* (1999), argues for the universal importance of the eternal-boy archetype that Barrie made famous in his fantasy.

Peter Pan is indeed a cultural icon, a shadow that haunts the fringes of contemporary culture. Such is a heavy burden to carry, especially for a boy who does not ever grow up. "All children, except one, grow up" (7): this famous opening from J. M. Barrie's novel *Peter Pan* captures the timelessness of the fantasy classic that also mirrors the continual cultural influence Barrie's work—as play and novel—has had on generations of playgoers, readers, and writers. Peter Pan does, indeed, live on. He is alive and well at the Great Ormond Street Children's Hospital and as a tourist attraction in Kensington Gardens. He was a crucial influence on Robert Baden-Powell, the founder of the Boy Scouts. He continues to be a perennial stage and screen star: Disney's *Peter Pan* (1953) and *Return to Never Land* (2002), Steven Spielberg's *Hook* (1991), and the live-action *Peter Pan* (2003) have reinterpreted the enigmatic boy for film audiences of all ages. Mary Martin starred in a live TV broadcast of *Peter Pan* in 1955; Sandy Duncan and Cathy Rigby owe their stage careers to him; Tinker Bell remains a spokesfairy for the Disney entertainment conglomerate. Peter Pan has influenced a vampire movie, *The Lost Boys* (1987), about adolescent undeads who cannot grow up; a documentary film, *Lost Boys of Sudan* (2004); and a graphic novel, *Echoes of the Lost Boys of Sudan* (2004), about the real-life tragedy of Sudanese orphaned boys. Peter sells peanut butter, lends his image to a tour-bus line, inspired an (in)famous pop star's ranch, and has morphed into the etherlands of cyberspace, where numerous websites pertain to Peter and his gang. Most recently, Johnny Depp, that oddly famous actor, plays Barrie in *Finding Neverland* (2004), based on Allen Knee's play, *The Man Who Was Peter Pan* (1998); the movie is an homage to the centennial celebration of *Peter Pan* and Barrie in particular. The 78th Street Theatre Lab opens its 26th season with the premiere of Trish Harnetiaux's *Straight on 'Til Morning*, a new play about Peter Pan that relocates Neverland in Brooklyn's blue-collar Williamsburg district. At 100 years, Peter Pan is as youthful as ever, entering the open windows of contemporary culture. Now, that is some influence.

THE *PETER PAN* INFLUENCE

All this interest in Barrie should not be *that* surprising, however. In *Secret Gardens*, Humphrey Carpenter states that "the effect of *Peter Pan* was . . . more immediate than that of any earlier work of children's literature, *Alice in Wonderland* included. . . . We are dealing here not just with a piece of imaginative creation by one man, but with a public phenomenon" (170). Alison Lurie, in *Don't Tell the Grown-ups*, provides a rationale for *Peter Pan's* popularity:

> In *Peter Pan* every wish comes true, from early fantasies of flying to the resurrection of the dead. . . . The whole play is an elaborate dream fulfillment of intense but contradictory wishes—to be grown up at once and never to be grown up; to have exciting adventures and be perfectly safe; to escape from your mother and have her always at hand. It is also, in some sense, deeply subversive, in that it demonstrates graphically that parents are timid and hypocritical and that it is far better to be young and live in Never-Never Land. (131)

Peter Pan's influence, in fact, has led Jacqueline Rose to posit that "*Peter Pan* is, therefore, more than one—it is repeated, reproduced, revived and converted in a seemingly endless spiraling chain" (103). This spiraling effect has grabbed hold of contemporary writers because those contradictory wishes of the play and novel inspire writers who find such ambiguity enticing. *Peter Pan's* reach is quite direct, as witnessed in Laurie Fox's novel. But this reach is also quite subtle and imbues the worlds of contemporary writers who are mining similar fantasy territory. In particular, two of England's most popular children's writers, J. K. Rowling and Philip Pullman, exhibit symptoms of the Peter Pan syndrome of influence. While neither Rowling nor Pullman is overly impressed with Barrie's boy creation, both are, ironically, heavily indebted to *Peter Pan;* they are simultaneously attracted and repelled by Barrie's creation—confronting, adapting, and eventually dispelling Peter Pan from their fantasy narratives.

Both Rowling and Pullman have castigated *Peter Pan*. Rowling is critical of Barrie's refusal to move Peter and Wendy from their innocent world to a more psychologically real one where characters have sexual desires, calling *Peter Pan* a "sinister" book for its avoidance of "hormonal impulse" (Interview, *BBC News*). Pullman has called the work "dreadful rubbish" (qtd. in De Bertodano) and has refused Great Ormond Street Children's Hospital's call for him to write a sequel, graciously declining by stating, "I wish Great Ormond Street very well, but I can't help feeling that they've got the process the wrong way round," for "it was Barrie who wrote it [*Peter Pan*], out of the pressures and fascinations and obsessions that attend any literary inspiration, and then gave it to them [Ormond]" (qtd. in Ezard 2). In spite of Rowling's and Pullman's critiques of *Peter Pan*, Barrie's work molds, to a substantial degree, both the Harry Potter and His Dark Materials series.

Barrie's work creates a fundamental problem that Rowling and Pullman explore in their novels: the issue of growing up in relationship to narrative closure, which truncates adolescent maturity, thus creating an overall sense of ambiguity. Sarah Gilead defines this ambiguity as "tragic" in *Peter Pan* because return leads to loss; the fantasy's closure does "not bring stability but, rather, generates further losses and returns" (98). Gilead concludes that endings like that in *Peter Pan* are subversive: "Instead of restoring or inverting conventional orders of significance, the return may function as the point at which the text most dramatically turns on itself to reveal its duplicities and discords" (102). By questioning the very nature of childhood while maintaining the idyllic desire of "the eternal boy" (110), *Peter Pan*, Jackie Wullschläger suggests, is a *fin de siècle* text that reflects "tragedy and disillusion" in its "creation of his [Barrie's] dream of eternal youth and its cruel unmasking" (111).

Both Rowling and Pullman, writing versions of *fin de siècle* stories nearly 100 years later than Barrie, cannot escape the cultural influence of *Peter Pan*, particularly this ambiguity about the child and supposed childhood innocence at the end of the twentieth and beginning of the twenty-first centuries. Rowling engages *Peter Pan* at its most attractive and tempting level for readers: the Harry Potter books are fantasies of escape from adulthood—quidditch the central flying-as-escape metaphor—that mildly subvert the child and adult worlds, while returning to a real world where growth to adulthood is encouraged. Yet Rowling's series, in which each succeeding volume becomes longer and more complex, demonstrates narrative fissure as Harry's maturation destabilizes the conventional narrative closure of each individual book in the series. Pullman, on the other hand, is also influenced by Barrie but in a more substantial way: His Dark Materials is a more subversive work than Rowling's, focusing on issues of identity, sexuality, morality, theology, and mortality. Whereas Rowling's series returns readers to the familiar and safe as it suggests an ultimate conflict between growing up and narrative closure, Pullman's series more dramatically denies thematic and narrative closure by requiring the child protagonists to grow up without adult guidance in an ambiguous world, thus extending Peter Pan's reach even further in contemporary children's literature. Both writers respond to *Peter Pan* as they create their own original fantasy spaces that are haunted by that boy who never grows up.

This anxiety over growing up permeates the works of Barrie, Rowling, and Pullman. Harold Bloom's theory of the "anxiety of influence," while challenged by many theorists, does address a fundamental fact—writers write in the shadows of those who have written before.[2] Bloom theorizes that writers must have "the persistence to wrestle with their strong precursors, even to the death" (5), revealing "immense anxieties of indebtedness, for what strong maker desires the realization that he [or she] has failed to create himself [or herself]?" (5). *Peter Pan*, as a foundational text in the canon of children's literature, sets into motion some of the most persistent questions about growing up in children's literature. Rowling and Pullman, who have an antipathy toward Barrie, channel this antagonism—this anxiety of influence—into original narratives about the ambiguity of maturation in children's literature.

An additional way to envision this influence is to situate Rowling and Pullman more specifically in the fantasy–fairy tale tradition, where influence, one may argue, is even more pronounced. In *Strategies of Fantasy*, Brian Attebery claims that "nearly all modern fantasy has made such raids on the recorded inventory of traditional narrative" (8), and "realistic fiction is similarly dependent on the devices of past storytellers, but fantasy is less able to disguise its dependence" (9). Fantasy, then, is vitally dependent on' past narrative forms and those writers who have come before. Attebery argues that the "fantasy genre may be viewed as the story of the imposition of one particular set of restrictions on the mode of the fantastic" (10), in effect an essential influence of precursorship. Attebery suggests that fantasy as genre revolves around a central fantastic mode that tends to dominate the fantasy work. Defining fantasy as a "fuzzy set" in which the genre is "defined not by boundaries but by a center," he asks: "From what center do we perceive it radiating?" (13) and concludes that fantasy radiates "from a few well-known and influential texts" (126). J. R. R. Tolkien becomes "our template" (14), an über text that pushes its influence into other works. Attebery acknowledges, however, that other works provide such influence. Children's fantasies and fairy tales, then, comprise another template that may radiate and influence the fantasy genre. Furthermore, Perry Nodelman reminds us that children's literature, by its very nature, is formulaic—providing the reader with "the pleasure of formula" (12)—which prompts an author to be creative within this formula, a sentiment supported by Vladimir Propp's notion of fairy tale functions in *Morphology of the Folktale* and Joseph Campbell's theory of the monomyth in *The Hero with a Thousand Faces*. As Nodelman notes, in particular, a formula may be followed in its basic structure but supplemented in a way that transforms the formula into an original act of storytelling. One such formula in children's literature centers around growth. "Much children's fiction deals with attempts to grow up without actually growing up," writes Nodelman, "to mature without losing the joy, optimism, and simplicity of youth, to be neither Peter nor Wendy but some combination of the two" (197).

It seems plausible that *Peter Pan* is one of those central texts that writers of children's fantasy must encounter and transform "into the revisionary insights of their own work" (Bloom 10). Rose would agree: "*Peter Pan*'s status is not, therefore, that of a children's book, but rather that of a concept or class—the whole category of children's literature out of which all these stories are produced" (86). Rowling and Pullman are no exceptions to this anxiety of influence. In the "Acknowledgments" to *The Amber Spyglass*, Pullman writes, "I have stolen ideas from every book I have ever read" (521). He lists Heinrich von Kleist, John Milton, and William Blake as central influences. *The Golden Compass* (first published in England as *Northern Lights*) begins with a quotation from Book II of *Paradise Lost*, and *The Amber Spyglass* begins with an excerpt from Blake's *America: A Prophecy*. Such stated influence is easy to identify. C. S. Lewis's *Chronicles of Narnia* is a central influence Pullman struggles with, especially when he claims that Lewis's influence on children's literature "is actually pernicious" (qtd. in Parsons and Nicholson 131).[3] But the unstated ones are equally persuasive. *Peter Pan* is also an important work to Pullman. The connections are obviously there. For example, the opening chapter of *The Golden Compass* introduces the reader to Lyra and her daemon, Pantalaimon. Lyra immediately refers to her daemon with the shortened name, Pan, evoking Barrie's namesake. Chapter 12 is called "The Lost Boy," further announcing the direct connection to *Peter Pan*. The relationship between Lyra and Pan echoes that of Wendy and Peter, but Pullman's creation of the co-protagonist Will in *The Subtle Knife* and *The Amber Spyglass* complicates the Lyra-Pan relationship by adding a flesh-and-blood romance between Lyra and Will, a direct response to the frustrated romance of Wendy and Peter.

With Rowling, the overt connection to *Pan* is not as obvious but is fundamentally present. In many ways the dominant radiating texts for Rowling may be Thomas Hughes's *Tom Brown's Schooldays* (1857), Anthony Buckeridge's Jennings series, Enid Blyton's Naughtiest Girl series, Elinor Brent-Dyer's Chalet School series, and the popular detective series of Nancy Drew and the Hardy Boys. These school stories are primarily realistic texts that seem to conflict with the fantasy setting in the novels. Yet the connection is there: Peter Pan and Harry Potter are the titles of their books, their names quite complementary; Harry Potter sounds suspiciously close to Peter Pan (the Ps, Ts, and Rs resonate), as do the Dursleys and the Darlings. Harry's nemesis in *Harry Potter and the Prisoner of Azkaban* is Peter Pettigrew, which may be a Peter Pan pun, as he is a character who *grew*. Chapter 1, "The Boy Who Lived," from *Harry Potter and the Sorcerer's Stone*, is a chapter title that could, with small modification, find itself in *Peter Pan*—The Boy Who Lives. Captain Hook haunts Peter; Lord Voldemort, Harry. Both boys are orphans and desire parents: Peter a mother, Harry both mother and father. Rowling's series is about growing up, Barrie's book about the ramifications of not growing up.

Rowling and Pullman write a variation on the *Peter Pan* formula which itself relies on the larger hero-quest structure that imbues much fantasy and fairy tale literature. These structural connections between *Peter Pan* and Rowling's and Pullman's series, we will see, become more pronounced when we examine some of the larger thematic concerns revolving around growing up that the books share.

How do these writers revise *Peter Pan* into something new, unique, and original? What do Rowling and Pullman bring to *Pan*? What do their fantasies *do* to the influence of the boy who lives? Rowling and Pullman rework the implications of Barrie's larger theme of (not) growing up by situating this theme in the larger context of maturation and sexuality. In addition, these writers confront an essential structural problem concerning narrative, that of closure. A key that connects *Peter Pan* to the Harry Potter series and His Dark Materials series is that of closure—or lack of closure—that leads to thematic ambiguity related to growing up. *Peter Pan* is such a phenomenon because it remains timeless, not necessarily because it is a canonical text that has captured the archetypal imagination (which may be true) and continues to be staged yearly during the holiday season, but because Peter Pan literally lives on. The text has no definitive closure, which gives the book the power to influence continually. This lack of closure becomes more complex when we examine how this creates and reflects the ambiguity of meaning that pervades the book.

A fantasy's closure is often dependent on return, and all three authors under discussion adapt the return-to-reality narrative framework, making their fantasies dependent on the "real" for their stability. Gilead reminds us that "return may be viewed as resolving a narrative rivalry between realism and fantasy and thus as analogous to a self that has worked out internal conflicts" (82). Gilead categorizes three types of return: 1) "the return as *Bildung"* (83) (one that educates, usually to complete the psychic growth of the protagonist); 2) "the return as narrative repression" (89) (one that "rejects or denies" the fantastic world); and 3) "the return as tragic ambiguity" (95) (one that rejects returns 1 and 2 for a "tragic mode that reveals, without an assuring sense of mediation, both the seductive force and the dangerous potentiality of fantasy") (82). In this mode of tragic ambiguity, argues Gilead, "return remains indeterminate" and is "dominated by a sense of loss unmitigated by a playful or softened tone" (95). Gilead concludes that in *Peter Pan*, "the return does not bring stability but, rather, generates further losses and returns. The children lose their powers of flight, their belief in the possibility of escape through fantasy, and also, perhaps, their belief in the inviolability of childhood itself" (98). That is why Gilead labels *Peter Pan* "a morbid book" (97) and may be why Rowling and Pullman tend to view the work somewhat negatively. But *Peter Pan*'s lack of closure gives the novel its enticing texture, making the book, to use Roland Barthes's concept, a writerly text, one that requires the reader to complete. In other words, *Peter Pan* urges—*demands* may be a more accurate word—readers and theater goers to participate in the text. At the end of Act IV of the play, Peter directly addresses the audience, asking them to help save Tinker Bell by clapping their hands if they "believe in fairies" (74). The novel *Peter Pan* works similarly; its writerly emphasis tempts other writers to complete the text, to revise, or as John Stephens and Robyn McCallum argue, to create a "reversion" that challenges the original version: "If outcomes of other kinds are to be achieved, a reteller has to struggle with and overcome material which is always to some extent intractable because of its combination of strong, familiar story shapes with already legitimatized values and ideas about the world" (x).

A common thread that connects Barrie, Rowling, and Pullman revolves around the Blakean notions of innocence and experience, which reinforce the tragic ambiguity of the narratives. U. C. Knoepflmacher argues that children's fantasies—particularly Victorian fantasies—have a precarious balance between the Blakean polarities of innocence and experience: "From the vantage point of experience, an adult imagination re-creates an earlier childhood self in order to steer it towards the reality principle. From the vantage point of innocence, however, that childhood agent may resist the imposition of adult values and stubbornly demand that its desire to linger in a realm of magic and wonder be satisfied" ("Balancing" 497). This tension also becomes manifest in the author:

> Torn between the opposing demands of innocence and experience, the author who resorts to the wishful magical thinking of the child nonetheless feels compelled, in varying degrees, to hold on to the grown-up's circumscribed notions about reality. In the better works of fantasy of the [Victorian] period, this dramatic tension between the outlooks of adult and childhood selves becomes rich and elastic: conflict and harmony, friction and reconciliation, realism and wonder, are allowed to interpenetrate and co-exist. ("Balancing" 499)

In *Ventures into Childland* Knoepflmacher writes that "Peter Pan can remain untainted by the City of Experience, sheltered and immune on his island of never-growing boys" (187), but Peter's Thel-like rejection of the experienced world leads to his stunted growth, which has generated a cottage industry of critical debate over sexuality in the novel.[4] Rowling and Pullman, however, seem intent on confronting what Barrie avoids: their works explore the complex implications of Blake's two contrary states of the human soul. This tension between innocence and experience, between adult and child, has prompted Rose to argue that children's fiction is an impossibility, with *Peter Pan* being the template for this unattainability. "Children's fiction is impossible," writes Rose, "not in the sense that it cannot be written (that would be nonsense), but in that it hangs on an impossibility, one which it rarely ventures to speak. This is the impossible relation between adult and child" (1). Rowling's and Pullman's series are the latest works that confront this conundrum which is *Peter Pan*, the impossibility of resolving growing up with narrative closure in children's literature. Both writers speak to the fissure between childhood innocence and adult experience.

PETER PAN AND J. K. ROWLING'S HARRY POTTER SERIES

The Harry Potter books are simply a phenomenon. Harry Potter has, in effect, become the new Peter Pan as cultural icon or archetype. *The New York Times* even had to create a new best-seller list to accommodate Rowling. This phenomenon is partly a result of Rowling's ability to tap into the innocence-experience dichotomy that frames much of children's literature. The Leaky Cauldron, a website that labels itself a "proud member of the Floo Network," reports that *The Scotsman* found that "'while *Peter Pan* and *Harry Potter and the Philosopher's Stone* were both recognized by every youngster polled, only 12 percent had read JM Barrie's tale . . . compared with 81 per cent who had read the first of JK Rowling's series'" ("At Least They're Reading").[5] In a 2003 BBC interview Rowling relates how she was taken aback by a woman who wrote her, pleading with her not to have Harry develop a desire for girls: "Please don't do that, that's awful. I want these books to be a world where my children can escape to." Rowling responds by referencing Enid Blyton's *Famous Five* books in which the characters "never had a hormonal impulse"; she admits that such supposed innocence "reaches its apotheosis in *Peter Pan* obviously, where it is quite explicit, and I find that very sinister." The Harry Potter books, then, can be seen as a response to *Peter Pan*—Rowling is writing a new chapter to the boy who would not grow up. *Peter Pan* denies the world of experience to Peter as he lives in Neverland, but Wendy, John, Michael, and the Lost Boys do return to the experienced world where they will mature and grow. Harry Potter, a lost boy himself, follows a similar pattern of return to reality and maturity.

The structure of the Harry Potter books reflects this movement from innocence to experience. Each novel follows a similar pattern: Harry is trapped at the Dursleys' in the Muggle world for the summer; he is transported via some inventive magical apparatus to Hogwarts, where he takes classes on magic and participates in Quidditch matches or other feats of athletic and intellectual abilities; eventually he must do battle with Voldemort around final exam time (successfully thwarting the evil one and passing his exams); he wins accolades at Hogwarts at the end of the school term; and finally he returns home to the Muggle world. The Potter books follow the return-to-reality framework that is organized around the conventional school year, which also is based on the movement of innocence to experience: students graduate to a new school level as they mature intellectually and physically. Brooke Allen contends that "the appeal of these tales is obvious: The fictional school provides an enclosed world with its own rules and standards. The reader can enjoy a certain measure of drama and even danger while resting assured that right will, in the end, prevail" (14). Though it appears that Rowling's series follows Gilead's return-as-education that teaches a lesson and reestablishes order to the magical world, the books also represent "the return as tragic ambiguity," a return that is integral to *Peter Pan*. At the end of the novel *Peter Pan*, Peter continues to visit the Darling household, first taking Jane to Neverland, and then Margaret. The novel ends with an infinite pattern: "When Margaret grows up she will have a daughter, which is to be Peter's mother in turn; and thus it will go on, so long as children are gay and innocent and heartless" (242). At the end of each Potter novel to date, Harry returns to a dysfunctional home (similar to Wendy and her brothers' return home, where they find their father in a literal dog house, suggesting that the Darling family is also somewhat dysfunctional, even having a dog as a nanny), but Harry's world, too, is not stable or closed—magic can infiltrate the Muggle world, for positive and negative effects.

Thus the narrative world of the Harry Potter books is simultaneously open and closed, making the books similar to Barrie's work. For example, Peter Pan can return to the Darling bedroom window at will to continue his adventures, even after Wendy has grown up, mothered a child, and lost her ability to return to Neverland. In this respect, Peter and Rowling's Voldemort operate in a similar fashion: both characters can traverse the magical and mundane worlds, crossing at will the threshold between the commonplace and the fantastic. In the Potter series, for example, Voldemort contacts Harry more frequently in the Muggle world, and this contact is seen in Harry's scar, which now throbs with pain as the evil one infiltrates the mundane world, thus signaling that Voldemort can break the barrier between the real and the magical worlds. The result is that the Harry Potter books have an odd overall structure that is often contradictory: each novel has closure as Harry advances at Hogwarts and returns to the Dursleys', yet Harry's larger mission to battle Voldemort continues beyond the school year. Of course, this lack of closure, on the one hand, is due to Rowling's casting of the Potter series in seven projected books. We can assume that at the end of book seven the narrative world will be closed in a way that *Peter Pan*'s is not, but that is mere speculation at this point.[6] What the series does, though, is allow Rowling to deny overall closure that creates a sense of tragic ambiguity as she orders her narrative world around the familiar structure of educational growth. While the narrator in *Peter Pan* tells the reader that "I solemnly promise that it will all come right in the end" (53), the reader recognizes at the end that all's not right with the world, for Peter Pan rejects growth and returns to Neverland, a place that is an impossibility for all but Peter, who can never be truly satiated by adventure. Each novel in Rowling's series, in turn, provides temporary closure that reassures the reader, but the narrative interest also resides in the unknown—will Harry Potter defeat Voldemort? Will Harry survive? Harry Potter may well rival Charles Dickens's Little Nell in the public's desire to know whether a character lives or dies. Book seven (and eight, if there is one) may allow critics to make more comfortable claims about the series, but the fact remains that as Harry Potter continues to grow up, his narrative world becomes increasingly dark and dangerous, with the conventional happy ending more tenuous with each new volume.

Rowling is able to create this narrative uncertainty by using dreams to create narrative instability, for dreams are otherworldly and blur distinctions between fantasy and reality. If a dream is seen as an illusion— as in the Alice books or the movie version of *The Wizard of Oz*—then the narrative world is, as Gilead suggests, one of repression or rejection of the fantasy. In *Peter Pan*, on the contrary, the dreamworld asserts its reality by slowly invading the Darling household. As diligent as Mrs. Darling is in "tidying up her children's minds" at bedtime (12), her dreams begin to become reality as "Peter breaks through" the window barrier that separates the real from the fantastic world of Neverland. In fact, it is in Mrs. Darling's own dream "that the Neverland had come too near and that a strange boy had broken through it" (18). When the dreamworld becomes real, consequently, the dangers of the imagination also become real: "Thus sharply did the terrified three learn the difference between an island of make-believe and the same island come true" (68). A similar concern is found in Rowling's books: Harry's dreams begin to cease being fantasy and become visions of events to come. In *The Sorcerer's Stone*, Harry tells Uncle Vernon and Aunt Petunia that he "had a dream about a motorcycle. It was flying" (25); indeed, the motorcycle brings Hagrid to the Muggle world. In *The Chamber of Secrets*, Harry's dreams turn to nightmares and he begins to hear tempting and threatening voices—"*Come . . . come to me. . . . Let me rip you. . . . Let me tear you. . . . Let me kill you. . . .*" (120)—which disturb his visions more. *The Prisoner of Azkaban* finally breaks the boundaries between dream and reality: Ron Weasley dreams about walking in a forest, pursued by some hoofed creature, and awakens to find Sirius Black with a knife. The dream cannot be explained away because Ron's bedroom curtains are shredded. Finally, in *The Order of the Phoenix* the dangers of dreaming become completely manifest: Harry's nightmare about Sirius Black is real, a premonition that he has no power to control. With Black's death, Harry has immense guilt and anxiety. Amy Billone argues that "Harry discovers that his dreams have deceived him—consequently, he has led all of his friends to their probable deaths and allowed his godfather to be murdered" (178). Similarly, Barrie writes of Peter's dreams: "Sometimes, though not often, he had dreams, and they were more painful than the dreams of other boys. For hours he could not be separated from these dreams, though he wailed piteously in them. They had to do, I think, with the riddle of his existence" (174). These dreams are a vehicle for Peter's survival; the night he does not dream, Hook is able to enter his chamber and poison his drinking cup.

Harry's dreams also suggest another tension that is at the heart of *Peter Pan* and the Potter books: the inability to fulfill desire, thus making the works tragic. Dreams are the road to the unconscious, Freud reminds us, and become *"disguised fulfilments of repressed wishes"* which further frustrate the dreamer (165; italics in original). Peter can never be fulfilled in Neverland's world of innocence because he rejects the experienced world of Wendy; in fact, Peter, it is suggested, has lost his ability to return to reality and can only visit temporarily Wendy's world, and Neverland, we should not forget, is a dreamscape for Wendy and her brothers. At the close of the novel Wendy, her brothers, and the adopted Lost Boys lose their magic, their ability to fly, and thus begin the process of maturation. They become Muggles, to use Rowling's term. Peter returns to Neverland, remaining eternal but not fulfilled: at the beginning of the novel he sobs because he cannot reattach his shadow; at the end he sobs because he is jealous that Wendy has grown up and given birth to Jane, who represents both the innocent who can fly with him to Neverland and the symbol of Wendy's sexual maturation. Barrie writes: "Wendy . . . felt at once that she was in the presence of a tragedy" (38), and Barrie repeats the word *tragedy* numerous times in the novel to emphasize such loss. *Peter Pan* creates a world of tragic ambiguity with its lack of closure that denies any wish fulfillment for Peter, who is simultaneously attracted and repulsed by Wendy as girl and then mother. Likewise, Harry's world is one of frustrated desire that becomes succeedingly tragic as the novels progress. He is abused by Dudley and the Dursleys in the Muggle world, but even when he is liberated by going to Hogwarts, he realizes that his scar, a symbol of his difference, will prevent him from enjoying the childhood innocence—as an orphan of murdered parents, he cannot be innocent, for the experienced world dictates his actions. Each time that Harry is close to satisfying some desire, it is denied. The Mirror of Erised is symbolic of this denial, for it can only reflect his parents' shadow, further reminding him of his loss—"He had a powerful kind of ache inside him, half joy, half terrible sadness" (*Sorcerer's Stone* 209)—and Dumbledore explains to Harry that the mirror "shows us nothing more or less than the deepest, most desperate desire of our hearts" (213). When he finally has a chance for a surrogate father in Sirius Black, Voldemort—evil incarnate and representative of the experienced world—takes Black from Harry.

The Potter series has a sense of "adjured closure" (to use Gilead's term) that mirrors the dominant theme that the series owes to Barrie— that of growing up. Growth traces a predictable narrative arc, following a character from childhood to adulthood to inevitable death. Growth is by nature tragic, for all must die, and contemplating the death of a child is even more tragic, bordering on the morbid. But that is the crux of stories of growth: children grow from innocence to experience, yet that growth presupposes an unsettling reality, death. Of course, *Peter Pan* complicates the growth narrative by stunting Peter so he can live on in innocence for eternity. But the other characters will grow, mature, and die, as seen in the death of Mrs. Darling and faithful Nana, who "died of old age" (235). Death hovers over *Peter Pan* in spite of Peter's eternal youth. And death, it seems, is intertwined with maturation into sexuality. As Gilead suggests, Peter is a contradiction, being "death itself as well as the desire for eternal childhood" (96). "Both boy eternal and rotting corpse," continues Gilead, "he arrives like a dream of immortality come true but also like a plague deadly to children—like ageing and death, he empties the nursery" (97). Rose writes that "between the lines of *Peter Pan*, we can see not only the question of origins (mothers and fathers), and of sexuality (boys and girls), but also the reference to death which is latent in the other two" (38).

Peter Pan, on one level, normalizes sexuality at the end by having Wendy grow to a literal mother of Jane and grandmother to Margaret, but the novel frustrates desire, on another level, by prohibiting Wendy's desire for Peter, as well as frustrating the desires of Tinker Bell and Tiger Lily, and some might add the desire Captain Hook has for Peter. Sexuality in *Peter Pan* is contradictory and troublesome and creates the ambitious texture of the novel that thwarts reader expectation. Rowling, on the other hand, creates a conservative heteronormative world: the novels slowly show Harry's growing desire for girls, whether it is for the brainy Hermione or for Cho. In *The Order of the Phoenix* Harry meets Cho under a mistletoe, and it is clear that Cho certainly wants to kiss—"I really like you, Harry"—but "he could not think. A tingling sensation was spreading throughout him, paralyzing his arms, legs, and brain" (457). Peter Pan remains paralyzed; Harry, we assume, will not. We can anticipate that Harry will eventually kiss Cho (or some other girl), and the plot of the series will follow Harry into puberty. Though Rowling dismisses Barrie's resistance to allowing children to mature, she is indebted to him for the strange mingling of this innocence and experience.

Thus we can see that Rowling, in part, constructs the Harry Potter series around the same polarities of reality and fantasy, innocence and experience, child and adult that Barrie explores. It may be that Rowling's greatest strength in the series is her ability to write for children rather than for adults, which aligns her even more closely with Barrie. Rose discusses the "impossible relation between adult and child" in which writers rarely "speak *to* the child" (1). Jack Zipes agrees: "There has never been a literature conceived *by* children *for* children, a literature that belongs to children, and there never will be" (40). Zipes emphasizes how the culture industry, controlled by adults, markets children's literature as a cultural commodity. And Knoepflmacher suggests that innocence (child) and experience (adult) "remain locked into a dynamic that acknowledges the simultaneous yet opposing demands of growth and arrest" ("Balancing" 497). Once again *Peter Pan* is the template for this tension, and we can see how Rowling consciously tries to write *for* the child—and the impossibility of such an artistic task. As soon as Rowling allows Harry to grow, for example, he no longer can be a child; the Potter books will find that their audience will have to grow too and that the readers may simply outgrow the Potter books before Harry does. Rowling's series may be a test case to examine Rose's notion of the impossibility of a true children's literature.

PETER PAN AND PHILIP PULLMAN'S HIS DARK MATERIALS SERIES

When we turn to Philip Pullman's His Dark Materials series, we can see this child-adult, innocence-experience polarity made more complex, reflecting, to a large degree, Barrie's work, "a classic in which the problem of the relationship between adult and child is unmistakably at the heart of the matter" (Rose 5). In a review of Pullman's series for *The New York Review of Books*, Michael Chabon articulates this fundamental tension:

> In fact the question of whether or not *His Dark Materials* is meant or even suitable for young readers not only remains open but grows ever more

difficult to answer as the series progresses. This indeterminacy of reader-
ship—the way Pullman's story pulses fitfully between the poles of adult
and children's fiction . . . [is] . . . itself a figuring- or working-out of the
fundamental plot . . . which turns . . . on the questions of what becomes
of us, or our bodies and our souls, as we enter the borderland of adolescence. (3)

Pullman's "working-out" of this child-adult tension through Blake's
states of innocence and experience, we will see, is influenced by
Peter Pan.

In *The Amber Spyglass*, Will Parry explains why the subtle knife,
which has the power to open windows to multiple worlds, shattered
into pieces: "The knife broke because I thought of my mother. So I've
got to put her out of my mind. But . . . it's like when someone says
don't think about a crocodile, you *do*, you can't help it . . ." (240). Or
to *not* think about *Peter Pan*. Pullman seems to admit, in this quotation,
that Barrie's work is an influence: motherhood and a devious crocodile
are certainly key elements in *Peter Pan*. But Pullman's series reminds
us at the beginning that it is much more serious in tone than Rowling's
work—i.e., Lyra and Pan find themselves helplessly watching as the
Steward conspires to poison Lord Asriel—and this darker, more urgent
tone, in turn, separates his work further from Barrie's and Rowling's
blending of satire and humor amidst worlds of violence and death. In
fact, Pullman's series seems closer in tone to Barrie's original interpo-
lated story of Peter Pan in *The Little White Bird* (1902), which became
Peter Pan in Kensington Gardens in 1906, two years after the play *Peter Pan*. In *Kensington Gardens* Peter suffers serious loss when he finally decides to return home to his mother, only to find his bedroom
window encased by iron bars; Peter leaves, sobbing, and Chapter 4
ends as follows: "There is no second chance, not for most of us. When
we reach the window it is Lock-out Time. The iron bars are up for life"
(40). Earlier in the story, Solomon Caw, a wise old bird, tells Peter that
he cannot fly anymore because he has lost faith by desiring to return to
his mother; thus, Peter's bird self must be lost so he can become fully
human. Peter's choice, to return, has implications ("'And never even go
to the Kensington Gardens?' Peter asked tragically"), and Solomon tells
him what exactly he will be: "'You will be a Betwixt-and-Between' . . .
and certainly he was a wise old fellow, for that is exactly how it turned
out" (17). Peter even tells the young girl Maimie, "I am not exactly a
boy; Solomon says I am a Betwixt-and-Between" (57). Peter Pan, then,

is eternal, but trapped Betwixt-and-Between the realm of child and adult and innocence and experience, and as a result, he becomes a tragic figure of unfullfillment. Pullman's response to Barrie is to maintain this tragic tone throughout the series but to reject Barrie's desire for eternal youth and innocence. As Pullman admits, his Lyra and Will books are about the importance of growing up.

To a larger degree Pullman and Barrie operate under similar conditions, exploring the ambiguity of maturation and growth. Peter Pan is certainly a tragic figure: he is eternal but simultaneously dead as a complex human who has not moved from innocence to experience to an advanced contrary state that Blake calls organized experience. *The Golden Compass* seems a direct response to the desire to keep children innocent and pure. Of course, from a theological perspective Pullman is revising Milton's notion of *felix culpa*, the fortunate fall that finds original sin elemental to being human. Pullman also engages Blake's *Marriage of Heaven and Hell*, with the poem's insistence that contraries lead to progression, that innocence can only exist simultaneously with the state of experience, the prolific and devourer (akin to creator and destroyer) entangled in a delicate balance. Pullman's first book in the series explores, to a large degree, the dangers of protecting innocence at the expense of experience. In other words, *The Golden Compass* explores the dangers of *Peter Pan*. Lyra and Pan are separate but unified, body and soul in the Cartesian duality. Pan is Lyra's shadow, completing her (she thinks). Though a supposed orphan, Lyra is happy in her world and content with her existence: "This was her world. She wanted it to stay the same forever and ever, but it was changing around her, for someone out there was stealing children" (62). But it is not Peter Pan who is enticing children to Neverland by blasting through a window or collecting fallen babies from their perambulators; instead, in Lyra's world these lost boys and girls are "severed" (21) by the Oblation Board, an arm of the organized Church. The sexual implications do not remain implied; they are made overt in the novel. To the Church, innocence is akin to sexual innocence; the Church attempts to deny original sin by preventing children from confronting puberty, thus allowing their daemon forms to remain flexible, not solidified into one particular form. Pullman provides a revised Genesis myth to account for the rationale for such horrific actions:[7]

"And the eyes of them both [Adam and Eve] were opened, and they saw the true form of their daemons, and spoke with them.

But when the man and the woman knew their own daemons, they
knew that a great change had come upon them, for until that moment it
had seemed that they were at one with all the creatures of the earth and
the air, and there was no difference between them:
And they saw the difference, and they knew good and evil; and they
were ashamed, and they sewed fig leaves together to cover their naked-
ness. . . ." (372)

Dust, a key motif in Pullman's series, is the physical symbol of this
fall into sexuality, "proof that something happened when innocence
changed into experience" (373). The Church, through the Gobblers,
kidnaps children so it can separate the child from the daemon, thus
preventing original sin from occurring at puberty.

This focus on innocence and experience in the context of sexual
maturation is at the heart of Pullman's series. Barrie acts like Pullman's
Church, cutting Peter Pan from his daemon (Wendy) and Wendy from
her daemon (Peter) and consequently keeping him innocent and pure
for eternity (while Wendy becomes a mother, losing her innocence).
But even Barrie's work demonstrates that Peter and his world are not
innocent—it is a violent, often sadistic world. Thus the ambiguity of innocence and sexuality in *Peter Pan*. Pullman finds creativity in such
ambiguity. In *The Golden Compass* Pullman explores the tension between Lyra and Pan, and then he complicates their relationship in *The
Subtle Knife* by bringing Lyra and Will together. In the first novel, Lyra
and Pan represent the innocence between human and daemon because their melding is natural (they are part of the same self, the body
and soul an apt analogy); however, the relationship between Lyra and
Will in *The Subtle Knife* is a result of the natural development into experienced desire that complicates the natural relationship with Pan.
Lyra realizes that she cannot live without Pan, *and* realizes that while
she can live without Will, she does not want to be separated from him.
In effect, Will and Lyra's relationship is a response to Wendy and Peter's frustrated one. In the second volume to the series, then, Pullman
traces the implications of growing up as Lyra and Will battle the Church
(the moral Authority), which is a battle to keep the Church from preventing children from growing up into sexual beings. In the second
volume of the series, the Magisterium (another office of the Church)
performs "intercision" (a kind of symbolic spiritual castration) on
young boys and girls so they can remain pure and "obliterate every
good feeling" (50). But this intercision kills the child or makes those
severed into zombies, as Mrs. Coulter, Lyra's mother and avid operative

in the Church, says, "But . . . they've undergone intercision. They have no daemons, so they have no fear and no imagination and no free will . . ." (199).

The final book in the series, *The Amber Spyglass*, explores the tension of innocence and experience as Lyra and Will fall in love—a sensual love—contrary to the frustrated sensuality between Peter and Wendy. Consummation of physical love is equated with death in Barrie and Pullman, but Pullman will not shy away from this reality. Peter Pan famously states that "to die will be an awfully big adventure" (132), and Pullman takes Peter's words literally as the characters enter the realm of the dead. Both Barrie and Pullman recognize the ambiguity of death: Barrie keeps Peter eternal but unnatural, for death is part of the life cycle. That Neverland is a kind of graveyard, where Wendy and the Lost Boys live underground in coffin-like houses, suggests that Barrie consciously or unconsciously was haunted by death. Pullman's world of the dead is a kind of limbo, where Roger, who is a victim of intercision, is described as an "unchanging dead" (*Amber Spyglass* 310). But the ghost of Roger is sad when he meets Lyra in the underworld because he notices that Lyra has changed, especially when she talks about Will. "Lyra began to explain, quite unaware of how her voice changed, how she sat up straighter, and how even her eyes looked different when she told the story of her meeting with Will and the fight for the subtle knife. How could she have known? But Roger noticed, with the sad, voiceless envy of the unchanging dead" (310). Death and sensuality are intertwined in Pullman's narrative world, and part of his larger theme about growing up concerns growing into sexual awareness that by its nature signals maturity and aging—and death. Pullman embraces death by negating it, for death in the Christian tradition as renewed life in heaven is a ruse (the dead, for Pullman, live in a limbo state of depressed consciousness); Lyra and Will guide the dead to the living world again, where they can dissipate into dust, a more secular take on ashes to ashes, dust to dust.

Lyra and Will's adventure in the world of the dead—a kind of Neverland—is essential for the development from innocence to experience, neatly following the hero's quest as defined in Joseph Campbell's monomyth. At the end of *The Amber Spyglass*, Pullman has Lyra and Will fall in love, and he describes their first kiss. Instead of getting a thimble and acorn, as do Wendy and Peter, Lyra and Will have a bonafide embrace: "The word *love* set his nerves ablaze. All his body thrilled with it, and he answered her in the same words, kissing her hot face over and over again, drinking in with adoration the scent of her body and her warm, honey-fragrant hair and her sweet, moist mouth that tasted of the little red fruit" (466). Dust begins to flow again: "The Dust pouring down from the stars had found a living home again, and these children-no-longer-children, saturated with love, were the cause of it all" (470). Whereas Barrie does not allow for the fulfillment of the desire that Wendy, Tinker Bell, and Tiger Lily have for Peter (because Peter cannot reciprocate this desire since he is a stunted innocent), Pullman does—but up to a certain point. Both Barrie and Pullman create a tragic sense in their narrative worlds because such desire is, finally, not fulfilled. Wendy and the Lost Boys return to London, and Peter is left alone—eternal, yet dead to growth and fulfillment. Lyra and Will do demonstrate their love for each other; however, Pullman does not subscribe to traditional happy endings and the two must remain apart, for daemons can survive only in the world in which they were born. Lyra and Pan must return to an Oxford of an alternate universe of a medieval past, Will to the contemporary reader's Oxford.

Thus Pullman's *His Dark Materials* simultaneously undercuts and negates Barrie's *Peter Pan* by rejecting stunted development, but also embraces Barrie's tragic sense of life in which desires are not satiated. At the end of *The Amber Spyglass*, Lyra and Will agree that they will meet each Midsummer's Day at the Botanic Garden. Lyra states: "What I thought was that if you—maybe just once a year—if we could come here at the same time, just for an hour or something, then we could pretend we were close again, because we *would* be close, if you sat *here* and I sat just *here* in my world" (507–8). This is Pullman's version of Barrie's spring cleaning. But Lyra provides a caveat: "And if we—later on—if we meet someone that we like, and if we marry them, then we must be good to them, and not make comparisons all the time and wish we were married to each other instead. . . . But just keep up this coming here once a year, just for an hour, just to be together" (508). Compare Lyra's plea to Barrie's description once Wendy and the Lost Boys return to London: "There could not have been a lovelier sight; but there was none to see it except a strange boy who was staring in at the window. He had ecstasies innumerable that other children can never know; but he was looking through the window at the one joy from which he must be for ever barred" (225). When Peter discovers that Wendy has grown up—and that she has become a literal mother with a child—he is repulsed: "He gave a cry of pain; and when the tall beautiful creature stooped to lift him in her arms he drew back sharply" (240). Will wants to embrace Lyra, but he must bar himself from her and close every window that has been opened by the subtle knife, thus shutting the portal that could bring him—like Peter Pan—to Lyra's world. By closing the window to Lyra's Oxford and by breaking the subtle knife, Will chooses not to be like Peter Pan but, consequently, creates for himself a tragic world of loss similar to Peter's. His Dark Materials and *Peter Pan* reflect Gilead's "return as tragic ambiguity" (82) because these returns remain "indeterminate" (95).

Such indeterminacy, finally, is seen in the act of storytelling itself that perpetuates into infinity. In Neverland, Wendy regales Peter and the Lost Boys with stories that sustain them like food. *Peter Pan* ends with the perpetual story: Wendy's adventures with Peter do end because she grows up, gets married, and has children—she enters the experienced world. But Wendy's child will continue the story, as will Wendy's child's child. The story goes on forever, as does Peter. Pullman's narrative world ends with Lyra and Will separating, Will returning to his mother with the scientist Mary Malone, and Lyra to her orphaned existence once again, hoping to build, as she says, "The Republic of Heaven" (*Amber Spyglass* 518). Though Lyra and Will have lost much in their adventures, including their parents, there is hope at the end for a better life. Pullman's closure, it appears, is more conventional than Barrie's: the story ends with Will and Lyra returning home. There can be no further adventures between the two. However, Pullman opens up the narrative world once again in *Lyra's Oxford*, a small, fifty-some page follow-up to His Dark Materials. In this way, Lyra becomes like Peter Pan, returning to the reader once again. Pullman writes at the beginning of *Lyra's Oxford* that "*this book contains a story and several other things. The other things might be connected with the story, or they might not; they might be connected to stories that haven't appeared yet. It's not easy to tell.*" At the end of his preface to the book, Pullman tells the reader that "*there are many things we haven't yet learned how to read*" (n.p.). The story subsequently continues, and closure is ultimately denied. Lyra's story, we understand, has not yet finished, and Lyra is still a child, her Pan still able to transform shapes. Lyra is yet the perpetual child, like Peter Pan.[8]

NOTES

1. Fox is not the first to tackle Barrie. Penelope Farmer's *The Summer Birds* (1962; revised 1985) explores *Peter Pan* from a feminist perspective, and Jane Yolen, in "Lost Girls" (from the collection of stories *Sister's Emily's Lightship*),

has the young women in Neverland discovering that Mrs. and Captain Hook's pirate ship is a more democratic space than Peter's homestead. And litigation has entered Neverland: Canadian author Emily Somma has published in Canada *After the Rain: A New Adventure for Peter Pan*, in which Peter leaves Neverland and finally grows up. The Great Ormond Street Children's Hospital has warned Somma to cease publication, arguing that the character Peter Pan is copyrighted. Somma has filed a counter suit. It is no coincidence, then, that Ormond has contacted prominent British children's writers—Philip Pullman and J. K. Rowling included—to write a sequel to the Pan story, thus insuring that the hospital receives additional royalties from Barrie's writing. The hospital has also contacted Walt Disney about Dave Barry and Ridley Pearson's *Peter and the Starcatchers* (2004), a comic prequel to *Peter Pan*.

2. I use Bloom's theory recognizing a great irony: he is vehemently dismissive of Rowling's work: "Can more than 35 million book buyers, and their offspring, be wrong? Yes, they have been, and will continue to be so for as long as they persevere with Potter," writes Bloom in *The Wall Street Journal*.

3. See Wood and Gooderham for detailed analyses of Lewis's influence on Pullman.

4. Blake's *The Book of Thel* may be seen as a template for this tension between innocence and experience. Thel, who is identified as a "virgin," desires to leave the Valley of Har to experience the wide world, which is a world of desire. After recognizing that fulfillment of desire—i.e., sexuality—will necessitate that she will eventually die, Thel rejects this temptation and "The Virgin started from her seat, & with a shriek / Fled back unhindered till she came into the vales of Har." Thel is not saved by innocence, however, for Blake suggests that she is incomplete, unfulfilled because she rejects experience. This rejection of experienced desire—or the embracing of naïve innocence—is also at the heart of much children's literature, *Peter Pan* in particular. Both Rose and James Kincaid enter into the complex discussion concerning *Peter Pan* and sexuality.

5. A great irony is that both Rowling and Pullman are not big fans of fantasy literature. Rowling admits her admiration for Tolkien, but when asked why she focused on magic in her novels, she responded as follows: "It chose me. I never really sat down & thought 'What shall I focus on?' and in fact, I don't really read fantasy—it's not my favorite genre" (Interview, *AOL Live*). Pullman insists that His Dark Materials is more realistic than fantastic: "I'm not writing about elves and goblins and so on. I couldn't care a fig for any of those things. Human beings are my subject matter. And although this story has Fantasy elements, I think at the core of it is something which is as realistic as I could possibly make it, which is the story about growing up" (qtd. in Kim Campbell).

6. There has been speculation by critics and fans alike that Rowling may kill off Harry at the end of the series. In a BBC Interview, Rowling fuels that conjecture by asking the interviewer, "How do you know he'll still be alive [at the end of book 7]?" Recently, Rowling has hinted that Harry will survive at the end

of book 7, but she is contemplating an eighth book to the series, which may not be so kind to Harry. Rowling admits that when Sirius Black was killed in *The Order of the Phoenix*, she had second thoughts but concluded that when "you are writing children's books, you need to be a ruthless killer." Peter Pan can also be considered a ruthless killer, who thinks that "to die will be an awfully big adventure" (132), and who has little regard for the lives of his Lost Boys, for "Peter had seen many tragedies, but he had forgotten them all" (119).

7. Rowling has been attacked by the religious right for her use of magic and images of witchcraft in the Harry Potter books. Interestingly, Pullman has avoided to a large degree such wrath, even though he clearly has an antipathy toward organized religion and many of the tenets of Christianity. Tom Stoppard has finished the screenplay for *Northern Lights* (*The Golden Compass*), and it can be expected that when Pullman's book comes out on film that a wider audience in America may lead to more discussion about Pullman's religious views.

8. I would like to thank Karlyn Crowley, Assistant Professor of English at St. Norbert College, for her judicious comments on the drafts of this essay.

WORKS CITED

Allen, Brooke. "A World of Wizards." *The New Leader* 1–15 Nov. 1999: 13–14.

"At Least They're Reading." *The Leaky Cauldron.* Feb. 2003. 9 July 2004 <http://the-leaky-cauldron.org/MTarchives/002563.html>.

Attebery, Brian. *Strategies of Fantasy*. Bloomington: Indiana UP, 1992.

Barrie, J. M. *Peter Pan*. Intro. Naomi Lewis. New York: Puffin, 1994.

———. *Peter Pan in Kensington Gardens and Peter and Wendy*. Ed. Peter Hollindale. Oxford: Oxford UP, 1999.

Barry, Dave, and Ridley Pearson. *Peter and the Starcatchers*. New York: Hyperion, 2004.

Billone, Amy. "The Boy Who Lived: From Carroll's Alice and Barrie's Peter Pan to Rowling's Harry Potter." *Children's Literature* 32 (2004): 178–201.

Blake, William. *The Book of Thel. William Blake: A Critical Edition of the Major Works*. Ed. Michael Mason. Oxford: Oxford UP, 1992. 175–79.

———. *The Marriage of Heaven and Hell. William Blake: A Critical Edition of the Major Works*. Ed. Michael Mason. Oxford UP, 1992. 8–20.

Bloom, Harold. *The Anxiety of Influence: A Theory of Poetry*. London: Oxford UP, 1973.

———. "Can 35 Million Book Buyers be Wrong? Yes." *The Wall Street Journal* 11 July 2000: n.p.

Campbell, Joseph. *The Hero with a Thousand Faces*. Princeton: Princeton UP, 1972.

Campbell, Kim. "Looking Through *His Dark Materials* for Light." *Christian Science Monitor* 15 Feb. 2001: 16.

Carpenter, Humphrey. *Secret Gardens: The Golden Age of Children's Literature.* Boston: Houghton Mifflin, 1985.

Chabon, Michael. "Dust & Daemons." *The New York Review of Books* 25 Mar. 2004. 21 June 2004 <http://www.nybooks.com/articles/17000>.

De Bertodano, Helena. "I am of the Devil's party . . ." *The Sunday Telegraph* 27 Jan. 2002. 19 Feb. 2002 <http://proquest.umi.com/pdqweb?TS=/// 1&Did=000000102586583&Mtd=17&Fmt=3>.

Echoes of the Lost Boys of Sudan. Ed. Susan Clark. Irving, TX: Echoes Joint Venture, 2004.

Ezard, John. "Hospital Challenges Writers to Make Peter Pan Fly Again." *The Guardian* 20 Aug. 2004: 1–4. 20 Aug. 2004 <http://www.guardian.co.uk/ uk_news/story/0,3604,1287109,00.html>.

Farmer, Penelope. *The Summer Birds.* New York: Yearling, 1987.

Finding Neverland. Dir. Marc Forster. Perf. Johnny Depp and Kate Winslet. Miramax, 2004.

Fox, Laurie. *The Lost Girls.* New York: Simon and Schuster, 2004.

Freud, Sigmund. *The Freud Reader.* Ed. Peter Gay. New York: Norton, 1989.

Gilead, Sarah. "Magic Abjured: Closure in Children's Fantasy Fiction." *Literature for Children: Contemporary Criticism.* Ed. Peter Hunt. London: Routledge, 1992. 80–109.

Gooderham, David. "Fantasizing It As It Is: Religious Language in Philip Pullman's Trilogy, *His Dark Materials.*" *Children's Literature* 31 (2003): 155–75.

Harnetiaux, Trish. *Straight on 'Til Morning.* Dir. Jude Domski. Perf. David L. Carson and Michael Colby Jones. 78th Street Theatre Lab, New York. 10 Sept. 2004.

Hook. Dir. Steven Spielberg. Perf. Dustin Hoffman and Robin Williams. Columbia/Tristar, 1991.

Kiley, Dan. *The Peter Pan Syndrome: Men Who Have Never Grown Up.* New York: Avon, 1984.

Kincaid, James. *Child-Loving: The Erotic Child and Victorian Culture.* New York: Routledge, 1992.

Knee, Allen. *The Man Who Was Peter Pan.* Dir. Bennett Windheim. The 42nd Street Workshop, New York. 28 Mar. 1998.

Knoepflmacher, U. C. "The Balancing of Child and Adult: An Approach to Victorian Fantasies for Children." *Nineteenth-Century Fiction* 37 (Mar. 1983): 497–530.

―――. *Ventures into Childland: Victorians, Fairy Tales, and Femininity.* Chicago: U of Chicago P, 1998.

The Lost Boys. Dir. Joel Schumacher. Perf. Jason Patric and Corey Haim. Warner, 1987.

Lost Boys of Sudan. Dir. Jon Shenk and Megan Mylan. New Video Group, 2004.

Lurie, Alison. *Don't Tell the Grown-ups: Subversive Children's Literature.* Boston: Little, Brown, 1990.

Maguire, Gregory. *Wicked: The Life and Times of the Wicked Witch of the West.* New York: Regan, 1996.

Nodelman, Perry. *The Pleasures of Children's Literature.* New York: Longman, 1992.

Parsons, Wendy, and Catriona Nicholson. "Talking to Philip Pullman: An Interview." *The Lion and the Unicorn* 23.1 (1999): 116–34.

Peter Pan. Dir. Clyde Geronimi and Wilfred Jackson. Perf. Bobby Driscoll and Kathryn Beaumont. Walt Disney, 1953.

Peter Pan. Dir. P. J. Hogan. Perf. Jason Isaacs and Jeremy Sumpter. Universal, 2003.

Propp, Vladimir. *Morphology of the Folktale.* Ed. Louis Wagner and Alan Dundes. Trans. Laurence Scott. 2nd ed. Austin: U of Texas P, 1968.

Pullman, Philip. *The Amber Spyglass.* New York: Knopf, 2000.

———. *The Golden Compass.* New York: Knopf, 1995.

———. *Lyra's Oxford.* New York: Knopf, 2003.

———. *The Subtle Knife.* New York: Knopf, 1997.

Return to Neverland. Dir. Donovan Cook and Robin Budd II. Perf. Harriet Owen and Blayne Weaver. Walt Disney, 2002.

Rose, Jacqueline. *The Case of Peter Pan; Or, the Impossibility of Children's Fiction.* London: MacMillan, 1984.

Rowling, J. K. *Harry Potter and the Chamber of Secrets.* New York: Scholastic, 1999.

———. *Harry Potter and the Goblet of Fire.* New York: Scholastic, 2000.

———. *Harry Potter and the Order of the Phoenix.* New York: Scholastic, 2003.

———. *Harry Potter and the Prisoner of Azkaban.* New York: Scholastic, 1999.

———. *Harry Potter and the Sorcerer's Stone.* New York: Scholastic, 1997.

———. Interview. *AOL Live.* 2000. 6 April 2001 <http://www.aol.co.uk/aollive/transcripts/jkrowling.html>.

———. Interview. *BBC News.* 19 June 2003. 9 July 2004 <http://news.bbc.co.uk/1/hi/ertertainment/arts/3004456.stm>.

Ryman, Geoff. *Was.* New York: Penguin, 1992.

Somma, Emily. *After the Rain: A New Adventure for Peter Pan.* Ontario: Daisy, 2004.

Stephens, John, and Robyn McCallum. *Retelling Stories, Framing Culture: Traditional Story and Metanarratives in Children's Literature.* New York: Garland, 1998.

Wood, Naomi. "Paradise Lost and Found: Obedience, Disobedience, and Storytelling in C. S. Lewis and Philip Pullman." *Children's Literature in Education* 32.4 (Dec. 2001): 237–59.

Wullschläger, Jackie. *Inventing Wonderland: Victorian Childhood as Seen Through the Lives and Fantasies of Lewis Carroll, Edward Lear, J.M. Barrie, Kenneth Grahame, and A.A. Milne.* New York: The Free Press, 1995.

Yeoman, Ann. *Now or Neverland: Peter Pan and the Myth of Eternal Youth: A Psychological Perspective on a Cultural Icon.* Toronto: Inner City, 1999.

Yolen, Jane. "Lost Girls." *Sister Emily's Lightship and Other Stories.* New York: Tor, 2000.

Zipes, Jack. *Sticks and Stones: The Troublesome Success of Children's Literature from Slovenly Peter to Harry Potter.* New York: Routledge, 2001.

13

The Blot of Peter Pan

David Rudd

"The Blot on Peter Pan" (1926) is an apocryphal account, related to a group of fictional children, of how Peter Pan came to be such a popular character. It was, J. M. Barrie tells us, thanks to a boy named Neil, to whom Barrie, the narrator, was godfather. In fact, Barrie tells us early on about Neil's christening, which he attended along with "the usual rabble of fairy godmothers, who took up their places in a circle on the rim of the font" and "gave their gifts, qualities such as Beauty," for example ("Blot" 84–85). By age four Neil had learned the art of playwriting from Barrie, whom he liked to imitate. Although Neil had problems with writing, the boy still managed to compose a play, using a new, coded language that depended on letters being sounded out—thus "MACC" = "Emma sees" (92)—and on pictorial representation. As a "curtain-raiser" to *Peter Pan*, Neil's play was incredibly successful, the audience being particularly impressed at Neil's own, strutting cleverness. As a result, Barrie rewrote *Peter Pan*, replacing the character's original "humility" with Neil's "cockiness"—this quality being "the blot on Peter Pan" (100). At the end of the story it is made clear that Barrie must have been the "bad fairy" godfather at Neil's christening. Barrie tells his child audience at this point that "if you were entirely good there would be no story in you; and the fairies are so fond of stories that they call giving you one bad quality 'Putting in the story'" (86). In other words, it is Barrie who gives Neil this quality in the first place, in order for the story to work as a story.

Barrie's tale thus conveys several things. First, there is the problem of establishing origins, which always tend to recede, explanations simply opening up earlier versions which themselves need explaining. Second, what we adduce as explanations of our behavior are usually post hoc rationalizations. This, as we shall see, is also one of Jacques Lacan's key points. For example, he argues that we only realize our lack of wholeness once we have language, but language does not merely name this earlier lack: it is language that creates it. Third, the statement, "if you were entirely good there would be no story in you," suggests that a "bad quality," or flaw, is essential to being storied. This brings to mind Lacan's comment about development proceeding "in a fictional direction" (*Écrits* 2), which, for Lacan, begins with the formation of the ego, itself a false mirror of the self that is conferred by others (as, for example, an appreciative audience at a play). It also seems significant that this quality is given to Neil at his christening, when Neil is officially named. That is, he is required to take up a place in the order of language (the Symbolic), represented by particular signifiers. From then on Neil is obsessed with letters–even going to bed with a "dictionary to hug" ("Blot" 91). However, to come to my fourth and last point, it is also made clear in Barrie's story that signification is both arbitrary—in that meaning may be presented by letters, by sounds, or pictorially—and is anything but a straightforward, transparent vehicle; rather, it often presents a barrier.

I am aware that some of these comments, especially those referring to Lacan, might also present barriers, but they should become clearer later. The point I want to establish here is that this short story of Barrie's could stand as a metonym for the entire *Peter Pan* oeuvre: it is forever confounded by the slippage of language, by the impossibility of establishing origins—which is why Jacqueline Rose found it so intriguing. Building on this, I want to argue that *Peter Pan* is less a case study of the impossibility of children's fiction—"a classic in which the problem of the relationship between adult and child is unmistakably at the heart of the matter" (Rose 5)—than a more general demonstration of the impossibility of coherent subjectivity, indeed, of a coherent reality, uncontaminated by fantasy. In exploring this thesis, like Rose, I shall be drawing on the work of Lacan, so a brief explication of some of his terms is necessary. In the process, not only will Lacan be used as a lens through which to view *Peter Pan*, but *Peter Pan* will also help us elucidate Lacanian psychoanalysis. So rather than have an undigestible slab of psychoanalytic theory, I shall prefer to layer it between slices of

Barrie's text, which should, hopefully, make for a more palatable concoction.

A central notion of Lacan's is that we don't exist simply in "reality." The subject is actually positioned in relation to three orders: the Imaginary, the Symbolic, and the Real. Very briefly, the Imaginary is concerned with notions of wholeness, of presence; it is forever seeking to identify with what look like comforting entities (the mother, a lover, a group, a philosophy, a religion). The Symbolic, in contrast, continually chops this wholeness up into differential signifiers. These signify not presence, but absence; that is, they represent the lack of the things themselves. For Lacan, we all have to move away from the Imaginary (which confers a false sense of wholeness) to take up our place in the Symbolic, where a signifier (our name) marks our place. It is this move that gives birth to the subject as such; but in coming into existence as a signifier, we simultaneously cease to exist as an object, a self. That is, in order to experience our being, we have to stand outside ourselves (in a system of words that pre-exists us), whence we lose that very being. We are now subject to a lack, a "want of being" (*manque à etre*). Moreover, for Lacan, lack is precisely what constitutes desire. We are, therefore, always trying to repair our sense of incompleteness. And yet, as a speaking being, this is impossible: the Symbolic can only perpetuate desire, never complete it. Because we are split in this way, between "being" and subject-hood, Lacan uses the symbol $, where S stands for the subject who is split, or "barred" from wholeness. The third order, the Real, occupied Lacan in his last years. This is what always stands outside symbolization. It is the excessive, messy stuff of the universe, which is liable to shock or excite us at any moment.

Existence is thus tenuous: at any moment the real might intrude, destroying our orderly existence—although, for Lacan, this can be a helpful jolt, for orderly existence itself rests on a lie, the flawed, incomplete world of signification. This is where fantasy helps, by concealing from us the symbolic world's inability to cover over the cracks in existence. Fantasy, then, is not mere escapism; rather, it is what gives direction to our existence as desiring beings. However, Lacan also makes the point that if we come too close to fulfilling our desires, we are in danger of an eruption of the real, that is, seeing the flaws, the inconsistencies.

In both the play and the novel of *Peter Pan*, we see that fantasy helps stitch together the tenuous middle-class lives of the Darlings. There is the nursemaid dog, Nana, for instance. There is also the scene in which the children re-enact their births, again hinting at an existence exceeded by the Symbolic, especially when the older son, John, acting as father, tells his younger brother, Michael, "brutally that they didn't want any more" children (*Peter and Wendy* 80). The Symbolic is also dependent for its continued existence on the Name-of-the-Father, the one who, in Lacanian terms, is seen to possess the phallus. But Mr. Darling, with his childish behavior in refusing to take the children's medicine, is found wanting. "Father's a cowardy custard," exclaims Michael; "O father!", adds Wendy (84), and Mr. Darling ends up "frightfully ashamed of himself" (85), later putting himself in the doghouse as a punishment. As a final example, we might note the presence of the night-lights as "the eyes a mother leaves behind her to guard her children" (86). On one level, this is a comforting image, but it also carries uncanny connotations of fragmentation and hints at what Lacan termed "the gaze," which is threatening because, again, it is made plain that the security of our existence depends on a point outside ourselves; that is, we are made consistent by the look of the Other, but this is a position that we ourselves can never inhabit; we can never see ourselves as others see us.

However significant the mother's look, Peter Pan turns out to be a more powerful presence. In line with the contradictory nature of fantasy outlined above, Peter Pan can be seen as a necessary screen that keeps the Symbolic (i.e., reality) intact. This is an example of a general principle of Lacan's Hegelian thinking; namely, that there is always an exception to the rule, which thereby proves that rule (Šišek, *Enjoy* 83–86); or as has already been noted, the truth of something always lies elsewhere, beyond the thing itself. So to sustain the claim that "all children grow up," there has to be one who does not: this being the mythical, eternal child. As Rose has noted, this construct is an adult creation, the child being seen to encapsulate an area of purity and innocence that, like the fetish, disavows the fact that children also must exist in the world of the Symbolic; that is, they too are split subjects, for whom sex and death are realities. They cannot be separated out in the Imaginary.

Rose reads *Peter Pan*—the iconic story—as a fetish for children's fiction in general, in that this literary creation stands as an exemplar of what all children's literature is about (innocence, the eternal child), while simultaneously deconstructing that notion. In more Lacanian terms, this sort of fantasy object gives consistency to our Symbolic world. Peter Pan is what Slavoj Šišek calls "the sublime object of ideology," seen to experience the "fullness of enjoyment" that is denied the rest of us (qtd. in Wright 167). However, coming too close to this fantasized object can be dangerous. For Peter Pan can also be said to feature as what is called an "anamorphosis," a term used (mostly of pictures) to indicate that different perspectives are contained within the same frame (in Lacanian terms, this is another example of an exception proving the rule). Lacan uses the famous example of Hans Holbein's *The Ambassadors*, where a blot, or stain, appears to float across the picture. However, viewed from the right angle, this blot resolves itself into a skull, which makes us read this picture of the important ambassadors, with their wealth and possessions, in a very different light, for they too are subject to death. In other words, the whole symbolic field is suddenly rendered differently. The skull provides an excess of signification that "quilts" or pins down reality in a particular way (Šišek, *Looking* 91).

Lacan argues that we all see in this distorted way, for that is what it means to be a subject—namely, to have our vision distorted by desire, by our *manque à etre*, our lack. To recap: in the Symbolic we are sundered from ourselves; consequently we continually try to plug this hole, to regain the wholeness we imagine we once had. And this gap in our wholeness, we are certain, was caused by the loss of a particular object, which Lacan terms the "*object a.*" It is seen as incapable of being symbolized, but can loosely be conceived as a part of the mother from the time when we felt united with her. Our striving to regain the *object a* is what keeps us moving on; it is the kernel around which we weave our fantasies. Thus it acts as both a remainder and a reminder of the mother—a rema(i)nder, in fact.

Peter Pan, then, is the blot, the stain in the Darling household. He is a mere shadow at first, but when viewed from the right angle (i.e., distorted by the children's desires), he becomes more distinct—and, as we shall see, bears some similarities to Holbein's skull. His manifestation is a result of our coming too close to our desires:

> [Mrs. Darling] dreamt that the Neverland had come too near and that a strange boy had broken through from it. . . . [I]n her dream he had rent the film that obscures the Neverland, and she saw Wendy and John and Michael peeping through the gap. (77)

The children are precipitated into the real of their desire, which is a more intimidating place than they had expected: "Thus sharply did the terrified three learn the difference between an island of make-believe and the same island come true" (110).

In a superficial way, Peter Pan seems to celebrate a selfish narcissism, characteristic of Lacan's Imaginary—"How clever I am," he crowed rapturously, "oh, the cleverness of me!" (91)—and it is of note that many abridgments of the story indulge this aspect. However, in doing so, they neglect the uncanny side of narcissism, which Freud explored: its auto-eroticism, animism, and misplaced omnipotence—in short, its fixated nature (most apparent in the original Narcissus) and its association with death. Peter Pan is similarly an uncanny figure; resisting the imposition of the Symbolic, he is trapped outside his mother's window, finding himself "barred" (167)—using that same Lacanian term. In *Peter Pan in Kensington Gardens*, this is more explicit: "there is no second chance, not for most of us. When we reach the window it is Lock-out Time. The iron bars are up for life" (40).

But to explore this further, another slice of Lacan is necessary. Lacan divides the shift into the Symbolic—the Oedipal stage—into two moves. First there is "alienation," when the child realizes that the mother is also a divided being, experiencing desire; the child tries, therefore, to fill out this lack by being everything that she desires. He/she tries to be what Lacan terms the maternal phallus. The word "phallus," of course, has been problematic from the beginning, so it is worth spending a few sentences clarifying what it is and isn't. It certainly isn't the penis, for the phallus is not a physical thing; rather, it stands for an absence, for something that both males and females lack. Hence it is better seen as that which signifies what everyone wants, which in our society, usually means power and authority. In other words, it marks our desire. In that we are all creatures who experience lack, no one actually has the phallus (it is closely associated with the *object a*, but whereas the former cannot be symbolized, the latter—being in the Symbolic—can). Peter Pan, of course, is made out to be particularly phallic:

> The name Peter Pan stood out . . . [Mrs. Darling] felt that it had an oddly cocky appearance.
> "Yes, he is rather cocky," Wendy admitted (75)

This is the blotted quality that Peter Pan acquired from Neil, of course, according to Barrie's later fictional account—the quality that gives Peter Pan his story-like quality, making him "the kind of boy the public wants" ("Blot" 99). And Peter Pan has this in excess: "To put it with brutal frankness, there never was a cockier boy" (*Peter and Wendy* 91).

Like the anamorphic spot, the phallus is that which "sticks out" (Šišek, *Looking* 91), around which we weave our fantasies, as noted earlier. However, returning to Lacan's model, the child soon realizes that it cannot be everything to the mother (the maternal phallus); her desire lies elsewhere—with the father, in fact. This brings about the second moment of the Oedipal, termed "separation," during which the father's interdiction is pronounced. In French, the Name-of-the-Father is *Nom-du-père*, allowing Lacan to make the pun *Non-du-père* to stress its prohibitory function: the father says "No" to this would-be incestuous link with the mother. In successfully resolving the Oedipal, the subject can then move from "being" the phallus to "having" it (i.e., he/she is promised power, recognition, a place in the symbolic order—although, beyond this, no one actually possesses the phallus, as noted above).

Peter Pan, I would suggest, does not complete this second move. Instead, he persists in trying to be all for the mother: the maternal phallus (the word "pan," of course, is Greek for "everything"). It is for this reason that the images of castration abound, forever threatening Peter Pan—as, for instance, at the beginning, when Nana seeks to ensnare him: "slam went the window and snapped it off" (*Peter and Wendy* 78). Fortunately it is only Peter's shadow that Nana has secured, but the Oedipal threat is clearly there.

It is because Peter tries to be the phallus for the mother that he always disappoints the females around him. When Wendy asks him, "[W]hat are your exact feelings for me?" he replies, "Those of a devoted son" (162). Peter Pan's perplexity at the attitude of Wendy and the other females is very close to the Lacanian question, "*Che Vuoi?* . . . [W]hat do you want from me?" (Šišek, *Looking* 91). But Peter doesn't really understand because he persists in trying to *be* the phallus, the *object a*—the utterly desirable lost object that makes him irresistible to all females. *Peter Pan in Kensington Gardens* explicitly says of Peter that "[i]n returning to his mother he never doubted that he was giving her the greatest treat a woman can have" (37). His identification with the *object a* is also made explicit when Pan is described as "very like Mrs. Darling's kiss" (77), the one at the corner of her mouth that neither Mr. Darling nor Wendy could ever obtain. Lacan describes this unsymbolizable "remainder" of the mother as being associated with edges, the boundary between inner and outer, and he explicitly mentions "lips" (Lacan, *Écrits* 314). So Peter, of course, easily "took Mrs. Darling's kiss with him. The kiss that had been for no one else Peter took quite easily. Funny. But she seemed satisfied" (218).

As Rose has noted, Peter Pan functions as an irresistible image of childhood for many people. He is innocent and seemingly entire unto himself—a mythical eternal being. However, he also has affinities with the primal father of Freud's *Totem and Taboo*, another exception who thereby allows the universal rule to function. This is the one man who has not been subject to castration, the one for whom all women are available, and who experiences uninhibited *jouissance* (Lacan's term for ecstatic, blissful enjoyment).[1] As such, in Freud's myth, this primal father (the "Great White Father," as Peter Pan styles himself), is the one man whom all the others want to kill (Hook, of course, comes to mind). In rejecting the paternal "No," this figure "is not subject to the law: *he is his own law*," as Bruce Fink puts it (*Lacanian Subject* 110). It should be emphasized, however, that such a figure is a necessary fantasy, who sustains our reality: as we are all limited by the Law, we therefore conceive of one figure who stands beyond it, exemplifying it. In Lacanian terms, such a figure is said to "ex-sist" rather than "exist." As Fink expresses it, "We obviously have a name for him, and thus in a sense he exists within our symbolic order; on the other hand, his very definition implies a rejection of that order, and thus by definition he ex-sists" (*Lacanian Subject* 110). The term "ex-sist" comes from Heidegger, for whom it is linked to "ekstasis," or ecstasy, meaning to be outside, or beside oneself—a position, as we know, that is precisely Peter Pan's: "He had ecstasies innumerable that other children can never know; but he was looking through the window at the one joy from which he must be for ever barred" (*Peter and Wendy* 214). Following this line of thought, Peter Pan might be said to exhibit the clinical structure of a psychotic:

> In a sort of way [Peter Pan] understands what [Wendy] means by "Yes, I know," but in most sorts of ways he doesn't. It has something to do with the riddle of his being. If he could get the hang of the thing his cry might become "To live would be an awfully big adventure!" but he can never quite get the hang of it, and so no one is as gay as he. (*Peter Pan* 153–54)

A psychotic, in Lacan's scheme, is someone who is trapped in the imaginary order, not recognizing the Symbolic. He has not accepted what Lacan calls the *vel* or forced choice, which runs along the lines of "Your money or your life" (Lacan, *Four* 211); that is, the symbolic order can be refused, but the result is to live in a hallucinatory, imaginary state. There is certainly mileage in seeing Peter Pan in these terms, though technically, following the classification of Fink, he seems to be closer to perversion, a position in which the symbolic order is recognized, but disavowed.[2] Rose describes the child sexuality that Pan exhibits as "bisexual, polymorphous, perverse," which is certainly apposite (4). Not only does he have "ecstasies innumerable" but he is also not delimited by a masculine structure—which would only come into play after becoming subject to the Law of the phallus.

It is therefore quite appropriate that he has traditionally been played by a female in the stage play. Marjorie Garber considers this issue extensively: "Why is Peter Pan played by a woman?", answering, "Because a woman will never grow up to be a man" (Garber 168). This is not quite correct, though, for Peter Pan will grow up to be neither (nor a transvestite, as she later argues); he simply will not grow up. The main point is that Peter Pan does not *have* the phallus; rather, he tries to *be* it. He is better depicted as "a Betwixt and Between," therefore, as the character Solomon Caws calls him in *The Little White Bird* (qtd. in Garber 174). He hovers between the Imaginary and the Symbolic, polymorphously perverse. Lacan liked to pun on perversion as being "père-version," and Peter Pan, in the absence of the Symbolic, certainly tries to enact his own law as the "Great White Father" (*Peter and Wendy* 157), requesting that he be addressed as "sir" and "captain." Even the sun rises for Pan's return: "the sun (another of his servants) . . . has been bestirring himself" (*Peter Pan* 105). Again, similarities with the primal father in Freud's *Totem and Taboo* come to mind.

From his own perspective, Peter Pan lacks nothing. He has no desires at all (desire being part of the Symbolic). Instead, Peter is fixated in the imaginary state of "demand," which as Richard Boothby says, has an "unconditional insistence that the Other satisfy needs—*now!*" (9). Demand expresses a move toward independence, away from the mother, but without full recognition of the consequences involved. It frequently has an aggressive side to it, too. Samuel Weber quotes Freud's famous example of the child symbolizing the mother's absence with his "*Fort-Da*" game. Here the child threw away a reel, then pulled it back, making these differential sounds, "fort" and "da" (gone, here). Freud pointed out that the child was enjoying the ego mastery of (seemingly) manipulating the mother in this way (131–35). But though these sounds mark the beginnings of language, they are not yet in the realm of the signifier (where we are left with a sense of emptiness, or lack—hence desiring). At this stage, the child still sees a one-to-one correspondence between the sounds it makes and the mother. The child still thinks he/she can hold onto the mother by ma-nipulating these signifiers.

Freud describes the child's *Fort-Da* game in connection with the rep-etition compulsion that he was seeking to theorize, which, again, aptly describes Peter Pan's fixated behavior, made explicit in the final chap-ter of the novel, "When Wendy Grew Up." Here we see the same cycle being played out with Wendy's own child, Jane, and her grandchild, Margaret (and we might then recall that, at the beginning, Mrs. Darling also remembered a Peter Pan from her childhood [75]). In other words, Peter Pan is compelled to repeat his actions. Freud saw this repetition as an attempt to ward off the unacceptable, as with traumatized sol-diers reliving their shell shock—in short, to ward off death.

Peter Pan's relation to death is quite complex. In *Totem and Taboo*, Freud mentions communing with the dead as one of the main taboos,[3] which Peter Pan certainly engages in: "when children died he went part of the way with them" (*Peter and Wendy* 75). *Peter Pan in Kens-ington Gardens* states that he sees to any child who has died, that "he digs a grave . . . and erects a little tombstone"—but this is for children who have expressly come looking for him, and perished "of cold and dark before Peter Pan *comes* round" (64). In *Peter and Wendy*, Peter Pan actually kills others, including his own Lost Boys, whom, we are informed, he "thins . . . out" (112). It seems apt that Joel Schumacher's film, *The Lost Boys* (1987), plays on the notion of the Lost Boys being connected with vampirism, with the living dead. Michael Patrick Hearn, too, has noted the connection between Peter Pan and the realm of the dead, picking up on the reference to Yeats' poem, "The Stolen Child" in chapter 3 of the novel—"Come away, come away!"—in which a child is seduced from the living by the fairies. As Hearn comments,

> In Celtic mythology, fairyland is called the Isles of the Blest, the Fortunate Isles, the Land of the Young, the Plain of Happiness. It is also known as the Land of the Dead. It is the home of perpetual Spring, eternal youth. (19–20)

"[C]lad in skeleton leaves" (*Peter and Wendy* 77), Peter Pan certainly has connotations of death from the beginning. In fact, the whole realm of Neverland, we are told, "wanted blood" (112). We see the boys parading with their daggers, wearing skins from bears "slain by them-selves" (77). Among the pirates we find Cecco, "who cut his name in letters of blood" (114) on a prison governor's back, and Smee, who "stabbed . . . without offence" (114) and has a cutlass called "Johnny Corkscrew, because he wriggled it in the wound" (118). Hook himself, of course, is an accomplished killer, and we are given an idle demonstration of this, as another pirate is arbitrarily chosen: "the hook shoots forth, there is a tearing sound and one screech, then the body is kicked aside" (115). Then there are the "redskins," adorned with scalps, with their tomahawks and knives; and Tiger Lily herself, who "staves off the altar with a hatchet" (116). But it is Peter Pan who is the biggest killer and maimer, who is responsible for Hook losing his right hand.

I mention all these images of mutilation because Lacan sees them as typical of the sort of images that bombard the Imaginary if it does not accept the Symbolic: fantasies of "castration, mutilation, dismemberment, dislocation, evisceration, devouring, bursting open of the body," which attack the narcissistic ego (*Écrits* 11). The ego itself, in seeking to retain its wholeness, tries to ward off such threats to its integrity. It is not made explicit, but when we are told that Peter Pan "had one of his dreams . . . and cried in his sleep for a long time, and Wendy held him tight" (*Peter and Wendy* 205), we might speculate that it is because of this anxiety about the *corps morcele* or "fragmented body" (*Écrits* 11), an augur of death. The Symbolic itself, of course, is precisely a cut into the artificial wholeness of the Imaginary: "the signifier . . . materializes the agency of death" (Lacan, qtd. in Boothby 136), slicing up the world such that it "manifests itself first of all as the murder of the thing" (Lacan, *Écrits* 104). In other words, it involves a process of symbolic castration.

This is what Peter Pan fears most: the order of the Symbolic, which is what instantiates death. For in entering it, Peter will become temporalized; he will lose his being and experience lack. Wendy's story is of note here; it is, we are informed, "the story they [the Lost Boys] loved best, the story Peter hated" (*Peter and Wendy* 163). His hatred would seem to arise from the story's concern with the temporal process, with parents and children, growing-up, and returning home. It is the process that eventuates in Wendy's maturation, to Peter Pan's horror, and of having her own child (Jane) and then grandchild (Margaret). Females, with their reproductive capacity, are particularly associated with mortality in Barrie's work, as against males with their art (Geduld; Jack) and it seems no coincidence that the crocodile, which has swallowed a clock (thanks to Peter), is specifically gendered female ("We shall see for whom she is looking presently" [116]). Peter, of course, remains locked in a state of eternal youth—in his ecstasy, certainly, but only to ex-sist, out of time, as a fantasy figure, as the sublime object.

Overall, Peter Pan lacks the quilting of the Symbolic that the paternal metaphor, the phallus, provides, so he has trouble not only with memory and chronological time, but with the linguistic order in general; thus we are told that he "was the only boy on the island who could neither write nor spell; not the smallest word" (*Peter and Wendy* 137). Aside from this, there is his confusion over words like "sewn" and "kiss." More generally, he doesn't seem to know what reality is: "The difference between him and the other boys at such a time was that they knew it was make-believe, while to him make-believe and true were exactly the same thing" (128). In short, as the narrator states elsewhere, "Peter did not know in the least who or what he was" (203).

The biggest threat to Peter Pan is Captain James Hook, who is highly cultured, with his "good form." Not only literate, he went to Eton and received a classical education (indeed, in earlier versions of the play, he was a schoolmaster named Pilkington). This background, coupled with his overtly "castrated" appearance (as Peter Pan says in the play, "I cut off a bit of him" [108]), makes him an excellent representative of the Law of the father. He actualizes Peter's anxieties, to the extent of stealing his mother figure, Wendy. This move, of course, underlines the fact that her desire does lie elsewhere (indeed, she has told Peter as much). Peter Pan then engages in what is the closest thing to a traditional Oedipal struggle, fighting with the father figure, Hook, over the desired mother. It is enacted with Peter Pan seeming to replace the father. For instance, we are told how, after helping dispatch his phallic rival, "Captain Pan" wears a new suit fashioned "out of some of Hook's wickedest garments," and that "on the first night he wore this suit he sat long in the cabin with Hook's cigar-holder in his mouth and one hand clenched, all but the forefinger, which he bent and held threateningly aloft like a hook" (*Peter and Wendy* 207). Michael Egan, who also notes these similarities, seems wrong, however, to claim that Peter Pan, after dispatching Hook, takes his place. This is the very thing Peter Pan refuses to do (partnering with the mother), which is why the Oedipal process is incomplete (Peter Pan resolutely wants a kiss to remain a more domestic, maternal image: a thimble or button). Moreover, it should be remembered that in Freud's conception of the Oedipal complex, it is resolved precisely by the child accepting that the father has the superior phallus; the child then forgoes his desire for the mother and looks elsewhere. Peter Pan, though, really does cause the death of the father figure, rejecting the *Nom-du-père* so that he can remain outside the Symbolic. His position becomes plain when the children, including the Lost Boys, return to the Darling household, where Peter Pan resolutely rejects this order, with its school, office-work, and manhood: "Keep back, lady, no one is going to catch me and make me a man" (*Peter and Wendy* 217). In short, as Rose notes, "it is too easy to give an Oedipal reading of *Peter Pan*" (35).

One more thing about Hook's fate that warrants attention is the fact that, as mentioned above, the crocodile is gendered female. Like all the other females, including the mermaids and Never Bird, the crocodile too seems to find Peter Pan irresistible. It is therefore an intriguing co-incidence that Lacan happens to refer to the mother as "a big crocodile," whose mouth you can "find yourself in" (qtd. in Fink, *Lacanian Subject* 56). Lacan continues, "You never know what may set her off suddenly, making those jaws clamp down. That is the mother's desire." However, what saves the person from being devoured by the mother (i.e., locked in an Imaginary unity with her) is the father, with his phallus:

> There is a roller, made of stone, of course, which is potentially there at the level of the trap and which holds and jams it open. That is what we call the phallus. It is a roller which protects you, should the jaws suddenly close. (qtd. in Fink, *Lacanian Subject* 56–57)

As noted above, in Peter Pan's case, it is the castrating father who is de-voured, allowing Peter to continue ex-sisting in the Imaginary.

It is of note that Fink stresses how difficult it is to get those who ex-hibit the clinical structure of perversion to shift from being the *object a* (*Clinical Introduction* 176). As a fantasized being, this person will con-tinually seek to plug the desire of others—that is, to disavow others' sense of castration, of lack. They try to be that very thing which will provide wholeness. In broad cultural terms, this sublime object is fre-quently the figure of the child (see Rose), the figure that elides con-cerns about slippage, about insecurity, about sex and death. Barrie's work stages (in both senses of the term) this dilemma for us: the prob-lem of coming too close to our desires (our *object a*); of letting the fan-tasy that provides consistency to us as subjects take us over entirely, such that we also become fixated, stuck in a limbo. Clearly Peter Pan occupies this betwixt-and-between position. His very name suggests ambiguity, as R. D. S. Jack has also noted: on the one hand there is Pe-ter, in the apostolic tradition, the rock, a solid signified; but on the other there is Pan, a loose signifier of "everything," which is less easily moored (159). Whereas "Peter" might have a place in the Symbolic,

"Pan" remains outside, trapped between the Real (unsymbolizable) and the Imaginary (self-sufficient).[4] But there is a danger that the Darling children might also lose their subjective status (their desires, their sense of lack), as Peter Pan becomes "everything" for them. Indeed, the danger is that, as one of the undead, he will eventually drain them so that they too become victims of his "thinning out" (the phrase having interesting associations with blood).

Wendy is the one who saves them, who helps reactivate their desires. Lacan always argued that those with a feminine structure (not necessarily women) are not so tied to the Symbolic, so it makes sense that Wendy is the one able to stand apart from the "lost boys," to remind them of their place, their relationships to others (their parents, and so on). Wendy reminds the Lost Boys of what they lack, thus reinstating the dialectical movement of the signifier. They might exist as barred subjects, split between being and lacking, at the mercy of their desires and mortality; however, in the Lacanian universe, to *realize* that this is the way things are is as much of an insight as we can hope for, henceforth changing our relation to our situation. This is what Lacan calls "traversing the fantasy," and there is a sense in which Wendy has done precisely this. She can see that everyday reality is not all there is, that it is the fantasy elements which make reality work, which mop up the excess that the symbolic order cannot handle. Moreover, it is the fantasy elements that make reality bearable: Peter Pan's existence as the exceptional child who does not grow up (including his annual return, which the Christmas play itself endorses) is what makes sense of, or quilts, our existence as split beings. The message, then, is to hold on to these fantasy islands, but without trying to realize them in any final sense—as, for instance, by actually trying to stop children from growing up. A more functional fantasy, perhaps, is expressed in the comment that Peter Pan is seen "in the faces of many women who have no children," hinting that Peter Pan's fantasized presence makes their sense of lack more bearable (*Peter and Wendy* 77). "Neverland," perhaps, itself contains this pun, with its injunction, never to land.

As I said at the outset, I have argued that *Peter Pan* enacts the whole problematic of sustaining a coherent subjectivity. Rose is right to focus on the figure of the child, in that childhood, at least since the Romantics, conventionally figures a being who stands, impossibly, outside normal social relations (pure, unsullied, natural), free of concerns about sexuality, origins, death, and the inadequacies of language: a being that ex-sists. As a fetish object, a blot, Peter Pan does two impossible things at once: he represents a being who seemingly erases all these problematic areas, as "youth . . . joy . . . a little bird that has broken out of the egg" (203), while as a fantasy, he simultaneously shows that these things are fantastic, based on a lie, on a symbolic order that is porous. Peter Pan thus lends shape to and materializes our desires while simultaneously being the cocky, anamorphic spot that sticks out, who viewed from the right angle, takes on the contours of a skull. He might have "all his first teeth," but he is also "clad in skeleton leaves" (*Peter and Wendy* 77) and is linked with death. A Lacanian reading helps spell out the inveterate ambivalence of this Peter Pan figure and indicates why he can never be a safe, cozy character, unless altered drastically. In the end, then, the message is that we must learn to live with these necessary fictions, of which Peter Pan is a powerful example, but we must remember to align ourselves with Wendy rather than Peter, with the bard rather than the barred.

NOTES

1. Karen Coats has recently published a Lacanian reading of Peter Pan that concentrates on the different characters' relation to *jouissance*.

2. According to Fink, this is exactly the position between alienation and separation in the Oedipal struggle (*Clinical Introduction* 175).

3. The other main taboo mentioned by Freud is incest, which Peter Pan, in terms of being the maternal phallus, could also be accused of.

4. Indeed, it can be argued that Peter Pan is not effectively represented by any signifier: he is himself. Certainly, as Rose has detailed, Barrie had great difficulty pinning him down.

WORKS CITED

Barrie, J. M. "The Blot on Peter Pan." *The Treasure Ship: A Book of Prose and Verse*. Ed. Cynthia Asquith. London: S. W. Partridge, 1926. 82–100.

———. *Peter Pan and Other Plays*. Oxford: Oxford UP, 1995.

———. *Peter Pan in Kensington Gardens; Peter and Wendy*. Oxford: Oxford UP, 1991.

Boothby, Richard. *Death and Desire: Psychoanalytic Theory in Lacan's Return to Freud*. New York: Routledge, 1991.

Coats, Karen. *Looking Glasses and Neverlands: Lacan, Desire and Subjectivity in Children's Literature*. Iowa City: U of Iowa P, 2004.

Egan, Michael. "The Neverland of Id: Barrie, Peter Pan, and Freud." *Children's Literature* 10 (1982): 37–55.

Fink, Bruce. *A Clinical Introduction to Lacanian Psychoanalysis: Theory and Technique.* Cambridge: Harvard UP, 1997.

———. *The Lacanian Subject: Between Language and Jouissance.* Princeton: Princeton UP, 1995.

Freud, Sigmund. *Totem and Taboo: Some Points of Agreement between the Mental Lives of Savages and Neurotics.* London: Routledge & Kegan Paul, 1960.

Garber, Marjorie. *Vested Interests: Cross-Dressing and Cultural Anxiety.* London: Penguin, 1992.

Geduld, Harry M. *Sir James Barrie.* New York: Twayne, 1971.

Hearn, Michael Patrick. "Introduction to J. M. Barrie's *Peter and Wendy.*" *Peter Pan: The Complete Book.* Montreal: Tundra Books, 1988.

Jack, R. D. S. *The Road to the Never Land: A Reassessment of J.M. Barrie's Dramatic Art.* Aberdeen: Aberdeen UP, 1991.

Lacan, Jacques. *Écrits: A Selection.* Trans. Alan Sheridan. London: Tavistock, 1977.

———. *The Four Fundamental Concepts of Psychoanalysis.* Trans. Alan Sheridan. London: Penguin, 1979.

The Lost Boys. Dir. Joel Schumacher. Perf. Kiefer Sutherland, Jason Patric, Dianne Wiest. Warner Bros., 1987.

Rose, Jacqueline. *The Case of Peter Pan; Or, the Impossibility of Children's Fiction.* London: Macmillan, 1984.

Šišek, Slavoj. *Enjoy your Symptom: Jacques Lacan in Hollywood and Out.* New York: Routledge, 1992.

———. *Looking Awry: An Introduction to Jacques Lacan through Popular Culture.* Cambridge: MIT Press, 1992.

Weber, Samuel. *Return to Freud: Jacques Lacan's Dislocation of Psychoanalysis.* Trans. Michael Levine. Cambridge: Cambridge UP, 1991.

Wright, Elizabeth. *Psychoanalytic Criticism: A Reappraisal.* Oxford: Polity, 1998.

IV

WOMEN'S TIME

14

The Kiss: Female Sexuality and Power in J. M. Barrie's *Peter Pan*

M. Joy Morse

Like Thomas Hardy, whom he succeeded as President of the Society of Authors, J. M. Barrie received the Order of Merit in the field of Letters. While Hardy is often credited with fictionalizing the New Woman of the *fin de siècle* and with calling attention to the painfully narrow lives of late Victorian and early Edwardian women, similar sympathies found in Barrie's works have been largely overlooked. Barrie's concern with the "woman question" and his pro-feministic sympathies lay just beneath the surface of what is generally known of the author. Close examination reveals that Barrie not only took an interest in the work of suffrage dramatist Elizabeth Robbins, offering her an alternative ending to one of her plays (John 96), but that he also created unconventional heroines in his own dramas throughout his writing career. In his 1891 farce, *Ibsen's Ghost,* Barrie acknowledges a woman's longing to break from accepted Victorian morality when his heroine, Thea, expresses her desire to be kissed by not just one but several different men (Jack 72). Barrie's charming 1914 single-act play, *The Twelve-Pound Look,* features a heroine, Kate, who has found contentment through the purchase of a typewriter by which she freed herself from a privileged, but unhappy existence as the wife of a pompous and tyrannical husband. In his 1920 *A Kiss for Cinderella,* Barrie depicts Nellie Bodie, a doctor and suffragette whose accomplishments are openly admired by a leading male character. The unconventionality of these heroines, however, is easily overlooked within the farcical nature of the dramas, especially since, despite minor stage success during their first productions, they have largely been forgotten under the shadow of his most famous story, *Peter Pan.*

The sole adult female character of *Peter Pan,* Mrs. Darling, appears to be a woman in complete conformity with the female passivity and submission expected of her as a Victorian woman.[1] It is likely this seeming conventionality that has caused her, until recently, to be of little interest to critics beyond her possible role as the object of Peter Pan's Oedipal desires—believed to be an outgrowth of Barrie's own feelings toward his mother. While other critics, such as R. D. S. Jack in his exploration of Barrie's life and works, *The Road to the Never Land,* have taken a more marked interest in Mrs. Darling (177–79), she has rarely been viewed as outside of the conventions of nineteenth-century womanhood.

In the 1911 novel originally entitled *Peter and Wendy,* Barrie provides the key to understanding Mrs. Darling beyond her seeming conformity, a Mrs. Darling whose unconscious conflict with Victorian social expectations gives rise to her role as the creator of Neverland and Peter Pan, products of her own fantasy world. While based upon the then unpublished play, it is in the novel alone that we discover the mysterious but persistently recurring kiss upon the corner of Mrs. Darling's mouth, an element not included in the 1928 published edition of the drama.

The omission of the kiss from the published play does not reflect its insignificance, but rather the difficulty of its visual depiction. Following us from cradle to grave, from the first kiss of our mother to the last kiss on our deathbed, a kiss as an act is both multivalent and mutable. Both a performance of assertion (for the giver) and of submission (for the receiver), the act of kissing not only encompasses a spectrum of power-positions, but also of sexuality. It is the self-same mouth that passionately (or submissively) kissed the lover that later offers a chaste kiss to the child. It is this mouth, according to Jacques Lacan, that also takes on the powerful role of the mirror from which the speech of the child will eventually be formed. While the kiss ascribed to Mrs. Darling has its own physical dimensions—"her sweet mocking mouth had a kiss on it . . . perfectly conspicuous in the right hand corner" (7)—and Barrie could perhaps have created a fixed object that represented the kiss on the dramatic version of Mrs. Darling's person, it would have lost the mercurial nature that it shares with the act of kissing. He chose, instead, to omit the kiss from the play.

In the novel, however, Barrie repeatedly draws our attention to Mrs. Darling's kiss and its evasiveness and ambiguity. He reveals in its first description that although Mrs. Darling's family could at times see the kiss, they could not "get" it. Barrie's focus upon an image of such seeming simplicity as the kiss of a wife and mother underscores not only the complexity that lay beyond the surface of the image, but also that of the woman upon whom the kiss appears. Like Alice's looking glass, Mrs. Darling's kiss provides a window into a world beyond her consciousness.

To comprehend the full ramifications of the kiss and the unconscious reality it represents, we must first explore the author's relationship with his mother, the relationship of nineteenth-century British culture with motherhood itself, and, finally, Mrs. Darling's relationship with her own reality and the unconscious fantasy world she creates in Neverland.

The emotional withdrawal of Margaret Ogilvy Barrie and the author's resulting fixation upon her has been well documented (Geduld 27; Griffith 30; Holbrook 81). In his biography of his mother, *Margaret Ogilvy*, Barrie describes his attempts to make his mother smile after the devastating death of her favorite son, thirteen-year old David. Clowning for his mother, who lay in the dark with her face toward the wall, was a business of deadly earnestness for the seven-year-old Barrie. In her biography he confesses, "I have been told that my anxiety to brighten her gave my face a strained look and put a tremor in my jokes . . . " (232). Although there can be no overlooking the painful effects of Margaret's emotional absence upon Barrie, there is also room to focus upon the empathy toward her suffering that his constant attentions reveal. Barrie describes his most triumphant moments with Margaret in this way:

> Her face beamed and rippled with mirth as before, and her laugh, that I had tried so hard to force, came running home again. I have heard no such laugh as hers save from merry children; the laughter of most of us ages, and wears out with the body, but hers remained gleeful to the last, as if it were born afresh every morning. There was always something of the child in her, and her laugh was its voice, as eloquent of the past to me as was the christening robe to her. (235)

In his impulse to include, within the vignette, the christening robe to which his mother spoke as though to her lost son, Barrie displays not only his own profound loss of a mother, but an unselfish acknowledgment of *her* pain as well. Additionally, the scene evokes the dichotomies of pleasure and suffering as well as the power and guilt that characterized motherhood in the Victorian bourgeois culture in which Margaret Ogilvie Barrie was raised and became a mother.

The ambivalent position of women and mothers in the late nineteenth and early twentieth centuries can be traced far beyond Barrie's age to the views of early Church fathers. An alignment of women with the "seductress" Eve was reinforced by the writings of St. Paul and St. Augustine, who viewed women as sexually voracious and the source of evil thoughts and sin. By depicting woman, whose lack of chastity could threaten the very fabric of a patrilineal society, as insatiable and irresponsible, Western patriarchy provided itself with a justification for the near-complete control of women and their bodies that dominated British culture and law through most of the nineteenth century.[2]

Despite the limitations such perspectives placed upon the preindustrial woman, she was in many ways a trusted and vital member of the cooperative household, working alongside her husband and, in some instances, directly with customers. The modest position of power given middle-class women through their role in production was undermined, however, by the Industrial Revolution and the notion of "separate spheres." As production moved into the public realm, men followed and found themselves in the hostile and unforgiving world of capitalism. While working-class women accompanied men into the commercial sphere, many working in factories and as seamstresses, the world of the bourgeois wife became defined by the home and her role within it. Eighteenth-century proto-feminist and author Mary Astell voices not only the practical motivations of a post-industrial man to procure a wife–the management of his home and the raising of his family–but the emotional as well, describing his desired mate as follows:

> One whose Beauty, Wit, or good Humour and agreeable Conversation, will entertain him at Home when he has been contradicted and disappointed Abroad; who will do him that Justice the ill-natur'd World denies him; that is, in any one's Language but his own, sooth his Pride and Flatter his Vanity.(41)

For the middle classes, whose values reverberated along all lines of British society, the bifurcation of the spheres in which the genders operated had prompted a transformation of the qualities of femininity.

As with the perception of women as sexually voracious, the image of woman as the pure and selfless "tender of the hearth" that Astell describes was highly advantageous to male interests. The philosophical foundation that supported the image of woman as "angel" well through the Victorian era emerged first as an element of seventeenth-century Puritan ideology. Nancy Armstrong, in her exploration of power and domesticity, describes the Puritan effort to reconstruct the home as a self-enclosed, politically independent unit in which the state had no role. In their treatises, Puritans put forward a concept of domesticity in which the home consists of the complementary male and female pairs. While still defined in opposition to men, women were endowed with virtues reciprocal to their male counterparts. Where he was active and assertive, she was passive and receptive; both, however, were principled and spiritual beings, and the home was the center of their emotional world (18–19).

The concept of female domesticity was celebrated and brought to mainstream English society in the eighteenth century by conservative Anglo-Evangelicals, such as Hannah More and William Wilberforce (Poovey 9). While the image of the home as a nexus of spiritual support and renewal had become a dominant image in nineteenth-century British culture, in a majority of homes, the Puritanical and Evangelical prescribed duties of the domestic husband as the emotional and moral leader had fallen by the wayside. The role of domestic spiritual authority, perhaps too burdensome in addition to the task of sole breadwinner, had been transferred to the bourgeois wife. "Unspotted from the world" and the corrupting influences of the public sphere, women were believed to be more naturally responsive and therefore more receptive to the teachings of religion. As a result, the Victorian woman found herself perceived as man's moral superior and awarded the role of spiritual leader of the family.

Women may have welcomed their status in the home, but it did not come without anxiety. The perceptive middle-class wife and mother could not help but intuit her inability to fully meet the standards of sexlessness and submission set before her. To her aid, however, came a multitude of conduct manuals, books created to offer young women advice on proper behavior, as well as women's magazines, novels, and poetry. Such writings extolled women's superior control in matters of the flesh as well as their responsibility to employ modesty to shield themselves from inappropriate advances. In his published letters to his daughter, Dr. John Gregory advises,

> There is a native dignity in ingenuous modesty to be expected in your sex, which is your natural protection from the familiarities of the men, and

which you should feel previous to the reflection that it is your interest to keep yourself sacred from all personal freedoms. (43)

Such stress on modesty, however, as Mary Poovey rightly points out, belied a need for sexual self-control and an awareness of a sexuality in need of restraint. Modesty was, in fact, "a woman's most effective lure. . . . Modesty is provocation; it whets the lover's appetite; it suspends both partners momentarily in the delicious foreplay of anticipation" (Poovey 22). The sexual promise of modesty, then, and not the sexlessness it sought to represent, was unmistakably at the heart of Victorian courtship. Sexuality, even when dressed in modesty, however, has always been a force of power, and the sexual appeal of Victorian women not only allowed them the "privilege of refusing," a term used by Gregory and others to describe the power-position held by women in their choice to accept or reject the advances of suitor, but also granted them power beyond courtship.

Marriage was the ultimate goal for the majority of young Victorian women who deplored the fate of spinsters, roughly 30 percent of British women in 1851, whose growing numbers had created the "surplus women problem" (Wolfee 44). Victorian marriages were, however, with limited exceptions, sexual unions.[3] It was the wedding night that was considered the "single greatest event of a woman's life, when she bestowed her greatest treasure upon her husband . . ." (Welter 154–55). Sex within marriage could be more than simply a gift bestowed or duty fulfilled in which one must "lie back and think of England"; it also offered a form of indirect power for wives. Not only did a wife's sexual appeal for her husband greatly aid her in her efforts of persuasion, but the threat of its denial could be of great influence upon a husband as well. Since men such as Dr. William Acton, an influential physician of the time, believed sexual desire to be necessary for the emotional and physical well-being of men, denial of it was feared to result in impotence (Hellerstein 177). The barring of the bedroom, when performed by Anne Brontë's tenant of Wildfell Hall, was an act so sensational that it "reverberated throughout Victorian England" (Gerin 1). In reality, however, by mid-century, middle-class women were, according to Acton, beginning to view the denial of sexual access to their husbands as a justifiable act (Tosh 155–56). Despite her public image, it would be naïve to ignore the sexuality of the Victorian wife or the power it provided her over her husband.

The nineteenth-century woman's unspoken sexual power, however, remained set against the fixed backdrop of male dominance. Beyond the earlier justification of the need for male control over their reproduction, women had long been viewed as less physically and intellectually capable versions of man who required the protection and rule of men for their benefit. The belief in the necessary subservence of woman to man remained a powerful force during Barrie's lifetime and found support from many quarters. From within the sciences, particularly the emerging fields of evolutionary biology, sociology, and anthropology, came new knowledge that ironically buttressed and supported the hierarchical relationship historically viewed as an integral component of "Divine order." The works of Charles Darwin, Herbert Spencer, and other biologists reinforced the perception of the male as active and sexually driven and females as passive and dependent.

Literature also made its contribution to the picture of female submission. In his polemic essay "Of Queen's Gardens," John Ruskin—whose own relationship to women could hardly be called untroubled (Rose 51–94)—urges: "She must be enduringly, incorruptibly good, instinctively, infallibly wise,—wise not for self-development, but for self-renunciation; wise, not that she may set herself above her husband, but that she may never fail from his side" (142). Both husband and wife were, in fact, strongly cautioned by conduct manuals and other sources not to allow the "design of providence" to be inverted. According to the conduct book *Lady Pennington's Advice to Her Daughter*, "A woman can never be seen in a more ridiculous light, than when she appears to govern her husband" (qtd. in Monaghan 106).

Ostensibly preoccupied with the public world, bourgeois husbands had, as a whole, allowed the home to fall under the dominion of their wives. Women found themselves in control of the rituals and practices of domesticity, which by Barrie's time, had become highly rigid. In addition to her sexual persuasions and domestic authority, women were ascribed the "power of influence," an authority they were told was not incompatible with their submissive role. As men's moral superiors, wives were viewed as an invaluable source of direction for their spouses. Through her discourse with her husband, a woman was assured, even by proto-feminists such as Harriet Martineau, not only of the improvement of her own mind through exposure to knowledge of the outside world, but also of her own ability to serve as her husband's moral center and "insinuate into his mind those softer graces and milder beauties, which will smooth the ruggedness of his character"

(Martineau 93). Men, for their part, were encouraged to turn to their wives with their fears and anxieties.

In his examination of Victorian masculinity within the context of domesticity, historian John Tosh points out, however, that by the late nineteenth century husbands had begun to chafe against the female administration of the household routine, the "tyranny of the five-o'clock tea" (180), and their emotional reliance on their wives. While still expected to retain the role of patriarch, for many, domestic submission to and emotional dependence upon their wives "was only acceptable to the man's sensitivities if the woman was constructed as mother instead of wife" (71). This devolution of the patriarch into the "patriarchal child" problematized the marital relationship not only for the husband, but for his wife as well.

It was believed, according to clergyman George Burnap in his 1851 lecture *The Sphere and Duties of Woman*, that a "true" woman "despises in man every thing like herself except a tender heart. It is enough that she is effeminate and weak; she does not want another like herself" (qtd. in Welter 159). This conflict could be further amplified, should the husband fail to prove himself worthy of his wife's respect. Mary Astell and Dr. Gregory, as well as conduct author Elizabeth Hamilton, strongly advised their female readers against marrying a man who was vastly inferior to them in intellect. While Hamilton laments "the misery of disappointment" brought upon a "woman who is capable of reasoning, and unites herself to a man of inferior capacity" (373–74), Gregory warns his daughters: "Heaven forbid you should ever relinquish the ease and independence of a single life, to be the slave of a fool" (109–10).

A man's ineptitude in the economic world could also impact marital harmony. According to historian John Wolfee, work was the sphere in which a man "obtained his dignity by demonstration of his independence, his honesty, and his competence" (26), so a lack of economic achievement could undermine a husband's self-image as well as the justification of his authority in the home. For those men who had earned their living through clerical work, establishing self-worth through economic success became increasingly difficult. By the mid-nineteenth century, women had begun to fill clerical positions, and as a result, the clerical positions became less well paid, less secure, and less masculine (Wilson 599–600). For a Victorian wife who could not respect her husband, confusion and guilt were inevitable.

In addition to economic success, the production of a child, particularly a son, was an important element in the formation of male Victorian identity, garnering a husband additional public authority (Tosh 3–4). Within the home, however, the transformation of the wife into mother greatly increased her already threatening authority. Hannah More emphasized the tremendous influence of mothers on British society: "in the case of our children we are responsible for the exercise of acknowledged *power*, a power wide in its extent, indefinite in its effects, and inestimable in its importance. On YOU, depends in no small degree the principles of the whole rising generation" (322). For fathers, however, the influence of mothers that warranted the well-known acknowledgment, "all that I am I owe to my angel mother," had become a locus of anxiety. Their own masculinity threatened by the domestic power of their wives, by mid-century both middle- and upper-class Victorian fathers began to fear that their sons' feminization under maternal influence would compromise their ability to compete in the marketplace. Charlotte Brontë portrays the male concern over feminized boys and the intended remedy of a public boarding school education in *The Professor*:

> He must go to Eton, where, I suspect, his first year or two will be utter wretchedness. To leave me, his mother, and his home, will give his heart an agonized wrench. Then, the fagging will not suit him; but emulation, thirst for knowledge, the glory of success, will stir and reward him in time. Meantime, I feel in myself a strong repugnance to fix the hour which will uproot my sole olive branch, and transplant it far from me. . . . The step must, however, be taken, and it shall be; for, though Frances will not make a milksop of her son, she will accustom him to the style of treatment, a forbearance, a congenial tenderness, he will meet from none else. (252)

Anxiety surrounding motherhood was not restricted to men alone, however. The selflessness and devotion expected of a Victorian mother created emotional burdens as well. The fear of negative influence upon a child, the loss of a son to boarding school, or more painfully, the death of a child were burdens that mothers were expected to accept as "God's will" (Welter 161–62), an acceptance that, if not successful in fully repressing negative feelings regarding motherhood, was highly effective in silencing their expression.

Given the tension that had come to surround the Victorian mother and female sexuality, as well as his intense experiences with his own mother, it is not surprising that Barrie's work focuses on motherhood. That Barrie's view of his own mother was heavily influenced by the Victorian anxiety regarding female sexuality is supported by biographer Harry M. Geduld's interpretation of Barrie's novel *Tommy and Grizel*: "The Margaret figure, the most complex of the prototypical characters, appears on the one hand a promiscuous woman, a Painted Lady, the defiled or debauched object of desire, and on the other as the virginal girl who is invariably a heroine" (30). Barrie's view of female sexuality, however, can be distinguished from Victorian stereotypes by his already stated sympathy toward his mother. The two conflicting images of sexuality that Barrie attributes to the Margaret figure reveal an understanding of the dichotomy of his mother's sexuality as both the source of her maternal power and the means by which she produced a son whose death proved her emotional undoing. Despite the reminder that "she still had another boy" (Barrie, *Ogilvy* 231–32), the devastated Margaret did not provide maternal support to her surviving children. For Barrie, Margaret's sexuality, like that of Victorian womanhood in general, is simultaneously powerful and life giving as well as self-destructive and selfish.

Margaret's failure to put aside her grief to meet the requirements of motherhood brings to the forefront Barrie's father's inadequacies as well. Blamed by Barrie, according to Geduld, for failing the young David by allowing him to visit the family home where his accidental death occurred (57–58), the elder David Barrie could also be accused of sexual irresponsibility. With his large family and lack of domestic servants, the senior Barrie may have been guilty of what nineteenth-century feminists believed to be the misconduct of husbands who put their wives' health at risk through repeated impregnation and the resulting dangers of childbirth and overburdening of children (Tosh 155).

As a handloom weaver, David Barrie, Sr., could only provide for the education of his seven children through great sacrifices to his family's domestic comforts. The economic strain of life in the Barrie home is revealed in the opening sentence of Margaret's biography, in which Barrie describes one of the great moments of his mother's life. He states, "On the day I was born we bought six hairbottomed chairs, and in our little house it was an event, the first great victory of a woman's long campaign; how they had labored for, the pound-note and the thirty three penny bits they cost" (Barrie, *Ogilvy* 225). David Sr.'s ability to provide for his family did not improve as his children grew. Not unlike the clerks squeezed out by lower paid women, his father's inability to keep up with the changes necessary to remain a vital component of the work force are described by Barrie:

> [O]lder folks are slower in the uptake. . . . Where had been formerly but the click of the shuttle was soon the roar of the "power," hand-looms were pushed into a corner as a room is cleared to dance. . . . Another era had dawned, new customs, new fashions sprang into life, all as lusty as if they had been born at twenty-one; as quickly as two people may exchange seats, the daughter, till now but a knitter of stockings, became the breadwinner, he who had been the breadwinner sat down to the knitting of stockings; what had been yesterday a nest of weavers was to-day a town of girls. (237–38)

While sympathetic to his father's plight, there is also a note of disgust at his lack of economic power and an unquestionable femininity in the image of the older man knitting. Barrie's disappointment with his father and his intense empathy for his mother and her struggles are reflected within his novel *Peter Pan*.

Barrie both begins and ends *Peter Pan* within the domestic sphere of another Victorian couple, the Darlings. With its effeminate name and diminutive size, the Darling home embodies the anxiety surrounding the nineteenth-century mother's familial dominance. Among the first episodes of the novel is Mrs. Darling's successful negotiation to raise the newborn Wendy despite her husband's protests, a victory reminiscent of Margaret Barrie's procurement of the hairbottom chairs:

> For a week or two after Wendy came it was doubtful whether they would be able to keep her, as she was another mouth to feed. Mr Darling was frightfully proud of her, but he was very honorable, and sat on the edge of Mrs. Darling's bed holding her hand and calculating expenses, while she looked at him imploringly. She wanted to risk it, come what might. (8–9)

There is, of course, never any mention of sending Wendy away, and Mrs. Darling's desire to raise her despite the "risk" appears to have won before Mr. Darling's calculations had even begun.

For Mr. Darling, however, the raising of a baby, the product of Mrs. Darling's sexual fecundity, plainly jeopardizes his already difficult struggle to ascend into a higher level of the middle class, in which he could enjoy being "exactly like his neighbors" (10). In the stage direction of the dramatic version of *Peter Pan*, Barrie refers to Mr. Darling as "a good man as breadwinners go," but follows with a description of his

lack of fulfillment and success as a clerk: "In the city where he sits on
a stool all day, as fixed as a postage stamp, he is so like all the others
on stools that you recognize him not by his face but by his stool" (qtd.
in Wilson 598).

Mrs. Darling has likely been unprepared for her husband's lackluster
career success. As a suitor, Mr. Darling demonstrated not only his re-
sponsiveness to her sexual charms, but an energy and ambition indicative of future economic achievement: "the many gentlemen who
had been boys when she was a girl discovered simultaneously that
they loved her, and they all ran to her house to propose to her except
Mr. Darling, who took a cab and nipped there first, and so he got her"
(7–8). While Mrs. Darling may have been misled by what was likely Mr.
Darling's single hour of creativity, she may also have been moved to
make her expeditious choice by the fear of spinsterhood that likewise
gripped novelist George Gissing's Monica Madden and can perhaps be
forgiven for faltering in judgment and ignoring the advice of conduct
authors by marrying "a man of inferior capacity." Despite her husband's underdeveloped potential, however, Mrs. Darling makes her
desire to present herself as a submissive and worshipping wife evident
in her reassurance that he is "admired" (30). The narrator's revelation
that "Mr. Darling used to boast to Wendy that her mother not only
loved him but respected him" (8), though, reveals the clerk's insecurity
regarding the sincerity of her declarations.

Mr. Darling's lack of a central role in his home, resulting from his failure as a breadwinner, is painfully evident in the fantasy games his children select. His sons do not dress up in his image and pretend to work
as he does. Instead, all of the children celebrate their mother's domestic sovereignty by playing at being born. When John, playing the role
of his father, attempts to block Michael from birth and the younger
child laments, "Nobody wants me," Mrs. Darling reprises her role in the
arrival of her children and intervenes: "'I do,' she said. 'I so want a third
child'" (24–25). As evidenced by the children's play, Mrs. Darling and
her sexual power are the central forces around which the Darling
home is constructed.

Despite Mr. Darling's failure to rule his home, we are told that
"[t]here never was a simpler, happier family" (12). The harmony of his
home, it becomes clear, is owed to a childlike subordinance on the part
of Mr. Darling. Given his wife's domestic power and his own financial
ineptitude, Darling had no choice but to take on the role of "patriarchal
child." His discomfort with his lack of paternal authority is demon-

strated by his attempt to assert his maturity and distinguish himself from his children. Boasting of his ability to take his medicine, he instead defers responsibility to his wife's surrogate, Nana, the canine nursemaid, and pours the medicine into the dog's bowl. When he is caught and denounced a "cowardy custard" by his own son, Mr. Darling endeavors to gain the role as "master in that house" by putting Nana outside (29–31). Echoing Barrie's father and the death of David Jr., Mr. Darling succeeds only in precipitating what Mrs. Darling perceives as the loss of their unprotected children.

Mrs. Darling's role in the removal of the children to Neverland is far more complex. While behaving in accordance with the letter of the laws of propriety allowing for female influence in the home, Mrs. Darling, as the wife of an unsuccessful and unmanly man, has failed to fully submit herself to her husband's authority. The narrator reveals that "[h]er romantic mind was like the tiny boxes, one within the other, that come from the puzzling East," but that Mr. Darling "got all of her, except the innermost box and the kiss" (7–8). That the kiss and the last box are not for her husband's possession is not due solely to failure on his part as a husband, however. Sheltered from the world by each subsequent box, the kiss and last most private box that houses it possess intrinsic qualities that make them incompatible with Mrs. Darling's adult role in Victorian society. Barrie hints at this in the opening paragraph of the story that immediately precedes the description of Mrs. Darling and her kiss. Having received flowers from a two-year-old Wendy, the mother exclaims, "Oh, why can't you remain like this for ever!" (7). Although *Peter Pan* is the story of a boy who would not grow up, it is significant that the desire to defer adulthood is first addressed to a girl and that it is Mrs. Darling who voices that desire.

The kiss is, in fact, inextricably tied to perpetual, childish freedom. When the family "romps," it is not Mrs. Darling, the mature matriarch, whom we see. Instead, the narrator observes that "gayest of all was Mrs. Darling, who would pirouette so wildly that all you could see of her was the kiss, and then if you had dashed at her you might have got it" (12). Expressive of a desire for freedom from the confines of adult female power and responsibility, like Peter Pan, the kiss represents both "youth" and "joy" (206). On the heels of this sighting of the kiss, Barrie portrays Mrs. Darling's initial encounter with Peter, a figure from her children's unconscious worlds she discovers while "tidying up her children's minds. It is the nightly custom of every good mother after her children are asleep" (12). While Mrs. Darling's initial contact with

Peter is made through Wendy, who at eight years old has already begun to transfer her desire for self-assertion to the male fantasy figure,
Peter immediately reawakens Mrs. Darling's repressed feelings for
freedom—feelings that, throughout her youth and adulthood, had
been confined to her kiss and innermost box: "thinking back into her
childhood she just remembered Peter Pan" (15).

Although irresistibly drawn to Peter, in her initial encounter with
him, Mrs. Darling expresses a distaste for his overt confidence (15).
While Mrs. Darling's use of the term "cocky" to describe Peter is clearly
intended as a reference to the assertive and aggressive nature of roost-
ers, neither aggression nor assertiveness was a trait incompatible with
masculinity, but both were instead aspects of manliness encouraged
during the days of empire building. Mrs. Darling's choice of terms
seems a surprising way to express objection toward a male character.
Her negative use of the term "cocky," however, reveals not only her
discomfort with her own strength and dominance in her home, but also
her feelings of connectivity with Peter. Should we fail to connect Peter
to Mrs. Darling and her desire for freedom from the confines of her social role, however, the narrator makes the link between the two undeniable: "If you or I or Wendy had been there we should have seen that
he was very like Mrs. Darling's kiss" (20).

Close examination of the bond between Peter and Mrs. Darling brings
to light an additional connection: their alignment with Margaret Barrie.
In the description of his mother's laugh in *Margaret Ogilvy*, Barrie
places particular emphasis on its eternal youthfulness and merriment.
Barrie's use of similar language in his description of Peter's laugh cannot be coincidental: "No one could look so merry as Peter, and the
loveliest gurgles was his laugh. He had his first laugh still" (43). Additionally, Peter's practice of crowing with excited self-praise can be
found within the pages of Margaret's biography, coming from her own
lips after triumphing over a peddler as well as Barrie, who had ordered
her to stay in bed, after making what she felt was a particularly good
trade (Barrie, *Ogilvy* 299). It is the connection between the youthfulness
of Mrs. Darling to which Barrie draws our attention and his mother's
girlishness, however, that most dramatically reveals Barrie's sympathy
toward the oppression experienced by Victorian adult women.

While Barrie constructs his story on several levels, it is useful at this
point to consider the possibility that the journey of the children to Neverland (and, in fact, the remainder of the novel) does not occur within
the reality of the Darling home but transpires within the dream-world of

Mrs. Darling's unconscious. This perspective is encouraged by the narrator's statement that "[w]hile she slept she had a dream. She dreamt that the Neverland had come too near and that a strange boy had broken through from it. He did not alarm her, for she thought she had seen him before" (18). Given this vantage point, it becomes clear that the characters of Neverland, as well as those in the Darling house, following Mrs. Darling's lapse into unconscious sleep, are the products of her repressions and represent some aspect of herself or her conscious world.

As a Victorian woman, Mrs. Darling's discomfort with her domestic power and her motivation to suppress such feelings are clear. Her wish that Wendy not grow into a woman like herself also indicates a dissatisfaction with the role of motherhood and a resentment of the selflessness it required. Critic Ellen Moers, in her discussion of Mary Shelley's novel *Frankenstein*, suggests that while maternal rejection, or even abandonment, was a nineteenth-century reality, it was such an unspeakable reality that Shelley could portray parental desertion only in a disguised form (214–24). Dissatisfaction with her maternal role, along with any recognition of the full extent of her domestic power, however, was a concept too debilitating for a Victorian mother to recognize consciously. Like Wendy, Mrs. Darling has unconsciously chosen to embody her desires for freedom from maternal sacrifice as well as guiltless self-assertion in the form of the fantasy figure Peter Pan. Having left his mother as an infant, Peter remains a pre-Oedipal child, free of the anxiety surrounding adult sexuality. In adopting as her doppelganger a male arrested prior to sexual desire, Mrs. Darling can grant full rein to her power. In this state, she can be "cocky," but without the fear of emasculating her husband and her sons.

In addition to the advantages of sexlessness and maleness, Barrie, meticulously careful in the naming of characters, has imbued Peter with profound cultural power as well. Naming the embodiment of rebellion against female limitations by joining Pan, from the Greek meaning "everything," with Peter, the foundation or "rock" of the Christian church, Barrie gives Peter the authority of both the classically pagan and the Christian, providing him unlimited scope and sway.[4]

As Mrs. Darling's primary alter ego, Peter rules over her unconscious world with near omnipotence: "Feeling Peter was on his way back, the Neverland had again woke into life" (71). Just as Mrs. Darling controls the physical and mental economies of her children, Peter, as leader of his male tribe, dominates his Lost Boys, "thin[ing] them out" if they began to grow (72) and limiting their knowledge to what he himself possesses (74). He, however, does so without apology. Under Peter's command, the masculinity of the boys not only remains intact, but is enhanced by their allegiance to this strong figure.

Only Captain Hook serves as a challenge to Peter's will. Although a comic figure as a pirate who cannot triumph over a young boy, Captain Hook, as critic Ann Wilson points out, possesses habits that reveal a boarding school education and upper-class background (600–601). By creating Hook as her husband's Neverland-double, Mrs. Darling has not only granted him the economic upward mobility that had eluded him in his real-world career, but takes him one step beyond his aspirations into the upper class. Having elevated her husband to a respectable level of economic success, Mrs. Darling, as Peter, can now openly battle for the authority she already possesses at home and, in so doing, justify her power. Despite Peter's symbolic castration of the pirate through the vagina-dentata-like mouth of the crocodile,[5] Hook remains a virile and imposing rival, thus allaying Mrs. Darling's anxiety regarding her sexuality and power.

The assumption of Peter's power by Mrs. Darling, however, has required the abdication of her sexuality and her role as mother. Despite his disavowal of mothers as "over-rated persons" (38), Peter (and the other male inhabitants of Neverland) is drawn to maternal images of womanhood intentionally absent from his reality. In an effort to sublimate her sexual/maternal power, Mrs. Darling has populated her island with dangerous and improper women. Described as "quite a common fairy" (44), Tinker Bell's attraction to Peter shares the transparency of her "skeleton leaf" gown that was "cut low and square, through which her figure could be seen to best advantage" (35). Equally drawn to Peter is Tiger Lily, who in an early version of the play, desires to be "caught" by Peter and made his squaw. Siren-like, the mermaids that inhabit Neverland lagoon present yet another menacing form of female sexuality. While they lavish Peter with sensual caresses, the mermaids make no effort to rescue him when he is "stranded" on Marooner's Rock (133) nor would they hesitate to pull the other characters to a watery death. Despite their potency, these lascivious female images fail to repress Mrs. Darling's desire for motherhood, and Peter is drawn to the image of Mrs. Darling with her children, arriving outside her window at the most satisfying moment in her day, the story-time hour in which she reigns guiltlessly supreme over the nursery.

It is clearly not feasible for Peter to integrate Mrs. Darling and her motherhood into Neverland. Within the oppressive culture in which she exists, it is equally impossible for Mrs. Darling to allow Peter into her world. Upon entering Mrs. Darling's dominion, Peter begins to disintegrate and become separated from his shadow. In her offer to reattach the shadow, Wendy promises a clever solution to the barrier between Peter and Mrs. Darling. By bringing Wendy, who represents the potential of future maternal power, into Neverland, Peter creates the possibility of attaining the maternal bond for which he longs, but free of adult sexuality. While Mrs. Darling cannot be any more ignorant of the reality that "Wendy was every inch a woman, though there were not very many inches" (40) than the narrator who voices this observation, this concern is initially side-stepped by Peter's transportation of Wendy to his domain, where both she and her sexuality are under his authority.

To combat the disruptive force of Wendy's entrance into Neverland, Mrs. Darling, through Peter, orchestrates her rebirth and arrested development at the pre-Oedipal stage by building a house around her in the image of a womb (Geduld 61). Her rebirth is immediately undone, however, with her adoption of the adult role as mother to the Lost Boys (98–99). The addition of even a sexless mother quickly reshapes Neverland into an echo of the Darling home. In her struggle for dominance within the underground den of the lost boys, Wendy is kept from the level of power possessed by her mother in the Darling home only through her inability to gain sexual control of Peter.

While the role of mother holds strong attraction for Wendy, a desire for power has, from the beginning, been at the heart of Wendy's interest in Peter. In their first meeting, Wendy presents herself as the epitome of motherliness. In introducing herself, Wendy not only calls upon the power of one middle name, Angela, which conjures up all the domestic power of the "angel of the house," but also her second middle name, Moira, a derivative of Mary, possessed of all the iconic power of the Virgin Mother. While Peter is deeply impressed, Wendy mistakes his motivation and attempts to emulate the sexual influence of wife over husband, making herself "rather cheap by inclining her face toward him" for a kiss (41). Peter responds by desexualizing the encounter and offering to return the thimble she has given him. Wendy, however, achieves a success in attaching Peter to herself that greatly outstrips the accomplishments of the other females. This success has come with his acceptance of the thimble, an image that, although innocently domestic, carries implications of which Peter appears unaware. The thimble, once an open-ended metal sheath, not only evokes the shape of a wedding ring, but also serves as a vaginal image, recalling female sexual power.

For Wendy, however, the promise of the thimble is not fulfilled. Instead, Peter continues his resistance to her sexual advances, stripping the power of sexuality from her role as mother. Wendy confesses the resentment of selflessness: "oh dear, I am sure I sometimes think spinsters are to be envied" (107). When Peter returns from his encounter with the Indians, who have named him the "Great White Father" as a reward for saving Tiger Lily, Wendy makes a final effort to use her maternal role to position Peter as her husband by stating, "Dear Peter . . . with such a large family, of course, I have now passed my best, but you don't want to change me, do you?" Peter responds:

> "I was just thinking," he said, a little scared. "It is only make-believe, isn't it, that I am their father?"
> "Oh yes," Wendy said primly.
> "You see" he continued apologetically, "it would make me seem so old to be their real father."
> "But they are ours, Peter, yours and mine."
> "But not really, Wendy?" he asked anxiously.
> "Not if you don't wish it," she replied; and she distinctly heard his sigh of relief. (145)

Ironically, had Wendy succeeded, Peter would have become the patriarchal child and she the "Great White Mother."[6] In so doing, she would have recreated the very dynamic that had originally set into motion the need for Neverland in Mrs. Darling's unconscious. As Peter has been created incapable of sexuality, Wendy's allure for him is limited to her maternal traits, and her efforts are therefore predestined to fail.

For Mrs. Darling, the fantasy of reintegrating her divided self through the interaction of Wendy and Peter has failed. She has, however, created another possibility for personal freedom. With the absence of the children from her imaginary home and with her husband's admitted culpability for the children's disappearance putting him literally in the doghouse, Mrs. Darling may rule over her home without guilt or fear. Like the parallel fantasy of Wendy in Neverland, however, her dream of guiltless matriarchy falls short. When Peter returns to the Darling home, he finds that instead of becoming more childlike and joyful in her freedom from maternal responsibility, Mrs. Darling and her kiss have been nearly destroyed: "The corner of her mouth, where one looked first, is almost withered up" (219). The narrator voices disapproval of her failure to embrace her freedom: "You see, the woman had no proper spirit. I had meant to say extraordinary things about her; but I despise her" (216). Too consciously consumed by her role as selfless wife and mother, even within her unconscious, Mrs. Darling is incapable of embracing her full power. While Mrs. Darling's unconscious has explored every option to supply her with an escape from the confines of her role as mother, for her such escape is impossible.

Still sleeping within the reality of the nursery, Mrs. Darling's dream begins to come to an end. Making a final attempt to bring herself and Peter together, she offers to raise him as her own son, a reality she must recognize, even unconsciously, as impossible. Finding her children returned to her, Mrs. Darling bars the windows against Peter and her rebellion. Her rejection, however, is incomplete while she still possesses the kiss that Peter personifies, and when she wakes, her family will remain vulnerable to the disruptive element of their mother's unconscious rebellion. Mrs. Darling's dream ends as she presents Peter with the kiss he personifies, turning her back on Neverland and giving herself over entirely to the role of wife and mother: "He took Mrs. Darling's kiss with him. The kiss that had been for no one else Peter took quite easily. Funny. But she seemed satisfied" (231). The kiss is not lost, however. Mrs. Darling has shared her dream with her daughter, and Peter's inevitable return to the fantasy world of Wendy and her daughter, and presumably all the women of her line, suggests that, as adults, each woman will explore the terrain of Neverland; each will attempt to clear a path beyond the confines of her domestic role in which she can acknowledge her full sexuality and power, as well as feelings of guilt and resentment toward her family. In so doing, each woman is able to test the limits of reality against the hope that one of them may encounter a future cultural climate conducive to the integration of all aspects of a woman's nature.

Like men such as Edward Carpenter, whose commitment to women's rights was inspired by the futility of his sisters' lives (Tosh 180–83), Barrie's observation of his mother's suffering as a Victorian wife and mother gave him a particular sympathy for the confinement of women within a culture of separate spheres. Through Mrs. Darling's kiss and her fantasy world of Neverland, Barrie emphasizes the need to rid society of the damaging and artificial compartmentalization of the female nature, shaped to fit the agendas of subsequent generations of men. The lack of an easily recognizable rebellion in Mrs. Darling and many of Barrie's other female characters has made them more palatable to audiences out of their sympathy with the needs of women. It has, however, also served to veil our understanding of Barrie's efforts as a writer whose works are rich, imaginative, and pro-feminist. While far more subtle and understated, Barrie, like Thomas Hardy, should be recognized as a writer whose sympathy for the plight of late Victorian and early Edwardian women, and the need for cultural reform, places him among the iconoclasts of his time.[7]

NOTES

1. The character of Peter Pan was first introduced in Barrie's 1902 novel *The Little White Bird*. The play, *Peter Pan; or, the Boy Who Wouldn't Grow Up*, was performed in 1904 and published as *Peter Pan* in 1928.

2. It was not until the years between 1870 and 1908, for example, that the Married Women's Property Acts were passed, allowing women to possess property that until that point was controlled by husbands after marriage under the system of coverture. British women were not enfranchised until 1919.

3. Barrie's marriage is often believed to have been unconsummated. According to Andrew Birkin, however, while it was rumored during his life that Barrie was impotent (dubbed "the boy who couldn't get it up"), it is likely that he and Mary Barrie had a sexual relationship in the early days of their marriage (180).

4. While R. D. S. Jack points to the tensions created through the joining of Peter, the founder of the Christian church, with the Greek word for "everything," emphasizing the power struggle between the two, he does not focus on the potential power of their partnership (159–62).

5. Marjorie Garber discusses in greater detail the phallic nature of Hook's hook and its removal by the female-engendered crocodile (178). The maternal aspect of the crocodile suggested by the ticking (biological) clock inside its belly should also be noted.

6. The Great White Mother was a title originally given to Queen Victoria in reference to her role as head of the British Empire.

7. My thanks to Alan Rauch for his encouragement and support and for his valuable feedback on early drafts of this paper.

WORKS CITED

Armstrong, Nancy. *Desire and Domestic Fiction: A Political History of the Novel*. New York: Oxford UP, 1987.

Astell, Mary. *Some Reflections Upon Marriage*. 4th ed. 1730. New York: Source Books P, 1970.

Barrie, J. M. *A Kiss for Cinderella*. 1920. *The Plays of J. M. Barrie*. New York: Scribner's, 1928.

——. *Peter and Wendy; Margaret Ogilvy*. New York: Scribner's, 1912.

——. *Peter Pan*. 1911. London: Puffin, 1968.

——. *The Twelve-Pound Look*. 1914. *The Plays of J. M. Barrie*. New York: Scribner's, 1928.

Birkin, Andrew. *J. M. Barrie and The Lost Boys: The Love Story that Gave Birth to Peter Pan*. New York: Potter, 1979.

Brontë, Charlotte. *The Professor*. 1857. London: T. Nelson, n.d.

Garber, Marjorie. *Vested Interests: Cross-Dressing & Cultural Anxiety*. New York: Routledge, 1992.

Geduld, Harry M. *James Barrie*. New York: Twayne, 1971.

Gerin, Winifred. Introduction. *The Tenant of Wildfell Hall*. By Anne Brontë. Ed. G. D. Hargreaves. London: Penguin, 1979. 1–18.

Gissing, George. *The Odd Women*. 1893. New York: W. W. Norton, 1977.

Gregory, Dr. John. *A Father's Legacy to His Daughters*. 4th ed. London: Cadell, 1762.

Griffith John. "Making Wishes Innocent: Peter Pan." *The Lion and the Unicorn* 3 (1979): 28–37.

Hamilton, Elizabeth. *Letters on the Elementary Principles of Education*. 2nd ed. Vol. 2. Bath: Cruttwell, 1801–1802.

Hellerstein, Erna Olafson, Leslie Parker Hume, and Karen M. Offen, eds. *Victorian Women: A Documentary Account of Women's Lives in Nineteenth-Century England, France, and the United States*. Stanford, CA: Stanford UP, 1981.

Holbrook, David. *Images of Women in Literature*. New York: New York UP, 1989.

Jack, R. D. S. *The Road to the Never Land: A Reassessment of J M Barrie's Dramatic Art*. Aberdeen: Aberdeen UP, 1991.

John, Angela. "Men, Manners, and Militancy: Literary Men and Women's Suffrage." *The Men's Share?: Masculinities, Male Support and Women's Suffrage in Britain, 1890–1920*. Ed. Angela John and Claire Eustance. London: Routledge, 1997. 88–107.

Martineau, Harriet. *Harriet Martineau On Women*. Ed. Gayle Graham Yates. New Brunswick: Rutgers UP, 1985.

Moers, Ellen. "The Female Gothic: The Monster's Mother." *A Norton Critical Edition: Mary Shelley's Frankenstein*. Ed. J. Paul Hunter. New York: Norton, 1996. 214–24.

Monaghan, David. "Jane Austen and the Position of Women." *Jane Austen in Social Context*. Ed. David Monaghan. Totowa, NJ: Barnes & Noble, 1981. 66–85.

More, Hannah. *The Works of Hannah More: First Complete American Edition*. Vol. 1. New York: Harpers, 1844.

Poovey, Mary. *The Proper Lady and the Woman Writer: Ideology as Style in the Works of Mary Wollstonecraft, Mary Shelley, and Jane Austen*. Chicago: U of Chicago P, 1984.

Rose, Phyllis. *Parallel Lives: Five Victorian Marriages.* New York: Vintage Books, 1983.

Ruskin, John. *Sesame and Lilies: Three Lectures.* Chicago: Donohue, Henneberry, 1866.

Tosh, John. *A Man's Place: Masculinity in the Middle-Class Home in Victorian England.* New Haven: Yale UP, 1999.

Welter, Barbara. "The Cult of True Womanhood: 1820–1860." *American Quarterly* 8 (1966): 151–74.

Wilson, Ann. "Hauntings: Anxiety, Technology, and Gender in Peter Pan." *Modern Drama* 43 (2000): 595–610.

Wolfee, John. "'Male and Female He Created Them': Men, Women and the Question of Gender." *Religion in Victorian Britain: Volume V. Culture and Empire.* Ed. John Wolfee. Manchester: Manchester UP, 1997.

15

The Female Figure in J. M. Barrie's *Peter Pan*: The Small and the Mighty

Emily Clark

> Race, gender, and class are not distinct realms of experience existing
> in splendid isolation from each other: nor can they be simply yoked
> together retrospectively like armatures of Lego.
>
> —Anne McClintock, *Imperial Leather*

Much of the critical conversation surrounding J. M. Barrie's novel *Peter Pan* in the last few years focuses on both imperial and feminist issues (particularly on Wendy as a maternal memsahib); however, the subject continues to bear further analysis. Although Wendy, Tinker Bell, and Tiger Lily certainly represent feminine archetypes, their struggle to address their double-consciousness as supposed racial and/or sexual subordinates and children during the course of the narrative questions any portrayal of them as simplistic.[1] What I especially believe warrants additional discussion is the manner in which Barrie's representation of Wendy's, Tinker Bell's, and Tiger Lily's physical attributes and dialogue not only reflects their oppression, but their appropriation of agency for themselves as well.

Anne McClintock's warning against compartmentalizing class, race, and gender underscores the complex tension present between Barrie's female characters as they form (or transform) their identities in Neverland. In addition to McClintock's argument against fetishizing social and cultural categories, Laura Donaldson also cautions readers against oversimplifying and generalizing gender identity and women's experiences:

> Historical colonialism demonstrates the political as well as theoretical necessity of abandoning the idea of women's (and men's) gender identity as fixed and coherent. Instead, it imbues us with a conception of gender as a site of conflicting subjective processes and makes it impossible to ignore the contradictory social positioning of white, middle-class women as both colonized patriarchal objects and colonizing race-privileged subjects. (6)

Both McClintock and Donaldson provide an astute guide to the complex gender and racial issues that arise in *Peter Pan*. Their arguments help underscore the ways in which Wendy, Tinker Bell, and Tiger Lily cope with a world that recognizes neither the scope nor the depth of their individual identities.

Toward the conclusion of the novel, Smee the pirate abducts Wendy and, as he binds her to the mast of the ship, whispers, "[S]ee here, honey . . . I'll save you if you promise to be my mother" (Barrie 134). Smee's brutal proposition, which conflates maternity and sexuality, epitomizes the multiple roles of mother, lover, woman, and child with which Wendy struggles throughout the text. In the "not" place, or theoretically invisible space, of Neverland, Wendy, Tinker Bell and Tiger Lily contend with the conflicting roles imposed upon them by Peter and the farce of Neverland's colonial society. Their successes and failures at navigating the margins of Neverland, where Peter functions as the central patriarchal authority figure, depends upon their ability to recognize the nontraditional methods of empowerment available to them.

Barrie makes it apparent from the outset of the novel that he intends to satirize the culture surrounding empire, which influences not only the geography of Great Britain, but domestic and social spheres as well. His description of the Darling nursery as well as Mr. Darling's tenuous role as the head of the household supports Peter Hunt and Karen Sands's argument in "The View From the Center: British Empire and Post-Empire Children's Literature" that "children's literature was, of course, the site of some subversion of the principles of empire, although the valorization of the home as the repository of values was . . . in itself a part of the inescapable matrix of imperialism" (45). The respective environments of the Nursery and Neverland mirror the confusion that Wendy, Tinker Bell, and Tiger Lily feel about themselves and the shifting adult world around them.[2] The Nursery, as opposed to the world of adults, represents English society, in which the roles of men and women, adults and children, and humans and animals seem inseparable. At the same time, Neverland, the token colony of masculine escapism, contains the Lost Boys, the Redskins, and the Pirates, all factions divided by their hold on territory, their intelligence, and often their ethnicity. Although the first portion of the novel focuses on the inversion of adult/child relationships (for example, Wendy and John administer medicine and advice to their parents), the majority of Barrie's criticism of gendered and racial stereotypes occurs in the looming and distant black continent of Neverland.[3] Here Barrie extends the confusion of the Nursery and establishes a feminine hierarchy based on physical size, voice, and agency that both silences and liberates Tinker Bell, Tiger Lily, and, especially, Wendy.

However, before Barrie introduces the reader to Neverland and its characters, he first defines Wendy as confident and able and as large as Peter. Wendy and Peter's dialogue in the Nursery while she reattaches his shadow, where she consistently refers to him as "my little man," establishes her strength and resistance to oppression (24). After Wendy successfully sews Peter back together, his reaction of "how clever I am!" without any acknowledgment of Wendy horrifies her (24). Her ensuing retreat back into her bed and refusal to encourage his arrogant attitude depicts Wendy as an unyielding proto-feminist, rather than merely a submissive future housewife. Thus, by rejecting Peter's self-perceived primacy as a male, Wendy takes her first stand against a patriarchal system that claims all victories for itself. She views her domestic accomplishments as a sign of both maturity and empowerment, not an indicator of Peter's male superiority.

According to Barrie, Wendy's transition from this powerful and more authentic place in the Nursery to her oppression in an imaginary home in Neverland occurs as a result of Peter's deft manipulation of her. When Wendy fails to respond to his threats to leave the Nursery, he beguiles her with the statement "one girl is more use than twenty boys" (Barrie 25). Wendy misconstrues this for an apology and an affirmation of the strength of women and girls; however, Peter's actual use for Wendy is self-serving and stifling to her as well as the other females in Neverland. He simply requires a mother and housekeeper more than he requires the Lost Boys. Wendy and Peter's exchange adds to the muddled relationships and roles in the novel, exemplified thus far by the Darling family. Additionally, with the narrator's explanation that "now Wendy was every inch a woman," Wendy and Peter's conversation institutes the idea that a "real" or a "complete" woman provides all for boys and men (25). Therefore, Wendy's failure to recognize that Peter does not value her as an individual, but as a useful possession, leads to her isolated captivity in Neverland.

Peter marks Wendy's arrival in Neverland, the site of her initiation into the sexual and racial hierarchy, by enclosing her in a small, pastoral home that makes her literally and figuratively invisible to the outer world. Her size no longer affords her a voice equal to Peter's, and he christens her a "nice motherly person," stripping her of her independent identity altogether (Barrie 67). In the Nursery, Wendy, a child mimicking a grown woman, exercised unusual authority over Peter, a child ignorant about the "real" world. However, in Neverland, Wendy discovers the difference between her experience of "reality," where she enjoys pretending to perform adulthood, and the false reality of Neverland. Wendy, a child in the Nursery, chooses to perform the positive aspects of female adulthood at will. However, Peter, a child consumed with pretending, forces Wendy to imitate both positive and negative aspects of adulthood in Neverland. For example, although Wendy commands the respect of the Lost Boys, she struggles to clothe and feed them in an illusory household with an often absent father figure.[4] This unusual situation causes Wendy to confront the marginalization of women into domesticity by an increasingly unstable and insecure British patriarchal society. Ann Wilson's argument that Neverland "is a place of a play within a play," a place both "nostalgic and gendered" and "a boy's world," augments the idea of Wendy as trapped in a seamlessly male-dominated environment where she no longer controls her performances of domesticity (600).

When confronted by Peter's and the Lost Boys' expectations of her, Wendy attempts to discontinue her pantomime of adult women's roles and protests: "I am only a little girl. I have no real experience" (Barrie 67). Peter invalidates her concerns, replying, "[T]hat doesn't matter," and forces her to maintain the dual position of mother and wife (67). Peter's dismissal of her supports Daphne Kutzer's assertion in *Empire's Children* that "the lack of women [in colonial spaces] reflects not only the limited possibilities for . . . women and the wishful thinking of men, but also the reality of imperial enterprise, which was almost entirely a male endeavor" (5). Therefore, Peter's reaction to Wendy immediately isolates her from the central society of Neverland in order to establish her as a non-threatening presence in his environment, which includes his territorial wars with the Redskins and Captain Hook.

Despite her seclusion, Wendy eventually recuperates her efficacy and individual identity by asserting her ability to terminate her performance in Neverland and return to the Nursery. Wendy's role as the gatekeeper to "reality" in Neverland provides her with the opportunity to regulate her future and that of her brothers, the Lost Boys, and Peter Pan. Once transplanted into the underground home, Wendy manipulates the duties of her maternal role, which include educating the boys, in order to gain control of her situation. In an attempt to remind John and Michael of their parents, Wendy educates them and, consequently, the Lost Boys, on the history of the Darling family:

> She tried to fix the old life in their minds by setting them examination papers on it, as like as possible to the ones she used to do at school. The other boys thought this awfully interesting, and insisted on joining, and they made slates for themselves, and sat round the table, writing and thinking hard about the questions she had written on the slate and passed around. (72)

As a result of Wendy's actions, two things occur: she establishes her command of the Lost Boys and her brothers, who quickly choose the Nursery over Peter's world, and she asserts her ability as a storyteller whose mastery of language trumps Peter's.

In addition to testing the boys, Wendy takes advantage of her position in Neverland as a narrator in order to inform Peter of her decision to return to the Nursery and embrace adulthood, no matter how difficult. She embodies Bruno Bettelheim's statement, "[A]s we awake refreshed from our dreams, better able to meet the tasks of reality, so the fairy story ends with our hero[ine] returning, or being returned to the real world, much better able to master life" (qtd. in Byrnes 55). As Wendy completes the account of her and her brothers' flight to Neverland, she reminds the Lost Boys of the unconditional love of human parents, thus enticing them to return with her to the Nursery, and also imagines her future as an "elegant lady of uncertain age," reaffirming her desire to pursue adult life outside of Neverland (105). Therefore, the nexus of maternal power, acceptance, and "reality" lures the Lost Boys, Peter's warriors, away from eternal childhood and redefines Wendy as an influential and visible figure in the child-colony.

As Wendy successfully recuperates her sense of self in preparation for her return to the Nursery, and eventually adulthood, Barrie offers readers two other feminine perspectives, that of Tinker Bell and Tiger Lily. The hierarchy denoted by the three different bodies of these girls/women clearly demarcates them as representative of the feminine stereotypes of middle-class housewife, lower-class prostitute or immigrant, and subaltern native. Their disconnected relationships to each other depend primarily on their desire for Peter and, in particular, Wendy's complex role as both colonial oppressor and victim.[5] While Wendy asserts an identity independent of Peter and escapes the margins of Neverland, Tinker Bell emerges from the margins of the underground home to temporarily inhabit a central place in the narrative, and Tiger Lily fails to transcend obscurity altogether. Therefore, as Barrie allows his characters to evolve, he defines three separate sets of margins within which the female characters struggle.

Peter governs Neverland and the narrative as its patriarchal, male center, with Wendy, Tinker Bell, and Tiger Lily inhabiting its theoretical borders, in that order. The chimeric world of Neverland exists as a shadow of the more dominant Nursery, which Wendy's, John's, and Michael's adventure brings to the forefront. Additionally, while the Nursery serves as both a touchstone of "reality" and the nucleus of the Darling family and Wendy's life, its presence lies on the outskirts of mainstream British life. Therefore, Barrie delineates a set of meta-margins that represent various hurdles each character must overcome in order to move forward toward a more voiced and empowered persona. While Wendy faces the smallest and simplest number of obstacles as a white, middle-class woman/child, Tinker Bell and Tiger Lily must address not only their femininity, but their linguistic silence and invisibility as well.[6]

Despite multiple analyses of Tinker Bell as lower-class, sexual, and silent, her diminutive stature and transparent body actually afford her extraordinary freedom. These characteristics release her from the constraints and codes of propriety that plague Wendy and allow her to inhabit a physically and socially independent space. Barrie's description of her somewhat marginal and hidden bedroom in the house under the ground epitomizes Tinker Bell's individuality and importance:

> There was one recess in the wall, no larger than a bird-cage, which was the private apartment of Tinker Bell. It could be shut off from the rest of the home by a tiny curtain, which Tink, who was most fastidious, always kept drawn when dressing, or undressing. No woman, however large, could have had a more exquisite boutique and bedchamber combined. (Barrie 70–71)

Unlike Wendy, Tinker Bell possesses her own room that provides her with a life independent from the domestic climate pervading the rest of the house. Her chamber, decorated according to her needs, rather than those of any husband or children, frees her to think and act of her own accord. Thus, this space provides her with temporary respite from the denigrating treatment of Peter, who consistently attempts to invalidate her existence by, for example, labeling her an "abandoned little creature" (101).

Tinker Bell's room, a model of cleanliness and privacy, provides an antithesis to Lois Rauch Gibson's argument that Tinker Bell and the other female characters "are all madonnas or whores, chaste, or common and profane" (178). Rather than living as a literal and figurative "public" woman, Tinker Bell consistently prefers privacy when dressing and carefully guards access to her voluptuous, yet minuscule and transparent body.[7] Her boudoir attests to her ultra-femininity, and although the narrator describes it as a sensual space, it further affirms her modesty and morals *despite* her constant use of offensive language and position as kettle-mender (that is, Tinker). Therefore, Barrie notes to the reader that Tinker Bell successfully balances her stereotypical femininity, alluded to in her clothing and reactions to Wendy, with her refusal to adhere to restrictive human standards for middle-class women (domesticity, maternity, asexuality). As a result, Tinker Bell competes with Wendy not only for Peter's attention, but for recognition in Neverland as well.

Both "women"—a human child and a mythical apparition—manipulate a form of language in order to assert themselves with Peter. While Wendy uses storytelling and knowledge as her tools, Tinker Bell capitalizes on the shock value of her swearing bells to interrupt Peter and expand the meaning of her body, which serves as her only vehicle for expression. Because Tinker Bell possesses no clear role in Neverland, in contrast to Wendy's maternal one, she struggles to make her vague and ephemeral appearances important. Her angry attempts to oust Wendy, who simultaneously represents Peter's maternal ideal and nemesis, showcase her ability as a nonhuman to step outside the bounds of acceptable human behavior. Tinker Bell's constant retorts of "you silly ass" function as a code for her hostility toward Peter (Barrie 28). He represents a patriarchal system in Neverland that fails to recognize her importance as a female with opinions and ideas rivaling his.

Additionally, Tinker Bell's replies signify a rejection of the "pretend" performances so common in Neverland.[8] Like Wendy's eventual assertion of the importance of reality, Tinker Bell's aggressive (and, therefore, stereotypically masculine) language and actions attempt to recuperate the "truth." Her actions function as a consistent reminder to both the reader and Peter of the multiple dimensions of femininity. Although she fails to strip Peter of his ignorance about the females in Neverland, she garners the validation and importance she seeks when she saves Peter's life using her body, the very object that unarguably threatens to hinder her influence in the colony.

Tinker Bell's uses of language as a form of resistance and her powerful physical invisibility both aid her in rescuing Peter, the only time she plays a central, rather than a liminal, role in the narrative. However, Barrie undercuts her report to Peter of Wendy's abduction as questionable and almost incomprehensible. Her voice, in "one ungrammatical sentence as long as the ribbons conjurers pull from their mouths," recounts to Peter the story of Wendy's and the children's disappearance (124). Nevertheless, despite its form, her "voice" significantly affects Peter, who not only believes Tinker Bell, but also prepares to react to the information and go to Wendy's aid. Because she causes change in the masculine world, Tinker Bell's unconventional narration of the incident creates another aspect of her identity: a purveyor of reality (much like Wendy). Almost immediately upon hearing Tinker Bell's explanation, Peter attempts to symbolically defer to Wendy by drinking his "medicine," which Hook poisoned. Tinker Bell warns Peter that Hook contaminated the drink, but he continues to question her access to knowledge in spite of the obvious veracity of her story about Hook's attack. Unable to convince Peter not to ingest the liquid, she interjects her body, her most useful and active instrument of expression, in between Peter and death.

The resulting scene, in which Tinker Bell lies dying, appealing to sleeping children to save her, diminishes her once again. Because she must rely on children's beliefs to revive her, her survival depends upon myth rather than truth and softens her previous message about feminine rebellion and independence. Although Tinker Bell recovers, she immediately fades into the background of the narrative as the pirate ship and Wendy's safety take precedence, once again making Tinker Bell a minor part of the larger human and imperial context. Her refusal to maintain a marginal presence, her emergence into the main adventure plot, and her return to her original place exemplify the difficulties she and Tiger Lily face as cultural outcasts. Despite their best efforts, Tinker Bell's and Tiger Lily's inability to permanently transcend their semi-human or non-white status confines them to the outskirts of Neverland and the narrative.

Barrie introduces Tiger Lily as a small, dark, inarticulate young woman who initially seems to function as a spectacle for the reader and the male community of Neverland. She exemplifies Donaldson's argument that "feminine 'to-be-looked-at-ness' transforms "woman" into a fetish whose idealization fixates upon her physical beauty; thus, she becomes an object" (26). However, despite Tiger Lily's physical visibility, her silence, and her general lack of representation in the text, her character briefly imparts a complex and nuanced way of navigating that world to the reader. Unfortunately, her struggles fail to result in the kind of agency that Wendy and even Tinker Bell develop. Instead, her character represents a marriage of both independence and oppression that forces her to consistently remain on the farthest boundaries of Neverland. Her name, an amalgam of human, animal, and plant characteristics, especially contributes to her liminality. Donaldson astutely describes Tiger Lily's significantly paradoxical traits as the truly "other" woman in Neverland:

> At first glance, Tiger Lily seems literally to embody her name: a "Tiger" evoking fierceness and Amazonian stature, and "Lily," beauty and whiteness. Since Never-Never Land had never never allowed women to immigrate there as "real" citizens, Tiger Lily also appears as a welcome antidote to the staunchly conservative maternalism of Wendy. (75)

Donaldson's commentary on Tiger Lily's name and, thus, her origin, pinpoints the other-worldliness that both inhibits and empowers her.[9] Additionally, Tiger Lily's heritage as a native princess adds to her unusual status, marking her differences both from her tribe and from the rest of Neverland.

The main disparity between Tiger Lily and the two other women— her royal birthright as the daughter of the Redskin chief—provides her with a kind of innate dignity in spite of her race and gender. Tiger Lily's lineage and, ultimately, her father's male authority provide her with her position of importance, rather than any specific act. However, in spite of this, like Wendy, she seeks to balance her authentic, individual identity with her precarious relationships with Neverland's boys. For example, although Tiger Lily reigns in the absence of her biological father, she defers to his white proxy, Peter Pan. Barrie limits their interactions to broken, trite exchanges that gloss over her significance as a woman and a princess: "'Me Tiger Lily,' that lovely creature would reply: 'Peter Pan save me, me his velly nice friend. Me no let pirates

hurt him.' She was far too pretty to cringe in this way, but Peter thought
it his due" (95–96). In a manner similar to Wendy's mother/child/lover
role in Neverland, Tiger Lily must balance her true self with the hollow
subaltern role that Peter expects her to fulfill.

However, unlike Wendy and Tinker Bell, Tiger Lily's place in the narrative relies heavily upon the small but visible parts of her body, rather
than what is left unseen (Wendy's isolation underground) or unheard
(Tinker Bell's voiceless bells). This dynamic regulates the rest of Tiger
Lily's brief appearance in the text, where she defines the limits of and
the connection between Neverland's racial and gendered factions. Barrie consistently describes her as beautiful, fierce, proud, and unpredictable: "bringing up the rear, the place of greatest danger, comes
Tiger Lily, proudly erect, a princess in her own right. She is the most
beautiful of the dusky Dianas and the belle of the piccaninnies, coquettish, cold, and amorous by turns" (51). This description categorizes
her not only as a woman victimized by Donaldson's term, "to-be-
looked-at-ness," but also with her argument that "she [Tiger Lily] becomes an object that satisfies rather than threatens impending castration" (26). Therefore, Barrie seemingly relegates a powerful female to
a role of sensual, harmless, and mute exhibit.

He describes this small woman as a rarity, a "Tiger-Lily" to be admired, conquered, and possessed. Tiger Lily, the only woman in a tribe
of "piccaninnies," a group Donaldson characterizes as "childish, dark,
and inferior," inhabits the decidedly feminine position of the jewel of
the tribe (86). However, the fact that she "staves off the altar with a
hatchet" despite the many men who "would [have] the wayward thing
for a wife" demonstrates her ability to resist the native men, if not Peter (51). Barrie suggests here that the oversexed native woman finds
the white man (or boy, in this case) irresistible and her racial peers re-
pulsive. However, the identification of Tiger Lily as a crucial component in the hierarchy of Neverland partially negates this problematic
representation of her.

McClintock's argument that "the female body is figured as marking
the boundary of the cosmos and the limits of the known world" precisely defines Tiger Lily's complex identity (22). While Tiger Lily's
voicelessness and eroticism portray her as a parody of the Indian or
Asian subaltern, she fosters a channel of communication between Peter, the Lost Boys, and the natives. Peter's rescue of Tiger Lily from the
pirates places her in much the same position as Wendy: because of Peter's actions, both women serve as liaisons between two worlds other-

wise separated. Every aspect of her presence points the reader toward an uninformed yet commonplace definition of indigenous populations in the colonies as animalistic, exotic, entertaining creatures. However, Barrie hides the linguistic and cultural obstacles that divide the white and non-white worlds that affect Tiger Lily. Although she ultimately fails to appropriate a lasting voice that extends beyond Neverland into the central Nursery, she manages to make the possibility and threat of her power known to the reader.

Peter's use of language and Tiger Lily's limited English vocabulary (as perceived by Peter and satirized by Barrie) contribute to both her oppression and her influence within the narrative. For example, as she faces her captors, "her face was impassive; she was the daughter of a chief, she must die as a chief's daughter. . . . She was too proud to offer a vain resistance" (80–81). She gains her freedom from the pirates when Peter manipulates his voice (a form of language) and therefore his identity, to convince them that he is Captain Hook ordering Tiger Lily's release. As a result of Peter's actions, she and her braves join the community of Peter and the Lost Boys, which exacerbates the complex liminality first denoted by her name.[10] Tiger Lily's new relationship to Peter both defines and blurs the already abstract boundaries between the native and non-native societies. The arrangement occurs not only as a product of Peter's use of language, but of Tiger Lily's choice not to speak when confronted with the prospect of death. Her actions as well as Peter's cause her to take on yet another confused role—that of cultural commodity and translator.

As one of three women living in or near Peter's home, Tiger Lily represents a new aspect of femininity not yet experienced by the main characters. Her addition to the household not only includes race in the dynamic of gender and class, but also underscores the conflicts that the girls/women face in Neverland. Barrie's depiction of Tiger Lily's (and Wendy's and Tinker Bell's) struggles to reconcile all of her functions reflects the increasing complexity of women's place in shifting British and World cultures. Tiger Lily's debt to Peter and her continuing role as the commander of her tribe further complicate her already questionable ability to exercise authority as a woman. Her newly formed subservient attitude toward Peter counteracts her former strength, undermining her chances to cause permanent change for herself. Tiger Lily now inhabits a tenuous and unsatisfying place similar to that of Wendy. Both children/women owe Peter gratitude for physically freeing them from Hook, although their freedom costs both of them a price: their moral and emotional independence. Wendy and Tiger Lily never achieve complete independence from Peter or from limiting and stereotypical gender roles, and Peter takes on an increasingly defiant identity. His desire to maintain his dominance in Neverland (which includes oppressing Tiger Lily and the Redskins) rather than live in the Darling household begins with the superior attitude he develops as a result of rescuing these females from Hook.

The dynamic that positions Peter as "great white father" inherently involves Tiger Lily as Barrie's main example of the subaltern. Her prostration before Peter, in which she and the other natives must reply "it is good," "Peter Pan has spoken," and then "shut up" in deference to him, further delineates her as linguistically, emotionally, and morally inferior to him (Barrie 96). Barrie defines her as an integral part of the cultural and social mechanism that perpetuates Peter as a child sovereign. Although, through Tiger Lily, he incorporates the Redskins into his own tribe of boy warriors, he neglects her significance as his native equal (that of commander). This, in conjunction with her unwillingness or inability to question his treatment of her and the Redskins, makes her a silent mediator between her world and Peter's. By adhering to a code of ethics that requires her to repay her debt to Peter, she enters into a relationship with him that both exposes him to her culture and promotes his primacy. Tiger Lily's encounters with Peter directly mimic much of what Gayatri Chakravorty Spivak labels "subject-effects" in her seminal argument, "Can the Subaltern Speak?"

According to Spivak, native "others" such as Tiger Lily possess no language according to Europeans because Westerners, represented by both Peter and Barrie, fail to imagine that these mysterious others possess the power or desire to speak (26). Additionally, Spivak identifies a hierarchy among the natives and establishes the importance of a cultural stratum she labels according to their liminality. This special group of people acts as a buffer between the white colonials and the local indigenous population (27). Tiger Lily fits Spivak's criteria for the subaltern who remains chiefly silent, yet functions as an interpreter between the colonizers and the colonized. Spivak's combination of language and hierarchy exemplifies the problems that all of the women, particularly Tiger Lily, experience when attempting to make themselves heard.

Tiger Lily's identity as an elite local ruler, the position that Spivak focuses on in her argument, as well as her gender, provides her with unusual access to Peter. He immediately recognizes her difference from the rest of the Redskins: her remarkable femininity, beauty, and position of importance among her warriors denote her prominence. Unfortunately, Barrie and Peter equate her moral identity with her physical one, a problem not at all unusual in the colonies that Neverland signifies. However, despite Barrie's eventual elimination of Tiger Lily from the main narrative and its conclusion in the Nursery, her body (rather than her voice) momentarily garners Peter's attention. Her character forces the reader to note one female's defiance of Western and racial stereotypes. Although Barrie describes Tiger Lily as something, or rather someone, that requires masculine protection, he also defines her as predatory, intuitive, and intelligent. For example, she leads the hunting braves, assesses and reacts to her environment when abducted, and conducts ethical warfare.[11] Although Barrie describes Tiger Lily as a revolutionary woman, he seems unable to resolve her conflicting traits and determines that she understands her circumstances, yet does not possess the desire or power to alter them.

Tiger Lily's racial, gendered, and physical liminality places her at the boundaries of whiteness, masculinity, and largeness and provides her with just enough agency to influence Peter's actions. However, her differences from both the "othered" natives and the other women are not enough to completely recuperate her from the confines of subaltern silence. The complex intersection of race and gender makes Tiger Lily minute in comparison to Peter, Wendy, and Tinker Bell. No opportunity exists to allow her to attain the position of a white woman, much less a white *man*. However, a connection to Peter offers Tiger Lily the chance to escape her linguistic and cultural exile. Therefore, her desire for Peter stems not from authentic sexuality, but perhaps from a wish to move to a more central position in Neverland. Perhaps she even acts in highly sexual ways to live up to what she imagines as Peter's expectations of her. Tiger Lily's physical merits outweigh all other aspects of her personality, and she capitalizes on Peter's and Wendy's perception of her as lovely, yet uncivilized. Because Barrie focuses on Tiger Lily's role as a mostly mute body on display, he speaks for her rather than letting her speak for herself.[12] Wendy notices Tiger Lily's extremely limited and narrow identity in Peter's eyes and, for a moment, studies the differences between this "other" woman and herself. Unfortunately, class distinctions, even in an imaginary place, hinder Wendy's capability to connect her own oppression with that of the tribal princess.

In one of the final interludes before Hook and his men invade the Lost Boys' territory, Wendy expresses an interest in Tiger Lily's plight as

Peter's subordinate. Barrie recounts that "Wendy secretly sympathized with them a little, but she was far too loyal a housewife to listen to any complaints against father" and that, despite her temporary pity for the braves, the difficulties of her own position (also as a subordinate) cloud these feelings (96). Wendy's maternal, middle-class, and white identity restricts her ability to forge any kind of bond with Tiger Lily, verifying the idea supported by Wilson and McClintock, among many others, that class, as well as race and sexuality, governs the text.[13] Tiger Lily's connection to the patriarchal center represented by Peter remains considerably more unsatisfying and unstable than Wendy's and Tinker Bell's. Unlike the other girls/women, Tiger Lily's character experiences scant transformation, and at the moment when change seems possible, she disappears altogether with no resolution. Tiger Lily, part woman and part animal, differs from Wendy, part woman and part child, and Tinker Bell, part woman and part myth, because in Peter's and Barrie's estimation, she possesses a one-dimensional identity. Tiger Lily's theoretical invisibility and physical smallness render her more inaudible than even the voiceless Tinker Bell, an equally independent woman who appropriates both unconventional space and language for herself.

In the end, Barrie's treatment of these three women/girls, all of whom struggle to find physical, emotional, and moral visibility, critiques the failure of the British Empire to cause positive change for anyone, including white men and middle-class white women. Wendy's, Tinker Bell's, and Tiger Lily's disruption of Neverland reveals erroneous ideas about race and gender and the failure of stereotypes to authentically incorporate the full continuum of women's experiences. Wendy's and Tinker Bell's success and Tiger Lily's failure to transcend the margins of Neverland reflect the confusing and shifting ideas about race, class, and especially gender during the *fin de siècle*. Wendy attains her freedom in Neverland as a result of her ability to return to "reality," however flawed and restrictive. Thus, Barrie depicts England and the Nursery as limiting, but preferable to the colonial Neverland of imaginary burdens. Tinker Bell, whose nonhuman status allows her to transgress many of the domestic responsibilities that hinder Wendy, turns a perceived weakness (voicelessness) into strength, but remains in Neverland. Unfortunately, although Tiger Lily holds an unprecedented position of power for a female as the Redskins' leader, her primitiveness, along with her gender, nullifies her tribal authority in the eyes of the Occident.

Wendy's, John's, and Michael's return to the Nursery signals the end of Tiger Lily's and Tinker Bell's roles in the narrative, thus refocusing the reader's attention on England and domesticity. The reassertion of the Nursery as central and Wendy's decision to embrace adulthood while maintaining a link to Neverland support Kutzer's argument that children's fiction often serves as adults' "unconscious desire[s] to maintain . . . earlier cultural codes" and "preserve the past" (xvi). Despite the resolution of the Lost Boys' fate and their incorporation into the Darling family, Peter continues to resist their defection from Neverland. Wendy then once again finds a way to reconcile her needs with those of Peter in order to maintain her authentic sense of self. She agrees to visit Neverland annually for "spring cleaning" in order to voluntarily indenture herself to him. This not only placates Peter, who remains both infantile and paternalistic, but also provides Wendy with continuous access to her idealistic childhood as she confronts the harsh adult world. Therefore, Barrie further encourages the idea of Neverland and the colonies as places of escape, where Wendy, her daughter Jane, and her future female progeny exchange "real" maternal responsibilities for "imaginary" exotic ones. This arrangement guarantees the survival of domestic subservience in Neverland despite Wendy's shifting roles in the "reality" of the Nursery.

The conclusion of the narrative, in which Wendy's voice remains loudest as the middle-class, white woman/child, reassures the reader that English domesticity continues intact and unquestioned. Peter's inability to remember Wendy after a while suggests a gap between the cultures of the Nursery and Neverland, where life continues unchanged. Peter's forgetfulness guarantees that Wendy, as well as each daughter, experiences the same journey every time she visits. This repetition allows each girl to "practice" performing femininity in preparation for their futures as wives and mothers. In Neverland they encounter patriarchal domination as well as varied female reactions to that system: for example, Tinker Bell and Tiger Lily during Wendy's initial visit. These trips not only support gendered stereotypes, but also provide a space for literal and figurative little women to explore their own agency, even perhaps their own feminist tendencies, without serious repercussions. The "spring" cleaning signifies not only a renewal of gender stereotypes, but of the girls' faith in themselves and their power to renounce Neverland for the possibilities found in their own Nurseries.

NOTES

1. See McClintock 11. She argues that the categories of both "women" and "postcolonial" encourage a "panoptic tendency to view the globe through generic abstractions."

2. See Kutzer xv. Barrie's female characters embody what Kutzer labels the "culture . . . not the politics of imperialism" and "the ethos that both produces imperialism and is engendered by imperialism."

3. "In the old days at home the Neverland had always begun to look a little dark and threatening by bedtime. Then unexplored patches arose in it and spread; black shadows moved about in them; the roar of the beasts of prey was quite different now, and above all, you lost a certainty that you would win" (Barrie 40–41).

4. "She told them to clear [make-believe tea] away, and sat down to her workbasket: a heavy load of stockings and every knee with a hole in it as usual" (Barrie 98). Barrie describes this scene as one in which no food appears on the table and Wendy referees between the boys as they all wait for Peter's nightly return.

5. See Donaldson's definition of the "Miranda Complex" (16).

6. See Wilson 608. She argues that "the figure of Tinker Bell, so innocuously presented as a disembodied fairy, is Barrie's management not just of the working-class but of the working-class immigrant for whom English was not a first language."

7. See Barrie 108. "'Tink,' he [Peter] rapped out, 'if you don't get up and dress at once I will open the curtains and everyone will see you in your négigée.' This made her leap to the floor."

8. Sharpe cites Elizabeth Cowie, who argues that, during empire, "the reproduction of women's gender roles constitutes a transaction that also gives value to a particular signifying system" (qtd. in Sharpe 68).

9. This takes into consideration Donaldson's argument that "although the text of *Peter Pan* imbues Tiger Lily with the possibility of challenging dominant interpretations of gender in *fin de siècle* imperial England, it also takes away this possibility of recuperating her within an implied enthymeme of the 'Picaninny'—that colonialist and paternalistic marker of a childish and less developed, therefore, unequal person" (76).

10. Barrie's description of Tiger Lily as both "dusky" and, like her brethren, able to "pass over fallen twigs without making a noise" highlights her dark skin and invisible status (51). Her name incorporates both the darkest and the lightest, the most feared and the most valued objects in the jungle.

11. "By all the unwritten laws of savage warfare it is always the redskin who attacks, and with the willingness of his race he does it just before dawn" (Barrie 112).

12. This idea comes, in part, from Edward Said, who argues against the validity of any Western representation of the Orient, claiming that the Occidental

writer consistently constructs an idea of the Orient that fits comfortably into his/her cultural schemas about the Other.

13. Wilson, in particular, makes a strong argument when she asserts that "similarly [to Tinker Bell], Tiger Lily and her braves seem to have limited abilities in English, marking xenophobia of the English middle class to the Other." (608).

WORKS CITED

Barrie, J. M. *Peter Pan*. 1911. New York: Bantam, 1985.

Byrnes, Alice. *The Child: An Archetypal Symbol in Literature for Children and Adults*. New York: Peter Lang, 1995.

Donaldson, Laura. *Decolonizing Feminisms: Race, Gender, and Empire-Building*. Chapel Hill: U of North Carolina P, 1992.

Gibson, Lois Rauch. "Beyond the Apron: Archetypes, Stereotypes, and Alternative Portrayals of Mothers in Children's Literature." *Children's Literature Association Quarterly* 13 (1988): 177 81.

Hunt, Peter, and Karen Sands. "The View From the Center: British Empire and Post-Empire Children's Literature." *Voices of the Other: Children's Literature and the Postcolonial Context*. Ed. Roderick McGillis. New York: Garland, 2000. 39–53.

Kutzer, Daphne. *Empire's Children: Empire and Imperialism in Classic British Children's Books*. New York: Taylor and Francis, 2001.

McClintock, Anne. *Imperial Leather: Race, Gender, and Sexuality in the Colonial Context*. NewYork: Routledge, 1995.

Said, Edward. *Orientalism*. New York: Vintage, 1979.

Sharpe, Jenny. *Allegories of Empire: The Figure of Woman in the Colonial Text*. Minneapolis: U of Minnesota P, 1993.

Spivak, Gayatri Chakravorty. "Can the Subaltern Speak?" *Marxism and the Interpretation of Culture*. Ed. Cary Nelson and Lawrence Grossberg. London: Macmillan, 1988. 21–35.

Wilson, Ann. "Hauntings, Anxiety, Technology, and Gender in Peter Pan." *Modern Drama* 43 (2000): 595–611.

Index

About the Contributors

Emily Clark, who received her Ph.D. from the University of North Carolina at Greensboro in 2004, is now a visiting assistant professor of English at the University of the Incarnate Word in San Antonio, Texas. Her specialties are modernism, postcolonialism, and critical theory.

Karen Coats is an associate professor of English at Illinois State University, where she teaches courses in children's and young adult literature and literary theory. She is the author of *Looking Glasses and Neverlands: Lacan, Desire, and Subjectivity in Children's Literature* (2004) as well as various articles on different aspects of children's and young adult literature.

Paul Fox received his Ph.D. in comparative literature from the University of Georgia. He has published on the subjects of decadent aesthetics and *fin de siècle* literature and is currently an assistant professor at Zayed University in the United Arab Emirates.

Irene Hsiao, having received her undergraduate degree in English and molecular and cell biology at Berkeley, is currently a graduate student at the University of Chicago. She studies ballads, dance, dreams, melancholy, and lyric poetry.

Cathlena Martin is a Ph.D. candidate at the University of Florida. She writes for the public radio program *Recess!* and has a newspaper column on children's culture. Her research interests include children's literature, new media, and revisionist fairy tales.

Jill P. May, professor of children's literature at Purdue University, teaches both graduate and undergraduate students. She has published many articles and five books, including *Children's Literature and Critical Theory* (1995) and *Exploring Culturally Diverse Literature for Children and Adolescents* (2005).

Karen McGavock, who was educated at Webster's High School in Barrie's hometown of Kirriemuir, received her Ph.D. in English literature from the University of Glasgow. Now at the Institute of Education at the University of Stirling, she has studied Lewis Carroll, C. S. Lewis, and J. K. Rowling, along with Barrie.

M. Joy Morse has a master's degree in literature from the University of North Carolina at Charlotte, where she teaches part time. While primarily working in the marketing industry, she reads and writes about Victorian literature for pleasure.

John Pennington is an associate professor of English at St. Norbert College, Wisconsin, where he specializes in nineteenth-century British literature, especially fairy tales. He is currently working on a full-length study of John Ruskin, George MacDonald, and Lewis Carroll.

Christine Roth, an assistant professor of English at the University of Wisconsin Oshkosh, is the editor of *"Many Recognitions Dim and Faint": Landscape and Literature, 1730–1850* (2005) and John Ruskin's *The Two Paths* (2004). She is presently completing a book on Cult-of-the-Little-Girl narratives in late-Victorian Britain.

David Rudd teaches children's literature at the University of Bolton, England, in the Department of Cultural and Creative Studies. He is the author of numerous articles about children's literature as well as two books, including *Enid Blyton and the Mystery of Children's Literature* (2000).

Clay Kinchen Smith began working with Donald Ault as an undergraduate at Vanderbilt and continued this association while completing his Ph.D. in cultural theories at the University of Florida, Gainesville. Currently, he is teaching at Santa Fe Community College, Gainesville.

C. Anita Tarr is an associate professor of English at Illinois State University, where she teaches children's and young adult literature with additional specialties in fantasy and science fiction, poetry, and women's studies. She has published on Virginia Woolf, J. M. Barrie, Robert Cormier, Scott O'Dell, and Marjorie Kinnan Rawlings.

Laurie Taylor, a Ph.D. candidate at the University of Florida, teaches and publishes on video games and digital media. She also writes a newspaper gaming column, an online gaming column, and radio programs for the public radio program *Recess!*

Rosanna West Walker, who received her doctorate in literature from the University of Oregon in 2005, focuses on American studies and folklore. Her next project analyzes the medical takeover of traditional midwifery.

Carrie Wasinger is currently at Northwestern University finishing her dissertation on gender and the figure of the child in Victorian literature. Her research interests include narrative theory, nineteenth-century children's culture, and Victorian popular fiction.

Donna R. White teaches young adult literature, linguistics, science fiction and fantasy, and writing at Arkansas Tech University. She is the author of *A Century of Welsh Myth in Children's Literature* (1998) and *Dancing with Dragons: Ursula K. Le Guin and the Critics* (1999) and is coeditor of *Diana Wynne Jones: An Exciting and Exacting Wisdom* (2002).

Kayla McKinney Wiggins is the chair of the English Department and the director of drama at Martin Methodist College in Pulaski, Tennessee. She is the author of *Modern Verse Drama in English* and a contributing author to many books and journals on drama, folklore, literature, and film.